Linen, Family and Community in Tullylish, County Down, 1690–1914

Linen, Family and Community in Tullylish, County Down 1690–1914

MARILYN COHEN

FOUR COURTS PRESS

This book was set in 10.5 on 12.5 point Ehrhardt
by Woodcote Typesetters for
FOUR COURTS PRESS LTD
Fumbally Lane, Dublin 8, Ireland
and in North America for
FOUR COURTS PRESS LTD
c/o ISBS, 5804 N.E. Hassalo Street, Portland, OR 97213

Note: Some of the material in the book appeared earlier in
'Religion and Social Inequality in Ireland',
Journal of Interdisciplinary History, XXV: 1 (1994), 1–21

A catalogue record for this title
is available from the British Library.

ISBN 1-85182-312-3

Printed in Ireland by
Colour Books, Dublin

Preface

The successful completion of this manuscript was assisted by many generous individuals and institutions. The research was funded by grants from the Joint Committee on the International Doctoral Research Fellowship Program for Western Europe of the Social Science Research Council; the Board of Foreign Scholarships under the Fulbright Hayes Act; and the Wenner Gren Foundation for Anthropological Research. I was assisted in numerous ways by an affiliation with the Institute of Irish Studies at the Queen's University of Belfast. Many scholars in Northern Ireland provided me with direction, and critique during my stay including William H. Crawford, Brenda Collins, Emily Boyle, Denis MacNiece, Anne McKernan and Leslie Clarkson. I would also like to thank Carla Keating for her hospitality during my visits to Dublin.

Most of the archival research was conducted at the Public Record Office of Northern Ireland. I was assisted by Trevor Parkhill and the staff who consistently helped me locate and reproduce documents. The collection of oral evidence and photographs was assisted by Michael P. Campbell who served as my initial contact in Tullylish. I am deeply grateful to the many residents of Tullylish who generously provided me with information, refreshments and other tokens of hospitality. Finally, I would like to thank the Ulster Folk and Transport Museum, the Ulster Museum, the County Down Museum and the Linen Centre at the Lisburn Museum for allowing me to reproduce photographs and for providing facilities to transcribe my taped interviews.

Coding and computer analysis of the census data were assisted by Robert Yaffee, the staff at the CUNY Computer Center and by Carole Turbin. I would like to thank William Roseberry and Louise Tilly for reading and commenting upon earlier drafts of this manuscript. I would like to thank Beth Brndjar for countless hours of childcare. Finally, I would like to thank my husband, Alan Serrins, whose support for this project has taken many forms over the years.

Contents

List of Illustrations

FIGURES

CREDITS

M.P. Campbell 8, 9, 10, 13, 16, 18, 19, 25; County Down Museum 3, 4, 21; E.R.R. Green 7, 17; Mr McElroy 11; Public Records Office of Northern Ireland 6; Mrs Sinton 14, 24; John Smyth 15; Ulster Museum, Belfast 20, 22, 23, 26, 27.

INTRODUCTION

New Perspectives on the Irish Linen Industry

> ... small communities, no matter how primitive, are never really isolated, and in the case
> of a nineteenth-century cotton-manufacturing town, its significant environment was,
> literally, the entire world ...'
>
> A.F.C. Wallace, 1972

This is a book about the industrialization of linen yarn and cloth in the parish of
Tullylish, located along the banks of the River Bann in northwest County Down.
While most of the mills and factories are now only artifactual reminders of linen's
prominence, it is easy to imagine the industry's dominance over the region for two
centuries. Alongside the mill premises, occupied workers' housing, schools and
churches, all built by former mill owners, remain. A close intersection between
workplace, family and community existed in these rural factory hamlets and towns,
where the linen industry provided the principle, if not the sole, source of employment for over two centuries.

Although much of Ireland's industrial development took place in such rural
places, the distinct texture of economic development and social life in them remains
underinvestigated. This book focuses upon the development of a capitalist linen
industry between 1700 and 1914 in one of Ulster's most significant rural industrial
parishes – Tullylish – located in the heart of the 'linen triangle'. The 11,707 acres of
arable land that comprised Tullylish were divided into nineteen townlands intersected by the Bann, which enters Tullylish in a northwesterly direction from neighbouring Seapatrick parish. The Bann was not a navigable river. However, it united
the mid-sections of Tullylish and neighbouring Seapatrick into one industrial region whose economic development depended upon it for sources of water power.

As our understanding of industrial capitalism deepens, linear trajectories are
being replaced by complex, multidimensional explanations that assume uneven paths
of development. The divergent rates and paths of capitalist development in the parish and in the linen industry generally provide evidence to refute teleological models. The best known unilinear model of capitalism in the Irish linen industry, that
offered by Conrad Gill in 1925, was based on a simplification of the English transition. His model stood alone for over half a century, with the entrenchment of empiricism

---

1 Anthony F.C. Wallace, *Rockdale* (New York 1972), p. xv.

in Irish historiography largely accounting for its tenacity.[2] Scholars are only now challenging Gill's teleological excesses, emphasising instead how detailed regional studies provide a tapestry of capitalist formations, each requiring historically specific theoretical treatment.[3] This analysis will explain the changing relationship between dispersed and centralized production in Tullylish. The centralized paths of industrial capitalism along the Bann differed substantially from those in the north, where dispersed domestic handloom weaving persisted into the twentieth century.

Explanation of these uneven paths of economic development is enhanced by historically contingent analysis. The methodology employed here is microhistory, which reduces the scale of analysis to focus on the particular.[4] My application of microhistory is guided by certain realist assumptions that diverse human experiences over space and time are substantially accessible and intelligible, and that attempts to explain human behaviour are as important as interpretation. I also assume that human beings make their own history, constrained by historically specific contingencies.

This perspective is the foundation for several interconnected theoretical problematics, which together comprise the backbone of the book. The first addresses the connections between historical and cultural specificity and the broader context of world capitalism. The second relates to what Philip Abrams has termed the 'problematic of structuring', which probes the persistent, central problem of human agency in social analysis.[5] The third explores the intersections between gender and class. The challenge and potential of microhistory lies in the conceptualization of questions, concepts and analytical units relating to these problematics. The microhistorian must theoretically define and explain spatial and temporal connections, and retain the inherent dialectic between detailed historically specific analysis, which yields a wealth of empirical detail, and abstract theoretical concepts and models of social change.

As a historical anthropologist, I was drawn to the methodological similarities between microhistory and anthropology. The affinity between their methods and perspectives, both of which emphasize historical context, is substantial, especially when both are conceived of as reflexive endeavours, inextricably shaped by the researcher's point of view.[6] Anthropologists, who are increasingly incorporating a

2 Conrad Gill, *The Rise of the Irish Linen Industry* (Oxford 1925). 3 W.H. Crawford, 'The evolution of the linen trade in Ulster before industrialization', *Irish Economic and Social History*, 15 (1988), 32–7; Anne McKernan, 'The Dynamics of the Linen Triangle: Factor, Family and Farm in Ulster, 1740 to 1825', Ph.D. diss., The University of Michigan, 1992; Anne McKernan, 'Contested Terrain: The Making of a Market Culture in Ulster Linens', in Marilyn Cohen (ed.), *The Warp of Ulster's Past: Interdisciplinary Perspectives on the Irish Linen Industry* (New York 1996). 4 Giovanni Levi, 'On Microhistory', in Peter Burke (ed.), *New Perspectives on Historical Writing* (University Park, PA 1991), p. 97. 5 Philip Abrams, 'History, Sociology, Historical Sociology', *Past & Present*, no. 87 (1980), p. 7. 6 Levi, 'Microhistory', p. 106; Marilyn Silverman and Philip H. Gulliver, 'Historical anthropology and the ethnographic tradition: a personal, historical, and intellectual account', in Marilyn Silverman and P.H. Gulliver (eds), *Approaching the Past: Historical Anthropology through Irish Case Studies* (New York 1992), p. 16.

revised conception of culture as process, have been pathbreakers in the attempt to forge interdisciplinary links with history. Although anthropologists often bring a distinct way of seeing and interpreting historical evidence, rooted in their traditional academic concern with cultural meaning, context, interpretation and the structure of social interaction, '"the past" is unlike other anthropological fieldwork sites.'[7] Despite the similarity in attempting to understand and explain 'others' (whether the 'other' is defined in terms of historical time or cultural space), analysis of the past illuminates how anthropology is broader than ethnology and more than a genre.[8] As anthropologists increasingly approach the past, new theoretical problems arise which focus our attention on the links between past and present, between locales and wider spatial and temporal contexts, structure and human agency, the varied meanings of contextualization, and the significant magnitude of cultural relativism.

In anthropology and sociology, contextualization has often been defined in functionalist terms, with explanations of human behaviour emerging from the operation of a coherent holistic system. While this functionalist understanding of contextualization has value, its synchronic 'logic of explanation' has often been oppositional to the recognition of culture as historical process.[9] Giovanni Levi suggests several alternative definitions of contextualization that emphasize instead comparison, the contradictions or 'incoherences' existing in all normative systems and the possibilities thus created for human agency and change.[10]

This book contributes to the anthropological literature on Ireland's past. As such, it fosters interdisciplinary research among scholars of Ireland. The quarter-century dialogue between history and the social sciences, that continues to generate rich theoretical debate, inventive methodologies and a voluminous literature, has only begun to influence Irish scholarship. There are few anthropological studies of Ireland's past, even fewer studies of capitalist development outside of agriculture, of Irish urban contexts, industrial worksites or of working class communities in the past.[11] The broad topics subsumed under the heading work and production have

7 Ibid., p. 55. 8 Ibid., p. 52. See also Philip H. Gulliver, 'Doing anthropological research in rural Ireland: methods and sources for linking the past and present', in Chris Curtin and Thomas M. Wilson (eds), *Ireland from Below* (Galway 1989), pp. 320–38. 9 Abrams, 'Historical Sociology', p. 4. 10 Levi, 'Microhistory', pp. 106–8. 11 Joan Vincent, 'Marriage, religion and class in south Fermanagh, Ireland, 1846–1920', in Owen Lynch (ed.), *Emergent Structures and the Family* (Delhi 1983); Thomas Wilson, 'From Clare to Common Market: perspectives in Irish ethnography', *Anthropological Quarterly*, 57, no. 1 (1984), 3; Hastings Donnan and Graham McFarlane, 'Social anthropology and the sectarian divide in Northern Ireland', in Richard Jenkins, Hastings Donnan and Graham McFarlane (eds), *The Sectarian Divide in Northern Ireland Today*, Royal Anthropological Institute of Great Britain and Ireland, Occasional Paper, no. 41 (1986); Curtin and Wilson, *Ireland from Below*; Marilyn Silverman and P.H. Gulliver, *In the Valley of the Nore* (Dublin 1986); Silverman and Gulliver, *Approaching the Past*; Chris Curtin, Thomas M. Wilson and Hastings Donnan (eds), *Irish Urban Cultures* (Belfast 1993); Marilyn Cohen, 'Proletarianization and Family Strategies in the Parish of Tullylish, County Down, Ireland, 1690–1914', Ph.D. diss., New School for Social Research, 1988; 'Paternalism and poverty: contradictions in the schooling of working class children in Tullylish, 1825–1914', *History of Education*,

provided fertile subject matter for interdisciplinary analysis since the organization of work and its varied meanings are socially constructed.[12] The production and circulation of commodities like linen were embedded in a variety of structures and symbolic systems that provided a context for its organization and meaning. A broad structural and cultural focus helps dismantle the ideological separation of work from other aspects of social life that appears under capitalism. In rural regions dominated by linen production, work was significant in cultivating a sense of identity and belonging to households and communities, while familial obligations helped create and reproduce forms of essential self-discipline.[13]

The analysis of work and working-class social life in Tullylish begins within the broad context of Ireland's political and economic domination by England in the seventeenth century, and the deliberate role played by the English state in promoting the Irish linen industry. Although analysis of the multifaceted role of the state is one of the least researched aspects of proto-industrialization, England's intervention in Ireland's proto-industries is well documented.[14] The development of the Irish linen industry was always linked with the process of empire building in Europe and particularly England. The flourishing Irish woollen industry was suppressed by the English state in 1699 in response to pressures from English woollen interests. Instead, the state sought to promote Irish linen and provisions. The competitive advantage of duty-free access to English and colonial markets after 1696 made it possible for imports from Ireland to drive foreign linen out of the English market. However, since Ireland remained constitutionally subordinate to England, its exports were vulnerable to changes in English commercial policy and overseas market demand. Markets for linen expanded more slowly than other textiles, and England restricted the types of linen imported from Ireland to maintain profitability in its own linen industry.[15] The Irish linen industry remained dependent for its growth on English and overseas markets throughout its long history, linking it to political and economic developments affecting trade in textiles elsewhere in world.

English hegemony was further extended by the plantation of Ulster and the revolution in landownership after the Act of Settlement in 1662. A heterogeneous

21, no. 3 (1992), 291–306; 'Urbanisation and the Milieux of Factory Life: Gilford/Dunbarton, 1825–1914', in Curtin, Wilson and Donnan, op. cit.; 'Religion and the reproduction of social inequality: Tullylish, County Down, 1901', *Journal of Interdisciplinary History*, xxv, no. 1 (Summer 1994); 'Rural paths of capitalist development: class formation, paternalism, and gender in County Down's linen industry', in L.J. Proudfoot (ed.), *Down: History and Society* (Dublin, forthcoming); Cohen, *The Warp*.   12 Patrick Joyce, 'The historical meanings of work: an introduction', in Patrick Joyce (ed.), *The Historical Meanings of Work* (Cambridge 1987), p. 2.   13 Tessie Liu, *The Weaver's Knot: The Contradictions of Class Struggle and Family Solidarity in Western France, 1750–1914* Ithaca 1994), p. 25.   14 Sheilagh C. Ogilvie, 'Social institutions and proto-industrialization', in Sheilagh C. Ogilvie and Marcus Cerman (eds), *European Proto-industrialization* (Cambridge 1996), pp. 33–7.   15 Denis O'Hearn, 'Innovation and the world system-hierarchy: British subjugation of the Irish cotton industry, 1780–1830', *American Journal of Sociology*, 100, no. 2 (1994), 598.

Protestant or Anglican ascendancy was created who retained political dominance for two hundred years. Throughout, I use the term hegemony, not to convey a monolithic domination by England or the Protestant Ascendancy, but rather as problematic, historically specific and contested. Hegemonies have specific material and cultural components that involve both coercion and consent. In the early modern period, land ownership ensured wealth, prestige, control over tenants and access to political office at the local and national level. Landlords' hegemony in the eighteenth century reflected a world view largely constructed in terms of paternalistic vertical social obligations. The idealized model of society featured the Anglican landlord living 'in the midst of his numerous family as a true father of his country, at once watchful of their good and advancing thereby his own'.[16]

The expansion of radical politics, secularism and industrial capitalism in the late eighteenth century threatened the class privileges of this landed ascendancy. In this changing cultural context, where new class divisions were emerging, Evangelical Protestantism 'offered the upper classes a creed which reaffirmed old values and supplied a rigorous defense of social and political conservatism'.[17] The twin values of improvement and respectability inspired a revised model of middle-class Protestant masculinity stressing the work ethic, independence, piety, chastity, sobriety, high-mindedness and dedication to family.[18]

In Tullylish, this model of social hierarchy, asymmetrical familial social obligation and deference was modified by an emerging capitalist class comprised largely of dissenting Quakers. Although, dissenters in the eighteenth century did not enjoy full civil rights, the entrepreneurial success of Quakers in the linen industry elevated them to positions of power in the region.[19] Quaker capitalists joined the Anglican county elite of landed gentry. However, Quakers reflected upon the contradictions between a commitment to simple living and their growing wealth, between individualism and communalism and between self-improvement and the social obligations of elites to the poor. This complex and often contradictory mix of Anglican deferential paternalism, Quaker individualism and Evangelical dedication to self-improvement through education, hard work and temperance provided the cornerstones of a historically-specific, rural, capitalist, cultural hegemony in Tullylish.

Contextualizing the Irish linen industry in this multifaceted way helps define the structural constraints that affected the decisions of ordinary people. Every individual and household in Tullylish were linked to historical forces shaping the linen industry in the region, nation and world. This study places subjects in Tullylish at the intersection of local and global process.[19a] Tullylish, part of Ireland's industrial northeast, was simultaneously part of the European periphery, England's semi-

16 S.J. Connolly, Religion, *Law, and Power: The Making of Protestant Ireland 1660–1760* (Oxford 1992), p. 129.   17 David Hempton and Myrtle Hill, *Evangelical Protestantism in Ulster Society, 1740–1890* (London 1992), p. 43.   18 Leonore Davidoff and Catherine Hall, *Family fortunes: Men and Women of the English Middle Class* (Chicago 1987).   19 J.C. Beckett, *Protestant Dissent in Ireland 1687–1780* (London 1948).   19a William Roseberry, 'Political Economy', *Annual Review of Anthropology*, 12 (1988), 161–85.

periphery and Ireland's core. Although linen provided a solid economic base for over two centuries, dependence upon a single industry demanded specific accommodations. Recessions and booms in market conditions impacted deeply upon communities and families along the Bann. Linen producing regions were sensitive barometers to these changes since their specialization and diverse linkages made them particularly vulnerable to external competition.[20]

All linen-producing regions in Ireland were dramatically affected by English technological innovations in the spinning and weaving of cotton and linen yarn. Although technology can be overemphasized in the history of industrial development, the impact of mill-based wet spinning on the subsequent development of the Irish linen industry was profound.[21] The mechanized cotton industry, its decline and the subsequent mechanization of linen yarn initiated a localized industrial revolution in northeast Ulster. Mill-spinning eliminated a centuries-old female occupation and, after 1825, displaced handspinners entered the new spinning mills exchanging their labour power for a wage, experiencing new forms of dependency, conceptions of time and labour discipline. The independence of male and female handloom weavers was substantially eroded by the subsequent extension of the putting-out system.

The links drawn between paths of industrial capitalism in Tullylish and English domination build upon the insights of scholars who connect economic innovation with world-systems and gender theory. Following Denis O'Hearn, innovations in leading sector industries like cotton are at the centre of economic change in core states because they are linked with complex global strategies to 'capture' innovations, 'suppress' them elsewhere, and 'protect' them at home to create and sustain competitive advantages.[22] At the microhistorical level, we can focus on how regional specificity in Tullylish mediated this global perspective. How and to what extent did forces associated with capitalist innovation in England shape the diverse paths of industrialization and strategies of Tullylish capitalists and producers? How did this rural region of 'revolutionizing industry' differ from urban industrial Belfast and other rural regions in Ulster where industrialization stagnated?[23] How were linen producing regions in Ireland hierarchically linked creating asymmetrical core/periphery relations within the semi-periphery? How were patterns of innovation in the linen industry gendered?

Other regional studies of the Ulster linen industry have revealed distinct paths of economic development, some leading to industrial capitalism and others to

20 Pat Hudson, 'The Regional Perspective', in Pat Hudson (ed.), *Regions and Industries* (Cambridge 1986), p. 36.   21 Charles Tilly, 'Flows of capital and forms of industry in Europe, 1500–1900', *Theory and Society*, 12, no. 2 (March 1983), 129, 137; E.R.R. Green, *The Lagan Valley 1800–50* (London 1949); Emily J. Boyle, 'The Economic Development of the Irish Linen Industry, 1825–1914', Ph.D. diss., The Queen's University of Belfast, 1977.   22 O'Hearn, 'Innovation', 595.   23 Hudson, 'Regional Perspective', p. 20.

de-industrialization and economic marginalization.[24] I will demonstrate that along the Bann in Tullylish, a successful 'take-off from the sites of proto-industry into the clear skies of self-sustaining growth' indeed occurred after 1825.[25] However, proletarianization, or the separation of the producer from the means of production, was an uneven process extending over most of the nineteenth century. This process reveals the complex relationship between centralization and dispersion, between labour-saving and labour intensive technology, and between gender and class formation. The proletarianization process in the linen industry illustrates how the existence of a 'sweated alternative' to the factory system undermines investment in labour-saving technology.[26] While factory spinning constituted the first wave accelerating the proletarianization of linen producers, I will show that a variety of options were open to displaced female handspinners in Tullylish that involved full or partial dependence upon capitalists.

Powerlooms did not spread until the second half of the nineteenth century. The spread of mill-based spinning generalized the putting-out system, illustrating the broad repercussions of mills in the countryside. The factors affecting the spread of powerlooms in the second half of the nineteenth century will be analyzed. Finally, I trace the decentralization of production processes in the 'making-up' of linen handkerchiefs from hemstitching factories into numerous homes, where female and child homeworkers performed a variety of sweated tasks.

Although I attempt to demonstrate what can be gained from accentuating the particular, and keeping theory close to the ground, I reject an extreme cultural relativism that denies comparison and the formulation of general theories of historical change. Irish studies have long suffered from such isolation. Tullylish provides an excellent case study for testing the limits of abstract models, comparison and relativism. I will argue that capitalism in Tullylish, defined as a specific form of class relationship between owners of the means of production and those who exchange their labour power for a wage, emerged in the late eighteenth century, when labour power among centralized bleach yard employees and the lowest strata of cottier weavers was becoming commoditized and control over production by the putting-out system was becoming formalized. In the early nineteenth century, just prior to the transition to mill-based spinning, the region between Gilford and Banbridge was singled out by contemporaries who noted the rapid advancement of the putting-out system and the extent to which weavers were abandoning their small plots of land to concentrate solely on weaving.

24 Eric L. Almquist, 'Mayo and Beyond: Land, Domestic Industry, and Rural Transformation in the Irish West', Ph.D. diss., Boston University, 1977; Leslie A. Clarkson, 'An anatomy of an Irish town: the economy of Armagh, 1770', *Irish Economic and Social History*, 5 (1978), 27–45; Leslie A. Clarkson and Brenda Collins, 'Proto-industrialization in a northern Irish town: Lisburn 1820–21', in *Proceedings of the International Economic History Conference*, 'A' Theme on Proto-industrialization: Report no. 8. Budapest: Akad. Kaido, 1982; E.R.R. Green, *The Lagan Valley 1800–50* (London 1949); McKernan, 'Dynamics'. 25 Liam Kennedy, 'The rural economy 1820–1914', in Liam Kennedy and Philip Ollerenshaw (eds), *An Economic History of Ulster 1820–1939* (Manchester 1985), p. 13. 26 Liu, *Weaver's Knot*, p. 8.

This study thereby follows the approach of scholars who push the emergence of capitalist social relations back in time to include periods of manufacture or rural industry. It contributes to the on-going debate surrounding the role of small-scale production to capitalist development, and the application of the proto-industry model to the Irish linen industry.[27] The proto-industry model has, over the last two decades, inspired a rich literature highlighting regional specificity, global economic linkages and comparison.[28] I argue that analysis of proto-industrial development in Tullylish requires analysis of regionally specific conditions that facilitate or inhibit the multiplication of large and small units of capital. Such analysis is obfuscated by naturalistic assumptions about the logic of the family mode of production, when conceived as inherently opposed to the accumulation of capital.[29] Elsewhere, I have criticized such assumptions, showing how these underestimate the complexity of capitalist development in Tullylish and the Ulster countryside.[30]

Analysis of domestic linen industry in Tullylish will, following William Roseberry, connect 'household economy and merchant capital not simply as a paradoxical symbiosis but as a constitutive and perhaps defining feature'.[31] Petty commodity producers of linen yarn and cloth in rural Ireland divided their time in varying proportions between textile production and agriculture on small plots of land. The interdependence between patterns of landholding, tenure, agricultural production and forms of rural manufacture have been repeatedly emphasized by those investigating proto-industrialization. While Conrad Gill's position that superior tenure patterns in Ulster largely accounts for its rapid industrialization has been subjected to debate, there is agreement that many Ulster landlords provided a stimulus to the development of the linen industry.[32] Ulster landlords sought to improve their estates and assure themselves of a more solvent tenantry by deliberately encouraging the growth of linen production and circulation.

27 Brenda Collins, 'Proto-industrialization and pre-famine emigration,' *Social History*, 7, no. 2 (May, 1982), 127–46; Almquist, 'Mayo and Beyond'; Clarkson, 'Anatomy'; Clarkson and Collins, 'Proto-industrialization'; L.A. Clarkson, *Proto-industrialization: The First Phase of Industrialization?* (London 1985); Kennedy 'Rural Economy'; McKernan, 'Dynamics'; Marilyn Cohen, 'Peasant differentiation and proto-industrialisation in the Ulster countryside: Tullylish, 1690–1825', *Journal of Peasant Studies*, 17 (1990), 414–32; Jane Gray, 'The Irish and Scottish linen industries in the eighteenth centuries: an incorporated comparison', in Cohen, *The Warp.*   28 Peter Kriedte, Hans Medick, Jurgan Schlumbohom (eds), *Industrialization Before Industrialization* (Cambridge 1981); Franklin Mendels, 'Proto-industrialization: the first phase of the industrialization process', *Journal of Economic History*, 32, no. 1 (1972), 241–62. For a useful review of recent revisions of the proto-industrialization model in Europe see the special issue on 'Proto-industrialization in Europe', *Continuity and Change*, 8, part 2 (1993); and Ogilvie and Cerman, *European Proto-industrialization.*   29 Cohen, 'Peasant Differentiation', Maxine Berg, *The Age of Manufactures, 1700–1820* (Totowa 1985), 133–4; Pat Hudson, 'Proto-industrialisation: the case of the West Riding wood textile industry in the 18th and early 19th centuries', *History Workshop*, 11 (1981), 37; Alice Littlefield and Hill Gates (eds) *Marxist Approaches in Economic Anthropology.* Monographs in Economic Anthropology, no. 9 (Lanham 1990); and Liu, *Weaver's Knot*, p. 58.   30 Cohen, 'Peasant Differentiation'.   31 Jay O'Brien and William Roseberry, 'Introduction', in Jay O'Brien and William Roseberry (eds), *Golden Ages, Dark Ages* (Berkeley, CA 1991), p. 5; Scott Cook, *Peasant Capitalist Industry* (Lanham 1984), pp. 4, 192; Gerald Sider, *Culture and Class in Anthropology and History* (Cambridge 1986), pp. 34–8.   32 W.H. Crawford, 'Ulster landowners and the linen industry', in J.T. Ward and

I conceptualize the emerging economic interdependence between landlord, bleachers and drapers during the late eighteenth century as a Protestant elite 'bloc', whose economic and political strategies provided the structural foundation for the genesis of rural industrial capitalism in the parish.[33] I argue that the basis for their power was both economic and cultural. The bloc's economic dominance emerged from ownership of the means of production – land, bleaching or finishing premises and merchant capital. However, if we ignore the fact that such ownership rested with Protestants – whose symbolic world emphasized individualism and personal achievement – and with men – those culturally enabled to seek their independent fortunes – significant cultural dimensions of their hegemony remain unanalyzed.

It is not coincidental that the period of fastest industrial growth in Tullylish, between 1841 and 1861, coincided with the Great Famine. While the multifaceted impact of the Famine has become an important theme in Irish historiography, the connection between an expanding capitalist linen industry and the Famine in northeast Ulster remains poorly investigated.[34] Here again, a widely known historical fact – that the Famine's impact was weakest in northeast Ulster – has resulted in overgeneralization and a poor understanding of the famine's processes west and east of the Bann. Microhistorical analysis of Tullylish provides an excellent case study for investigating the connections between the Great Famine, proletarianization, urbanization and enlightened paternalism and the linen industry. The parish was divided between two Poor Law Unions: Banbridge which included the industrializing mid-section along the Bann, and Lurgan, which included the handloom weaving townlands to the north. Through an examination of the divergent effects of the Famine in both Unions including a detailed analysis of the Johnston estate, I will analyze how divergent regional economic structures and gender conceptions mediated mortality, internal migration, evictions, industrial development and proletarianization in Tullylish.

With mill-based spinning, the centre of the Irish linen industry shifted to urban Belfast. The bulk of our knowledge concerning the industrial revolution in northeast Ulster focuses upon Belfast and the Lagan Valley.[35] We know more about the connection between urbanization and the linen industry, the condition of the working class and attempts to organize them in Belfast, than we do about these processes

R.G. Wilson (eds), *Land and Industry* (New York 1971); 'The influence of the landlord in eighteenth century Ulster', in L.M. Cullen and T.C. Smout (eds), *Comparative Aspects of Scottish and Irish Economic and Social History 1600–1900* (Edinburgh 1977); Leslie A. Clarkson, 'Pre-Factory industry in Northern Ireland', in Pat Hudson (ed.), *Regions and Industries* (Manchester 1986), pp. 260–1; W.A. Maguire, *The Downshire Estates in Ireland 1801–1845* (Oxford 1972).   33 Antonio Gramsci, *Selections from the Prison Notebooks* (New York 1971), pp. 157–8, 366.   34 For an anthropologically informed perspective on the Famine see, Joan Vincent, 'A political orchestration of the Irish famine: County Fermanagh, May 1847', in Silverman and Gulliver, idem.   35 Green, Lagan Valley : E.R.R. Green, 'Belfast entrepreneurship in the nineteenth century', in L.M. Cullen and P. Butel (eds), *Negoce et Industrie en France et en Irlande aux XVIIIe XIXe Siecles* (Paris, 1980); J.C. Beckett et al., *Belfast: The Making of the City* (Belfast 1983). For a broader economic perspective see Kennedy and Ollerenshaw, idem.

in rural industrial regions not visited as often by state officials or reformers.[36] The villages and towns in rural industrial Tullylish and Seapatrick formed part of an urban hierarchy headed by Belfast, that shared many of the same social problems as other British urban industrial cities.

A distinct type of urbanization and urbanism emerged in rural villages and towns built and guided by paternalistic linen entrepreneurs. These settlements, which were often 'an amalgam of factory-dominated neighbourhoods or "villages"' reflected the distinct challenges faced by rural capitalists in the early Victorian period to ensure sufficient sources of power and labour.[37] Capitalist strategies to overcome these obstacles often included the provision of housing and, at times, the institutional framework for complex communities.

Such rural factory settlements in Ireland and elsewhere flourished in the early years of industrialization 'when industrial discipline had to be imposed for the first time, and an industrial society created *de novo* in a rural land-scape'.[38] In Ulster, the rapid advancement of the linen industry between 1825 and 1880, nurtured the growth of numerous factory settlements that have not received the scholarly attention they deserve. The case study of Gilford/Dunbarton presented here represents a historically specific example of 'new towns' or industrial developments built adjacent to existing older villages and towns in the late eighteenth and early nineteenth centuries. The built environment of the town, as it emerged during the second half of the nineteenth century, reflected its specific production and commercial functions and the specific ways status-class and religious sect were configured.[38a]

There have been few attempts beyond my own to extend Denis McNiece's pioneering research on worker's housing in several factory towns in Ulster.[39] My analysis builds upon the theoretically sophisticated literature on employer paternalism as a form of cultural hegemony in the nineteenth century. This hegemony took historically and culturally specific forms. To analyze cultural hegemony in Tullylish, I link together the theoretical insights of Patrick Joyce, feminist analysis of Victorian familial

36 Emily Boyle, 'The economic development of the Irish linen industry', in Beckett, idem.; R.A. Butlin (ed.), *The Development of the Irish Town* (New Jersey 1977); P. Froggatt, 'Industrialisation and health in Belfast in the early nineteenth century', in Mary O'Dowd and David Harkness (eds), *The Town in Ireland* (Belfast 1979); A.C. Hepburn and Brenda Collins, 'The structure of Belfast, 1901', in P. Roebuck (ed), *Plantation to Partition: Essays in Honour of J. L. McCracken* (Belfast 1981); L.M. Clarkson, 'Population change and urbanisation', in Kennedy and Ollerenshaw, idem.   37 Patrick Joyce, *Work, Society and Politics* (New Brunswick 1980), p. 145.   38 Ibid., p. 146.   38a Marilyn Silverman and P.H. Gulliver, *Merchants and Shopkeepers: A Historical Anthropology of an Irish Market Town*, 1200–1991 (Toronto 1995)).   39 Denis S. McNiece, 'Industrial villages of Ulster, 1800–1900', in Peter Roebuck (ed.), *Plantation to Partition*, op. cit.; Bessbrook Spinning Co. Ltd., and J.N. Richardson, Sons and Owden, Ltd., *Bessbrook: A Record of Industry in a Northern Ireland Village Community and of a Social Experiment 1845–1945* (Belfast n.d.); Charlotte Fell Smith, *James Nicholson Richardson of Bessbrook* (London 1925); Herdsmans Ltd., *1835 to 1935 – At the Works of Herdsmans Ltd. Sion Mills, Co. Tyrone* (privately printed, n.d.); S.A. Royle, 'Industrialization, urbanization and urban society in post-famine Ireland c. 1850–1921', in B.J. Graham and L.J. Proudfoot (eds), *An Historical Geography of Ireland* (London 1993); Cohen, 'Paternalism and Poverty'; and 'Urbanisation'.

models of social inequality and the mediation of upper-class status in Ulster by Protestantism.[40] The investigation of nineteenth-century factory culture focuses upon several questions that highlight the tension between paternalistic structures generated by employers and working-class agency. How did the centrality of work in the linen mills and factories influence the formation of social classes, occupations, households, social institutions and the network of social relationships among coworkers, kin and neighbours in the community? How did this close interdependence, born of dependency upon low wages, generate consensus with gendered notions of a work ethic, independence, self-improvement and respectability at its core? What forms of ambivalence among the working class existed relating to these work-centred identities and ideologies, and how was subjectivity linked to differentiation along occupational, gender and religious lines?

This analysis of employer paternalism as a form of cultural hegemony incorporates the insights of feminist scholars who have linked Victorian employer paternalism with cultural conceptions of gender rooted in the patriarchal family.[41] Such gender conceptions were not monolithic, fixed in time or oppressive in unvarying degrees. The paternalistic employer, as a historically specific type of hegemonic masculinity, was both individualized, remote from other men, and an icon signifying the public omnipotent father. As figures of authority within the family, fathers were expected to provide their dependent wives and children with the physical necessities of life, train their sons for future adult breadwinning roles and oversee their children's spiritual and moral development. Such familial responsibilities were extended to factory workforces by paternalistic employers.

An important goal of this book is to push women's history in Ireland beyond the 'herstory' stage to a level where gender is at the centre of analysis mediating social structures, social practices, ideologies and identities.[42] This goal dovetails with interdisciplinary perspectives since the analysis of gender has been from its inception a transdisciplinary endeavour, grappling with its omnirelevance in all aspects of social life.[43] First, I build upon more than two decades of scholarly research into women and work that has uncovered how gender shapes class relations, the work process, the wage form, workplace conflicts and the complex links between the workplace, family and community life. Although it is well known that women were central lynchpins in the Irish linen industry, our understanding of the theoretical connections between gender and the sexual division of labour, class formation, capital accumulation, regional development, community networks, unionization,

40 Joyce, *Work, Society and Politics.* 41 Sonya Rose, *Limited Livelihoods* (Berkeley, CA 1992), pp. 33–49; Judy Lown, *Women and Industrialization* (Minneapolis, MN 1990). 42 Margaret MacCurtin and Donncha O'Corrain (eds), *Women in Irish Society: The Historical Dimension* (Westport, CT 1979); Margaret MacCurtin and Mary O'Dowd (eds), *Women in Early Modern Ireland* (Edinburgh 1991); Maria Luddy and Cliona Murphy (eds), *Women Surviving* (Dublin 1989); Chris Curtin, Pauline Jackson and Barbara O'Connor (eds) *Gender in Irish Society* (Galway 1987). 43 Shulamit Reinharz, *Feminist Methods in Social Research* (Oxford 1992), p. 250.

work ideologies and family strategies is limited.[44] Placing gender at the centre of Ireland's localized textile-based industrial revolution, will necessarily suggest new questions and perspectives.

Women remain a poorly understood segment of the Irish working class. Most of Irish labour historiography remains embedded in male models that focus on androcentric definitions of work, men's work and attempts to organize men into trade unions.[45] This bias emerges partly from conventional dichotomous opposi- tions between male/public/work verses female/private/home that have margin- alized women's labour history generally. While the majority of Irish female linen industry workers were, indeed, young single daughters who conformed to Victorian cultural norms regarding the sexual division of labour and female employment pat- terns, a significant minority diverged from these norms. Further, since the majority of female linen industry workers were not members of trade unions in the period analyzed here, we need to investigate alternative gendered forms of social organiza- tion, conceptualized by Ava Baron as 'women's separate world of homosocial bonds', to reveal them as active agents in the workplace and home.[46]

Because the industrial labour force in the linen industry was predominantly fe- male, it provides an ideal context for examining women's contributions to the in- dustrialization process in Ireland and the relationships between women, work and family. Research investigating these connections in Ireland is in its infancy and has largely concentrated on rural women engaged in agricultural production.[47] Handloom

44 Cohen, 'Proletarianization'; 'Survival Strategies'; 'Rural Paths'; Marilyn Cohen, 'From Gilford to Greenwich: the migration experience of female-headed households at the turn of the century', in Patrick O'Sullivan (ed.) *The Irish World Wide, Vol. 4, Irish Women and the Irish Migrations* (Leicester 1995); Joanna Bourke, 'Women and poultry in Ireland, 1891–1914', *Irish Historical Studies* (1987), 293–310; 'Dairymaids and housewives: the dairy industry in Ireland 1890–1914', *Agricultural History Review*, xvi (1990); '"The best of all home rulers": the economic power of women in Ireland, 1880–1914', *Irish Economic and Social History*, xviii (1991), 34–47; *Husbandry to Housewifery* (Oxford 1993).   45 James Connolly, *Labour in Irish History* (New York 1919); James Connolly, *Selected Writings* (Harmondsworth 1973); Desmond Ryan, *James Connolly* (Dublin 1924); Samuel Levenson, *James Connolly* (London 1973); W.P. Ryan, *The Irish Labor Movement* (New York 1920); P. Berresford Ellis, *A History of the Irish Working Class* (London 1972); J. Dunsmore Clarkson, *Labour and Nationalism in Ireland, Studies in History Economic and Public Law*, vol. CXX, no. 266 (New York 1952); Emmett Larkin, *James Larkin: Labour Leader 1876–1947* (Cambridge, MA 1965); Nora Connolly O'Brien, *James Connolly, Portrait of a Rebel Father* (Dublin 1975). Some information on Irish Women's trade union activities can be gleaned from Barbara Drake, *Women in Trade Unions, Labour Research Department* (London 1920); Norbert C. Soldon, *Women in British Trade Unions 1874–1979* (Dublin 1978); Mary Daly, 'Women in the Irish workforce from pre-industrial to modern times', *Saothar*, 7 (1981), 74–82; 'Women work and trade unionism', in MacCurtain and O'Corrain (eds), *Women in Irish Society*; Rosemary Owens, '"Votes for ladies, votes for women": organized labour and the suffrage movement, 1876–1922', *Saothar*, 9 (1983), 32–47; Mary Jones, *These Obstreperous Lassies: A History of the Irish Women Workers Union* (Dublin 1988).   46 Ava Baron, 'Gender and labor history: learning from the past, looking to the future', in Ava Baron (ed.), *Work Engendered* (Ithaca 1991), pp. 8–12; Rose, *Limited Livelihoods*, p. 9.   47 Bourke, 'Homerulers'; 'Women and Poultry'; 'Dairymaids and Housewives'; *Husbandry to Housewifery*.

weaving was a collective enterprise where the labour and earnings of women were essential. However, an androcentric bias existed in the culture shaping the types of work performed by women, their identities and signifying hierarchical relation-ships between genders and generations. Similar to the Choletais region in France, handloom weaving involved a hierarchical organization of tasks and status favour-ing the male household head over women and children. Embedded in this distinc-tion was a cultural construction of masculinity partly in terms of skill or craftsmanship in weaving linen cloth and femininity in terms of assisting or sup-porting this main activity.[48] The cultural association between skill and masculinity proved to be tenacious influencing occupational sex segregation, asymmetrical wage scales and the formation of trade unions throughout linen's history.

Although a considerable descriptive literature relating to the types and condi-tions of work performed by female linen operatives exists, many unanswered ques-tions relating to their work experience remain.[49] These questions demand that we historicize the analysis of patriarchy and gendered identities in linen producing households, historicize the theoretical relationship between unwaged work and the reproduction of a capitalist linen industry, adopt a broad definition of work which includes unwaged work and how it articulated with the labour market, and analyze women-centred networks and how these shaped workplace culture and community life.

Since Betty Messenger's pioneering *Picking Up the Linen Threads* published in 1975, only a small number of scholars have worked on these questions.[50] This book asks how, why, under what circumstances and with what consequences Irish women were assimilated into the linen industry over a period of two centuries. In consider-ing the intersection between class and gender, I will analyze how conceptions of masculinity and femininity influenced the kinds of paid and unpaid work performed by women emphasizing that new technology, occupations, skills and pay scales were

48 Liu, *Weaver's Knot*, pp. 234–6.   49 Betty Messenger, *Picking Up the Linen Threads* (Belfast 1980); Marilyn Cohen, 'Working conditions and experiences of work in the linen industry: Tullylish, County Down', *Ulster Folklife*, 30 (1984), 1–21; Irene Margaret Thompson, 'Dust and Sensitivity in the Linen Industry: Investigations into the Health of Linen Workers', M.D. diss., The Queen's University of Belfast (1952); D.L. Armstrong, 'Social and economic conditions in the Belfast linen industry, 1850–1900', *Irish Historical Studies*, 7, no. 25, 235–69; Thomas Oliver, *Dangerous Trades* (London 1902); C.D. Purdon, *The Sanitary State of the Belfast Factory District during Ten years (1864–1873 inclusive), Under Various Aspects* (Belfast 1877); Hilda Martindale, *From One Generation to Another, 1839–1944* (London 1944). 50 Messenger, *Linen Threads*; Collins, 'Proto-industrialization'; Gray, 'Rural Industry', pp. 590–611; Jane Gray, 'Gender and plebian culture in Ulster', *Journal of Interdisciplinary History*, 24, no. 2 (1993), 251–70; Collins, 'Sewing and Social Structure', 242; Nuala Kelly, 'Women knitters cast off', in Chris Curtin, Pauline Jackson and Barbara O'Connor (eds), *Gender in Irish Society* (Galway 1987); Andrew Finlay, 'The cutting edge: Derry shirtmakers', in Curtin, Jackson and O'Conner idem; Leslie A. Clarkson and E. Margaret Crawford, 'Life after death: widows in Carrick-on-Suir, 1799', in Margaret MacCurtin and Mary O'Dowd (eds), *Women in Early Modern Ireland* (Edinburgh 1991); L.A. Clarkson, 'Love, labour and life: women in Carrick-on-Suir in the late eighteenth century', *Irish Economic and Social History*, 20 (1993), 18–34; Cohen, 'Survival Strategies', 303–18; Cohen, 'Gilford to Greenwich'; Hepburn and Collins, 'Industrial Society'.

subject to gendering. Scholars have shown that the types and patterns of work performed by women differed according to stages in their life cycle. While Irish working class women were no exception, following Carole Turbin, we should not assume that female linen industry workers were homogeneous or ignore the substantial minority of working-class women who diverged from conventional patterns and norms.[51]

Further, since most of our knowledge of women's waged work and working conditions in the linen industry focuses on spinning mills and weaving factories, the largest employers of women, I include all the phases of linen production where women were employed including rural flax scutching mills, the making-up phase of production, homework and bleachgreens.[52] I argue that conceptions of gender are central to the analysis of women's work and State attempts to regulate working conditions. Finally, since the reproduction of working-class families often depended on supplemental earnings, the unpaid labour of women and children and non-market resources, these will be included to illuminate the multifaceted ways women contributed to household and community survival.

In an industry notorious for paying low wages, a central question to be addressed is how poverty constrained household and community survival strategies. The concept of strategies will be used throughout this book retaining the tension between agency and structural determination.[53] The decisions made by members of the working class were fundamentally shaped by the structure of the local economy, class stratification and unequal generational and gender relations. The analytical utility of family strategies has been enhanced by scholars who have addressed problems which arise from assumptions of functional interdependence. Others have probed into the levels of meaning in this military metaphor to answer the fundamental question of how families can have strategies. Laurel Cornell has specified three elements: a policy or long term goals; a strategy or the ability to identify opportunities, mobilize resources and take advantage of these; and tactics, the everyday choices made throughout the duration of engagement.[54]

None of these elements are gender neutral. Policy goals were partly economic, relating to size and security of income, and partly cultural, relating to gender specific standards of respectability. Strategies included job recruitment patterns, waged and unwaged contributions by household members and gender specific self-help networks. Job recruitment practices in the linen industry reflected the prevalence

---

51 Carole Turbin, 'Beyond conventional wisdom: women's wage work, household economic contribution and labor activism in a mid-nineteenth century working class community', in Carol Groneman and Mary Beth Norton (eds), *To Toil the Livelong Day* (Ithaca 1987), pp. 48–9; 'Beyond dichotomies: interdependence in mid-nineteenth century working class families in the United States', *Gender and History*, 1, no. 3 (1989), 297; *Working Women of Collar City* (Urbana 1992).   52 Cohen, 'Working Conditions'; and Cohen, 'Proletarianization'.   53 Louise A. Tilly, 'Individual lives and family strategies in the French proletariat', *Journal of Family History* (Summer, 1979); 'Beyond family strategies', *Historical Methods*, 20, no. 3 (1987); Nancy Folbre, 'Family strategy, feminist strategy', *Historical Methods*, 20, no. 3 (1987).   54 Laurel L. Cornell, 'Where can family strategies exist', *Historical Methods*, 20, no. 3 (1987), 120–3.

of a family labour system, another connection between workplace and home characteristic of the linen industry and small factory towns and hamlets in Tullylish.[55] Finally, tactics that were operationalized on a daily basis, emerged from the myriad of social interactions organized by wives and female household heads who exclusively managed household budgets. These overlapping relations between co-worker, kin and neighbours were shaped by the contingencies of class, religion and gender.[56]

The book is divided into parts corresponding with the historical division of the linen industry before and after the spread of mill-based spinning. The first part focuses upon capitalist class formation during the 'long eighteenth century' between 1690 and 1825. The second part concentrates on the nineteenth century encompassing the period between 1825 and 1914. Evidence was derived from a variety of archival, oral and secondary sources. The backbone of archival data for social historical analysis was the 1901 Irish Census, and 1901 Census Enumerator's Schedules linked with other nominal lists including wage books, school attendance registers, valuations and an Outdoor Relief Register for the Banbridge Board of Guardians (see Appendix 1). This quantitative data were supplemented by business records, estate papers, school records and correspondence, Board of Guardian records and Gilford Town Commissioners records. Finally, Parliamentary Papers relating to the linen industry, Factory Inspectors Reports and investigations into wages and cost of living among the working class were used as were the annual reports of Commissioners of National Education in Ireland.[57]

As an anthropologist, I wanted to retain a concrete focus on real people who experienced and coped with the dominance of linen over their lives. Consequently, doing 'the archive in the field' meant combining archival evidence with extensive interviews.[58]

---

55 Leslie Clarkson, 'The city and the country', in Beckett, idem, p. 156; Mary Blewett, *The Last Generation* (Amherst 1990), p. 147.   56 Rosemary Harris, *Prejudice and Tolerance in Ulster* (Manchester 1972); Elliott Leyton, 'Opposition and integration in Ulster', *Man*, IX (1974), 185–98; Anthony Buckley, *The Gentle People: A Study of a Peaceful Community in Ulster* (Cultra 1982); Hastings Donnan and Graham McFarlane, 'Social life in rural Northern Ireland', *Studies* (Autumn, 1985); Hastings Donnan and Graham McFarlane, 'Informal Social Organisation', in J. Darby (ed.), *Northern Ireland: Background to the Conflict* (Belfast 1983); Hastings Donnan and Graham McFarlane, '"You get on better with your own": social continuity and change in rural Northern Ireland', in Patrick Clancy, Sheelagh Drudy, Kathleen Lynch, and Liam O'Dowd (eds), *Ireland: A Sociological Profile* (Dublin 1986); Donnan and McFarlane, 'Social Anthropology'; Graham McFarlane, 'Dimensions of protestantism: the working of protestant identity in a Northern Irish village', in Curtin and Wilson (eds), *Ireland from Below* (Galway 1987); Richard Jenkins, 'Ethnicity and the rise of capitalism in Ulster', in Robin Ward and Richard Jenkins (eds), *Ethnic Communities in Business* (Cambridge 1984); Richard Jenkins, 'Northern Ireland: in what sense "religious" in conflict', in Richard Jenkins, Hastings Donnan and Graham McFarlane, *The Sectarian Divide in Northern Ireland Today*. Royal Anthropological Institute of Great Britain and Ireland, Occasional Papers no. 41 (1986); Vincent, 'Marriage, Religion and Class'; Thomas M. Wilson, 'Culture and class among the "Large" farmers of eastern Ireland', *American Ethnologist*, 15 (1988), 678–93; Cohen, 'Religion and Social Inequality'.   57 For a thorough discussion of source relating to the Irish linen industry see Cohen, *The Warp*.   58 Joan Vincent quoted in Silverman and Gulliver, op. cit., p. 54.

These oral histories serve two purposes. One follows Paul Thompson's early empirical inspiration to 'imagine what evidence is needed, seek it out and capture it'.[59] This approach to oral history collects additional qualitative facts for a 'structural reading' of evidence relating to family strategies, socialization practices, self-help and women-centred networks.[60] Oral evidence was gathered to explore workers' perceptions and reactions to their working conditions, to the division of labour in the home, to poverty and to factors working to both unite and divide the community. This evidence served to both expand a largely quantitative database and better illuminate existential differences. It highlights the ways a narrow employment base, low wages, social class stratification, religious discrimination and patriarchy shaped the experiences and perceptions of the various men and women interviewed.

A second purpose, less bound within empiricism, was to use popular memory to help reveal the hidden history and ambiguities of Irish working-class and women's subjectivity. Here I integrate the insights of Luisa Passerini and the Popular Memory Group.[61] Passerini's usage of 'subjectivity' provides a useful conceptual tool for exploring the contingencies of human agency at the level of consciousness. By posing the connection between structural 'coercion' and subjectivity, defined broadly to include attitudes, behaviour, language, identity, self-consciousness as problematic, Passerini provides clues for interpreting ambiguities in the forms of working-class consensus.

Cultural readings 'focus on the ways in which the account makes sense of a structured experience or life history' revealing the socially differentiated and ambiguous nature of symbolic meanings and representations of reality.[62] A cultural reading emerges from a number of questions. How did the working class interpret class stratification and limited life chances? How did women evaluate their double oppression and contributions to household survival? How did children evaluate their contributions and sacrifices for their household's maintenance? How did gendered work ideologies reveal the ambiguity between consensus and spontaneous subjectivity reflected in contradictory attitudes to waged and unwaged work.

Tullylish epitomized rural industrial regions in Ulster whose narrow economies were based upon the linen industry, which was, in turn, dependent upon foreign markets and cheap female labour. The historically specific structures of class, gender, and religious stratification provide the warp through which working-class experiences and identities were woven creating a tapestry of social life in these working class communities that extended over two centuries.

---

59 Paul Thompson, *The Voice of the Past: Oral History* (Oxford 1978); p. 7. See also Appendix 1.   60 Popular Memory Group, 'Popular memory: theory, politics, method', in Richard Johnson, Gregor McLennan, Bill Schwarz, David Sutton (eds), *Making Histories* (Minneapolis, MN 1982), p. 227.   61 Luisa Passerini, 'Work ideology and consensus under fascism', *History Workshop*, 8 (1979), 83–108; Popular Memory Group.   62 Popular Memory Group, 'Popular Memory', p. 227.

PART I

THE LONG EIGHTEENTH CENTURY:
PROTO-INDUSTRIALIZATION IN TULLYLISH, 1690–1825

I

Dependency and Domestic Industry: Contextualizing the Eighteenth-Century Irish Linen Industry

> The Irish Sea separated two different worlds and so the factors in the rise and development of the linen industry in such a colonial atmosphere, where its promotion with government support and under the aegis of the Linen Board, was designed originally to strengthen the Protestant interest, differ in degree from those of a comparable industry in Britain.
>
> William H. Crawford, 1971[1]

DEPENDENT DOMESTIC INDUSTRY: IRISH LINEN AND ENGLISH DOMINATION

The micro perspective in history and anthropology problematizes the linkages between localities and major historical transformations, such as the rise of capitalism, so that particular consequences become visible. This chapter contextualizes the eighteenth-century Irish linen industry as an example of colonial proto-industry by connecting it to political and economic dependence on England. It also explores the particular nature of dependency in linen producing regions along the River Bann. Last: it describes the eighteenth-century production and circulation system.

Although narrow or bandle linen had for centuries been produced in Ireland, its commercial expansion was wholly dependent upon trade access to English markets. The Irish linen industry illustrates the combined effects of English mercantilist policy and commercial interests on Irish economic development, and its consequent dependent industrialization. After 1696, and throughout the eighteenth century, linen from Scotland and Ireland was deliberately encouraged by granting it duty-free access to English markets. The vast majority of Irish linen cloth was exported to England and the American colonies to clothe the English lower classes and American slaves. Linen came largely to supplant, though not to eliminate, imports to England from the Continent reducing its dependence on foreign sources.[2] By

1 W.H. Crawford, 'Ulster landowners and the linen industry', in J.T. Ward and R.G. Wilson (eds), *Land and Industry* (New York 1971), p. 117. 2 Ireland, like most European countries, grew flax, hand spun yarn and wove linen cloth for hundreds of years. See William Carter, *A Short History of the Linen Trade, Volume I: To the Time of the Industrial Revolution* (Belfast 1952), p. 3; W.H. Crawford, *Domestic Industry in Ireland: The Experience of the Linen Industry* (Dublin 1972), p. 1.

1725, linen was second in importance only to provisions in the list of Irish exports and accounted for almost one-third of their total value.[3] By the second half of the eighteenth century, more than 90 per cent of Irish linen exports were destined for England.

Another consequence of English colonial domination that facilitated the growth of the linen industry was the introduction of the English estate system and Cromwellian Settlement in the seventeenth century. The plantation of Ulster, which aimed after 1607 to impose English civilization on the conquered native Irish, divided the six counties at its disposal into a large number of discrete estates. These estates were transformed into manors on the English model by granting patents that transformed landowners into landlords through a confirmation and legitimization of power over their tenants.

By the seventeenth century, these early modern manors reflected the social changes associated with the first period of the enclosure movement in England between 1460 and 1640. As production for the market expanded, attempts by landlords, the new gentry, and yeoman to consolidate and improve their estates and holdings undermined the role of the community as decision maker in production. In Ireland, the 'Orders and Conditions' of the plantation scheme stipulated that leased farms be enclosed and compact rather than fragmented under the rundale system.[4] Manorial patents in Ulster were instruments of colonization designed to give each landlord the legal authority necessary to operate an effective local government with many new manors designed to correspond with parishes.[5]

Although the global changes resulting from the Cromwellian Settlement in Ireland are well known, local experiences were variable. The manor of Gilford (Magill's Ford) was created in 1680, during the life of the first John Magill (Johnston). The Johnstons of Gilford were of Scottish origin and first came to Ireland in the 1640s. In a 1678 charter, all of the 800 acres granted to Captain John Magill, inherited by his grandson John, 'shall be from henceforth taken for one entire manor to be known and called by the name of the Manor of Gilford'.[6] The patent creating the manor of Gilford transformed John Magill into a landlord with the power to make tenures, hold a Court Leet and Court Baron, authority to hold and keep two fairs in the town of Gilford, and to hold a weekly market in Gilford each Monday. Gilford remained the chief residence of the Johnston family until the mid-nineteenth century.[7]

The parish of Tullylish was noted in both the 1422 and 1546 valuations; in the

---

3 According to Cullen, 'the Irish linen industry was perhaps the most remarkable instance in Europe of an export-based advance in the eighteenth century'. See L.M. Cullen, *An Economic History of Ireland since 1600* (New York 1972), p. 53.   4 W.H. Crawford, 'The significance of landed estates in Ulster 1600–1820', *Irish Economic and Social History*, 17 (1900), 49–51; D. McCourt, 'The decline of rundale, 1750–1850', in Peter Roebuck (ed.) *Plantation to Partition*.   5 Crawford, 'Significance of landed estates', pp. 44–7.   6 (PRONI), T.1282, Parkanaur MSS. vol. X, p. 2; See also M.P. Campbell, 'Gilford and its mills', Review: *Journal of the Craigavon Historical Society* 4, no. 3 (1981–2), 20.   7 (PRONI), T.426, Myles MSS., p. 59.

1609 charter of Dromore Cathedral, it formed part of the Corps of the Deanery.[8] From the twelfth century, the Baronies of Upper and Lower Iveagh in County Down, that included Tullylish, were in the possession of the Magennis sept.[9] Despite the loyalty of the sept throughout the reign of Elizabeth, they played a prominent role in the 1641 Rebellion against the English led by Sir Arthur Magennis, Lord Viscount Iveagh. Under Art Oge and Edmund Boy Magennis, rebels marched on Lurgan, which they attacked and burned. Under Hugh Roe, rebels marched into Lisnegarvey (Lisburn) where numerous English and Scotch settlers died. The early church at Tullylish was also probably destroyed in the rebellion; it was described as ruined in the 1657 inquisition.[10]

After the rebellion was crushed by Oliver Cromwell, various inquiries were held that gave witness to local incidents in Tullylish, and resulted in the seisure and distribution of the Magennis sept's lands.[11] Every soldier who fought received a land debenture for a holding in proportion to the arrears of pay due to him at the rate in Ulster of 4s. to the acre.[12] Through this process, the ancient territory of Clanconnell fell to Lord Deputy Fleetwood's troop of horse and the company of his regiment of foot commanded by Captain John Barret. One small portion of 41 acres in Tullylish fell to the lot of Captain Sterne's troop.

Since most soldiers had no desire to become colonists, their officers saw an opportunity for the easy acquisition of large estates. They bought up the men's grants and established themselves as landlords while the soldiers returned to England. Captain John Barret, an officer in Fleetwood's Regiment, sold the land he had bought to Sir George Rawdon, Captain Magill, William Leslie and William Waring.[13] The area was then planted with colonists from southwest Scotland and the north of England, many of whom were Church of Ireland, resulting in the large proportion of this denomination in the diocese of Dromore and its immediate surrounding area.[14] Together transplanted British Protestant landowners and tenants comprised a 'bridgehead' group, or enclave of people from the dominant centre in England, who shared a 'harmony of interest' and desire to reproduce English hegemony.[15] The origins of the eighteenth- and nineteenth-century Protestant landowning class in Tullylish emerged from this change in landownership from the Catholic Magennis sept to New English and Scots beneficiaries.

A key strategy among these beneficiaries to encourage the settlement of British tenants on their estates was to grant favourable terms of tenure. John Magill, born in Scotland and an officer in Cromwell's army, acquired an extensive estate in

8 *Clergy of Down and Dromore* (Belfast 1996), p. 240. 9 E.D. Atkinson, *Dromore, An Ulster Diocese* (Dundalk 1925), pp. 4–5, 16. 10 Ibid., pp. 20–1; *Clergy of Down and Dromore*, p. 240. 11 (PRONI), D.695/96, Waring MSS., 25 May 1690; and T.370/A Downe Survey. 12 Dean Myles, *Historical Notes on the Parish of Tullylish* (n.d.), p. 10; and E.D. Atkinson, *An Ulster Parish: Being a History of Donaghcloney* (Dublin 1898), p. 23. 13 (PRONI), T.370/A, Downe Survey; D.695/131, Waring MSS.; and M.P. Campbell, *A History of Tullylish* (Lurgan 1985), pp. 12–15. 14 Atkinson, *Dromore*, p. 40. 15 Johan Galtung, 'A structural theory of imperialism', *Journal of Peace Research*, 8, no. 2 (1971), 81–3.

Tullylish, Donaghcloney and Dromore where he established his Gill Hall Estate. John Magill left no male issue, and according to his will, left all of his lands to the son of his only daughter Susanna who married William Johnston, a Lieutenant of the Dragoons stationed in Dromore.[16] Sir John Magill (Johnston) reputedly 'established a very respectable Protestant yeomanry on his estate by granting considerable parts of it in perpetuity to Scotch adventurers'.[17]

In the decades that followed the Cromwellian Settlement, there was an increased immigration from Britain. Immigrants from central and southern Scotland settled in north Ulster, while those from northern England settled in mid-Ulster, especially in the Lagan Valley and north Armagh. In mid-Ulster, the linen industry developed along commercial lines based on the imported skills of these northern English linen weavers originating from areas dominated by weaving and small-scale commercial agriculture. Settlement in Ireland attracted many British weavers who attempted to improve the terms of their tenancies based on the growing manufacture of cloth indicated by a yarn surplus and the cheapness of land.[18] These weavers brought with them the ability to weave coarse cloth, such as was woven in north Yorkshire and parts of Cumberland, and fine linen woven in Manchester.[19] They also usually sponsored themselves and brought insufficient funds for large-scale investments in land. Consequently, they sought to diversify agriculture with textile production.[20] The new immigration of skilled linen weavers from northern England and France provide part of the answer as to why linen came to be concentrated in the north of Ireland.

According to David Hempton and Myrtle Hill, 'it is on the canvas of the original settlement patterns that the various shapes and shades of Ulster religion are primarily to be located'.[21] As elsewhere in Ulster, Protestantism in Tullylish was not a 'parochial monolith', but rather comprised of diverse sects.[22] Although Scots Presbyterians were the most powerful of the dissenting sects in numerical and organizational terms, another group of migrants from northern England, the Quakers, assumed power in the parish. Originating from Cumberland, Yorkshire, Lancashire and Westmorland, Quakers settled in small groups or as individual families on land leased to them as a result of negotiations between proprietors and the Society of Friends as a corporate body from the 1650s. The areas in Ulster where they settled were Lurgan, Lisburn, Kilmore, Magheralin, Banbridge and the townland of

16 (PRONI), D.1549, Bundle 71, Burgess Estate Papers, The Will of John Magill, 5 January, 1676; T.426, Myles MSS., p. 53; T.1282, Parkanaur MSS., vol. III, p. 91.   17 (PRONI), T.426, Myles MSS., p. 54; and T.1282, Parkanaur MSS., vol. III, p. 91.   18 W.H. Crawford, 'Ulster landowners and the linen industry', in J.T. Ward and R.G. Wilson (eds), *Land and Industry* (New York 1971), p. 118.   19 William H. Crawford, 'Economy and Society in Eighteenth Century Ulster', Ph.D. diss., The Queen's University of Belfast, 1982, p. 83; 'Drapers and bleachers in the early Ulster linen industry,' in L.M. Cullen and P. Butel (eds), *Negoce et Industrie*, p. 113.   20 Peter Gibbon, *The Origins of Ulster Unionism* (Manchester 1973), p. 14.   21 David Hempton and Myrtle Hill, *Evangelical Protestantism in Ulster Society, 1740–1890* (London 1992). p. 4.   22 David Hempton, 'Religious Minorities', in Patrick Loughrey (ed.), *The People of Ireland* (Belfast 1988), p. 155; J.C. Beckett, *Protestant Dissent in Ireland 1687–1780* (London 1948).

Moyallon owned by the Johnstons in Tullylish. Quakers made important contributions toward establishing the linen industry, some fifty years before the Protestant French Huguenots led by Louis Crommelin arrived.[23] Many Moyallon Quakers invested in bleaching and finishing mills along the Bann in the early eighteenth century.

Another reason for the concentration of the linen industry in Ulster was the more favourable terms of land tenure given to tenants in the north referred to as the 'Ulster Custom'. The Ulster Custom was defined by the 'Three F's' – fair rent (which influenced the other two), fixity of tenure and free sale by the tenant of his interest in the farm. Here too, the roots of the custom lie with the Ulster plantation. While immigration from Britain to Ireland increased during the course of the seventeenth century, the rate of flow was at first slow and sporadic. Landlords found it difficult to attract and hold tenants; hence attractive terms to new British colonists, such as the granting of leases, became commonplace. British tenants, who were required to introduce British husbandry practices such as enclosure, planting orchards and digging ditches, were thus guaranteed the enjoyment of these improvements throughout the duration of their leases. When their lease expired, there was widespread recognition of the right of a tenant to sell his lease to another or lay claim to renewal by their show of good faith and offer to pay the current value of the farm in increased rent.[24]

This differed from the situation of Catholic tenants – the vast majority outside of Ulster – who were still labouring under the Penal Code forbidding Catholics from holding land for long terms of years including life. Catholic tenants, therefore, did not have the same security of tenure; they were subject to rackrenting, or were penalized for improvements because the lease might be offered to a higher bidder when it expired. Such a system was as fatal to the development of manufacture as it was to agriculture.[25]

Liam Kennedy argues that claims relating to the benefits of the Ulster Custom and its causal implications for the development of the linen industry in Ulster are exaggerated. The tenant right payment was a lump sum (often substantial) paid by an incoming tenant to an outgoing tenant, and, as such, was not confined to Ulster or to areas associated with progressive farming. Incoming tenants effectively paid two rents – one to the landlord and one to the outgoing tenant. Nevertheless, tenant right was beneficial to the tenant because it was a payment or 'form of insurance' within the class of tenant farmers rather than between tenant and landlord and because the selection of successors rested largely with tenants rather than landlords. Kennedy concedes that the custom did 'facilitate some capital accumulation'

23 Carter, *Short History*, p. 6; Crawford, 'Drapers and bleachers', 113; Cullen, *Economic History*, p. 60; Leslie Clarkson, 'PreFactory industry in Northern Ireland', in Pat Hudson (ed.), *Regions and Industries* (Manchester 1986).   24 Crawford, 'Influence of the landlord', 194; W.H. Crawford, 'Ulster as a mirror of the two societies', in T.M. Devine and David Dickson (eds), *Ireland and Scotland 1600–1850* (Edinburgh 1983), p. 63.   25 Conrad Gill, *The Rise of the Irish Linen Industry* (Oxford 1925), p. 24.

in east Ulster aiding capital formation in agriculture, and diverting some capital from agriculture to handicraft production. However, since the sums involved were too small to make a major contribution, he concludes that a strong connection between the Ulster custom and the development of the linen industry in the countryside cannot be substantiated.[26]

Since low level investment by tenants cannot be quantitatively measured, it is difficult to argue with Kennedy's conclusion. However, the Ulster Custom was a factor in the differentiation of proto-industrial producers since it 'left an investible surplus in the hands of tenants'.[27] Crawford argues that after 1740, when the pace of economic development quickened, many leaseholders began to prosper at the expense of their undertenants since there was more profit in subletting land to weavers than in farming.[28] Therefore, the Ulster Custom allowed for small-scale capital formation and investment by those who leave scant evidence in historical records.

THE PRODUCTION AND CIRCULATION OF LINEN IN THE EIGHTEENTH CENTURY

Within this economic and political context, a particular system for producing and circulating linen cloth emerged and flourished in Ireland. Throughout the long eighteenth century between 1700 and 1825, linen yarn and cloth were produced in the Ulster countryside.[29] In comparison with Scotland, Irish linen producers were more likely to hold land where they grew food and flax resulting in near self-sufficiency regarding raw materials except flaxseed.[30] These proto-industrial producers were small tenant farmers, subtenants, cottiers, farm labourers and their families. Initially, weaving and spinning were by-industries to agriculture, with earnings

26 Liam Kennedy, 'The rural economy 1820–1914', in Liam Kennedy and Philip Ollerenshaw (eds), *An Economic History of Ulster 1820–1939* (Manchester 1985), pp. 38–410. In his critique of Mokyr, Kennedy argues for the importance of low-level capital formation in agriculture and industry. See Liam Kennedy, 'Why one million starved: an open verdict', *Irish Economic and Social History*, 11 (1984), 102–3; and Joel Mokyr, *Why Ireland Starved: A Quantitative and Analytical History of the Irish Economy, 1800–1850* (London 1983), p. 83. 27 Kennedy 'Rural Economy', pp. 40–1. 28 Crawford, 'Ulster as mirror', p. 63. 29 Primary sources include Walter Harris, *The Ancient and Present State of the County of Down* (Dublin 1744); Arthur Young, *A Tour in Ireland* (London 1892); Sir Charles Coote, *Statistical Survey of the County of Armagh* (Dublin 1804); Revd John Dubourdieu, *Statistical Survey of the County of Down* (Dublin 1802); Edward Wakefield, *An Account of Ireland, Statistical and Political* (London, 1812). Secondary sources include Gill, *Rise of the Linen Industry*; John Horner, *The Linen Trade of Europe during the Spinning Wheel Period* (Belfast 1920); E.R.R. Green, *The Lagan Valley 1800–1850* (London 1949); H.D. Gribbon, *The History of Water Power in Ulster* (Newton Abbot 1969); John W. McConaghy, 'Thomas Greer of Dungannon 1724–1803, Quaker Linen Merchant', Ph.D. diss., The Queen's University Belfast, 1979; Crawford, 'Economy and Society'; 'Drapers and bleachers'; 'Ulster landowners'; 'Influence of the Landlord'; *Domestic Industry*; 'Rise of the Linen Industry'; 'Evolution of Ulster towns'. 30 Alastair Durie and Peter Solar, 'The Scottish and Irish linen industries compared', in Rosalind Mitchison and Peter Roebuck (eds), *Economy and Society in Scotland and Ireland 1500–1939* (Edinburgh 1988), p. 211; Jane Gray, 'The Irish and Scottish linen industries in the eighteenth century: an incorporated comparison', in Marilyn Cohen (ed.), *The Warp of Ulster's Past* (New York 1996).

providing supplemental money for the rent and perhaps additional food not produced on the farm.[31] Money brought into the household through weaving reduced
the amount of land needed for growing food for the household or for sale. As a
result, small plots were further subdivided.[32] The importance of this combination
of agricultural and textile production to tenants was noted by John Cary as early as
1704:

> The Rents of Ireland grow due at two times of Payment, viz 1st of May, and
> 1st of November; the first becomes payable whilst their Cattle are Lean, which
> puts the Tenants under great straits, and forces them to sell very low, if they
> are pressed for Mony [*sic*]; but the second payment is more easily made their
> Fat Cattle being sold and their Harvest over. This is the state of that part of
> the Kingdom that depends on Feeding and Tillage; but where the Linnen
> Manufacture is, the Tenants are much easier; they spin in the Winter nights,
> and at other leisure times, which being wove into Cloath, and Whiten'd early
> in the Year, provides mony for their first Payment without selling their Cattle
> before fatted for a market.[33]

Linen production was usually organized along domestic lines with the family
functioning as the dominant force behind work discipline. Household members acted
as an androcentric production unit: the male head worked the land, his sons, if any,
wove cloth and helped him during harvest seasons. The female members were responsible for various preparatory processes; they helped to harvest and prepare the
flax, spun it into yarn to be used by the weavers, or sold and wound yarn onto
bobbins. This household production revealed familial cooperation but within the
confines of patriarchal hierarchy and a sexual division of labour. After the spread of
the fly shuttle in 1808, this rigid division of labour softened somewhat as women,
typically young daughters, increasingly turned to linen weaving. Following Anne
McKernan, women were encouraged to weave as the fly shuttle and the putting-out
system spread.[34]

Yarn spinning always had a commercial side linked to demand for yarn by weaving households within Ireland and the market in England where Irish linen yarn
was imported for use as warp by Lancashire cotton weavers. Because of yarn's
commercial importance, women were as economically important to the household

31 Brenda Collins, 'Proto-industrialization and pre-famine emigration', *Social History*, 7, no. 2 (1982),
pp. 130–1.   32 Young, *A Tour*, vol. 1, pp. 148, 150.   33 John Cary, *Some Considerations Relating to the
Carrying on of the Linen Manufacture in the Kingdom of Ireland* (London 1704), p. 12.   34 Anne
McKernan, 'War, gender, and industrial innovation: recruiting women weavers in early nineteenth century Ireland', *Journal of Social History*, 28, no. 1 (1995), 109–24; Anne McKernan, 'The Dynamics of
the Linen Triangle: Factor, Family and Farm in Ulster, 1740 to 1825', Ph.D. dissertation, The University of Michigan, 1992, pp. 264–9. Gay L. Gullickson, *Spinners and Weavers of Auffay* (Cambridge
1986), pp. 57–61 argues that in the Caux region of France a similar division of labour was found prior to
the spread of mill-spinning. Thereafter, displaced spinners turned to weaving in increasing numbers.

as men, for they earned needed cash to pay the rent or to lease larger plots on which to grow flax.[35] However, gender inequality was general.[36] Yarn spinning was a poorly remunerated task with lower status than weaving. Contemporaries, who took note of the wages earned by spinners, reported that they could earn from 3*d.* to 6*d.* per day while weavers earned from 1*s.* to 5*s.* depending on demand and type of cloth.[37]

The importance of spinners to a household at times led to taking in of itinerant spinners, who in return for board, lodging, and sometimes a small wage, spun for a weaver. Brenda Collins has shown that weaving households often were characterized by a flexibility of membership with extended kin, journeymen weavers, and itinerant spinners evident in the surviving 1821 Census Enumerators' Schedules.[38] Such co-residing non-kin were economic parts of the household and subject to the familial authority of the male household head.

Handloom weaving was a complicated and tedious process.[39] Setting up or 'mounting' a loom involved tying each warp thread to the warp beam, feeding these threads through the 'mails' on the 'headles' and between the teeth of the 'reed' before being tied to the 'cloth beam'. The amount of time needed to complete these tasks varied with the fineness of the cloth, and could take at least a week if several thousand threads were involved. After the warp was mounted, the weaver prepared the exposed warp threads to give them both strength and ease during weaving. First, a thin dressing of flour and water was carefully brushed onto the threads and, after they dried, they were rubbed thoroughly with tallow. Both of these substances were removed later during the bleaching process. Because of the inflexibility of linen yarn, weaving 'shops' needed to be kept cool and damp to help prevent yarn breakage.

Bobbins of spun yarn for the shuttle were prepared by women and children of both sexes by winding thread onto spools called 'pirns' from a large revolving wheel frame called a 'swift'. These pirns were then inserted into the shuttle. If broad cloth

35 Eric L. Almquist, 'Mayo and Beyond: Land, Domestic Industry, and Rural Transformation in the Irish West', Ph.D. diss., Boston University, 1977, p. 69; Collins, 'Proto-industrialization', 133–4; Gullickson, *Spinners and Weavers*, p. 82. 36 Jane Gray, 'Rural industry and uneven development: the significance of gender in the Irish linen industry', *Journal of Peasant Studies*, 20 (July): 590–611; Gray, 'Incorporated Comparison'; Hans Medick, 'The Proto-industrial family economy: the structural function of the household and family during the transition from peasant society to industrial capitalism', *Social History*, 3 (1976), 291–315; Gay L. Gullickson, 'Love and power in the proto-industrial family', in Maxine Berg (ed.), *Markets and Manufacture in Early Industrial Europe* (London 1991), pp. 205–6. 37 The wage data provided here has been chosen from the areas closest to the parish of Tullylish. Young, *A Tour*, 128, reported that spinners in Lurgan earned 3–4*d.* per day. In 1802, Dubourdieu, *Statistical Survey*, p. 234, noted that spinners could earn from 3–4*d.* per day, and when they worked for others, they were paid so much per hank. Finally, Coote, *Statistical Survey*, p. 255, reported that in Co. Armagh, women's wages were 6*d.* per day and children's wages from 3–6*d.* per day, '... but in some branches of the linen manufacture, if they had constant employment, they could earn 10*d.* per day'. Yarn prices in various markets close to Tullylish were given in 1816 by John Horner, *Linen Trade of Europe*, pp. 177–8. Wage data for weavers was taken from Young, Dubourdieu and Coote. 38 Collins, 'Proto-industrialization', 133–4. 39 Eighteenth century handloom weaving processes are described in Crawford, *Domestic Industry*, pp. 31–3; and Horner, *Linen Trade of Europe*, p. 57.

was woven before the use of the fly-shuttle, two weavers were needed to throw the shuttle from side-to-side across the cloth. For most of the eighteenth century, only handshuttles were used and these were thrown with changing hands through the 'shed' formed between the warp threads. The work was exhausting, but a weaver, at this time, was able to control the hours he worked. This independence was highly regarded by weavers who typically relaxed for a day or so after market day and gradually increased their hours to the point of staying up all night as the next market day approached.[40] If the household did not have a sufficient number of sons to be weavers, journeymen, apprentice weavers, or extended kin would be employed. Collins has pointed out that like farm servants, journeymen weavers were often young unmarried men who readily entered and left such situations.[41]

Finally, the cloth was bleached both to remove the impurities added by the weaver during weaving and to whiten the cloth that was brown when removed from the beam. Bleaching was a very lengthy, tedious and uncertain process only attempted during the summer months since it was feared that frost would damage the cloth. Each piece of cloth was boiled up to seven times in a potash solution and then spread on the grass or bleach yard where it was watered and whitened by the sun all summer.

Early in the eighteenth century, bleaching was removed from the hands of household women, and centralized with production tasks performed by men.[42] Given the time required, bleaching was the first process to be taken over by capitalists who were better able to afford the required investment in time and technology. Significant advances were made both in the machinery and chemicals used in bleaching during the eighteenth century.[43] Irish bleachers were among the first to experiment with sulfuric acid (oil of vitriol) in bleaching, and washmills and rubbing boards were of Irish origin. Beetling engines for finishing linen cloth were also introduced in 1725.

The circulation process for linen yarn and cloth was dominated by men. In the first half of the eighteenth century, linen drapers in the north purchased brown or unbleached webs in markets and fairs from weavers, arranged with bleachers to bleach them, and took the white webs to Dublin for sale to Dublin factors. As the production of flax, linen yarn and cloth grew during the eighteenth century, a network of smaller specialized markets in the linen trade developed. Encouraged by

---

40 E.P. Thompson, 'Time, work-discipline and industrial capitalism', *Past & Present*, no. 38 (1967). 41 Collins, 'Proto-industrialization', 133. 42 Gribbon, *History of Water Power*, pp. 85, 102–9. 43 Ibid., pp. 82–4; and Crawford, 'Drapers and bleachers', 114–15. Washmills were an adaptation to linen of old woollen tuck mills. It was there that the cloth was washed in big wooden tubs with large wooden 'feet' pushing the cloth forwards and backwards. Rubbing boards were corrugated wooden boards that rubbed one another as they were pushed backwards and forwards, and between which the soaped linen was drawn. Beetling engines were large diameter wooden rollers over which linen was slowly rotated while smooth-ended vertical wooden planks or beetles, packed tightly together but free to move up and down, pounded the cloth to flatten and close the fibres for a smooth finish.

local landlords, Lisburn and Lurgan were the first towns to establish brown linen markets. Brown linen was sold by independent weavers to drapers who were often also bleachers. According to the Reverend John Dubourdieu, in County Down, '... where a weaver finds his own yarn, his profits are greater; indeed, independent weavers were able to make more money than those who wove yarn provided for them'.[44] The wages weavers could earn varied according to the type of cloth woven and demand.[45] Both weavers and drapers maneuvered to get the best price. In addition to drapers, brown linen woven in more remote areas was purchased by jobbers who bought webs from weavers at their homes or at fairs to carry to the central markets. These brown linen markets contributed to urban growth, helped sustain a market economy in the countryside and established the authority of the linen drapers who operated in them.[46]

Once the linen was bleached, it was taken to the White Linen Hall in Dublin which opened in 1728, to Belfast's White Linen Hall which opened in 1782, or to factors in London, the greatest reception and distribution centre for the linen trade. Three times a year, English merchants attended Dublin's White Linen Hall to buy from the Irish drapers or their factors. In the early period, Belfast and Newry were collecting centres for dispatching white cloth to Dublin. With the industry's expansion in the 1780s, White Linen Halls were established in Newry and Belfast with the latter quickly becoming the leading northern port.

---

44 Dubourdieu, *Statistical Survey*, p. 233. This was confirmed by Coote for Co. Armagh, *Statistical Survey*, p. 254. 'Weavers are generally paid for their day's work one shilling; but when there is a brisk demand, and large orders out for linens, they can average 2s.6d. per day at task work. Those weavers who sell their own webs at market and rear their own flax will often times make 5s. a day of their labour, when the demand is brisk'.   45 The earliest wage data for weavers is found in Young, *A Tour*, p. 128, who noted a range from 10d. to 1s.4d. per day. Dubourdieu, *Statistical Survey*, p. 233, noted for Co. Down a range of 1s.4d. to 1s.6d. a day for fine linen and 1s. to 1s.3d. for coarse cloth.   46 Crawford, *Domestic Industry*, pp. 9–12; W.H. Crawford, 'The evolution of the linen trade in Ulster before industrialization', *Irish Economic and Social History*, 15 (1988), 33; and McConaghy, 'Thomas Greer', p. 20.

2

Landlords, Bleachers and Drapers: The Formation of an Elite Bloc

> From Tanderagee to Guilford there is the closest neighbourhood of opulent linen merchants ... many of these are held by the respectable society of Quakers, and their establishments in the linen trade are the most considerable in the county ... The delightful improvements in this view, and the verdure of the lands, are finely contrasted with the white webs, which cover so extensive an area, this whole country being occupied by wealthy bleachers.[1]
>
> Sir Charles Coote, 1804

LANDLORD TENANT RELATIONS IN TULLYLISH

This chapter analyzes the structural emergence of a Protestant elite bloc in Tullylish consisting of prominent bleachers, drapers and the Johnston family (descendants of John Magill, the original grantee) as principal landlords. Although the Johnstons were relatively small landlords by Irish standards, their estate along the Bann, formed part of one 'pole of capital' in the Ulster linen industry where a regionally specific combination of geographical, technical, marketing and human resources were concentrated.[2] Like other Ulster landlords, the Johnstons' interest in expanding their ground rent and securing a stable tenantry, became inextricably tied to the advancing linen industry.

A 'bloc' can be understood as a 'binding together' of various groups on economic, political or ideological grounds for a variety of purposes.[3] For example, after the Cromwellian Settlement, Protestants from all social ranks can be conceptualized as a bloc who possessed a common sense of privilege *vis-à-vis* Catholics and a sense of belonging to a 'Protestant nation' resting on the Acts of Settlement considered worthy of defense.[4] The ideological links often drawn by contemporaries between Protestantism, British connection, economic prosperity, social stability and enlightened thought were reflected in the cultural and religious attitudes of most Ulster Protestants.[5]

---

1 Sir Charles Coote, *Statistical Survey of the County of Armagh* (Dublin 1804), pp. 358–9.   2 Liam Kennedy, 'The rural economy 1820–1914', in Liam Kennedy and Philip Ollerenshaw (eds), *An Economic History of Ulster 1820–1939* (Manchester 1985), p. 14.   3 Antonio Gramsci, *Selections from the Prison Notebooks* (New York 1971), p. 74.   4 J.C. Beckett, *The Anglo-Irish Tradition* (Ithaca 1976), pp. 64–5.   5 David Hempton and Myrtle Hill, *Evangelical Protestantism in Ulster Society, 1740–1890* (London 1992), pp. 3–4.

However, within this Protestant bloc, there existed significant religious cleavages between Anglican and Dissenter, unequal access to civil and property rights along gender and religious lines, and fundamental class distinctions between landlords, who owned the means of production in land, and those who held rights to its use. In Tullylish, as elsewhere in East Ulster, tenants were a heterogeneous group of men leasing plots of varying size under varying terms. On top were the substantial tenants who held in fee simple at a low fixed rent. It was hoped by landlords that these men would invest money, provide leadership and assist in social control. Such favourable tenure arrangements facilitated capital formation among those interested in capital investment in the linen industry. Large tenants who benefitted from favourable terms of tenure emerged as Ireland's gentry, a class of entrepreneurial landholders. Below this group were freeholders who took leases lasting for the lives of named persons with a proviso that renewal could take place at the termination of each life on payment of a renewal fee equal to one year's rent. Finally, there were lease holders who held for a fixed term of years. These were mostly Irish Catholics who were limited to 31 year leases until 1771 under the Penal Laws.[6]

In Ireland, there was relatively greater scope for upward mobility among tenants profiting from industry and commerce than elsewhere in Europe, and they often adopted the lifestyle and position of Protestant landlords.[7] Because large tenant/entrepreneurs on the Johnston estate shared with their landlord elite status and privilege based upon gender, wealth, Protestantism and an economic interest in promoting the linen industry, I conceptualize them as a historically specific elite bloc who established hegemonic predominance in the parish by the mid-eighteenth century.

In the eighteenth century, owning land affected all aspects of rural life, and conferred high social status, respectability and masculinity. Therefore, landlords initially were the most dominant group in this tripartite bloc. The role of smaller landlords, like the Johnstons, whose estates did not include major marketing towns, differed from that of others who facilitated the growth of the linen industry by providing good market facilities, improvements in the infrastructure, giving gifts of spinning wheels, serving on the Linen Board, or by sporadic investment in manufacture.[8] Their contributions were largely confined to granting favourable leases to encourage settlement, facilitate capital investment and population growth on their estates.[9] The Johnstons were principal landlords to numerous weavers, bleachers and drapers who contributed to the linen industry's eighteenth-century dynamism.

---

6 William H. Crawford, 'Economy and Society in Eighteenth Century Ulster', Ph.D. diss., The Queen's University of Belfast, 1982, p. 41.   7 S.J. Connolly, *Religion, Law and Power: The Making of Protestant Ireland 1660–1760* (Oxford 1992), p. 62.   8 W.H. Crawford, 'Ulster landowners and the linen industry', in J.T. Ward and R.G. Wilson (eds), *Land and Industry* (New York 1971), pp. 119–22; G.E. Kirkham, '"To pay the rent and lay up riches": economic opportunity in eighteenth-century north-west Ulster', in Rosalind Mitchison and Peter Roebuck (eds), *Economy and Society in Scotland and Ireland 1500–1939* (Edinburgh 1988), pp. 96–9; Anne McKernan, 'The Dynamics of the Linen Triangle: Factor, Family, and Farm in Ulster, 1740 to 1825', Ph.D. diss., University of Michigan, 1990.

Every estate had evolved its own system of relationships that protected a land-lord's interests, profits and established a secure rent-paying tenantry.[10] Evidence from the Johnston estate suggests that small estates were very similar in their tenure arrangements to larger estates in County Down. Like much of Down and the Barony of Lower Iveagh, Tullylish possessed hilly lowlands and clayey soils suitable for commercial agriculture.[11] Most of the land in the County was held in fee simple or leased for lives and years renewable forever.[12] In 1802, average rents were 20s., or one pound per Irish acre. In 1808, Edward Wakefield gave a figure of two guineas per acre for a lease of twenty-one years.[13]

For the Johnston estate, rent rolls, leases, and surveys for both the first and second half of the long eighteenth century cast light on three interrelated topics: security of tenure, size of holdings and rent. There were three ways a tenant could hold land from a landlord: by a written lease, year-to-year with a specific commencement and termination date and at will. However, the majority of tenants held leases with varying terms. Until 1771, under the Penal Laws, Roman Catholics could not hold leases for more than thirty-one years. In that year, the term was increased to sixty-one years for bogland and in 1778, all restrictions were removed.[14] Leases also varied between terms of years and lives renewable forever. The number of lives chosen by the lessee could be one, two or three with a concurrent term of years such as twenty-one, thirty-one, or forty-one.

As numerous scholars have shown, the typical lease on Ulster estates in the eighteenth century was long, usually for two or three lives. According to W.A. Maguire, in England, three lives was equivalent to twenty-one years, but in Ireland it was equivalent to thirty-one, and usually much longer extending to perhaps twice that.[15] As was true of other well-documented estates, nearly all of the Johnston estate was leased in the eighteenth century, usually for long terms like three lives or in perpetuity.[16]

One result of long leases was that much of the land was removed from the land-lord's control in terms of regulating subdivision, subletting of holdings and being able to take advantage of the sharply rising rents in the second half of the eighteenth century. However, subdivision and subletting were not contradictory to landlords'

9 Peter Roebuck, 'The economic situation and functions of substantial landowners 1600-1815: Ulster and Lowland Scotland compared', in Rosalind Mitchison and Peter Roebuck (eds), *Economy and Society in Scotland and Ireland 1500–1939* (Edinburgh 1988), p. 85.   10 William H. Crawford, 'The influence of the landlord in eighteenth century Ulster', in L.M. Cullen and T.C. Smout (eds), *Comparative Aspects of Scottish and Irish Economic and Social History 1600–1900* (Edinburgh 1979), p. 196.   11 Scholars have demonstrated that proto-industry can coexist with commercial agriculture. See Gay L. Gullickson, *Spinners and Weavers of Auffay* (Cambridge 1986), p. 65; McKernan, 'The Dynamics', p. 14; and Jane Gray, 'Rural Industry and Uneven Development in Ireland: Region, Class and Gender, 1780-1840', Ph.D. diss., Johns Hopkins University, 1992, p. 75.   12 Revd John Dubourdieu, *Statistical Survey of the County of Down* (Dublin 1802), p. 30.   13 Edward Wakefield, *An Account of Ireland, Statistical and Political* (London 1812), pp. 255–6.   14 W.A. Maguire, *The Downshire Estates in Ireland 1801–1845* (Oxford 1972), p. 110.   15 Ibid., 118.   16 (PRONI), D.1594/76, Burgess Estate Papers.

interests in this period, serving both economic and political purposes. The economic purpose was straightforward – an increase in holdings meant an increase in rents, especially since the rentable value of smaller plots always tended to be greater per acre than that of larger ones.[17] As early as 1731, this rule was operative on the Johnston estate. Very large estates of over 100 acres, paid very low rents of between 1s. and 2s. per acre. Small farmers holding under ten acres paid rents ranging from 5s. to 16s. with the range between 10s. and 16s. the most common rent per acre.[18]

As linen manufacture prospered during the eighteenth century in the core weaving district, it separated more and more from agriculture. This led to competition between farmers and weavers for land after 1740 when the linen industry began to advance. Landlords in fine linen weaving districts attempted to reclaim for themselves the profits reaped by tenants who sublet small plots to weavers on short leases. Whenever head leases fell due landlords only renewed to farmers occupied land while reclaiming for themselves the land sublet to undertenants. Since weaving produced more income per acre than farming, weavers outbid farmers for small holdings. This reduced the number of substantial farmers since demand for small holdings by weavers who had a regular source of income encouraged both primary and principal tenants with large holdings to sublet parts of their farms. With long leases, there was little a landlord could do to prevent this beyond inserting a clause against alienation. When a lease expired, the landlord could increase his profits by only reletting the portion of land actually occupied by the sitting tenant and leasing the remainder directly to the occupying subtenants.[19]

As the linen industry spread, weavers competing for holdings forced up the value of the land. On the whole, weavers were able to pay these increased rents, and because they did not need to subsist by their holdings alone, they needed only small holdings for which they paid full value. Landlords could gain by the increasing number of small highly valued plots leased to weavers. Further, a diversified income, not tied solely to agriculture, decreased the likelihood of rent arrears. Consequently, Ulster evolved into a society of small tenant farmers dependent upon the production of linen.

The rents paid for such small farms were very high in the later part of the eighteenth century, especially if there was a good market town nearby. Tullylish was very close to four: Lurgan, Tandragee, Portadown, and Banbridge, and quite convenient to several others including the port at Newry. Consequently, we find high acreable and annual rents on the Johnston estate by the late eighteenth century.

The political purpose served by subletting and subdivision was also straightforward – the more forty shilling freeholders on a landlord's estate, the larger his voting constituency. After the abolition of the forty shillings franchise in 1829, there

17 Peter Gibbon, *The Origins of Ulster Unionism* (Manchester 1978), p. 29.   18 In 1731, the most common acreable rent for land without tenements in Loughans was 6s. Land in Drumaran with tenements ranged from 10s to 16s per acre.   19 Crawford, 'Influence of the landlord', 195–6; 'Ulster as mirror', 63.

was much less political incentive for landlords to grant leases.[20] There was an increased tendency away from leases, with Johnston beginning to show more concern with subdivision after 1829.[21]

By leasing land on favourable terms, landlords were able to play an important supporting role in economic growth during the eighteenth century. An expanding linen industry benefitted landlords in several ways. They could collect direct duty on linens if they were sold in markets where the landlord maintained toll rights. Throughout the eighteenth century, many landlords furnished adequate market facilities, granted long leases as an incentive to linen drapers to settle, and encouraged the establishment of bleachgreens that required a substantial capital investment. A cycle beneficial to landlords was established in which low rents contributed to capital accumulation among bleachers whose bleachgreens further encouraged settlement. Landlords were also active in infrastructural projects such as constructing roads and canals, and promoted the industry, as did Samuel Waring or Hawkins Magill of Gilford, through the institution of the Irish Linen Board.[22]

The strategies of landlords in increasing their ground rents changed during the eighteenth century. Early on, when their primary concern was to establish a secure and hopefully prosperous bridgehead tenantry, landlords like John Magill and the Johnstons attracted tenants by granting long leases for low rents, especially on large farms. Smaller farms had larger acreable rents, but even these were low relative to the second half of the eighteenth century. In the later period, continued growth of the linen industry caused land values to soar; the small holdings demanded by proto-industrial producers brought handsome profits to landlords. Their rent rolls increased both in terms of the number of tenants and rent per acre, especially as leases expired.[23]

While there is no evidence that the Johnstons directly invested in or helped finance through loans the building of mills or other commercial premises on their estate, the low rents and long leases granted to drapers and bleachers were a substantial incentive to manufacturing in the parish.[24] Indeed, many landlords agreed that the linen industry held the promise of prosperity for their region.[25] Landlords

20 Maguire, *Downshire Estates*, pp. 129–31; McKernan, 'The Dynamics', pp. 330–3. 21 (PRONI), D.3044/A/4/18/1/3,4,5, Clanwilliam Meade Papers, Gill Hall Estate. 22 Crawford, 'Influence of the landlord', 200; Crawford, 'Ulster landowners'; Eric L. Almquist, 'Mayo and Beyond: Land Domestic Industry and Rural Transformation in the Irish West', Ph.D. diss., Boston University, 1977; Roebuck, 'Substantial Landowners', pp. 85–8; Francis X. McCorry, *Lurgan: An Irish Provincial Town, 1610–1970* (Lurgan 1993), p. 31; McKernan, 'Dynamics', p. 46. 23 Maguire, *Downshire Estates*, pp. 138–45. 24 Pat Hudson, *The Genesis of Industrial Capital* (Cambridge 1986), p. 89. According to Roebuck, 'Substantial Landowners', 85, even large Ulster landowners rarely invested directly in the linen industry. 'Although proprietors recognized the need to promote activities, such as the manufacture of linen yarn and cloth, which might supplement farming incomes, they were unable (according to one well-informed contemporary) to provide "any great help ... from their purses".' 25 Crawford, 'Ulster landowners', 121; Roebuck, 'Substantial Landowners', p. 87; Kirkham, 'To Pay the Rent', pp. 96–8; McKernan, 'Dynamics', pp. 28–110.

often turned a blind eye to tenants who used their leases as a pledge or mortgage to borrow money for such investment. Those who did so were often large tenants who were themselves middle-level landlords as well as bleachers or drapers.

THE FIRST INDUSTRIAL CAPITALISTS IN TULLYLISH: BLEACHERS

By the early eighteenth century, the parish of Tullylish had become known for its bleach yards along the Bann. The water of the River Bann was highly esteemed for the whitening of linen, and for ten miles along the Bann from Gilford to beyond Banbridge numerous bleach yards were located. Walter Harris described the village of Gilford in 1744, making reference to the many bleach yards in its vicinity. The bleach yard of the Quaker John Nicholson at Hall's Mill near Gilford was the only one exceptional for its size.[26] Due to the prime location of greens in Tullylish, bleachers along the Bann attracted linen from as far away as Dunganon as well as from Portadown, Tandragee and Richhill.[27] Arthur Young reported that bleachers received 3*s.* a piece for coarse linens, 4*s.* to 5*s.* for middling, and 6*s.* a piece for bleaching fine linen.[28]

Joseph Schumpeter defines the 'creative response' to economic change as doing something outside the range of existing practice. Within the context of capitalism, creative response means entrepreneurship – doing new things or doing old things in new ways to earn profits. Such entrepreneurship need not be spectacular. It exists 'in even the humblest levels of the business world' where it is of considerable import 'though it may be difficult to find the humble entrepreneurs historically'. What is central to creative response is that it generates permanent change.[29]

The recognition of creative response during the period of manufacture has only just begun. Although technical changes in bleaching during this period stopped short of fully mechanizing production, significant productivity increases through mechanization and the appliation of chemicals and changes in industrial discipline occured.[30] During the eighteenth century, the bleaching sector was at the centre of creative response in the Irish linen industry. By 1725, bleaching had passed beyond the reach of ordinary weaving households, who did not have the resources to wait the long period of time required to bleach linen before sale. As a result, weavers preferred to sell their webs brown. The early bleach yards assisted by the Linen Board provided this necessary service for an agreed upon price. Between 1722 and

26 Walter Harris, *The Ancient and Present State of the County of Down* (Dublin 1744), pp. 105–6.   27 John W. McConaghy, 'Thomas Greer of Dungannon, 1724–1803, Quaker Linen Merchant', Ph.D. diss., The Queen's University of Belfast, 1979, p. 70.   28 Arthur Young, *A Tour in Ireland* (London 1892), p. 131.   29 Joseph Schumpeter, 'The creative response in economic history', *Journal of Economic History*, 7, no. 2 (1947), 150–1.   30 John Rule, 'The property of skill in the period of manufacture', in Patrick Joyce (ed.), *The Historical Meanings of Work* (Cambridge 1987), p. 101.

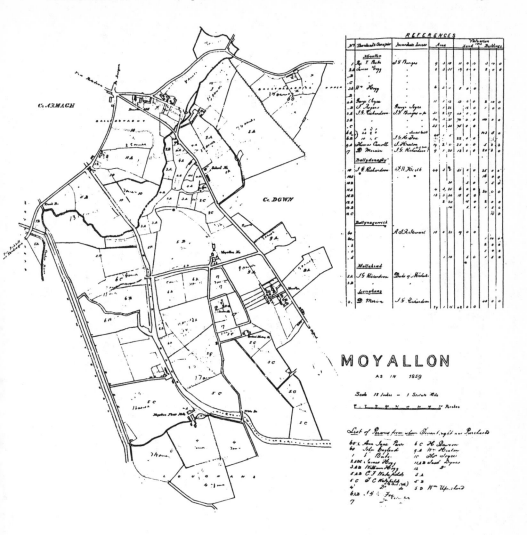

1   Survey map of Moyallon, 1859

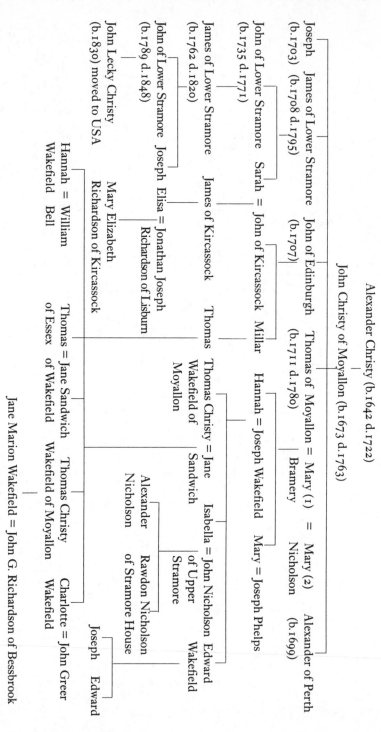

2   The Christy family of Moyallon

Source: D.2714/5/1, Gilford Geneologist. Note first cousin marriage which is characteristic of endogamous communities

1728, the Linen Board gave out £10,000 in grants for the establishment of bleach yards.[31]

Creative response is also a gendered process. In the early eighteenth century, bleachers were essentially artisans, or skilled workers who were by definition male. Mechanization, tied to the harnessing of water power, both strengthened and changed the position of bleachers. The harnessing of water power required capital, a form of property under male control, to build dams, cut water courses, and install water wheels. Once these expenditures in altering the environment were made, bleachers benefitted from a continuous source of power at little cost.[32] They could then proceed to purchase machinery that increased their productivity.

Innovators in the Ulster linen industry, whose agency reflected creative response, possessed a combination of personal and social qualities including masculinity and Protestantism. In Tullylish, the larger part of this wealthy entrepreneurial class were Quakers whose religious distinctions strongly influenced the regional economy and forms of elite cultural hegemony. In 1654, William Edmonson, an ex-Cromwellian soldier and the founder of Irish Quakerism, moved to nearby Lurgan establishing with his brother the first settled meeting of Friends in Ireland.[33] As Protestants from the north of England, Irish Quakers served in Cromwell's army, received land grants and formed part of an emerging Protestant bloc, whose ascendancy the state was determined to maintain.

However, in the seventeenth century, the inclusion of Quakers in this bloc was problematic since they were easily singled out, ridiculed and persecuted for their refusal to display deference by removing their hats, pay tithes, rates, assessments or worship in public churches. Irish Quakers led very disciplined lives, emphasizing simplicity in dress, speech, house decor and behaviour. Discrimination funneled their energies into restricted forms of economic activities.[34] Although their commercial activities brought Quakers into frequent interaction with other Irish, they were strictly endogamous. Finally, Quakers were influenced by the Evangelical movement and displayed in their monthly meetings a consistent concern for the poor, literacy, education, independence and industry which enhanced their upward mobility and economic power and respectability.[35]

By 1696, the Quaker community in Lurgan was large enough to have its first meeting house built.[36] A Scottish Quaker, Alexander Christy, arrived in 1675 to the townland of Moyallon in Tullylish, and acquired it from John Magill about 1685 (see figure 1). The townland of Moyallon contained 404 acres and 18 perches, all of

31 Conrad Gill, *The Rise of the Irish Linen Industry* (Oxford 1925), p. 49.   32 Gribbon, *Water Power*, p. 87.   33 William C. Braithwate, *The Beginnings of Quakerism*, revised by Henry C. Cadbury (Cambridge 1970), p. 210.   34 R.H. Campbell, 'The influence of religion on economic growth in Scotland in the eighteenth century', in T.M. Devine and David Dickson (eds), *Ireland and Scotland 1600–1850* (Edinburgh 1983), p. 227.   35 Phil Kilroy, 'Women and the reformation in seventeenth-century Ireland', in Margaret MacCurtin and Mary O'Dowd (eds), *Women in Early Modern Ireland* (Edinburgh 1991), p. 185.

3   Members of the Richardson family visiting Moyallon National School

4   Moyallon Meeting House

which was formerly set at the low rent of 6s. per English acre. Most of the Johnstons' thirteen tenants in Moyallon were Quakers who were medium to large farmers.

In the north Armagh/northwest Down region, there were many Quaker innovators who helped establish diaper and damask weaving in the region and who made major contributions to the bleaching end of production.[37] Alexander Christy is credited with introducing the linen industry and the bleaching of linen to the Moyallon district.[38] Christy's five grandsons (figure 2) were prominent in the bleaching of linen both in Scotland and Ireland. Alexander, Joseph and John all ran successful businesses in Scotland with the assistance of skilled tradesmen from Ireland. James and Thomas remained in Tullylish. The continued growth of the Quaker community at Moyallon, prompted a meeting house and small graveyard to be built there in 1736 and enlarged in 1780.[39]

Alexander's grandson, Thomas Christy, became the wealthiest and most powerful draper/bleacher in Tullylish, exemplifying the rapid vertical mobility of Quakers in the region and their inclusion by the mid-eighteenth century in the local elite bloc. On 8 September 1764, Richard Johnston leased in fee forever eighty acres in Moyallon to Thomas Christy at the low rent of 11s.4½d. per acre. On 5 August 1771, his former master Joseph Richardson 'demised granted and released' to Thomas Christy twenty-five acres in Stramore formerly in the possession of Thomas and James Christy. James continued to live at Stramore, and Thomas took up residence in the old Moyallon House that faced 'the shaded avenue to the meeting' house enlarged by him in 1780. In 1788, reflecting the emphasis placed on literacy and education, Thomas Christy built the first school for boys in Tullylish[40] (see figures 3 and 4). Over one-quarter of the land in Moyallon was owned by the Christy family including part of the east bank of the Newry Canal and part of the new dam located there.[41] While much of Thomas Christy's wealth, like other Quaker families, was earned through the linen industry, he probably also profited by lending money on mortgages to landowners and dealing in land. By the time of his death, Thomas Christy held property in Counties Down, Armagh, Tyrone, the City of Dublin and in North Carolina.[42]

The success of many Quakers as capitalists, rooted in their social restriction, their philosophy of economic individualism and the reinvestment of profit, generated a contradiction between collectivism and individualism. This contradiction did not apply solely to Quakers. Quakerism was one of several variants of the domi-

36 Jane Marion Richardson, *Six Generations of Friends in Ireland* (London 1894), p. 5.   37 William H. Crawford, 'Drapers and bleachers in the early Ulster linen industry', in L.M. Cullen and P. Butel (eds), *Negoce et Industrie*, p. 114.   38 Ibid., 115; Richardson, *Six Generations*, 184; George R. Chapman, *Historical Sketch of Moyallon Meeting*, Preparative Meeting Clerk, Friends Meeting House, Moyallon, p. 3; and (PRONI), D.2714/5/1, Gilford Genealogist.   39 Chapman, *Historical Sketch*, p. 3.   40 (PRONI), ED.6/1/3/1, Correspondence National Schools regarding the establishment of Moyallon National School.   41 (PRONI), D.1594/115, Burgess Estate Papers, Copy of Francis Atkinson's Survey of Moyallon, 23 November, 1764.   42 W.H. Crawford and Brian Trainor, *Aspects of Irish Social History 1750–1800* (Belfast 1969), pp. 70–1.

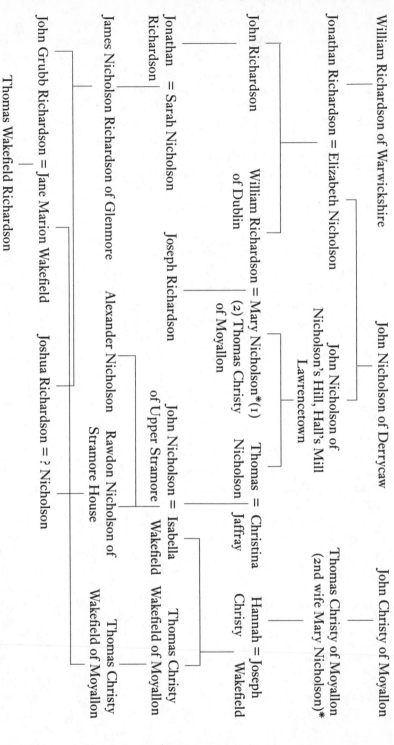

5   Intermarriages between three prominent Quaker families in Tullylish

Source: D.2714/5J1 Gilford Geneologist

nant Puritanism that chastised idleness, emphasized that one's work was one's calling or an expression of God's will, considered diligence to be a religious duty, and held frugality and honesty in high esteem.[43] Although strict individualism would later lead many Quakers to oppose trade unions and State regulation of working conditions, they were strongly influenced by the Evangelical movements of the late eighteenth century. Methodism spread in Ulster after 1756 establishing strong footholds in Tandragee, Moira, Banbridge, Lurgan and Portadown.[44] The Evangelical commitment to philanthropy, social justice, education and temperance led to numerous humane endeavours among the poor by both Methodists and Quakers.

Bleachers in Tullylish prospered and their profits enabled some to become exporters relying on the extension of credit. Bleachers were also one of the earliest employers of waged labour in the linen industry. As such, they joined landlords as owners of the means of production who stood in a relationship of exploitation *vis-à-vis* their employees. They also were the first to introduce factory discipline in the early form of rational spatial organization to route raw materials between various groups of workers and to control the movements of people and merchandise.[45] At first, bleachers employed male weavers during the summer months only, and, after 1800, permanently, as cloth was bleached all year rather than simply between March and mid-August.[46] The artisan bleachers, calender men, lappers and other bleach-green workers enjoyed a status that was 'a degree higher than the weaver'.[47]

In addition to grants from the Linen Board, where did the bleachers find their initial capital? One important source, suggested by William Crawford, came from mortgaging the titles to their properties. For example, the Quaker John Nicholson, whose bleachgreen at Hall's Mill in Tullylish was noted by Harris in 1744, obtained at least £1,500 by mortgaging a variety of holdings. This money, plus awards of £100 in 1728, and £50 by the Linen Board, was most likely invested in the construction of a drying house, and to purchase two large coppers, eight kieves, a wringing engine and a cold press to equip the bleachgreen.[48] Thus, as in the West Riding, land was the major security for raising loans since it was the principal source of credibility, respectability and financial status.[49]

Among the close-knit endogamous Quaker community, capital could also be raised by turning to kin or by strategic marriages.[50] The numerous intermarriages

---

43 Frederick B. Tolles, *Quakers and the Atlantic Culture* (New York 1980), pp. 55–65. S.J. Connolly points out that the majority of Catholic churchmen in the eighteenth century fully absorbed the conventional economic and social of their day and shared a similar outlook on most moral issues to Protestants. See S.J. Connolly, 'Religion, work-discipline and economic attitudes: the case of Ireland', in T.M. Devine and David Dickson (eds), *Ireland and Scotland 1600–1800* (Edinburgh 1983), pp. 237–8. **44** C.H. Crookshank, *History of Methodism in Ireland, Vol. 1: Wesley and his Times* (Belfast 1885). **45** Michele Perrot, 'The three ages of industrial discipline in nineteenth-century France', in John Merriman (ed.), *Consciousness and Class Experience in Nineteenth-Century Europe* (New York 1979), p. 151. **46** Gill, *Rise of the Linen Industry*, pp. 144–5. **47** Wakefield, *Account*, p. 734. **48** Crawford, 'Drapers and Bleachers', 116; and McConaghy, 'Thomas Greer', p. 112. **49** Hudson, *Genesis*, p. 19. **50** Crawford, 'Drapers and Bleachers', 117; McCorry, *Lurgan*, p. 28; Hudson, *Genesis*, pp. 20–1; Leonore Davidoff and Catherine Hall, *Family Fortunes: Men and Women of the English Middle Class, 1780–1850* (Chicago 1987), pp. 198–271.

among prominent Quaker families in Moyallon engaged in the linen industry helped lay the foundation for commercial contacts and business structure (see figure 5). An enterprising young man such as Thomas Christy Wakefield who wanted to build a flour mill on his Moyallon property, could turn to Thomas Christy of Essex for £2,500 of the capital needed, charging it on his property at five per cent interest.[51]

One bleacher in Tullylish, who was able to invest capital derived through leasing a strategic portion of Johnston's estate was Thomas Purdy. On 18 August 1691, Sir John Magill leased in perpetuity to Thomas Purdy, clothier, 'as long as water runs and grasse grows', the Corn and Tuck Mill of Gilford with all the houses and seven acres of land adjoining the mill and part of the townland of Ballymacanallon adjoining the village of Gilford. For the first three years, his rent was 2s. per acre or £11 per year, for the next seven 3s. per acre or £15 per year, and, finally, 4s. or £20 per year.[52] All subsequent leases on the Johnston estate required that corn grown by tenants be ground at Purdy's corn mill. Although the extent to which this covenant was enforced is unknown, Purdy received all profits from those who complied. Purdy was sufficiently prosperous to have established a bleachgreen prior to the date of his will in 1728.

Although bleachers and landlords often shared an interest in profiting from the expanding linen industry, conflicts over the use of land could and did emerge. Landlords could attempt to exercise their power as landowners, impeding schemes to alter the physical environment on their estate to meet bleachers' need for water power. One such example occurred between landlord Richard Johnston and bleacher George Law. The power held by wealthy bleachers and drapers by the late eighteenth century could rival that of landlords, and Law was fully prepared to challenge Richard Johnston's opposition to his plans to alter the water courses along the Bann. Law's wealth had increased after 1 May 1777 when the Purdys (John Purdy Sr, John Purdy Jr, and Thomas Purdy) leased in perpetuity the water corn mill, corn kiln, the use of the water courses and weirs, and dwelling houses on the north side of the mill to linen drapers George Law and James McCreight for £85.[53] In the 1780s, Law gained increasing control over the Purdys' land, and, in 1784 James McCreight conveyed his moiety of the corn mill and other properties to George Law. Law was also part owner of a large bleach mill, beetling engine and green in Lenaderg, and possessed other land at Coose in Tullylish.[54] In 1786, Johnston brought suit against Law who wished to 'sink and widen' the mill race leading to his bleachgreen. The case was settled in Law's favour for £100, giving him the freedom to make his alterations and supply his bleachgreen and corn mill with water power, if he promised to repair all damage to the land, weir and race.[55]

By the mid-eighteenth century, bleachers along the Bann were generators of innovation, attempting to improve factor conditions relating to the organization of

51 (PRONI), D.1252/9, Carleton Atkinson & Sloan Solicitors, Wakefield (Richardson) Estate Papers.   52 (PRONI)., MIC.102/1, p. 10.   53 (PRONI), D.1594/137, Burgess Estate Papers.   54 (PRONI), MIC.102/1.   55 (PRONI), MIC.102/1.

labour, technology and infrastructure. For example, time had always been the principal problem in bleaching since whitening linen was a very lengthy process. In the earliest days, cattle urine and manure were used as an alkali and buttermilk for an acid or souring agent. Linens were washed by hand, trampled by foot, and dried in the open air.[56]

Water powered machinery for washing linen in wash mills and rubbing was introduced to lessen the time required for washing linens early in the 1730s. In 1727, Hamilton Maxwell introduced water powered beetling machinery for finishing linen.[57] Bleachers along the Upper Bann including Thomas Christy are credited with the adaptation of woollen tuck mills to linen wash mills.[58] Thomas Christy in particular is credited with inventing the drying house where cloth was dried after starching and blueing eliminating some of the time and risks involved with exposure to the atmosphere.

Important chemical discoveries were also made in the eighteenth century. In 1764, Dr James Ferguson successfully applied lime for bleaching and in 1770, he applied sulfuric acid (vitriol) used by the Scotch scientist Francis Home in 1756. Irish bleachers, including those in Tullylish, were among the first to make use of vitriol.[59] Reducing the time involved in bleaching, reduced its cost bringing cheaper cloth to the market to be sold. Vitriol was in itself a significant time saver reducing the length of the bleaching process from seven or eight months to four.[60] Still, productivity was limited to only two lots of goods in one season, and there were risks of damage in the application of chemicals to the cloth.

Like other Quakers, the Christys showed a keen interest in applying scientific methods and experimentation to bleaching. James Christy, a man 'always alert to technical changes' and (as Arthur Young noted) contributed some of his own, in 1756 proposed to the Linen Board a policy which aimed at eliminating the secretive nature of the bleaching process.[61] Christy was a leading partner in the Moyallon Vitriol Company, set up in 1786 to meet the demand for vitriol by bleachers in the area.[62] By 1808, Thomas Christy Wakefield of Moyallon had begun to use a hydrometer to determine more precisely the strength of the alkali. Earlier, the testing of alkali strength was a skill controlled by the foreman bleacher who also decided when the linen was ready for souring and rubbing. Foreman bleachers used to reach their conclusions 'by tasting the liquor', a risky method causing frequent and costly accidents.[63]

---

56 Gill, *Rise of the Linen Industry*; E.R.R. Green, *The Lagan Valley 1800–50* (London 1949), p. 69. 57 Green, *Lagan Valley*, p. 69. 58 Crawford, 'Economy and Society', p. 91; 'Drapers and Bleachers', p. 115. 59 William Charley, *Flax and its Products in Ireland* (London 1862), pp. 3–5; Young, A *Tour*, p. 131; and John Curry, *Elements of Bleaching* (Dublin 1779). 60 S.H. Higgins, *A Short History of Bleaching* (London 1924), p. 63; and A Working Man, *Hints to Bleachers Containing Remarks on the System at Present Adopted for Bleaching Linen Goods; Also Remarks on Finishing Linen Goods as Practiced in the North of Ireland* (Lisburn 1859), p. 49. 61 See Young, *A Tour*, p. 131, where he notes how secretive bleachers were in the eighteenth century. 62 McConaghey, 'Thomas Greer', p. 69; and Crawford, 'Drapers and bleachers', 115. 63 Wakefield, *Account*, p. 693.

These risks and the application of technological and chemical innovations required that bleachers possess a relatively large amount of capital. Bleachgreens became increasingly concentrated both in terms of both region and the availability of investors with the fixed capital outlay – £2–3000 pounds by 1800.[64] By 1783, the twenty bleachgreens between Gilford and Banbridge bleached 90,000 pieces of linen annually, an average of 4500 each.[65] By 1808, Thomas Christy Wakefield reported that the average had risen to 8000 pieces each. At that time, yard wide linens cost 8s. and cambrics 7s., yielding a profit of 8.33 per cent.[66] An 1803 statistic reports 238,500 pieces of linen bleached annually in the sixty-six bleachgreens in County Down.[67] If we multiply Wakefield's 8000 pieces by twenty, the Gilford-to-Banbridge greens bleached a total of 160,000 pieces annually – 67 per cent of the County's total capacity.

The first complete listing of bleachers and merchants in Tullylish did not appear until 1824. We cannot know who owned the twenty bleachgreens in Tullylish existing in 1808, nor can we know which greens disappeared in the competitive environment of the late eighteenth century. Only twelve bleachgreens in Tullylish were listed by Pigot in 1824, a reduction of eight from 1808. This suggests that the concentration of bleaching capital was well advanced by the early nineteenth century.[68]

THE ACCUMULATION OF MERCHANT CAPITAL: LINEN DRAPERS

As the production of flax, linen yarn and cloth grew during the eighteenth century, a network of markets specifically for the linen trade developed. Brown linen was sold at these markets by independent weavers to drapers, the last group of men in the elite bloc. While drapers and bleachers increasingly merged as the eighteenth century progressed, in the early days of the linen industry dealers, drapers, and bleachers were distinct as Crawford explains:

> Dealers were often small merchants, even shopkeepers, who bought and sold brown linens as they might other commodities. The term draper described those dealers who bought brown linens and sent them as white linens after bleaching either to be sold at the Dublin White Linen Hall or directly to English factors. Bleachers were usually the owners of bleachgreens who contracted with a draper to bleach his linens. Whenever they were substantial enough to deal in linens on their own account, they preferred to be recognized as linen drapers since that term suggested men of some capital where as some bleachers were little more than farmers with a good supply of water available on their lands.[69]

64 Gill, *Rise of the Linen Industry*, p. 246; and Green, *Lagan Valley*, p. 62.   65 Crawford, 'Economy and Society', p. 103.   66 Wakefield, *Account*, p. 693.   67 Crawford, 'Economy and Society', p. 103.   68 Ibid., p. 92; Gribbon, *Water Power*, p. 87.   69 Crawford, 'Economy and Society', p. 92.

Similar to other groups engaged in linen production and trade, drapers were a heterogeneous group ranging in wealth from hawkers and small draper/weavers to large draper/bleachers. There were manufacturing drapers emerging from 'below' (i.e. weavers), and gentlemen drapers who had never been weavers. Drapers usually held from ten to twenty acres of land. Those holding less than this were probably once weavers, while those with considerably more land probably were not. Despite the conventional distinction between the two groups in the mid-eighteenth century, there was much upward and downward mobility.[70] Drapers usually spent most of their time travelling, attending markets and making trips to Dublin.

Drapers were engaged in a distinct type of entrepreneurial activity – creating new markets for yarn and linen cloth. By the mid-eighteenth century, organized drapers promoted the emergence, growth and regulation of brown linen markets which replaced the older fairs.[71] Those who resided near market towns were able to capitalize on the growth of proto-industrial production and increasingly took over the marketing of linen cloth. By the 1780s, the credit resources of northern drapers were sufficient enough to allow them to break away from Dublin's dominance as the centre for white linen. Many of the wealthiest merchants and later industrialists in Ulster rose from the ranks of drapers.

Following Gerald Sider's call for a 'more historically dynamic perspective on merchant capital' and its social worlds, I argue elsewhere that the term merchant be deconstructed to include small manufacturers or weaver/drapers, hawkers, large bleacher/drapers and merchants.[72] It cost little at that time to purchase a few looms and a small stock of yarn. Small drapers or manufacturers were petty entrepreneurs, with their roots among proto-industrial producers, who had accumulated enough capital to become petty capitalists providing looms and yarn to a few (maybe as few as one or two) proletarianized cottier weavers.

Sider's agenda must also include the gendered division of labour since yarn was produced by women while commerce was dominated by men. Following Jane Gray, buying cheap yarn produced by women in the peripheral yarn counties in the west facilitated the accumulation of merchant's capital among manufacturers large and small in the core linen triangle in east Ulster.[73] Although manufacturers were not part of the elite bloc, they are an example of Marx's 'really revolutionary path' in the

---

70 Gill, *Rise of the Linen Industry*, pp. 149, 151.   71 Anne McKernan, 'Contested terrain: the making of a market culture in Ulster linens', in Marilyn Cohen (ed.), *The Warp*.   72 Gerald Sider, *Culture and Class in Anthropology and History* (Cambridge 1986), 191; Cohen, 'Peasant differentiation', 54–5. Liana Vardi presents a similar analysis for linen merchant-weavers in the French village of Montigny in the Cambresis region. She argues that as a group, merchant weavers came from the middle ranks of the peasantry raising initial capital from their landed assets. Liana Vardi, *The Land and the Loom* (Durham, NC 1993), pp. 161–80.   73 Gray, 'Rural Industry', 237. For a similar argument relating to the silk industry in England see Judy Lown, *Women and Industrialization* (Minneapolis, MN 1990), pp. 212–13. 74 Karl Marx, *Capital* (New York 1974), 334–6.

transition to capitalism whereby the producer is enabled to become merchant and capitalist extracting profits at both the points of production and exchange.[74]

Bleachers and draper/bleachers were another example. Those drapers who operated purely in the circulation sphere extracted merchant capital by subtracting from the price of labour the means of subsistence produced by farmer/weavers on their small plots of land. However, to the extent that drapers small and large began to put-out yarn to weavers, they entered the sphere of production and contributed directly to proletarianization. Those drapers dominating Banbridge market were on the cutting edge of this process, aggressively seeking to overcome trade barriers and the competition posed by British mill-spun yarn by reorganizing production through the putting-out system prior to 1825.[75]

> Between Banbridge and Guilford some of the first manufacturers who invested large capital in the linen trade established themselves and here the great experiment of placing the linen trade of Ireland on a new foundation was tried.[76]

THE ELITE BLOC AND EIGHTEENTH-CENTURY COMMERCIAL URBANIZATION

Urbanization in the eighteenth century provides a useful framework for analyzing the unified interests of the elite bloc of landlords, drapers and bleachers. Historians have laid the groundwork for probing the links between the linen industry and urbanization in eighteenth-century Ulster.[77] A microhistorical perspective deepens their contribution. How and by what means was space used, created or appropriated to fit the temporal requirements of drapers and bleachers in Tullylish? What was the nature of the urban hierarchy in the region and how did it change? What was the relationship between proto-industrialization and urbanization?

One feature of proto-industrial theory that has been strongly criticized is its overemphasis on rural industry neglecting urban centres as coordinators and sites of proto-industry in their own right. Paul Hohenberg and Lynn Lees alternately suggest that 'proto-industry flourished not as town or country, but as a complementary system involving both rural and urban places and the various elements of a regional urban hierarchy.'[78] As elsewhere in Europe, towns in eighteenth-century

75 Samuel Lewis, A *Topographical Dictionary of Ireland* (London 1837), p. 177; E.R.R. Green, *The Industrial Archaeology of County Down* (Belfast 1963), p. 6.   76 *Reports of Assistant Commissioners on Handloom Weavers, Industrial Revolution: Textiles*, IUP ser., ix (1839–40), p. 659.   77 W.H. Crawford, 'The Evolution of Ulster Towns', in Peter Roebuck (ed.), *Plantation to Partition*, op. cit.; 'Economy and Society'; Marilyn Cohen, 'Urbanization and the milieux of factory life: Gilford/Dunbarton, 1825–1914', in Chris Curtin, Hastings Donnan and Thomas M. Wilson (eds), *Irish Urban Cultures* (Belfast 1993).   78 P.M. Hohenberg and L.H. Lees, *The Making of Urban Europe* (Cambridge, MA 1985), p. 130.

Ulster were an outgrowth of the vast expansion of merchant capital and marketing networks. This urban network of brown linen and yarn markets was connected by a complex system of roads, canals and river navigations. Although most linen weavers lived in the countryside, where they were better able to maintain their independence, residence close to good market towns was highly desirable and reflected in the high rents weavers were willing to pay for small plots in their vicinity.

The extra-regional economic and political forces that propelled the Irish linen industry also nurtured the urbanization process as small villages expanded into commercial towns. Banbridge in adjacent Seapatrick parish provides an poignant example of commercial urbanization as an outgrowth of the interests of the local elite bloc. Banbridge's grew from a small village in 1690 to one of the principal linen market towns in Ulster a century later due to alterations made to its built environment to suit the needs of linen drapers. In 1744, the town of Banbridge held 'some of the greatest Fairs for Linen Cloth ... five times a year, constantly attended by Factors from England.'[79] Soon after, in 1750, the physical layout of Banbridge was altered. Its four principal streets were widened and the Earl Of Hillsborough encouraged building by granting leases at nominal rents. By 1817, Secretary of the Linen Board James Corry described Banbridge as the largest linen market in County Down with annual sales of brown linen valued at £53,976. While this figure was well below the markets of Armagh, Dungannon, and Lisburn, it rivalled the older Lurgan with £96,200 and surpassed Newry.[80] In addition, the Marquess of Downshire, who as landlord stood to gain in terms of tolls and rents from encouraging trade at Banbridge, built a market place in 1815 for meal and grain, a brown linen hall in 1817 and a market house for linen yarn and cloth in 1834.[81] By the end of the long eighteenth century, Banbridge served as the capital of the linen trade in County Down and a service centre for its rural hinterland and smaller towns such as Gilford in the region.

An integral aspect of capitalism is the spatial alterations associated with its development. The elite bloc of Tullylish and elsewhere in Ulster were all involved in varying degrees in altering space to meet the temporal needs of producing and circulating linen yarn and cloth. Landlords built market places, brown linen halls, market houses, improved infrastructure, and encouraged capital investment. Such investment directly contributed to the emergence and growth of towns in Ulster.[82]

While the connection between urbanization and the temporal needs of linen drapers for a more rational and concentrated organization of markets is clear, the role of bleachers in the urbanization process has less often been investigated. One reason is that many bleachgreens were small and settlements in their vicinity were

79 Harris, *Ancient and Present State*, p. 83. **80** W.S. Kerr (section on the linen trade) in Captain Richard Linn, *A History of Banbridge* (Banbridge 1935), p. 166. **81** Crawford, 'Evolution of Ulster Towns', 146; Lewis, *Topographical Dictionary*, p. 177. **82** Crawford, 'Evolution of Ulster Towns', 144.

on the order of hamlets rather than villages or factory towns.[83] Nevertheless, given the number of centralized bleachgreens along the Bann between Gilford and Banbridge that were employers of labour on an increasingly permanent basis, it is reasonable to conclude that population settlements were encouraged.

Thus, the second half of the eighteenth century was a period of transition in Tullylish, when capitalism was emerging, but not yet hegemonic. In 1825, as the long eighteenth century came to a close, the area between Gilford and Banbridge was noted out for the extent to which the relations of production were changing. The Select Committee on the Linen Trade in Ireland stated that in this region, '... there are people possessed of a certain capital who employ a good number of weavers among them'.[84] Capitalist development in Tullylish during the eighteenth century demonstrates the complexity of social forces at the top of the social pyramid contributing to capital accumulation and capitalist class formation. It is to those forces emanating from the 'bottom' that we now turn.

83 W.H. Crawford, 'The evolution of the linen trade in Ulster before industrialization', *Irish Economic and Social History*, 15 (1988), 32–53 refutes Gill's claim for the importance of weaver's settlements near bleachgreens.   84 H. C., *Report from the Select Committee on the Linen Trade of Ireland*, v (1825), p. 104.

3

The Social and Economic Differentiation of Linen Producers

The peculiar advantage of the linen business is, the opportunities of earning it affords not only to weavers, but to every woman and every child; and although individually that earning may be small, in the aggregate it forms a considerable object and probably has done more than any mere political regulations could do to keep off the necessity of entering into measures for the permanent support of the poor.[1]

The Reverend John Dubourdieu, 1802

An adaptive response to economic change occurs when an economy, sector or firm reacts by adding additional labour or expanding within its existing practice.[2] During the eighteenth century, production of linen yarn and cloth expanded in this adaptive way. Producers divided their time between spinning, weaving and farming small plots of land. Rent was paid through the sale of yarn and cloth, and since weavers were not wholly dependent on farming for their living, only small plots of land were leased to each individual household. Small plots served both to cheapen the cost of labour, and to deter proletarianization. Finally, control over the means of production including land, flax, spinning wheels and looms ensured weavers varying degrees of control over the work process.

The interpenetration between rural industry and agriculture, characteristic of the pre-modern linen industry in Europe, has led to various attempts by scholars to extend and amend the proto-industrial hypotheses in each historical context. This chapter contributes to this debate in several ways. First, I challenge a central theoretical assumption of the family-economy model as it relates to peasant and proto-industrial households. Second, I analyze the historically specific factors contributing to class differentiation among linen producers in Tullylish. I argue that the long eighteenth century was a transitional period when a combination of long leases and an expanding market economy for linen simultaneously encouraged and undermined the household as unit of production. Third, I stress that our conceptualization of rural producers effects the way we analyze their role in the development of capitalism.[3]

1 Revd John Dubourdieu, *Statistical Survey of the County of Down* (Dublin 1802), p. 242.   2 Joseph Schumpeter, 'The creative response in economic history', *The Journal of Economic History*, 7, no. 2 (1947), 150.   3 Marilyn Cohen, 'Peasant differentiation and proto-industrialisation in the Ulster countryside: Tullylish 1690–1825', *Journal of Peasant Studies*, 17, no. 3 (1990), 413–32.

Despite clarity regarding the historicity of family farms in Ulster after the plantation, certain transhistorical theoretical presumptions about peasantries generally and the logic of family economy have left their imprint on Irish scholarship.[4] All variations of the family economy model begin with the presumption of a pre-capitalist, self-sufficient, bounded, family household guided by the logic of simple rather than expanded reproduction, and operating outside of or displaying resistance to capitalist market forces and social relations. Many who share these assumptions draw inspiration from A.V. Chayanov's equilibrium model for peasant economy.[5] Models based upon these pre- or anti-capitalist assumptions theoretically eliminate peasant entrepreneurship. Peasants are thus treated as 'prey' rather than 'predators' during the transition to capitalism, with forces of change originating from groups outside their ranks.[6]

The transplantation of this family economy model to the proto-industry model occurred principally through Hans Medick's characterization of the 'ganze Haus' as a social formation in which family economy, defined in neo-Chayanovian terms, intersected with an expanding world market dominated by merchant capital.[7] The part played by proto-industrial households in the transition to capitalism is necessarily a conservative and passive one because they generate expansion of the proto-industrial system only by remaining tied to a family mode of production inherently opposed to accumulation.[8] Further following Jane Gray, a focus on the household as a bounded entity both reifies it and denies the existence of heterogeneity and conflict along gender and generational lines.[9]

In this chapter I focus on how an expanding linen trade allowed certain categories of linen producers to accumulate profit, while others either retained their independence or were proletarianized. Alongside activities promoting capitalism initiated by the superordinate elite, forces eroding family economy emerged through petty entrepreneurship and class differentiation at the bottom of the social class pyramid.

SOCIAL DIFFERENTIATION AMONG LINEN PRODUCERS

There is an abundance of evidence that confirms the heterogeneity of linen producers in eighteenth-century Ulster. Most scholars agree that this heterogeneity was

4 K.H. Connell, *Irish Peasant Society* (Oxford 1968).   5 A.V. Chayanov, *The Theory of Peasant Economy*, D. Thorner et al. (ed.) (Madison, WI 1986).   6 Sidney W. Mintz, 'A note on the definition of peasantries', *Journal of Peasant Studies*, 1, no. 1 (1973), 94.   7 Hans Medick, 'The proto-industrial family economy: the structural function of household and family during the transition from feudal society to industrial capitalism', *Social History*, 3 (1976), 291–315.   8 Cohen, 'Peasant Differentiation'; Jean H. Quataert, 'A new view of industrialization: "Protoindustry" or the role of small-scale, labor-intensive manufacture in the capitalist environment', *International Labor and Working-Class History* no. 23 (1988), 3–22.   9 Jane Gray, 'Rural industry and uneven development: the significance of gender in the Irish linen industry', *Journal of Peasant Studies*, 20, no. 4 (1993), 590–611; Tessie P. Liu, *The Weaver's Knot* (Ithaca 1994), pp. 22–44.

the result of social and economic processes such as class and gender, rather than demographic ones. In pre-Famine Ireland, there were sharp distinctions emphasized by the people between those who held land, regardless of how small, and those who did not, even though smallholders, cottiers and the landless did not differ substantially in lifestyle.[10] They were all the rural poor. However, when we focus on the rural poor, finer distinctions emerge. Those holding between five and ten acres of land were often independent farmer/weavers. Cottier weavers comprised a group at the bottom who were essentially proletarians. They worked as part time weavers or agricultural labourers leasing a cabin with a patch of land, a 'dry cot' or cottage without land, or purchased 'con acres' on which one crop of potatoes or oats was grown. Their existence depended on 'a patch of land, a crudely built cabin, and sometimes supplies of yarn'.[11]

This lowest strata of weavers, who have left scant evidence of themselves, remained impoverished during this period of expansion. Since cottiers often rented patches of potato ground from manufacturers, who were themselves tenants, they do not usually appear on the rent rolls of landlords. The principal source of evidence for their existence are the reports of contemporaries who attest to the extent of small holdings and middle-level landlords in County Down (and elsewhere in Ireland), evidence from estate papers and the 1821 Census.[12] Census Enumerators listed a household as landless if they held less than two acres of land. Of the 40 surviving Tullylish households in the 1821 Census, nearly one-third held no land. In nearby Derryhale, County Armagh, of the 121 households, 42 per cent were landless. The only additional evidence relating to the prevalence of cottiers in Tullylish comes late in the 1836 Poor Law Report which addressed questions relating to subletting. Plots of land in Tullylish, 'are chiefly held by the tenants from the head landlord, except in the cases of very small lots held by cottiers which latter system is very general in the parish'.[13]

Anne McKernan has made an indepth analysis of landless weavers on the nearby Richhill estate in County Armagh. She is reluctant to conceptualize this group as proletarians because they retained control over some means of production, notably a garden and spinning and weaving implements. She also suggests, based upon the young ages of the majority of landless weavers, that this household form was new to the Richhill estate in 1821.[14]

'Independent farmer/weavers' were above cottiers in their standard of living due to economic and ideological independence. This group, the Irish variant of the 'Kaufsystem', were not, according to McKernan, common in the Ulster country-

10 Samuel Clark, *Social Origins of the Irish Land War* (Princeton 1979), pp. 34–40.   11 Liam Kennedy, 'The rural economy 1820–1914', in Liam Kennedy and Philip Ollerenshaw (eds), *An Economic History of Ulster 1820–1939* (Manchester 1986), pp. 32–3.   12 For Tullylish see (PRONI), T.238/13, Crossle MSS. Part B; For nearby Derryhale townland in Kilmore Parish, County Armagh see T.1228/2.   13 H.C. *Reports From Commissioners, Poor Laws-Ireland*, Appendix (F), xxxiii (1836), pp. 335–6.   14 Anne McKernan, 'The Dynamics of the Linen Triangle: Factor, Farm and Family in Ulster, 1740–1825', Ph.D. diss., University of Michigan, 1990, p. 256.

side before 1750.[15] It was not until the third quarter of the eighteenth century that a division of labour between farming and weaving households occurred in Ulster's linen triangle. By the late eighteenth century, however, independent farmer/weavers became the largest category of weavers.

Unlike cottiers, who were usually dependent upon manufacturers for yarn, the independence of farmer/weavers rested partly upon female members of the household who spun at least part of the needed yarn. This product was a central lynchpin, along with leasing land, supporting the higher standard of living and social status of male independent farmer/weavers. However, spinning was not equal in status to weaving, a skilled male occupation. The division of labour between weaving and auxiliary tasks signified both the patriarchal structure of social relations between women and men and between parents and children and the centrality of work in the formation of gendered identities.

Weavers of fine linen earned higher wages (from 9s. 4d. to 10s. 6d. a week) than weavers of coarse linen (who earned from 7s. to 8s. 9d. per week), and those who wove cloth from yarn they obtained on their own made higher wages still.[16] John Horner estimated that prior to 1825, a family would need a daily wage of at least 1s. a day or 7s. a week to meet ordinary needs.[17] These figures suggest that coarse linen weavers lived at the subsistence level, while weavers of fine linen, such as those in Tullylish, were able to provide a higher standard of living for their families.

This higher standard of living is evident in the houses of independent weavers. According to Sir Charles Coote, such weavers lived in stone houses each with a kitchen, dairy, several small bedrooms, and a workshop, all 'remarkable for comfort and cleanliness'.[18] In addition to the basic diet of potatoes, oatmeal and milk noted by Arthur Young, better off weavers enjoyed meat once a week, tea for breakfast, bacon, herring, butter, and produce from their gardens.[19] Independent weavers also dressed better than poor cottiers, with their wives and daughters wearing 'cotton or linen gowns'.[20]

Such men formed the 'core of the oral and literary cultures of the communities in which they lived'.[21] In many areas, including that around Banbridge, male weavers founded reading societies or clubs in which books were purchased by subscriptions and shared, poetry written by local 'bards' was read aloud, and debate on political, economic and religious issues flourished. The prevalence of book clubs reflect high literacy rates among men in Antrim, Down and Londonderry. Within this region, south and mid-Antrim and north and northeast Down had higher literacy rates still. Country reading societies used their small subscriptions to maintain lending

---

15 Ibid., p. 188. 16 Dubourdieu, *Statistical Survey*, p. 238. 17 John Horner, *The Linen Trade of Europe During the Spinning Wheel Period* (Belfast 1920), p. 50. 18 Sir Charles Coote, *Statistical Survey of the County of Armagh* (Dublin 1804), pp. 133–4. 19 William H. Crawford, *Domestic Industry in Ireland: The Experience of the Linen Industry* (Dublin 1972), pp. 26–7. 20 Edward Wakefield, *An Account of Ireland Statistical and Political* (London 1812), p. 740. Wakefield was referring specifically to weavers in Moyallon, and his source of information was Thomas Christy Wakefield. 21 Peter Gibbon, *The Origins of Ulster Unionism* (Manchester 1975), p. 30.

libraries, and served as loci for social gatherings, story telling, debate, and politici-zation.[22] While County Down was less noted for these societies than County Antrim, in nearby Banbridge, the Banbridge Reading Society was founded in 1795 with a monthly subscription of one shilling. It had a membership of 120 individuals and a catalogue of 568 books.[23]

Such cultural activities suggest that independent weavers earned enough for discretionary time devoted to leisure spending. Their leisure time also indicates the control exercised by male weavers over the production process. Indeed, independ-ent male weavers controlled the social relations of work within their household, reproduction of these relations over time, and the marketing of their webs. House-hold members, for the most part, produced the yarn and cloth under the direction of the male head while wives provided the other essential domestic services. Typical of a pre-capitalist work rhythm, weavers could relax and work at a slower pace just after market day and increase their pace as the next market day arrived. Some stopped working once enough had been produced to ensure subsistence.[24] Under pressure, weavers were known to work all night, and in general, worked hardest in the first half of the year. After June, when prices dropped, some worked in bleach yards or tended their small plots before returning to the loom.[25] This independence was integral to the plebian culture of northeast Ulster, and the encroachment that the putting-out system embodied was resisted.[26]

It is not surprising that less is known about women's work culture. Patriarchal social relations of the eighteenth century subjugated women to male authority and to an asymmetrical division of labour within the household. Eighteenth-century women had the responsibility of housework and childcare, and they spun when they had 'spare' time. While men worked hard both at the loom and on their land, the rhythm of women's work was distinct. The high level of men's cultural and leisure pursuits depended on the provision of essential services by their wives such as cooking food, caring for children and maintaining the home. Eighteenth-century women, like their sisters a century later, had little leisure time. When they were not involved with household work they spun, mended or worked in the fields. When women sought social interaction, the more public arenas such book clubs, hunts or pubs were not open to them. Theirs was a more private home-centred world. In ways similar to spinners from the Caux region in France, Irish handspinners 'gathered to work not to relax'.[27] Contemporary descriptions of women's 'work' are

22 John Hewitt (ed.), *Rhyming Weavers and Other Country Poets of Antrim and Down* (Belfast, 1974); Nancy J. Curtin, *The United Irishmen: Popular Politics in Ulster and Dublin, 1791–1798* (Oxford 1994); Jane Gray, 'Folk poetry and working class identity In Ulster: an analysis of James Orr's "The Peni-tent"', *Journal of Historical Sociology*, 6, no. 3 (1993), 251–75. 23 Hewitt, *Rhyming Weavers*, p. 32. 24 Arthur Young, *A Tour*, p. 132. 25 Crawford, *Domestic Industry*, pp. 33–4. 26 Gray, 'Rural Industry', 178–83; Gray, 'Folk Poetry'; Jane Gray, 'Gender and plebian culture in Ulster', *Journal of Interdis-ciplinary History*, 24, no. 2 (1993), 251–70; Liu, *Weaver's Knot*, pp. 235–7. 27 Gay Gullickson, *Spinners and Weavers of Auffay* (Cambridge 1986), p. 84; and Gay Gullickson, 'Love and power in the proto-industrial family', in Maxine Berg (ed.), *Markets and Manufacture in Early Industrial Europe* (London 1991), pp. 205–26.

often blurred with 'amusements' suggesting the lack of distinction between work and leisure characteristic of a specifically female task-oriented work rhythm as Edward Wakefield described:

> The women in the weaving districts are much accustomed to visiting each other, and these visits are called keating. A young female with her spinning wheel on her head travels a considerable distance to the house of an acquaintance, where others are assembled, who spin, sing and converse during the whole evening; after which they cheerfully return to their own homes without participating in any refreshment excepting potatoes and milk.[28]

Manufacturers were a petty-capitalist and petty-landlord class employing small numbers of cottier weavers and marketing their cloth. Because this entrepreneurial group emerged from proto-industrial producers, they fundamentally contradict neo-Chayanovian assumptions relating to their presumed anti- or precapitalist economic logic. Manufacturers accumulated enough money in the eighteenth century to increase the size of their holdings, set up proletarianized cottier weavers in small cottages on tiny plots, provided them with looms, and become early putters-out. Their employees often paid their rent in work, and the success of the first manufacturers encouraged others to follow suit.[29] These manufacturers no longer engaged in weaving themselves. Like the wealthier drapers, they took the cloth produced by their weavers to brown linen markets and sold it, thus dominating their cottier employees at both the points of production and exchange. By 1800, manufacturers formed the majority of 'weavers' selling yarn and cloth in brown linen markets.[30] Within the context of an expanding eighteenth century linen industry, this group of men, eager for upward mobility, prospered.

Manufacturers have also left scant documentation of their existence. Although contemporary evidence refers to them, the title 'manufacturer' does not appear frequently in the census or in estate papers. This is because official records listed them as weavers.[31] In the 1821 Census of Derryhale, Thomas Stanley, who is listed as a farmer and linen merchant, held only three acres. Both his wife and daughter were flax spinners suggesting both humble origins and the contributions of women to the social mobility of the male household head and the household.[32] In 1825, a linen merchant at Lambeg, County Antrim, reported that manufacturers near Dromore and Hillsborough were of 'a considerable number and business conducted on a considerable extent'.[33] Occasionally, there is a lease like that of 7 June 1798, between Sir William Johnston of Tullylish and William McDowell, a 'draper weaver',

28 Wakefield, *An Account*, p. 739; Gray, 'Rural Industry', 151–2; Gray, 'Plebian Culture', 260.   29 Crawford, *Domestic Industry*, pp. 14–15.   30 Ibid., p. 6.   31 Conrad Gill, *The Rise of the Irish Linen Industry* (Oxford 1925), p. 146.   32 (PRONI), T.1228/2, MSS Census of 1821, Kilmore Parish, Co. Armagh.   33 H.C. *Report From the Select Committee on the Linen Trade of Ireland*, vol. x (1825), p. 126.

who leased a house and garden in Drumaran for three lives.[34] Finally, among the numerous drapers who rented land from Sir William Johnston in 1795, there was James Orr, who leased only six acres, and William Trouten who leased five acres, two roods and thirty perches. These can be separated from the large wealthy draper/bleachers including Thomas Christy Wakefield of Moyallon with eighty acres.

Manufacturers, who did not have large reserves of liquid capital, were obliged to take risks to obtain profits. If the market turned down, their small capital, which was tied up in stock of yarn, could be wiped out. The ability of manufacturers' to accumulate stocks of yarn depended upon the low wages paid to female handspinners in the yarn spinning regions west of the Bann. Since manufacturers employed cottiers dependent on yarn put-out to them, purchasing sufficient yarn was a significant capital expense. To the extent that this expense was kept low, manufacturers' profited from selling webs.[35]

Evidence suggests that many manufacturers did not survive the enormous socio-economic changes associated with mill spinning in the early nineteenth century. Since handspinners could not compete with cheaper mill-spun yarn, manufacturers were deprived of sources of yarn. Petty-capitalists did not have access to sources of capital sufficient to build spinning mills or bleachgreens. Others could not survive sudden changes in the market or in technology, or compete successfully with the larger drapers and bleachers in the competitive environment of the early nineteenth century.[36]

DIFFERENTIATION, SUBDIVISION OF LAND AND POPULATION GROWTH

The links between an expanding market economy for linen, landlord tenant relations and demographic change also contributed to the social differentiation of producers. Since long leases effectively removed much of an estate from a landlord's control, he could do little to curb subdivision or subletting among his tenants. Contemporaries both noted and lamented the extent of subdivision and subletting in Ulster which they connected to deteriorating methods of husbandry and the spread of the linen industry. For example, Dubourdieu listed subletting of land to undertenants and the provision of a share of land to each child as the chief reasons for the extent of small farms in County Down.[37] Referring to County Armagh, Sir Charles Coote wrote that, 'the pursuit of manufacture, and the population very

34 (PRONI), T.1007/291/218, Burgess Estate Papers.   35 Gray, 'Rural Industry'.   36 *Pigot's Provincial Directory* (London, 1825), pp. 385–6. Hugh McCall, *Ireland and her Staple Manufactures* (Belfast 1870), p. 209, states, 'The effect of centralising the manufacture of linens was most unfavourable to many small capitalists. Makers who only had a few weavers at work would not compete with the extensive men in the trade'. See also Liana Vardi, *The Land and the Loom* (Durham 1993), pp. 199–202 who describes a highly competitive market economy for linen in the Cambresis region of France in the late eighteenth century that forced some merchants out of the trade and back into farming.   37 Dubourdieu, *Statistical Survey*, pp. 39–40.

numerous, are the causes of the small size of farms, which are of so little extent as to leave the average of the county at less then 5 acres'.[38]

In the eighteenth century, holding land was important means of production, helping to ensure independence and subsistence. Nearly all medium and large farms had the household head listed as farmer in the 1821 census. These households either lived solely from farming, combined farming with shopkeeping or were successful linen merchants. Such households were middle class or wealthy 'gentry' families. In most of these wealthy families, members were not involved in producing yarn or cloth. None in Tullylish were so employed, but five farms in Derryhale with twenty or more acres did have household members producing cloth or yarn. The combination of a medium-sized farm with members engaged in linen production could suggest humble origins. But even if the origins of some of these families were humble, medium and large farmers were a class apart from the small farmer/weavers and the landless.

Dubourdieu makes a distinction between those whose farms alone supported the family and those 'such as are held by weavers and other tradesmen, and are not sufficient for their maintenance without the intervention of some other occupation unconnected with agriculture'.[39] He also suggests that twenty acres were necessary for such self-sufficiency and we can use this guide to distinguish between these middle class farmers and those below who combined farming with linen production. Both Liam Kennedy and Anne McKernan agree that the independent farmer/weavers of east Ulster needed between five and ten acres of land.[40] Using this estimation, 38 per cent of Tullylish households and 22 per cent of Derryhale households in the 1821 census held under five acres, which was insufficient to ensure independence. While those who held under ten acres had their heads of the household listed as farmers, as did every person holding two acres or more, in reality they were land poor and dependent upon the income derived from linen production.[41]

Within this historically specific context, a contradiction emerged – household members tried to secure small plots of land to ensure independence, while cultural practices governing the division of land amongst children at marriage had the opposite effect of increasing dependence upon earning wages. McKernan, however, has questioned this contradiction, arguing that the 'rampant subdivision of farms' portrayed and lamented by contemporaries is 'not consistent with the maintenance and reproduction of the classic farmer-weaver mode of production'.[42] She uses evidence from the Richhill estate in northeast County Armagh to demonstrate the predominance of independent farmer-weavers, while attempting to account for the coexistence of 'dependent forms of production' such as landless and land poor weavers. The main thrust of her argument is that the farmer-weaver mode of production (Kaufsystem) and proletarianization can coexist. She concludes that the majority of

38 Coote, *Statistical Survey*, p. 136.   39 Dubourdieu, *Statistical Survey*, p. 39.   40 Kennedy, 'Rural Economy', 32; McKernan, 'Dynamics', p. 245.   41 Gullickson, *Spinners and Weavers*, p. 4.   42 McKernan, 'Dynamics', p. 239.

households had enough land to ensure independence up to 1821, and that the cause and effect relationship between linen production and subdivision is more problematic than evidence from contemporaries would have us believe.[43]

McKernan's argument against rampant subdivision rests partly upon the calculation of average acreage per household determined to be 14.7 acres on the Richhill estate. This average did not significantly decrease between 1766 and 1821 suggesting the reproduction of the 'farmer-weaver mode of production'. McKernan cautions the reader that the use of averages hides the complexity of subdivision, and she adjusted her calculations accordingly to exclude the landless. The landless are, however, only one of two outlying categories that can distort average acreage figures. Elsewhere, I have demonstrated that the use of averages can present a distorted picture of rents on estates, since large holdings leased to principal tenants in perpetuity for low acreable rents will, when averaged in with total rent figures, suppress the true extent of rent increases.[44] In this case, the inclusion of large holdings of 50 or more acres can inflate average acreage per household and hide the complexity of subdivision.

Although the Johnston estate in Tullylish was located close to the Richhill estate, there were significant subregional differences, particularly those resulting from the development of bleaching along the River Bann. Rent rolls for the Johnston estate between 1731 and 1814, however, provide comparative evidence. Evidence of subdivision can be seen by the leasing of fractional holdings, the listing of all a tenant's fractional holdings by a professional surveyor, and 'the presence side by side, of holdings of exactly equal size occupied by tenants of the same surname', suggesting familistic subdivision.[45] One can also see the leasing of small plots to joint tenants. For example, a survey of part of Richard Johnston's estate in Drumaran called the Turfbog undertaken in 1760 lists several small plots leased to two joint tenants – sometimes kin and sometimes not – suggesting the persistence of rundale agrarian practices on the estate.[46] Another survey undertaken in 1809 lists eighteen holdings held by nine tenants. None of the holdings exceed six acres and most were under two. Some tenants held separate fragments of land which together only amounted to a tiny farm. For example, John Madole held four parcels which totalled only three acres. His kinsmen Archibald, who was listed immediately after him, held two fragments which totalled two acres, one rood indicating familistic subdivision.[47]

---

43 Ibid., pp. 238–54. 44 Cohen, 'Peasant Differentiation'. 45 Maguire, *Downshire Estates*, pp. 120–1. 46 (PRONI), T.1007/90, Burgess Estate Documents. Late eighteenth century leases for both the Johnston and Clanwilliam estates show leases between the landlord and two to four joint tenants. See D.1594/148 Burgess Estate Documents; D.3044/A/4/7/1 Clanwilliam Meade Papers, Gill Hall Estate. McCourt, 'Rundale', 123, argues that rundale practices were still extensively practiced in Ulster at this time. The extension of agricultural production after the 1750s was partly achieved by reclaiming waste, a solution consistent with the rundale practice of permanently settling partnership groups, already experiencing population pressure, on their summer (booley) grounds. 47 (PRONI), T.1007/233, Burgess Estate Papers.

Rent rolls dating from 1731, 1795, and 1814 for the Johnston estate provide better evidence.[48] A principal landlord's rent rolls present an incomplete account of the extent of subdivision and subletting on his estate, since they list only those tenants leasing directly from him.[49] It is well known that large tenants were frequently themselves middlemen landlords in Ireland. While Johnston's rent rolls make scant mention of Thomas Christy's or 'Purdy's tenements', their names were not recorded.[50]

If, following McKernan, an average acreage per household is calculated including all tenants large and small on the Johnston estate, high averages of 34.3 acres per household in 1731, 12.9 acres in 1795, and 16.7 acres in 1814 are obtained. If we exclude the five largest tenants with fifty or more acres, who together held 64 per cent of Johnston's estate in perpetuity, the average falls to 16 acres in 1731 and to just over 10 acres in 1795 and 1814. Although this revised average is nearly identical to McKernan's, it is inconclusive evidence regarding the extent of subdivision on the estate. A closer examination of Johnston's rent rolls reveals a steady decrease in the size of holdings, especially among farms under ten acres as table 1 reveals. The proportion of small farms under ten acres (with those under five acres accounting for the change) rose from 38 per cent in 1731, to 52 per cent in 1795, to 61 per cent in 1814 suggesting increasing dependence on petty commodity production.[51] Further, there is a decrease in the proportion of holdings larger than fifteen acres after 1731 suggesting subletting. Many tenants with the same surname are listed with side by side plots suggesting familistic subdivision.

Table 1: Size of holdings on the Johnston Estate, 1731–1814

Size of holding*	1731		1795		1814	
	No.	%	No.	%	No.	%
1 – 5 acres	4	13	9	26	22	37
5 – 10 acres	8	25	9	26	14	24
10 – 15 acres	4	13	5	15	5	8
15 – 20 acres	5	16	4	12	5	8
over 20 acres	11	34	7	20	13	22
Total	32	100	34	99	59	99

Source: PRONI, D. 1594, Bundle 69, D.1594/76; T.1007/237 Burgess estate papers. * Data relating to size of holdings was not given for every tenant.

48 (PRONI), T.1007/233, Burgess Estate Documents, Part of Drumaran, County Down Surveyed by John Couzins, October, 1809; T.1007/237, Burgess Estate Documents, Rent Roll of Sir William Johnston, 1814.   49 (PRONI), T.1007/237, Burgess Estate Papers.   50 (PRONI), D.1594/148 and T.1007/237, Burgess Estate Papers.   51 (PRONI), D.1594, Bundle 69, Burgess Estate Papers; D.1594/76, Burgess Estate Papers; T.1007/237, Burgess Estate Papers.

In the second half of the eighteenth century, proto-industrial producers paid sharply increasing rents for these small holdings in Tullylish. Rent rolls for the Johnston estate also reveal a steady increase in rents per acre in the eighteenth century. The 1795 Rent Roll listed acreable rents for all thirty-two holdings which were not held in perpetuity. Fifty-six per cent of the acreable rents were between one and two pounds and six per cent were over two pounds per acre. This is in sharp contrast to 1731 where only two were above a pound per acre. The 1795 Rent Roll also contains a category of the current yearly rent and the current value of that holding. Because of the prevalence of long leases, thirty of sixty-two, or half of the tenants were paying rents below the value of the land.[52]

In eighteenth-century Tullylish, subdivision and subletting can be understood partly as household strategies to maximize their economic position *vis-à-vis* the expanding land and linen markets. Linen production ensured that less land was required per household permitting families to divide their land between their sons as they reached maturity. Finally, as the rents per acre were always higher on small holdings, it was profitable for tenants to sublet their land and profit from the sky-rocketing land market. The producers' strategy was to secure a small holding, preferably with a lease, that granted some degree of security of tenure which functioned as a means for providing food, some flax and if large enough, independence. Throughout the eighteenth century in Tullylish, weavers were able to secure such leases.[53] Security of tenure as an active strategy meant that in spite of high rents, some categories of proto-industrial producers would not see all of their money absorbed in ever-increasing rents, thus facilitating low-level capital accumulation. However, both economic and cultural forces undermined independence based upon retaining ten acres of land, thus contributing to the larger process of class differentiation.

PROTO-INDUSTRIALIZATION AND POPULATION GROWTH

Contemporaries were quick to link the spread of the linen industry and subdivision to population growth. The demographic impact of the link between rural industry and agriculture forms the basis of one powerful proto-industrial hypothesis. The feedback hypothesis between domestic industry, subdivision of land, early marriage and population growth that was taking place during the late eighteenth century in Ireland has been subjected to much testing throughout Europe.[54] It suggests that

---

52 Ibid.   53 W.H. Crawford, 'The influence of the landlord in eighteenth century Ulster', in L.M. Cullen and T.C. Smout (eds), *Comparative Aspects of Scottish and Irish Economic and Social History 1600–1900* (Edinburgh 1977), p. 196.   54 Lutz K. Berkner and Franklin F. Mendels, 'Inheritance systems, family structure and demographic patterns in Western Europe 1700–1900', in Charles Tilly (ed.), *Historical Studies of Changing Fertility* (Princeton, NJ 1978), pp. 215–16; Ogilvie and Cerman, *European Proto-industrialization*.

the combination of handicraft production with agriculture undermines the population equilibrium found in peasant societies where marriage and procreation depend on the transmission of the family's land to one son only. Other sons are forced to find alternative employment, emigrate or remain celibate while a dowry is provided for one daughter. With proto-industry, the quantity of land necessary for a household is greatly reduced (in some cases it may not be necessary at all) and, therefore, the incentive for postponing marriage or remaining celibate is undermined.[55]

If we eliminate static notions of population 'equilibrium' as a universal characteristic of peasant societies, we can address how domestic industry affects demographic change in a particular historical context. There is little doubt that the population of pre-famine Ulster was growing rapidly during the second half of the eighteenth century and that this growth was partly connected to the expanding linen industry.[56] Jane Gray has argued that the western yarn districts were more deeply enmeshed into this proto-industrial cycle than those in the core weaving districts of Armagh and Down. However, even this core district, enormous population increases occurred in the decades prior to the Famine.[57]

County Down's population growth before the Great Famine was quite remarkable. According to Dubourdieu, the number of houses rose from 19,270 in 1751 to 38,351 in 1791, an increase of 4817 houses every ten years.[58] The 1821 census, which also listed aggregate statistics for 1813, showed that the number of houses in County Down had risen to 53,310 in 1813, and to 62,425 by 1821. The corresponding number of people rose from 287,290 in 1813 to 329,348 in 1821, an increase of 42,058 in that ten year period.[59] County Down contained 544 square miles and 348,550 Irish acres. The average number of inhabited houses per square mile was 109 4/5, with 598 inhabitants per square mile and 5 4/5 acres per household. This was a very high population density indeed, surpassed in Ireland only by Counties Dublin, Louth, Armagh and Monaghan. In terms of acres per inhabitant, only Armagh and Monaghan had less than Down's 1.06.[60]

In Ulster where producers had the opportunity of earning additional income through domestic industry, the formation of new households depended as much on employment in the linen industry as on inheritance systems. The existence of domestic industry encouraged household formation since members could be maintained on less and less land increasing their dependence on a monetary income derived from yarn and cloth production.[61]

55 Brenda Collins, 'Proto-industrialization and pre-famine emigration', *Social History*, 7, no. 2 (1982), 135.
56 The link between textile production and population growth in Ireland was first systematically tested by Eric L. Almquist, 'Mayo and Beyond: Land, Domestic Industry, and Rural Transformation in the Irish West', Ph.D. diss., Boston University, 1977, pp. 197, 288–9. However, Joel Mokyr, *Why Ireland Starved: A Quantitative and Analytical History of the Irish Economy, 1800–1850* (London 1983) p. 63, concluded that cottage industry, was not a significant factor in marriage behaviour.   57 Gray, 'Rural Industry', p. 92.   58 Dubourdieu, *Statistical Survey*, p. 243.   59 H.C. *Abstract of the Population of Ireland*, vol. 14, 1822, p. xiii.   60 Ibid.   61 H.J. Habakkuk, 'Family structure and economic change in nineteenth century Europe', *Journal of Economic History*, 15, no. 1 (1955), 10.

HOUSEHOLD COMPOSITION AND DIFFERENTIATION

Use of the 1821 census to analyze the household in terms of political economy focuses attention on relations of production, division of labour and possibilities for accumulation. Households in Tullylish revealed a fairly rigid division of labour by gender. Females were overwhelmingly spinners and winders while males were weavers and labourers. However, in six of forty Tullylish households, young daughters between the ages of ten and eighteen were listed as weavers. McKernan has discussed the complex factors drawing females into the traditionally male preserve of weaving in the early nineteenth century.[62] Her Richhill sample revealed 16 households that contained one female linen weaver suggesting that the rigid sexual demarcation between female spinning and male weaving relaxed before the end of the proto-industrial period.[63] She also draws an important connection between the expansion of the putting-out system and the appearance of female weavers. This insight is especially relevant for regions close to Banbridge in Tullylish where the putting-out system was more advanced than in Richhill prior to the advance of mill-based spinning in 1825.

Census data for Tullylish also supports Brenda Collins' argument about extending family production and the possibilities for accumulation through flexible household membership. In Tullylish, 23 of 40 households included co-resident extended kin or non-kin. In Derryhale, 34 per cent of households were similarly composed. Of the 23 in Tullylish, eleven had either kin or non-kin members who were spinners or weavers. Some of these were listed as lodgers, in which case they received food and lodging, while others were 'dieters' who received their lodging while paying for their meals. In Derryhale, 32 of the 121 households had extended kin or non-kin who were weavers or spinners. Looking at the occupations of extended household members, 15 per cent were linen weavers, 12 per cent were yarn spinners, 4 per cent were apprentices to linen weaving, and 1 per cent were bleachers. Those remaining were domestic servants. By taking in extended kin or non-kin, households could significantly extend their productive capacity and total income while incurring only minimal costs associated with reproducing each new member.[64]

In conclusion, on the eve of the huge transformation to factory spinning that occurred after 1825, the Tullylish area was indeed one of the 'economic nerve centers of proto-industry'.[65] Factors combining to generate capital accumulation among groups at the bottom of the social ladder should not be dismissed, even though they elude precise measurement. In the context of rapid economic expansion during the

62 Anne McKernan, 'War, gender, and industrial innovation: recruiting women weavers in early nineteenth century Ireland', *Journal of Social History*, 28, no. 1 (1995), 109–24. 63 McKernan, 'Dynamics', p. 269. Her data from the 1821 census suggests that the sexual division of labour was more flexible than that argued by Gray between 1780–1840. See 'Rural Industry', 147. 64 Collins, 'Proto-industry', 134. 65 Kennedy, 'Rural Economy', 14.

eighteenth century, both class and gender differentiation eroded family economy. Thus, the family economy of independent farmer/weavers 'was being stabilized under unstable conditions'.[66] Manufacturers emerged from the ranks of petty commodity producers accumulating profits through the exploitation of both their cottier employees and the low wages earned by female handspinners elsewhere to become petty-capitalists and petty-landlords. Cottier weavers were essentially proletarians whose total dependence upon the wages and yarn provided by manufacturers was, perhaps, held at bay through retaining patches of land.

These paths of capital accumulation in Tullylish caution us against teleological models of capitalist development and conceptualizations of modes of production based upon simple reproduction. In Tullylish, as in the Cambresis region in late eighteenth century France, the expansion of rural industry could not have occurred without peasant entrepreneurship.[67] Henceforth, the development of industrial capitalism in Tullylish was as much related to British technological imperatives as to primitive accumulation.

66 William Roseberry, 'Potatoes, sacks and enclosures in early Modern England', in Jay O'Brien and 1 William Roseberry (eds), *Golden Ages, Dark Ages: Imagining the Past in Anthropology and History* (Berkeley, CA 1991), p. 42.   67 Vardi, *Land and Loom*, p. 11.

PART II

THE NINETEENTH CENTURY:
RURAL INDUSTRIAL CAPITALISM IN TULLYLISH, 1825–1900

4

Dependency and Industrial Capitalism: Contextualizing the Nineteenth-Century Irish Linen Industry

The physical condition of the weavers appears to me to be worse off then that of any class of Irishmen. The length of time they continue at work, and the damp, unwholesome cabins they work in (a disgrace to any country that would permit such a state of things) appears one great cause of this inferiority ... I could not pass a weaver by without knowing him to be one; and I never saw a weaver that had not dyspepsia written in his countenance.[1]   C.G. Otway, 1840

Oh, had I the power to restore,
The reel would still crack and the spinning wheel snore,
Mill yarn would sink down as it never had been,
Trade flourish as fair as it ever was seen,
A swab with a steam loom would never appear
Our country to steep in affliction and fear.[2]
Ulster handloom weaver, 1853

DEPENDENT INNOVATION: CONNECTIONS BETWEEN COTTON AND LINEN

In both law and technology there was a close relationship between cotton and linen, but as the eighteenth century closed, this linkage was usually to the detriment of linen. The cotton fibre was much easier to process, allowing technological innovation to advance far more rapidly. By the last quarter of the eighteenth century, cotton was a 'leading' sector at the centre of innovation in England. Machinery for spinning coarse cotton yarn suitable for warp was possible by the 1770s on Richard Arkwright's small multi-spindle frames, and in ten years, mule spinning enabled the production of fine cotton yarn. As a result, linen was no longer required for warp, and the cheaper lighter cotton cloth displaced linen in the tropical markets, especially with raw materials produced by slave labour. While linen stagnated during 1770–80s, due to depression and the American War of Independence, the semi-autonomous Irish parliament acted to encourage and protect cotton manufacture.

1 H. C. *Reports of Assistant Commissioners on Handloom Weavers*, part III, vol. xxiii (1840), Report of C.G. Otway, p. 622.   2 Quoted in Henry Patterson, 'Industrial labour and the labour movement, 1820–1914', in Liam Kennedy and Philip Ollerenshaw (eds), *An Economic History of Ulster* (Manchester 1985), p. 161.

New spinning technology and water-driven mills were introduced leading to the displacement of linen by cotton in Ireland, and the necessity to develop similar technology for spinning linen yarn.

Denis O'Hearn argues that innovation involves far more than technological invention. Innovations, defined sociologically to include changes in the social relations of production, are at the centre of major economic change. Such changes are linked with the power of core states since innovation is part of a larger process of reproducing global stratification or 'world-system hierarchy'.[3]

Cotton spinning in England was a 'core' innovation, a centre of creative response in which new technologies and reorganization of work were used to create and sustain world hegemony in England. Actions by the English and Irish parliaments encouraged and protected the smaller Irish cotton industry. As in England, the cotton industry in east Ulster, with its dependence on water power, coal driven steam power, and imported raw materials, ushered industrial capitalism into the Lagan Valley. Cotton yarn spinning was concentrated in factories, requiring creative responses – changes in the relations of production, and considerable fixed capital formation.

However, the Irish cotton industry was not simply a regional equivalent of the English. In England, innovation in the spinning sector led to other innovations in engineering, steam power and powerloom weaving. In Ireland, cotton spinning did not revolutionize weaving but further developed the system of putting-out mill-spun yarn to handloom weavers in Belfast and its hinterland.[4] Although capitalist relations of production were thereby extended, production remained decentralized, relations of production were not transformed, and expansion was achieved through such adaptive responses as additional labour or looms.

Irish muslin weavers earned low wages in comparison to English weavers.[5] However, in Ireland, muslin weavers earned relatively high wages (as much as three times those of linen weavers), and cotton yarn was far easier to weave than linen yarn. The result was that in the vicinity of Belfast and in the Lagan Valley as far as Moira and Hillsborough, cotton almost entirely replaced linen.[6]

The rapid expansion of the Irish cotton industry posed a competitive threat to the cotton industry in England. Ireland formed part of the England's semipheriphery, and its industrial growth was subjugated to meet the needs of capital accumulation in England. The Irish cotton industry was deliberately peripherialized by the English state creating Irish dependency for sources of cotton wool, for mill-spun yarn

3 Denis O'Hearn, 'Innovation and the world-system hierarchy: British subjugation of the Irish cotton industry, 1780–1830', *American Journal of Sociology*, 100, no. 3 (1994), 595; Denis O'Hearn, 'Irish linen: a peripheral industry', in Marilyn Cohen (ed.), *The Warp*.   4 Philip Ollerenshaw, 'Industry, 1820–1914', in Liam Kennedy and Philip Ollerenshaw (eds), *An Economic History of Ulster, 1829–1939* (Manchester 1985), p. 66.   5 O'Hearn, 'Innovation', 603.   6 E.R.R. Green, *The Lagan Valley 1800–1850* (London 1949), p. 99.

put-out to dispersed poorly remunerated Irish handloom weavers and by periodically dumping yarn and later cloth in Ireland. When, by the 1820s and 30s, Belfast cotton spinners could not compete in cotton, they turned to spinning flax. Thus, the industrial revolution in the Irish linen industry began as a subordinate, dependent, adaptive response to innovation in the English cotton industry.[7]

Nevertheless, competition and innovation in the cotton industry forced similar technological changes in the linen industry. The first response came again from England, where two Darlington men, John Kendrew and Thomas Porthouse, in 1787 patented flax spinning machinery. Six months later, John Marshall of Leeds decided to try out this new machinery. As a result of Marshall's investment, Leeds became a centre for mill-spun linen yarn, which spread to Aberdeen and Dundee by 1792. The whole coarse linen trade was thereby captured by England and Scotland eliminating Ireland almost entirely. Henceforth, Ireland concentrated on fine linen production.

GENDER AND INNOVATION: MILL-BASED SPINNING OF FLAX

The innovative process is never gender neutral. Feminist scholarship has revealed a close connection between cultural conceptions of gender, the development and implementation of new technology, definitions of skill, and the social relations of work.[8] Sex/gender systems influence the global and national environment for innovation including access to cheap sources of labour, raw materials, capital, markets infrastructure, and human knowledge.

Female labour always dominated the spinning sector and was considered less skilled than weaving. Unlike the cotton industry where mule spinners were male, wet spinning frames for flax spinning were designed to be worked by women. The operation of wet spinning frames required little formal training, and a strict gendered division of labour existed between female operatives and male mechanics, who built and maintained them.[9]

Scholars have analyzed why the mechanization of linen yarn and cloth production in Ireland lagged behind Scotland.[10] The first objective of machine flax spin-

---

7 O'Hearn, 'Innovation', 587–621; David Dickson, 'Aspects of the rise and decline of the Irish cotton industry', in L.M. Cullen and T.C. Smout (eds), *Comparative Aspects of Scottish and Irish Economic and Social History 1600–1900* (Edinburgh 1977), p. 111. 8 Ava Baron, 'Contested terrain revisited: technology and gender definitions of work in the printing industry, 1850–1920', in Barbara Drygulski Wright, Myra Marx Ferree, Linda H.Lewis, Gail O. Mellow, Maria-Luz Daza Samper, Robert Asher, Kathleen Claspell (eds), *Women, Work and Technology* (Ann Arbor, MI 1987), p. 61; Sonya Rose, *Limited Livelihoods* (Berkeley, CA 1992), pp. 22–30. 9 Rose, *Limited Livelihoods*, p. 27. 10 Alastair Durie and Peter Solar, 'The Scottish and Irish linen industries compared, 1780–1860', in Rosalind Mitchison and Peter Roebuck (eds), *Economy and Society in Scotland and Ireland* (Edinburgh 1988), p. 217; Jane Gray, 'The Irish and Scottish linen industries in the eighteenth century: an incorporated comparison', in Marilyn Cohen (ed.), *The Warp*.

ners in the late 1780s was to displace coarse yarns produced by handspinners since mills could produce cheaper yarn cheaper of equal quality. Fine yarn spinners were safe for the moment, but by the mid-1820s, all but the finest handspinners were driven out of the market both in Ireland and in the linen districts of Europe.

The long flax fibre is composed of short ultimate fibres held together by the gummy substance pectose. Before the 1820s, spinners drew out and twisted these long fibres producing medium yarns. However, to produce fine yarn, the ultimate fibres also needed to be drawn out and twisted. James Kay found that by long immersion of rovings in cans of cold water, the pectose softened sufficiently to allow the fibres in the drawing process to slip past each other. Machinery for spinning was redesigned, soaking cans were replaced by troughs of water, and hot water was soon found to be even more effective than cold. This latter refinement only required a quick wetting. It produced a chemical reaction that parted the ultimate fibres allowing very fine yarns of 60 and 100 leas to be spun by machine.[11]

Initially, Irish handspinners had two advantages. First, women could spin yarn of any weight while machines could only produce coarse yarn of five leas, severely restricting the market. Second, handspinners were usually part-time workers and members of proto-industrial households. Because they partially reproduced themselves, Irish handspinners worked cheaper than spinners in Britain and cheaper than urban proletarians who required a subsistence wage of about 6s. a week. To these higher variable capital costs were added the costs of machinery that far exceeded the cost of hand implements. These factors inhibited technological innovation in the linen industry since there was little incentive for capitalists to invest in fixed capital to raise productivity. Even with bounties for constructing spinning mills offered after 1803 by the Linen Board and England's technological challenge, few spinning mills were built in Ireland during the first two decades of the nineteenth century. Attempts at dry spinning failed since the method could not produce the fine yarns needed by Irish weavers.[12]

The links between proto-industrial production and the sexual division of labour had enabled Irish household members to produce their yarn and cloth cheaply. This fact led some witnesses before a Select Committee formed in 1825, such as millowner Thomas Crosthwate, to conclude that attempts to reorganize yarn production would fail.[13] He and other influential men of the time, did not think the putting-out system, dominant in England, Scotland, and the Belfast area, was superior to the domestic system of production. Others, such as Dublin factor James Twigg, advocated the admission of cheaper, superior, and foreign mill-spun yarn, along with the permanent split between farming and weaving, despite the more regular payment of rents by weavers in the north.[14]

11 W.G. Rimmer, *Marshalls of Leeds, Flax Spinners 1788–1886* (Cambridge 1980), pp. 169–73; Emily J. Boyle, 'The Economic Development of the Irish Linen Industry, 1825–1913', Ph.D. diss., The Queen's University of Belfast, 1977, pp. 22–4.   12 Durie and Solar, 'Linen Industries Compared', 217–18.   13 H.C. *Report From the Select Committee on the Linen Trade of Ireland*, vol. v (1825), p. 18.   14 Ibid., 'Testimony of James Twigg', p. 35.

By 1825, reliance upon cheap female labour was a strategy that Irish capitalists could no longer afford. In that year, James Kay of Preston invented the wet spinning process enabling fine counts of yarn to be spun by machine and threatening the future of the Irish linen industry.[15] According to Emily Boyle, in 1825, it cost approximately 3s. 1d. to spin a bundle of 100 leas yarn in an English mill compared with 10s. 9d. by an Irish handspinner. Ireland was the obvious market for English fine mill-spun yarn; technological innovation was, thus, essential to preserve the home market.[16]

Although many expressed reluctance to change a formerly successful profitable system of production, the regulation affecting the importation of British and foreign yarns was abolished. Thereafter, the response by Irish linen capitalists was swift. Entrepreneurs with capital such as bleachers, cotton mill owners, and manufacturers began to erect spinning mills or convert cotton mills to linen.[17] In 1835, there were twenty-two linen yarn spinning mills in Ireland. By 1840, there were thirty-eight, and sixty by 1845, leading Emily Boyle to conclude that 'wet flax spinning was an instant success in Ireland'.[18]

THE IMPACT OF MILL SPINNING: GENDER AND REGIONAL MEDIATIONS

According to Joseph Schumpeter, a 'primary wave' of economic growth is predicated upon a limited group of leading sectors where innovation is concentrated. A primary wave persists until an innovation is generalized. Thereafter, the prosperity generated by the primary wave induces a 'secondary wave' that further extends economic growth.[19] In the Irish linen industry, mill-based spinning of linen yarn induced a primary wave of economic growth in the northeast that permanently transformed the domestic organization of production.

Such economic growth was predicated upon the proletarianization of female handspinners. Marx argued that, 'the history of ... expropriation, in different countries, assumes different aspects, and runs in various phases in different order of succession, and at different periods'.[20] The historical specificity of the expropriation process in any context also reflects the sexual division of labour.[21] Mill-based spinning of linen yarn initiated a large-scale primitive accumulation process that further reduced the independence of male weavers through a generalization of the putting-out system and proletarianized many female handspinners who now produced linen yarn as operatives in the new spinning mills.

After the spread of mill spinning, women's contributions to their household's

15 Green, *Lagan Valley*, p. 112.   16 Boyle, 'Economic Development', pp. 24–5.   17 Green, *Lagan Valley*, p. 116.   18 Boyle, 'Economic Development', p. 34; Durie and Solar, 'Linen Industries Compared', 218.   19 Joseph Schumpeter, 'The creative response in economic history', *Journal of Economic History*, 7, no. 2 (1947), 149–59.   20 Karl Marx, *Capital*, vol. 1 (New York 1967), p. 716.   21 Thomas Dublin, *Transforming Women's Lives* (Ithaca, NY 1994), p. XV.

budget through handspinning declined. If the household resisted proletarianization by retaining their small plots of land, women continued to contribute needed cash through raising and selling pigs, poultry and occasionally through agricultural labour.[22] In industrializing regions, such as Tullylish, former handspinners worked as operatives in the new spinning mills, as winders for manufacturers or husbands, or as linen weavers. Similar to the Choletais region in France, the availability of female labour in Ireland shaped the types of employment opportunities in an area.[23]

Cheaper mill-spun yarn undermined the earnings of handspinners whose prices and numbers diminished over the next thirty years. According to Boyle, handspinners could only produce one bundle of yarn every four weeks, while a mill could produce four bundles per week per person. In the mid-1830s, one bundle of 100 leas yarn mill-spun cost about 2s.4½d. compared with just under 4s.10d. spun by a woman in her home. Consequently, domestic spinners had to sell their yarn far below cost to compete with mills, and as a result, their wages fell by up to 90 per cent between 1815 and 1836.[24]

This situation could not fail to hurt the vast majority of proto-industrial producers in the short term. However, the long-term impact was mediated by region and gender. In the yarn spinning counties west of the Bann, where the linen industry had a different rhythm from those east of the Bann, handspinners saw their prices reduced as demand for their yarn withered.[25] Further, cloth woven from handspun yarn could not compete with cloth woven from cheaper mill-spun yarn. The combination of declining markets for yarns and cloth and distance away from mills and putters-out, resulted in the collapse of rural industry in counties west of the Bann. As Brenda Collins concluded, 'it was essentially changes in the market for hand-spun yarn which was the employment of women, subordinate family members ... which affected the viability of the farming-weaving households of the Northwest'.[26]

What occurred in the northwest was peripherialization and de-industrialization. In east and southern Ulster (except Cavan and Monaghan where a substantial decline in the number of weaving households also followed), machine-spun yarn did not destroy the household as a textile-producing unit. Profound changes arose, again pivoting on the female members of the household, as handloom weaving expanded as a form of homework organized by the putting-out system. Areas in the core fine linen triangle region of east Ulster were closer to sources of mill-spun yarn.

22 Mary Cullen, 'Breadwinners and providers: women in the household economy of labouring families, 1835–6', in Maria Luddy and Cliona Murphy (eds), *Women Surviving* (Dublin 1989), pp. 85–115.   23 Tessie Liu, *The Weaver's Knot* (Ithaca, NY 1994), p. 42.   24 Boyle, 'Economic Development', p. 48.   25 For a discussion of the prevailing 'east-of-the-Bann bias' in analyses of the Irish linen industry and the 'different angle of vision' required for counties west of the Bann see, Joan Vincent, 'Linen in the Irish Northwest: unfinished business or lived experience in the 1830s', in Cohen (ed.), *The Warp*.   26 Brenda Collins, 'Proto-industrialization and pre-famine emigration', *Social History*, 7, no. 2 (1982), 138–9; Eric L. Almquist, 'Mayo and Beyond: Land, Domestic Industry, and Rural Transformation in the Irish West'. Ph.D. diss., Boston University, 1977.

Although employment opportunities for displaced spinners were greatest in east Ulster, we should not conclude that their households did not suffer. In 1841, spinners comprised 21.4 per cent and weavers 19.8 per cent of the inmates at the new Lurgan Workhouse.[27] Women and children of both sexes turned to handloom weaving in substantial numbers as it was the most important source of employment for displaced spinners. As an attempt to offset the loss of earnings from spinning and decreased earnings from weaving, households employed two or more handlooms to increase their output.[28] Not surprisingly, this increase in the supply of weavers and competition from cheaper cotton cloth kept the wages of handloom weavers low. Nevertheless, the continuing contributions of female weavers, both in terms of skill and earnings, were central to the survival of their households.[29]

Tessie Liu has considered why the new sweated trades in the Choletais region of France employed mostly women. She suggests that within weaving households, gender constitutes a class divide structuring differential relations to ownership and skill. This division along gender lines structured the process of proletarianization.[30] The increasing number of female handloom weavers in the Irish linen industry marked a further relaxation in the sexual division of labour that began with the fly-shuttle. When a skilled occupation is mechanized, deskilled, or experiences a decline in wages, women are often employed in greater numbers. Feminization does not, as Gay Gullickson observes, usually increase the status of women who perform the same tasks as men, but 'the status of men in those occupations would decline, now that they could conceivably be seen as performing women's work'.[31] Technological innovations enabled women in Ulster to weave, just as wages, status and independence in handloom weaving were declining. Further, since women remained responsible for many domestic tasks including childcare, they had to integrate weaving with the rhythm of their daily domestic routine.[32]

Another option for displaced handspinners in areas close to mills or putters-out, was to work as winders. In the vicinity of Banbridge and Gilford, many women worked as winders either for their husbands, for putters-out or for thread manufacturers cropping up in the area. Winding illustrates the dependence between the availability of cheap female labour and new sweated occupations in the linen industry. The importance of winding as a source of employment for women in Seapatrick was emphasized by the Reverend James Davis, Presbyterian minister of the First Congregation of Banbridge, in 1836.

27 Francis X. McCorry, *Lurgan: An Irish Provincial Town, 1610–1970* (Lurgan 1993), p. 75. 28 Liam Kennedy, 'The rural economy, 1820–1914', in Liam Kennedy and Philip Ollerenshaw (eds), *An Economic History of Ulster, 1820–1939* (Manchester 1985), p. 5; Henry Patterson, 'Industrial labour and the labour movement, 1820–1914', in Ibid., pp. 159–60. 29 *Reports on Handloom Weavers*, Report from Mr Otway, p. 617. 30 Liu, *Weaver's Knot*, p. 41–2. 31 Gay Gullickson, 'Love and power in the proto-industrial family', in Maxine Berg (ed.), *Markets and Manufacture in Early Industrial Europe* (London 1991), p. 221. 32 Dublin, *Transforming*, p. 29.

... in this parish in which there is so much employment given to women and children in the winding of yarn, their earnings would be more than in many others; if women have no employment but the spinning of yarn they will not make more, on an average, then 2*d* or 2$\frac{1}{2}$*d* per day, and possibly their children nothing; a very middling winder of yarn will make 3$\frac{1}{2}$*d* a day, a good one 4*d* or 5*d*, when diligently employed all the time; in several families there are two winding wheels, by which among the wife and children 7*d* a day might be earned, which would be 3*s.*6*d* per week; This is an average sum, as sometimes they may be disappointed of yarn, and sometimes not equally diligent, equal to £9.2*s*.8*d* in the year.[33]

In areas where winding was available, female proletarianization revealed both the complexity and unevenness of the process. When women worked as winders for putters-out, they were proletarianized since they exchanged their labour power for wages. However, because they worked at home, they were not subject to the same centralized working conditions as in a factory. Winders, who were still tied to a disintegrating dispersed proto-industrial system, enabled manufacturers to squeeze additional profits from sweated workers who partly absorbed the costs of reproducing themselves. If women worked within the domestic system as winders for their husbands, who in turn were employed by putters-out, they were still part of the process in which capitalist relations of production were extending to all aspects of production, albeit indirectly. Finally, where employment in the new spinning mills was available, women joined the ranks of the industrial proletariat adjusting to new relations of production.

Regional variations can be illustrated by comparing the Barony of Upper Iveagh in County Down, which did not industrialize, and Lower Iveagh, which did. In 1836, labourers in Upper Iveagh interviewed by the Poor Law Commissioners were concerned that their wives could not earn more than 1*d*. per day at spinning since the opening of the mill at Castlewellan. Like their husbands, who were once farmer/weavers, these women turned to agricultural pursuits such as selling eggs to supplement their household incomes since rents were still high.[34] Before 'linen weavers confined themselves exclusively to their trade, but that now the linen trade is so bad that most of the weavers work as agricultural labourers whenever they can obtain employment, and that it is only when they cannot get employment in the fields and on wet days that they work at the loom'.[35]

33 H. C. *Reports from Commissioners: Poor Inquiry Ireland, 1836*, Appendix D, vol. xxxi, 1836, Evidence of the Revd James Davis, p. 335.   34 Ibid., Appendix D, p. 91; Cullen, 'Breadwinners and Providers, 104.   35 *Poor Inquiry*, Appendix D, p. 67.

MILL-BASED SPINNING AND THE PUTTING-OUT SYSTEM

The mechanization of spinning fundamentally changed the organization of production and generated enormous capital accumulation. However, as in the cotton industry, weaving again remained unmechanized and decentralized, resulting in adaptive response – the generalization of the putting-out system. In the early nineteenth century, to the extent that weaving households maintained control over the production of raw materials, they were able to resist putting-out. However, increasing numbers reluctantly yielded their independence to manufacturers.[36] Men with capital, such as bleachers and drapers, bought mill-spun yarn from factories and employed weavers at an agreed upon price. Within fifteen years of the introduction of fine mill-spun yarn, the majority of Ulster's weavers were employed by manufacturers.[37] Brown linen markets also withered (with certain exceptions such as Ballymena and Lurgan) as petty manufacturers and weavers ceased to sell cloth on their own account. The large manufacturers who took their place sold their linen by private contract.

According to Liam Kennedy, unlike cotton weavers, whose wages fell dramatically between 1800 and 1830, the wages of linen handloom weavers are harder to trace prior to 1840. Various factors affected the wages of those working for merchants and manufacturers including the type of cloth woven, piece rates, the productivity of the weaver (affected by circumstances outside of his/her control), the number of hours worked and the general price level. At the household level, earnings were obviously affected by its size and composition. For those weavers who remained independent, earnings depended partly on their commercial judgment in procuring supplies of yarn and selling their cloth.[38] In 1800, only the most skilled weavers earned in excess of 10s. per week. Coote and Dubourdieu give a low of 1s. for coarse cloth, and a high of 1s.6d. for fine cloth. However, when demand was brisk, Coote reported weavers could earn as much as 2s.6d. a day and independent weavers as high as 5s. a day.[39] Using Wakefield's average of 7s. per week, this was a decline from 1800, when 8s.9d. per week was the average wage. By the late 1830s, the average wage was about 6s. per week, but between 1810 and 1830, prices also dropped by one third. While it is difficult to specify real wage cuts, working conditions for weavers worsened with twelve to fourteen hour days not uncommon indicating a significant loss of control over the work process.

Thus, between 1825 and 1846, the material constraints faced by proto-industrial producers changed. Wages were declining, as were prices between 1810 and 1830, the hours of work were increasing, and rents were still high. It is significant that when farmer/weavers expressed their opinion, they considered their circum-

36 Kennedy, 'Rural Economy', 7; Gray, 'Folk Poetry'.   37 William H. Crawford, *Domestic Industry in Ireland: The Experience of the Linen Industry* (Dublin 1972), p. 51.   38 Kennedy, 'Rural Economy', 8–9.
39 Revd John Dubourdieu, *Statistical Survey of the County of Down* (Dublin 1802), p. 233; and Sir Charles Coote, *Statistical Survey of the County of Armagh* (Dublin 1804), p. 254.

stances to be much worse when employed by manufacturers then when they worked independently as the following lengthy quotation by Reverend Davis confirms:

> The great majority of small farmers, some years ago, were in the habit of connecting the weaving of linen with the management of their little farms; and regarding their farms merely as places of accommodation, they looked to the profits of their trade to enable them to pay their rent and all other demands. At the time of which I speak 19/20ths of the tradesmen were able to weave on their own account, and all of the profit on the webs wrought came to themselves. For some years past 19/20ths of them weave to extensive manufacturers, who are not able to weave for themselves, and the wages are so low, that in general it requires close, constant, and hard work, to clear from 7*s* to 8*s* or 9*s* in the week, and in doing so it requires a great part of another person's time in the family to attend them; many of them fall considerably short of these sums if the yarn happen to be bad, or if they be not exceedingly diligent. At the same time I believe the manufacturer pays them as high wages as the state of the market will afford, but their earnings by the loom no longer enable them to pay high rents, high tithes, and high cess, and the farm seldom does more then merely increase their difficulties. Thus, whilst the operative tradesman in the linen business is getting exceedingly poor, extensive manufacturers are monopolizing the trade and are getting exceedingly rich. For if they have but a single shilling of clear profit on every web woven to them their yearly gain will be very considerable; so that whilst they are most eminently useful in giving employment to thousands and thousands, the principal benefit settles with themselves and whilst there may be as much money in the country as there was 16 or 20 years ago, it is far from being so equally divided among the community; the operatives in the linen trade are becoming more and more dependent, the money is leaving the hands of this useful class of men, and is accumulating, to an immense extent in the hands of their employers.[40]

The Assistant Commissioners on Handloom Weavers confirmed the disturbance and suffering caused by the generalization of the putting-out system. While the middle class generally applauded the new system of production, impoverishment was the immediate consequence for producers. The average earnings of handloom weavers between 1837 and 1839 were 9*d.* to 1*s.* per day including men and women ages fourteen to seventy. These wages were low relative to the past, and relative to Scotland and England. During the eighteenth century, weavers who worked on their own account were able to earn higher wages than those who worked for manufacturers. After 1825, those who worked for manufacturers earned higher wages.

40 *Poor Inquiry*, Appendix E, p. 335.

By 1840, there were four groups of weavers in Ulster. The first were independent weavers who still worked by the old Kaufsystem of owning land and marketing their cloth at the remaining markets. The second were cottier weavers who worked for manufacturers and did not hold land. The third group worked for manufacturers while leasing land. Finally, the fourth group of weavers worked for manufacturers in weaving shops or manufactories.

Only the first group were still resisting proletarianization. In the vicinities of Lurgan, Ballymena, Ballymoney and Coleraine independent farmer/weavers were still to be found along with handspinners, comprising most of the handspinners in the 1841 census.[41] Many of these weavers were highly skilled men who had a 'great dislike' for taking work from manufacturers and resisted it 'until forced to do so by absolute necessity'.[42] The majority of independent weavers near Lurgan held farms of from five to fifteen acres; those in north Antrim held from one to eight acres and had one to three looms. A farm with five to fifteen acres was still large enough to provide food and security enabling weavers to maintain their independence. Nevertheless, most were facing insuperable odds due to market and wage fluctuations.[43] By 1840, there were few districts in Ulster where manufacturers who put-out yarn had not penetrated.

Weavers who retained small plots of land continued to pay high rents for their one to three acres in the Lurgan area. In this region, most of the weavers were also engaged as agricultural labourers for one month per year during seed and harvest time when wages were the highest. This group was fully employed including their children of both sexes who began weaving at age twelve. By the time children were sixteen, they earned 'as much as a man of 30'. A vivid account of working conditions among domestic weavers near Lurgan was provided by cambric weaver Edward Hamilton:

> I put my boys on the loom at 12, and my girls at 11; the girls can weave as well as the boys. After a year's teaching they can earn 1s a day on 1500 lawns. They are paid 6s.6d the piece for weaving, and can weave a piece in a week by 16 hours a day work. I have a wee girl who never gets off the loom from day light in the morning until 10:00 at night. She is only 13 years of age. She can earn 8d or 10d a day. The work is light 1300 lawns. On a 1500 lawn I could only make 1s a day. The youngsters could make more than I could on a 1700 lawn. I could make 1s.6d a day ... the expenses of light, dressing, tallow and winding the weft we have to deduct out of our earnings; besides a day in going to the office with and bringing home on each web.[44]

41 Boyle, 'Economic Development', p. 249. 42 *Reports on Handloom Weavers*, p. 664; Patterson, 'Industrial Labour', 162. 43 *Reports on Handloom Weavers*, p. 665. 44 Ibid., p. 666.

In the nineteenth century, cottier weavers were a mixed group containing some formerly independent weavers, some young persons who acquired the skill of weaving from their parents but did not possess capital, and cottier weavers under the old system. The condition of cottiers varied. Where a family had two or three looms and worked constantly, they could be fairly comfortable. Those with only one loom, those who wove coarse linen, or those with many young children would be 'found in the most abject state of misery and distress'.[45]

Last were those weavers who were employed in shops or manufactories. They experienced the full change to proletarian status and factory discipline. 'This system which is exceedingly distasteful to the operatives, particularly in those establishments where the strictness of factory discipline is attempted to be enforced', had the advantage of regularity of employment, production and quality.[46] Wages, which were calculated by the piece, were generally low, varying according to the type of cloth woven.

Thus, complex divisions between centralized and dispersed production existed in the linen industry in the pre-Famine period. The replacement of handspinning by mill spinning concentrated the linen industry in northeast Ulster, especially in the greater Belfast vicinity. By 1835, at least ten of twenty-two flax spinning mills were within a twenty-mile radius of Belfast. By 1850, thirty-three of the existing sixty-eight spinning mills were situated in Belfast and its hinterland. Outside the Belfast area, flax mills were most heavily concentrated in Counties Armagh, Down, South Antrim and East Tyrone. Only five mills were west of Dungannon and only six were located south of Ulster.[47]

Spinning mills were usually built in port towns like Belfast or in areas with easy access to a port by means of navigable waterways like the Newry Canal and the Lagan Navigation. Also, the northeast had a large number of linen weavers, bleachgreens, a well established system of distributing semi-finished and finished goods and better banking facilities than elsewhere in Ireland. These facilitated the easier acquisition of flax, the distribution of yarn and provided better sources of credit for investment in the industry.[48]

This geographical concentration of mills and factories in the greater Belfast vicinity has resulted in an overemphasis on urban industrial development by scholars. In urban Belfast, spinning mills were able to take advantage of a large, often skilled workforce that were accustomed to factory discipline. Rural mill owners, such as those in Tullylish, confronted distinct challenges addressed in chapter 3.

45 Ibid., p. 735.   46 Ibid., p. 739.   47 Boyle, 'Economic Development', p. 51.   48 Ibid., p. 52.

5

From Independent Handloom Weavers to Barefoot Spinners: Gender, Working Conditions and State Regulation

... she would like to have a shorter time to work even if she were to get less wages for it. Two or three slaps on the side of the head is the most she ever got when she was late with her share [of the bobbins]. Can read. Has never written since she left the day school 4 years ago. Doesn't go to night school. It will be too late for her to get to bed. She gets up at 4:00 sometimes and always at half past. She is glad that she has been sent to the mill, for she earns her mother money.[1]

Evidence given by Sarah Pollack, age 12, doffer, Messrs. T & A Mullholland's Tow and Flax spinning mill, 1833

The Irish scutching mills are illbuilt, illkept, unhealthy sheds packed with dangerous machinery, unfenced, revolving rapidly, and liable to entangle and perhaps destroy any person coming within its reach ... In most of the mills men and women, boys and girls work from daylight usually until 9:00 and frequently till 12:00pm. The atmosphere in which they work is one thick constant cloud of dust and fine particles of straw and flax.[2]   Sub-Inspector Hayden, 1862

When the days work is done ... you need a whole change of clothing before you go out ... I have seen my very suspenders when I could wring water out of them. I would wish to say the women suffer more than the men, for natural modesty prevents them taking off as much garments as what a man can do ...[3]

Powerloom weaver, 1914

... home work will always ... find itself justified, for it indisputably allows the married woman to contribute her share to family maintenance in a way congenial to herself, and on lines which are consonant with the beauty and stability of family life.[4]   Ada Heather-Bigg, 1894

Sylvia Walby argues that the empiricist assumptions framing many historical accounts of factory legislation are superficial because they fail to reveal underlying

---

1 H.C. *First Report of the Central Board of his Majesty's Commissioners for inquiring into the Employment of Children in Factories*, vol. iv (1833), p. 90. 2 H.C. *Half Yearly Reports of the Inspector of Factories, Industrial Revolution: Factories*, IUP ser., vol. ii (1862), p. 305. 3 H.C. *Report of the Departmental Committee on Humidity and Ventilation in Flax Mills and Linen Factories* (cd 7433), vol. xxxvi (1914), p. 192. 4 Ada Heather-Bigg, 'The wife's contribution to family income', *Economic Journal*, 4 (1894), 58.

gender relations.[5] While humanitarian concern with the reproduction of the workforce and poor working conditions are important, what remains unexplained is 'why
the legislative attempts to remedy the situation should have contained such a marked
distinction between men and women'.[6] State involvement in regulating the working conditions of women and children was predicated upon assumptions about the
'natural' consequences of sexual difference elaborated in the late eighteenth and
early nineteenth centuries. Women and children were not conceptualized as 'free
agents' since both were presumed to be dependent on men.[7]

This chapter focuses on connections between gender construction in the middle class paterfamilias and state regulation of the production processes in the linen
industry. By the 1830s, belief in 'natural' differences, complementary roles and separate domains for men and women had become commonplace in the English middle
class.[8] Among this class, the male head of the family – the husband, father and
master – retained dominance through the ownership of property, patrimonialism,
patrilineality and representing his dependents in the public domain. Women's sphere
was by 'nature' the domestic, and the concern expressed by middle-class reformers
over married women working in textile factories reflected the view that women's
primary duty was to home and family. These cultural conceptions of gender were
salient to patterns of state regulation, the categorization of job tasks, structures of
authority, wage scales, status and forms of contract in the linen industry.[9] Working
class women were culturally defined in domestic terms while they were simultaneously preferred employees in the new textile factories as table 2 shows.

Table 2: Number of females per 100 males in the flax industry in Belfast
by age groups

Year	10–14	15–19	20–24	25–44	45–65	>65
1881	396	415	566	269	135	65
1891	259	380	518	329	133	91

Source: Board of Trade Report by Miss Collet on Changes in the Employment of Women and Girls in
Industrial Centers, Part I: Flax and Jute Centers, vol. 88 (1898), p. 56.

5 Sylvia Walby, *Patriarchy at Work* (Minneapolis, MN 1986), p. 102; Judy Lown, *Women and Industrialization* (Minneapolis, MN 1990), pp. 172–209.   6 Walby, *Patriarchy*, p. 112.   7 Sonya Rose, *Limited
Livelihoods* (Berkeley, CA 1992), pp. 55–6; Leonore Davidoff and Catherine Hall, *Family Fortunes: Men
and Women of the English Middle Class, 1780–1850* (Chicago 1987), p. 74.   8 Davidoff and Hall, *Family
Fortunes*, p. 149.   9 Alison MacEwen Scott, 'Industrialization, gender segregation and stratification
theory', in Rosemary Crompton and Michael Mann (eds), *Gender and Stratification* (Cambridge 1986),
p. 157.

SPINNING MILLS

In 1835, there were only twenty-two flax spinning mills in Ireland with 3370 work-ers. By 1845, the number had trebled to sixty mills with more than 17,088 work-ers.[10] The earliest investigation of working conditions in Belfast was held in 1833. Early Factory Inspectors Reports confirm that the majority of flax spinning mill employees were female, many of whom were children. In stark contrast to the eight-eenth-century prototype of linen producers as independent, skilled, male handloom weavers, the nineteenth-century image of the proletarianized linen mill operative was that of a young girl – the barefoot spinner.

A brief description of the work process in spinning mills will help clarify the discussion to follow. Flax that had been previously scutched elsewhere, was 'roughed' or rough sorted in mills by hand. Handfuls or 'pieces' of flax weighing ¼ lb. were subjected by male 'roughers' to an initial combing dividing the flax into three lengths – coarse and strong root ends, fine and strong middle and still finer but less strong tops. These were collected into separate heaps or 'stricks' of three or four hundred to the cut.

Next, the flax was 'hackled' and sorted. Hackling was done both by machine and by hand. When performed by machine, the operative was a male child who was paid very little. Machine hackling was performed when stricks of flax were spread out and placed between a pair of short iron bars called holders that held it firmly like a hackler's hand. A number of these holders were fixed to a cylinder a few inches apart. The ends of the flax fell upon an inner cylinder covered with sharp teeth. This revolved slightly and combed the flax while the outer cylinder moved in the opposite direction. First, the root end and then the top was hackled in one or two machines. After hackling, the 'tow' or short fibres were separated from the fine soft 'line' fibres.

When the flax was hackled by hand or 'dressed' it was the work of highly skilled, relatively well-paid adult men. With hand hackling, a series of increasingly finer combs were used. The first tool was a 'ruffer', a crude comb with iron or steel teeth seven inches long that tapered to a fine point. The tin covered wooden stock with teeth was screwed to a board fixed to the hackler's bench with the teeth inclining from him. A 'slopping board' at a still greater inclination was placed behind the teeth to prevent the flax from entering them too far. The hackler grasped a handful of flax by the middle, spread it out as flatly as possible between the forefinger and thumb, and wound the top end around his right hand to prevent it from slipping. Then he proceeded by a circular sweep of his hand to lash the root end of the flax into the teeth of the ruffer beginning at the near end and working up to-wards his hand. He then ruffed the top end in a similar fashion.

10 Emily J. Boyle, 'The Economic Development of the Irish Linen Industry, 1825–1913', Ph.D. diss., The Queen's University of Belfast, p. 37.

The next tool used was similar to the ruffer called a 'common 8', with closer set shorter pins of five inches. Here the flax was laid on the hack board over pins with the left hand and slight lowering of the right hand that caused the flax to enter the pins sufficiently. Increasingly finer combs were used such as the 'fine eight', 'ten', 'twelve', and 'eighteen', to split the filaments of flax into the line and tow that adhered to the teeth. After hackling, the flax was sorted or separated into various divisions according to the degrees of fineness judged by the eye and hand of the sorter. The hackling and sorting processes required skill, a masculine attribute. This skill was considered to be crucial since flaxdressers' proficiency and judgement determined the future quality of the yarn.

The shorter fibres called tow, produced in the above processes, were collected in bags, shaken out by machine, carded, and combed by young female operatives, who reduced it to a large ribbon ready for drawing. 'Drawing' and 'spreading' also performed by females, were the next processes for both tow and line. Each strick of flax was subdivided into two or three portions. These were arranged longitudinally on a feeding cloth called a 'creeping sheet' on the spreading machine with ends of successive portions overlapping each other about three quarters of their length. The flax was drawn forward through a part of the spreader called a gill frame (after *aiguille*, the French word for needle) and deposited in the form of a ribbon called a 'sliver' into a tall can capable of holding 1000 yards. Long flax was drawn out to sixty times its original length and cut flax twenty times.

This machine sought to imitate the fingers of a handspinner, who was able to draw out the flax while diminishing its thickness. This was accomplished by a set of rollers called the holding or back rollers that delivered the flax to another set of rollers called the drawing rollers. These moved at a greater speed increasing the length and diminishing the thickness of the flax. Between these sets of rollers was a set of screwgills of separate bars or rods called 'fullers' armed with closely ranged steel needles. These restrained and regulated the drawing of fibres by rollers preventing the sliver from becoming bumpy or irregular. Finally, the delivery rollers deposited the sliver into cans.

The drawing frame combined eight slivers and drew them out into one length equal to the sum of their united lengths. The ribbon produced had great uniformity. There were usually three drawing frames; one combined eight slivers, one twelve and the third fifteen. The principle was the same as with the spreading machine, but there was no creeping sheet since the sliver had sufficient coherence to be drawn directly from the cans by the back rollers of the drawing machine.

The roving frame was the last preparatory process before spinning. This frame was also similar to the drawing frame but the sliver was now twisted into a 'rove' or loose thread by means of a flyer that wound the rove onto bobbins. When full, the rove bobbins were taken by 'doffers' to the spinning room. There the rove was drawn down to the last degree of fineness and twisted into cylindrical cords called yarn.

In handspinning, the woman would moisten the fibres with her saliva to make them adhere to each other and to make them more pliable. With wet spinning, the fibres were made wet by hot water of 120 degrees F. which made the yarn finer, smoother and more uniform. The hot water was contained in a trough that ran the whole length of the spinning frame. Throstle spinning at full speed produced 5000 revolutions per minute producing twenty-seven hanks per spindle per week. The roving was twisted into yarn by a twirling of the spindle. Three rollers delivered the roving at a proper degree of fineness through a guided eyelet vertically to the spindle receiving the requisite twist by the rapidly revolving spindle. The yarn was thus consecutively drawn and twisted onto a bobbin equally distributed by the up and down motion of the bobbin. If thread was being produced, instead of yarn, a compound cord was produced by doubling and twisting two or more single lines of yarn by a frame that closely resembled the throstle frame.

Full bobbins were then conveyed to the reeling room where the yarn was unwound and measured on reels.[11] The number of leas, or 300 yard lengths per pound, gave the yarn its description. For example, No. 20 yarn would equal 20 leas per pound. Bunches of bundles of each description were arranged according to their fineness, dried by steam in lofts, folded, and made ready for sale.

Because cultural conceptions of femininity assumed girls to be weaker, more passive, and more helpless than boys, 'they seemed indisputably in need of legislative protection'.[12] Reformers' concern initially focused on female wet spinners who worked in very unpleasant conditions. First, the hot water created a very hot humid environment in the spinning rooms often in excess of 100 degrees F. Second, water was thrown off by the spindles in the form of a fine spray that saturated the spinners and accumulated on the floors, requiring spinning room workers to keep their feet bare so as not to ruin their shoes.

Wet feet caused an inflammation of the big toe called onychia, skin irritation, swollen ankles, and varicose veins.[13] Spinners were also soaked from the waist down despite 'oil cloth petticoats' or aprons, and frequently were in contact with the hot water and oil integral to the operation of their frames. The contrast between the hot damp environment of the mill and a raw damp climate outside lowered their immunity to colds, coughs and bronchitis.[14]

Worse conditions were reported in remote flax and tow mills located in small villages or near small secluded streams than those in urban areas like Belfast. Urban factory owners had greater familiarity with provisions of the 1833 Factory Act and were more likely to be visited by Factory Inspectors. Most did not employ children under nine, restricted the working hours for those under twelve to nine hours a day and for those under eighteen to twelve hours. The small mills employing twenty or

11 The measurements for yarn were: 300 yards = 1 lea, 10 leas = 1 hank or 3000 yards, 20 hanks = 1 bundle or 60,000 yards. 12 Catherine Gallagher, *The Industrial Reformation of English Fiction 1832–1867* (Chicago 1985), p. 128. 13 D.L. Armstrong, 'Social and economic conditions in the Belfast linen industry 1850–1900', *Irish Historical Studies*, 7, no. 25 (1951), 235–69. 14 *Children's Employment Commission*, Report before Mr. Stuart; Evidence of Rosan Curran, p. 129.

less people were owned, according to Inspector James Stuart in 1837, by 'ignorant and illiterate' men whose workforce was comprised of whole families. Child labourers were often under age, working without certificates of school attendance, and were employed for more hours than the law allowed.[15]

In the 1830s, wages in Irish flax spinning mills were lower than those paid in Leeds or Scotland as table 3 shows. Also, there was a greater percentage of workers under twenty-one with Belfast employing 81.7 per cent, Leeds 68.9 per cent and Scotland 62.4 per cent.[16] These two factors were interdependent since low wages compelled parents to send their children to work as soon as possible. In the early reports by Leonard Horner, Inspector of Factories for the Belfast area, many 'irregularities were pointed out involving certificates of age which indicate the pressure parents were under to have their children begin work'.[17] This opinion was shared in 1843 by Sub-commissioner Thomas Martin, who reported to the Children's Employment Commission:

> ... in Ireland, so inadequate, as a general rule, is the workmen's pay to their hand-to-mouth wants, that they are driven to the necessity of sending out their children, at the earliest ages possible, to such employers as will receive them. Nine years, eight, seven, six, and under, nay five, are not thought too early ages for children to be thus placed; and I am bound to say, with advantages to them for the time being ... It enables their parents to give them better fare ...[18]

The prevalence of women and children in the early spinning mills, raised concern whether earning wages would erode gender and generational relationships in the paterfamilias based upon their economic and familial dependence.[19] One response by linen industry employers was to reconstitute older patriarchal relations in the new mills by ensuring that positions at the top of the organizational pyramid were occupied by men. They also permitted children to be employed by their parents, with whom they negotiated wage contracts.[20]

For example, at William Barbour's linen cloth and thread manufactory, established at Lisburn in 1825, children who worked as weighers, shoe thread ballers, thread twisters, and pirners, were hired and paid by the principal workers. The wage contracts were sometimes with their parents and sometimes with the children, but payment was generally made to the parent. Also, advances were sometimes made to the parents on account of their children's wages often used to buy clothes for the winter. One man, who employed two of his children as pirners, was

15 H.C. *Reports of the Inspector of Factories*, vol. xxxi (1837), pp. 63–4.   16 Boyle, 'Economic Development', p. 40.   17 H.C. *Reports of the Inspectors of Factories*, vol. xxxx (17 August 1835), p. 4.   18 *Children's Employment Commission*, Appendix to the Second Report Part II, Thomas Martin Esq., 'Report on Trades and Manufactures in the North of Ireland', *Industrial Revolution: Children's Employment*, IUP ser., vol. xi (1843).   19 Lown, *Women and Industrialization*, p. 61.   20 Ibid.

Table 3: Ages and weekly wages of male and female flax workers in Belfast,
Scotland and Leeds, 1834

MALES

Age	Scotland		Belfast*		Leeds	
	No.	Ave. wage	No.	Ave. wage	No.	Ave. wage
>11	14	2s.9¼d.	8	2s.1d.	54	2s.10½d.
11–15	776	3s.10¾d.	96	2s.8½d.	416	4s.1d.
16–20	216	7s.6d.	13	5s.8¼d.	134	9s.11½d.
21–25	121	13s.¹¹⁄₂d.	19	14s.9d.	70	17s.1¾d.
26–30	156	14s.7d.	12	13s.8½d.	74	19s.1d.
31–35	148	15s.3½d.	7	14s.2½d.	53	19s.2½d.
36–40	131	14s.5½d.	7	11s.4d.	66	18s.2d.
41–45	115	14s.2d.	8	14s.6d.	64	19s.5½d.
46–50	102	13s.10¾d.	1	8s.	37	18s.3¾d.
51–55	51	14s.3½d.	1	13s.	35	17s.7d.
56–60	48	15s.11½d.	–	–	22	14s.9d.
61–65	22	9s.1¼d.	–	–	8	13s.6¾d.
66–70	13	8s.10½d.	1	9s.	11	16s.1¼d.
*Total**	2,053		183		1,053	

FEMALES

Age	Scotland		Belfast*		Leeds	
	No.	Ave. wage	No.	Ave. wage	No.	Ave. wage
>11	178	2s.1d.	10	1s.11½d.	45	2s.9½d.
11–15	1,433	3s.10¾ d.	197	2s.11d.	634	4s.
16–20	1,742	5s.6¾d.	163	4s.11d.	596	5s.9¾d.
21–25	918	6s.¾d.	31	4s.6d.	184	6s.4¾d.
26–30	440	5s.7¾ d.	8	4s.7½d.	57	6s.2d.
31–35	144	5s.4¾d.	1	5s.	14	6s.2½d.
36–40	145	5s.2½d.	1	5s.6d.	9	6s.3d.
41–45	52	5s.1½d.	1	4s.3d.	6	6s.
46–50	36	5s.9¾d.	–	–	4	6s.2d.
51–55	31	6s.	–	–	1	6s.
56–60	14	6s.8d.	–	–	2	6s.
*Total**	5,141		412		1,552	

Source: Supplementary Report From Factories Commissioners, Part I, 1834, Vol. 19, Dr. Mitchell's Report. *Workers over age 61 were not included. Based upon 1 flax mill, 2 cotton.

poor earning 7s. a week. His two children earned 1s.6d. giving him 8s.6d. per week
to support a family of six. While his children were healthy, due to the improved
food purchased with their wages, they still ate little animal protein, subsisting on
three meals of potatoes and stirabout with milk or buttermilk.[21] While the piecerate
system drove parents to work their young children hard, they remained under their
care at the factory, coming and leaving with them. This system was beneficial to
parents and capitalists enabling the latter to avoid labour costs associated with training, supervising and paying child workers.

Following Neil Smelser, changed relations of production in textile factories did
not wholly eliminate the pre-capitalist androcentric family structure. However, parents were subordinate to capitalists, who controlled hours, wages and the labour
process.[22] Parents could not always protect their children from corporal punish-
ment, as the quote by Sarah Pollack introducing this chapter illustrates. At T. & A. Mullholland's Tow and Flax Spinning Mill, the overlooker 'used to beat the children and
had the leave of the fathers and mothers to do so' before strict orders were made that such
practices should cease.[23]

Parents also could not protect their children or themselves from the unhealthy
conditions prevalent in flax mills. The nature of the flax fibre created dangerous
dust in the preparing end of production, and wet, hot, oily atmospheres in wet
spinning rooms. Attempts to regulate these conditions were made periodically
throughout the nineteenth and twentieth centuries with varying degrees of success. The wet conditions in spinning rooms proved easier to correct and were less
detrimental to the health than flax dust (which was never adequately eliminated),
resulting in respiratory problems and death in an unknown number of people.

Throughout Great Britain, the education of factory children in the early nineteenth century was minimal. Most of the young persons employed in Belfast's spinning mills could not write. Evidence from children emphasized their fatigue due to
long hours spent working, preventing them from concentrating in school. Others
were too poor and their families could not afford to keep them in school.[24]

This lack of schooling was addressed in the Factory Act of 1844 (7 and 8 Vic. c.15)
that extended new regulations to women workers and established the halftime system of education for child workers. Under this Act no child was to be employed in
a factory for more than six and one half hours a day or ten hours on three alternate
days. Attendance at school was to be certified by the school master whose voucher
was to be obtained each Monday by the mill owner. Fees of 2d. per week could be
deducted from the child's wage to pay the school master's salary. Penalties for non-

21 Ibid., p. 23.   22 Neil Smelser, 'Sociological history: the industrial revolution and the British working class family', *Journal of Social History* (1967), pp. 17–35; Michael Anderson, 'Sociological history
and the working-class family: Smelser revisited', *Social History*, 3 (1976), p. 325.   23 *Children's Employment Commission*, p. 90.   24 Ibid., p. 129; Hilda Martindale, *From One Generation to Another
1839–1944* (London 1944), p. 111.

compliance, meaning employing a child without a school attendance certificate, were 20s. to £3 for an employer and 5s. to 20s. for a parent.[25]

The 1844 Act also included the first reference to flax spinning. It required that in wet spinning rooms, where women, young persons, or children were employed, 'means shall be taken for protecting the workers from being wetted, and when hot water is used, for preventing the escape of steam into the air of the room'.[26] Women above eighteen were now to work the same hours as young persons below eighteen – twelve hours a day or sixty-nine hours per week.

Nevertheless, unhealthy conditions persisted. C.D. Purdon, who investigated spinning mills during the 1860s and 70s, drew attention to the health affects of poor working conditions in spinning rooms. When first entering the factory, a young girl could expect to experience 'mill fever' after a few days. The cause of mill fever was the smell of the oil, the steam and the heat. The symptoms that lasted for two to eight days were 'rigors', meaning nausea, vomiting, head ache, thirst and fever.[27] Prolonged exposure to the heat in wet spinning rooms averaging 79–82 degrees F., caused fainting, risk of injury from the machinery and bronchitis. Purdon concluded that the mortality of women would have been higher if not for most leaving work at marriage.[28]

In the 1860s and 70s, particular concern among those favouring the extension of the Factory Acts, was expressed about working mothers. Contemporaries claimed that pregnant linen industry employees usually continued to work right up until a few days prior to delivery and resumed fulltime work within a month. Sub-Inspector Cameron reported, 'I have known a female worker leave off work on a Saturday afternoon, give birth to a child, and return to her work at 6 o'clock on Monday morning'.[29] According to Dr Newitt, such deliveries were more difficult and various ailments resulted from returning to work too soon including prolapse of the womb, uterine displacement, and ulceration of the cervix.

Carol Dyhouse has argued that in addition to the correlation between high-density urban living, inadequate sewage disposal, artificial feeding of infants, and high rates of infant mortality made by contemporaries in the nineteenth century, it was widely accepted that the infants of working mothers were more likely to die due to neglect and ignorance.[30] Such concern about the prevalence of working mothers in urban Belfast by reformers and trade union organizers reflected cultural conceptions that married women's proper place was in the home. Fears about the moral repercussions to society when domestic responsibilities were neglected were commonly expressed.

25 *Children's Employment Commission*, pp. 213–18.   **26** *Report, ... on Humidity and Ventilation*, p. 5.   **27** Dr Newitt, 'The diseases that prevail among workers in flax', in C.D. Purdon, *The Sanitary State of the Belfast Factory District During Ten Years (1864–73 inclusive)* (Belfast 1877), pp. 14–15.   **28** Purdon, *The Sanitary State*, p. 7.   **29** H.C. *Factory Inspectors' Reports, Industrial Revolution: Factories*, IUP ser. vol. xvii (1876–77), p. 84.   **30** Carol Dyhouse, 'Working-class mothers and infant mortality in England, 1895–1914', in Charles Webster (ed.), *Biology, Medicine and Society 1840–1940* (Cambridge 1981), pp. 73–98.

For example, Mary Galway, organizer of the Textile Operative Society of Ireland, considered the number of married linen industry workers to be 'deplorable', the effects of which were 'bad for the State, for the community and the family'. Trade union organizer James Connolly drew attention to the large number of married linen industry workers in Belfast stating that most working-class women returned to work as soon as possible after their children were born.[31] Factory Inspector Hilda Martindale was disturbed by the 'dirty' home and 'ill-nourished delicate' children of a spinner who 'frankly admitted to me that she knew nothing of housework or the rearing of children preferring work in a factory, and returned there as soon as after her confinement as possible'. It was Martindale's view that, 'neglected and delicate children, dirty and ill-kept homes were the natural concomitants of the employment of married women'.[32] Finally, it was the view of Sub-Inspector Cameron that 'women who are much engaged in mills and factories make very bad housewives, and their children are sadly neglected, the very young suffering most'.[33]

Since childcare was the responsibility of individual women, during the day, working mothers would leave their infants with childminders, a situation decried by contemporaries as causing increased rates of diarrhea, and high infant mortality.[34] While infant mortality was indeed high, the diets of poorly paid linen workers in general were inadequate, consisting of tea and bread four times a day supplemented by potatoes, milk, bacon and, occasionally, meat for dinner. Newitt stated that child care was often in the hands of kin, who were either mothers or mothers-in-law.[35] despite the prevalence of poor nutrition and hygienic conditions, it is likely that most childminders looked after and fed babies a diet that they believed would sustain them.

In 1891, Inspector E.H. Osborn, who was appointed to supervise the administration of the Cotton Cloth Act, made an inquiry into the conditions of work in flax mills and linen factories and the mortality of textile operatives.[36] Osborn's description of working conditions was virtually the same as those in 1833 except that workers endured them for successively fewer hours after 1847, 1850, 1853 and 1874.[37] Death rates among workers continued to be higher then non-textile workers due to the damp, heat, and poor ventilation.

As a result of Osborn's inquiry, in 1894, various regulations relating to fans for ventilation, limitations on humidity levels and heat and insulation of steam pipes were enacted. Also spinning frames were to be provided with 'splash boards', to

31 Mary Galway, 'The linen industry in the north', in William G. Fitzgerald (ed.), *The Voice of Ireland* (Dublin and London, 1929), p. 297; James Connolly, *Selected Writings* (London 1973), pp. 193–4; Nora Connolly O'Brien, *James Connolly, Portrait of a Rebel Father* (Dublin 1975), pp. 129–30.   32 Martindale, *From One Generation*, p. 119.   33 H.C. *Factory Inspectors' Reports, Industrial Revolution: Factories*, IUP ser., vol. xvii (1879–77), p. 83.   34 Ibid., p. 21; Rose, *Limited Livelihoods*, p. 71.   35 Newitt, 'Diseases', 14–15.   36 H.C. *Factory Inspectors' Reports, Industrial Revolution: Factories*, IUP ser., vol. xxiii (1894), p. 190.   37 Ibid., p. 193; George Henry Wood, 'Factory legislation, considered with reference to the wages etc., of the operatives protected thereby', *Journal of the Royal Statistical Society*, LXV (1902), pp. 285–6, 292.

shield the worker from the spray, waterproof aprons were to be worn by spinners and the floors were to be drained. Further revisions in the Acts were made in 1896 and 1903, including the provision of suitable toilets and cloakrooms so that operatives working in humid rooms could change their clothes.[38]

Finally, spinning and weaving of flax were certified by the Secretary of State as 'dangerous trades' in 1905. This necessitated improvements in ventilation, heat, purity of the water used for humidity, and splash guards. It was found that the body temperature of operatives rose in the hot humid conditions to levels above normal with increased pulse rates and respiration. Regulations aimed to alleviate these conditions by requiring that sources of heat from troughs of water, pipes and power sources be controlled through better ventilation.[39]

SCUTCH MILLS

Dusty conditions in flax spinning and scutching mills were more difficult to correct and even slower to be regulated. Most dust was produced in the preparatory processes antecedent to spinning. Prior to the mechanization of flax scutching, this process was performed by women at home. With the encouragement of the Linen Board in the application of waterdriven machinery, mechanized scutch mills multiplied in number and importance in the late eighteenth century. By 1802, every parish in County Down had a scutch mill, and the 1836 Ordnance Survey Memoirs show two flax scutching mills in the parish of Tullylish.[40]

Flax scutching was performed in country mills driven by water power, and often owned by farmers who performed this initial preparatory process for the surrounding area. Scutch mills were simple, cheap, and efficient. They were usually single story rectangular stone structures with a breastshot water wheel. This drove a horizontal shaft having a series of scutching 'stocks' and perhaps a 'targing' stock for tow arranged along it at intervals.[41]

By the first half of the nineteenth century, the bruising or breaking process was mechanized. The flax was bruised by passing it between two rollers. This broke the woody part of the flax sufficiently to allow for finer cleaning. The labourer sat opposite the frame and inserted a handful of flax straw between the lowest and middle rollers. This was drawn in and bruised and passing upwards between the top most pair was bruised a second time. This process might be repeated two or three times according to the general thickness of the flax and how it had been steeped. The bruised or rolled flax was then evened off in 'stricks' and forwarded to the scutchers.[42]

38 H.C. *Factory Inspectors' Reports, Industrial Revolution: Factories*, IUP ser., vol. xxv (1896), p. 108. 39 Ibid., pp. 8–10.   40 Harry D. Gribbon, *The History of Water Power in Ulster* (Newton Abbot 1969), pp. 103–5; (PRONI), O.S.M., MIC.6/173, 20 October 1834.   41 W.A. McCutcheon, 'Water powered corn and flax scutching mills in Ulster', *Ulster Folklife*, 12 (1966), 44–6.   42 Ibid., 47.

Scutching of bruised flax was done by means of a horizontal shaft with wooden blades attached. This shaft revolved and the blades hit the flax straw vertically, splitting and cleaning it. The more effectively the woody part of the flax was broken by the rollers, the less scutching time was needed.

While scutching flax was technologically simple, the mills were quite dangerous and produced large quantities of dust. Women and young boys often performed the bruising, rolling and stricking of flax for the male scutchers. In fact, these two ancillary processes were considered to be the most dangerous since hands or clothing were easily caught and dragged into the rollers at times resulting in the amputation of limbs and even death.[43] For example, in 1876, Sub-Inspector Cameron reported that Dennis McSermon, age eleven, 'was sent to my hospital here from the scutch mill ... where the muscles of the right forearm hanging in strips, the hand and fingers all comminuted from being caught in the rollers'. This young boy had replaced his pregnant mother (who left work earlier due to the onset of labour) at the rollers.[44]

Scutch mills had not been regulated under earlier Factory Acts since the work was considered agricultural in nature rather than pertaining to manufacture. Due to the dangerous dusty conditions, their isolation and dilapidated appearance, Factory Inspectors began regularly reporting on scutch mills after 1862. Henceforth, they remained a constant source of concern.[45] Inspectors Cameron and Woodgate repeatedly refered to the dangerous unfenced machinery, the lack of proper ventilation and their 'filthy condition'.[46]

Usually scutch mills operated on a seasonal basis from September to February or March, however they could be kept open all year if the summer months were devoted to 'targing' or dressing the tow left over from the previous winter's scutching. When they were seasonal, scutch mills were seen to be more accessory to agriculture than to textile manufacture; hence they were exempted from the regulations of the Factory Acts, even though women and children were employed. Under the 1878 Act, scutch mills were required to have a sufficient system of ventilation, but this was almost impossible to enforce. The reasons for evasion included both the isolation of the mills and the fact that many of the occupiers were relatively poor farmers, not themselves landlords, who could not afford to install a ventilation system to meet the requirements of the Factory Acts. When pressured, after inadequate fans became clogged and broke down, some occupiers simply chose to close the mill.[47]

The farmer who had a scutch mill not only scutched his own flax but let out the

43 Dr D. Hamilton, in *The Sanitary State*, p. 40.   44 *Factory Inspectors' Reports*, IUP ser. (1876–7), p. 84.   45 Marilyn Cohen, 'Working conditions and experiences of work in the linen industry: Tullylish, County Down', *Ulster Folklife*, 30 (1984), 3–4.   46 See the reports of Inspectors Cameron and Woodgate in *Factory Inspectors' Reports, Industrial Revolution*, IUP ser., vols. xvii and xviii (1876–7) (1878–81).   47 H.C. *Half Yearly Reports of the Inspector of Factories, Industrial Revolution: Factories*, IUP ser., vol. 18 (31 October 1879), pp. 68–71.

use of it to other farmers who often carried their flax on their backs to be scutched. This practice was, according to Sub-Inspector Cameron, the root of another serious problem – the farmer, who sent his flax to be scutched at his neighbour's mill, also sent the labour to be employed. This labour frequently included his children who were expected to help, just as any farmer expected his children to assist with the daily agricultural routine. However, to Factory Inspectors, whose responsibility was to enforce the restrictions on the hours and ages of child labourers, the sight of young children carrying stricks of flax was cause for alarm. The justification offered that 'they were only the "bit weans" of some farmer who has on the day brought his flax to be scutched and whose family are as a matter of course assisting in the operation' was not, in their view, sufficient.[48] Also, because the operation of scutch mills was seasonal, the hours of work began at daylight and ended at dark, when continuation required candle light. Wages were paid by the piece and workers received a percentage on the finished flax of so much per stone. Consequently, scutch mill operatives sought to work as long as possible.

Improvements in working conditions were made in the area of fencing machinery, but ventilation systems remained inadequate. The flax dust produced in the scutching, and the subsequent preparatory processes in spinning mills, was called 'pouce'. For relief from pouce, scutchers often drank whiskey carried in their pockets to clear their throats and chests. Such drinking was, of course, frowned upon by the Factory Inspectors because of the dangerous machinery and because of its 'moral' effects on the women and children employed alongside men for long hours.[49]

Scutch mill workers were usually subjected to pouce for only six or seven months, but roughers, hacklers, carders, spreaders, drawers and rovers in spinning mills were subjected to it for long hours all year. In fact, women engaged in the latter four processes inhaled a very fine dust considered to be the most injurious of all. The respiratory problems produced were associated with a dry throat, cough, dyspnoea and premature death. According to Dr Purdon in 1877, in some operations, like carding tow, conditions were so bad that 'if a girl under 18 years of age gets a card she very rarely, if constantly employed at it, lives beyond 30 years'.[50]

In spite of the extreme risks to health that many mill workers preparing flax faced daily, no attempts to regulate dusty conditions in spinning mills were made until 1891. One reason is that a significant proportion of preparing-end workers, such as roughers and flaxdressers, were adult men. Victorian reformers were reluctant to interfere with the working conditions of adult men who were considered free agents and responsible for the material well-being of their families. In 1891, Inspector Osborn found that some mills only had windows for ventilation, and even when powerful fans were provided, conditions were persistently dusty. After his report, exhaust fans to draw the dust forward and down from the face of the worker were to

48 Ibid.   **49** H.C. *Half Yearly Reports of the Inspector of Factories, Industrial Revolution: Factories*, IUP ser., vol. xvii (31 October 1875), pp. 82–3.   **50** Purdon, *Sanitary State*, pp. 5–6.

be installed, and children and young persons were required to wear 'respirators' or filtering masks. Respirators were hated by the employees because they became dampened with saliva, foul smelling and unsanitary. Further reports and recommendations were made in 1906 that reveal the benefit of good exhaust systems installed close to the origin of the dust. These were expensive however, and many factory owners objected to the regulations.[51] Consequently, pouce remained an unresolved health problem.

BLEACHGREENS

Although the bleaching and finishing sectors were innovative during the eighteenth century, during the nineteenth century, the processes remained remarkably unchanged.[52] First, each web of linen was marked by women with red thread for identification and stitched together to make one long piece of linen many thousands of yards in length. The resulting long piece of linen was then placed into a 'pot' where it was boiled in a solution of lime for eight to ten hours. Thereafter, the linen was drawn through a tank of water. The webs were then unsewn and bundled separately to be washed in the 'brown mills' with water. Next, the linen was steeped in 'kieves' in a 'sour' or acid solution of dilute hydrochloric acid to convert the residues into a soluble salt. It was then washed again, boiled in soda lye that combined with the waxes and fats in the fibre and liquefied them, washed again, and placed on the grass to be exposed to the atmosphere. The linen was then rubbed in soap and water, boiled in lye, washed and grassed again.

After sufficient boiling, the whitening process began by the use of bleaching powder or 'dip' in which the cloth was left for one night. It was then washed and treated with a weak sulfuric acid, and boiled in soda lye until proper whiteness was achieved. After the cloth was white, it was starched and dried on steam heated rollers. The webs were re-stitched together, stretched, passed through a water mangle between rollers to impart the proper moisture for absorbing starch and passed into and through a tank filled with a mixture of starch and 'blue' for whitening.

Linen cloth was then passed over heated rollers to dry, unsewn and taken to the finishing house. There it was placed on the 'beetling beams' where it was subjected to the pounding wooden 'beetles' to close the spaces between the threads. Finally, it was stretched to its full width and 'calendered', a process in which the cloth passed through a series of vertically stacked rollers to obtain its patent finish.

Linen was more difficult to bleach than cotton because there was more colour-

---

51 H.C. *Report To His Majesty's Secretary of State for the Home Department on the Draft Regulations for the Processes of Spinning and Weaving Flax and Tow, and the Processes Incidental Thereto*, vol. xv (1906), p. 6.

52 Alfred S. Moore, *Linen: From the Raw Material to the Finished Product* (London 1914), pp. 85–92; W. T. Charley, 'Linen', in *British Manufacturing Industries* (London 1876), pp. 102–9; and oral interview with Albert Uprichard, former bleachgreen owner, July 1983 by author.

ing matter to bleach out and the straw and various pastes used by handloom weavers to prepare and strengthen the yarn had to be removed. In comparison with cotton cloth, that only lost one twentieth of its weight, linen lost one-third. While grass bleaching (exposing cloth to the atmosphere), was considered to be the secret of Ireland's soft white linen, as it was not damaging to the cloth, more and more chemicals were used to reduce the amount of time involved.

The next extension of the Factory Acts took place in 1860 when bleach and dye works were first regulated. Less evidence exists for working conditions in bleachgreens than for the other branches of the linen industry. One reason is that the work was considered relatively healthy and did not attract as much attention from Factory Inspectors. Dust was not produced and much of the work took place in the open air. However, an equally significant explanation relates again to Victorian cultural conceptions of gender.[53] Feminist scholars have repeated shown the connection between gender conceptions and the classification of jobs in relation to skill. Such classifications do not always reflect the amount of training or ability required for competency, with women's work classified as semi- or unskilled simply because women perform it.[54] Prevailing assumptions that skill, technological competence and strength were inherently male traits shaped the sexual division of labour in all mills and factories depressing women's wages, status and authority.[55]

The production process in Irish open-air bleachgreens required skill, strength and night shifts, all of which were masculine preserves. Unlike the other branches of linen production, the labour force of bleachgreens consisted largely of adult males over the age of eighteen, who most reformers agreed 'could continue to set their own terms in an employment contract without "interference" from the state'.[56] According to Factory Inspector Robert Baker in 1862, 'With adult male labour nobody desires to interfere. Men have to work and live by it, and bring up and educate their families, and with them every execution is voluntary ...'[57] These views were not, however, always shared by male bleachgreen workers, who frequently worked at night and also wished their hours to be regulated by the state.[58]

The Children's Employment Commission Report in 1843 contained evidence from several bleachgreens in Ireland. Children of both sexes were employed at bleachgreens working thirteen or fourteen hours a day averaging 72 hours a week. While employers hired children, no separate contracts were made with them and

53 Catherine Hall, 'The early formation of Victorian domestic ideology', in Sandra Wallman (ed.), *Fit Work for Women* (New York 1979), pp. 15–32; Leonore Davidoff, 'The role of gender in the "First Agricultural Nation": agriculture in England 1780–1850', in Rosemary Crompton and Michael Mann (eds), *Gender and Stratification* (Cambridge, 1986), p. 191.   54 Anne Phillips and Barbara Taylor, 'Sex and skill: notes towards a feminist economics', *Feminist Review*, 6 (1980), p. 79.   55 Cynthia Cockburn, 'The Relations of Technology', in Rosemary Crompton and Michael Mann (eds), *Gender and Stratification* (Cambridge 1986), pp. 77–8; MacEwen Scott, 'Industrialization', p. 157.   56 Rose, *Limited Livelihoods*, p. 57.   57 H.C. *Half Yearly Reports of the Inspectors of Factories, Industrial Revolution: Factories*, IUP ser., vol. xi (1861–4), p. 135.   58 Ibid., p. 243.

their wages were paid to their parents. The employers maintained that 'no branch is unhealthy' and the earnings of children 'enable parents to give them a better diet'.[59]

Due to the number of children and women employed, in the early 1850s, a Commission was set up to inquire whether the provisions of the Factory Acts should be extended to bleachgreens. The 1854 report outlined the processes and conditions of work where women and children were employed. Women and girls were employed largely at bleachgreens where cambric handkerchiefs or fine cotton goods were bleached. Their work consisted, with few exceptions, in attending to the frames on which these goods were stretched to their proper breadth, and in the process of drying by means of stoves where temperatures ranged from 85–95 degrees F. When trade was brisk or when a quantity of goods was required by a customer on a certain day, the hours could extend from 6a.m. to 8, 9, or 10p.m., and occasionally through the night. But, usually, women worked from 6a.m. to 6p.m. with two and one half hours for rest and meals. The intense heat necessitated these and other breaks where the women could go outside to cool off. As a result of the changes in temperature, the same health problems faced by wet spinners frequently occurred.[60]

Boys under eighteen were relatively few and mostly worked at the beetling engines where they took their turn at night work. Only 271 boys under eighteen were employed at the thirty-nine greens visited by the Commissioners. Most of them were between the ages of fourteen and eighteen, but a few were twelve and thirteen. Since much of the dangerous machinery had been fenced, this work was considered safe and easy. Only their hours were at issue and boys were given 'frequent intervals of rest'.[61]

In the 1854 report, numerous bleachers along the Bann between Gilford and Banbridge were asked to provide evidence. Of the nine that did, only two close to Banbridge employed women in any numbers. None of the Tullylish bleachers employed women to any significant degree. J. & W. Uprichard, bleachers of linen, diaper, and damask employed ninety people of which only seven were women employed in the lapping room. Of the fourteen boys employed, ten worked at the beetling engines taking their turn at night work every other night. At this time, boys worked 6pm to 6am working the machines for one half hour in every three. The rest of the time they could sleep, and because they were allowed so much sleep, Uprichard did not consider night work injurious to them. Messrs. Houghton and Fennell at Banford Green near Gilford employed only one woman and eleven boys under eighteen among their seventy employees. However, like the other beetlers, the boys took their turn at night work every other week earning from 8*d*. to 1*s*. per day. Adult men earned 2*s*. per day at task work like beetling, and day men earned 1*s*. per day.[62]

59 H.C. *Children's Employment Commission, Appendix to the Second Report of the Commissioners, Part II, Industrial Revolution: Children's Employment*, IUP ser., vol. xi, 1843, Evidence of Messrs John and William Langtry.   60 H.C. *Report of the Commissioners Appointed to Inquire How Far It May Be Advisable to Extend the Provisions of the Acts for the Better Regulation of Mills and Factories to Bleaching Works, Established in Certain Parts of the United Kingdom of Great Britain and Ireland*, vol. 18 (1854–5).   61 Ibid., p. 30.   62 Ibid., p. 77.

One possible reason why so few women were employed at both Tullylish bleachgreens is that male bleachers earned slightly higher wages than both male spinning mill workers and weavers enabling more of their wives to remain home. As far back as 1812, Wakefield noted that bleaching was a higher paid and higher status job.[63] In 1845, bleachers earned an average of 8s. per week while weavers earned 7s. per week.[64]

As the following passage illustrates, the family labour system was normative at bleachgreens enabling sons to follow fathers or other male kin. One male worker stated, 'I reared all my family in the bleach-works.'[65] When the family labour system included wives, daughters assumed housekeeping responsibilities.

> I am a beetler and work from 6 in the morning till 11 at night from Monday to Friday. Saturday we leave off at 6pm. I have five children in all. For this I get 10s.6d a week; my wife works here also and gets 5s a week. The oldest girl, who is 12, minds the house. She is also cook and all the servant we have. She gets the young ones ready for school. A young girl going past the house wakes me at half past five in the morning. My wife gets up and goes along with me. We get nothing (to eat) before we come to work. The child of 12 takes care of the little children all the day, and we get nothing till breakfast at eight. At eight we go home. We get tea once a week; at other times we get stirabout sometimes of oatmeal, sometimes of Indian meal as we are able to get it. In the winter we get a little sugar and water to our Indian meal. In the summer we get a few potatoes, planting a small patch ourselves; and when they are done we go back to stirabout ... I am always very much tired when I have done at night. We may see a bit of flesh meat sometimes but very seldom.[66]

Bleachgreen owners often opposed regulation by the state. In the Second Report from the Select Committee on Bleaching and Dying Works, a large successful Quaker bleacher, Jonathan Richardson, expressed strongly that he was against the extension of the Factory Acts to bleachgreens. He explained that work performed inside bleachgreens was dependent on outside work that was inherently limited by the uncertain weather. Frost or snow might delay or prevent field work from commencing on time, or at all, resulting in workers falling into debt.[67] Rather then

63 Edward Wakefield, *An Account of Ireland Statistical and Political* (London 1812), p. 734. 64 H.C. *Report from Her Majesty's Commissioners of inquiry into the State of the Law and Practice in Respect to the Occupation of Land in Ireland* (Devon Commission), Evidence of John M'Carten of Waringstown, vol. 19 (1845). 65 H.C. *First Report of the Select Committee Appointed to Inquire into the Circumstances Connected with the Employment of Women and Children in the Bleaching and Dying Establishments in England, Scotland, and Ireland and to Consider How Far it May be Necessary or Expedient to Extend to These Establishments Provisions Regulating such Employment*, Evidence of Jonathan Richardson, vol. 11 (1857), pp. 187–8. 66 H.C. *Factory Inspectors' Reports, Industrial Revolution: Factories*, IUP ser., vol. xii (1865–7), p. 468. 67 *Select Committee on Bleaching and Dyeing Establishments*, Evidence of Jonathan Richardson (1857), pp. 187–8.

shorten the hours of women, Richardson would have preferred replacing them with machines. Between 1855–7, he dispensed with 109 women who worked the stoves, knowing the hardship this would bring to them and their families.[68]

Despite bleachgreen owners' protestations, the Factory Acts were amended in 1860 to cover bleaching and dyeing works that did not bleach cloth in the open-air. This eliminated overtime for women and boys under the age of eighteen. However, the vast majority of bleachgreens in Ireland were of the open-air variety. Even Inspector Baker, who was critical of the longer hours from 6am to 8pm, and the lack of provisions for the schooling of children permitted under the Bleaching and Dyeing Works Act, made an exception for Ireland because the open-air nature of the work made it more like 'exercise' than 'labour', and because young children were relatively well educated.[69] Sub-inspector Darkin, also pointing out the weaknesses of the Act, advocated repealing the myriad of Acts relating to finishing of cloth and the passage of a single comprehensive Factory Extension Act.[70] This was finally accomplished in 1870.

There were no other investigations of bleachgreens in Ireland by the Factory Inspectors after the 1850s indicating that conditions were considered satisfactory, even by the zealous Inspector Hilda Martindale. In her 1908 Report she described bleach works in Northern Ireland in idyllic pre-industrial terms – rural mill hamlets where generations of workers lived in mill-owned cottages on the estate of the resident manager and worked in 'excellent' buildings with 'large and airy' rooms.[71]

HANDLOOM WEAVERS

During the first half of the nineteenth century, proletarianization advanced unevenly with the weaving of linen cloth remaining unmechanized. Although some weaving was carried on in manufactories, most was performed in the homes of petty commodity producers organized through the putting-out system. In 1845, in the region surrounding Lurgan (including the northern townlands of Tullylish), the Devon Commission reported that 'there are a vast number of small farms, if farms they can be called, that are held by men who cultivate them and weave also'.[72]

The Children's Employment Commission report in 1843 contained evidence on children employed in handloom weaving manufactories. Since these were not yet mechanized, they represent a transitional form between domestic weaving sheds and powerloom factories. Weavers who were concentrated under one roof were fully

---

68 Ibid., Evidence of George McComb, pp. 203–5.   69 H.C. *Half Yearly Reports of the Inspector of Factories, Ending 30 April, 1863, Industrial Revolution: Factories*, IUP ser., vol. ii (1861–4), p. 377.   70 H.C. *Half Yearly Reports of the Inspector of Factories, Ending 31 October, 1864, Industrial Revolution: Factories*, IUP ser., vol. xii (1865–7), pp. 143–5.   71 H.C. *Annual Report of the Chief Inspector of Factories and Workshops for the year 1907*, vol. 12 (1908), p. 150.   72 *Devon Commission*, Evidence of Lieutenant Colonel William Blacker, p. 455.

dependent upon the wages paid by the capitalist. However, the androcentric focus characteristic of the eighteenth century proto-industrial system persisted. Children as young as seven of both sexes were employed between 6am and 8pm mostly as winders of bobbins for their weaver parents. Again, contracts were made with parents who were fully responsible for their supervision. According to Messrs. William Orr & Co. in Belfast, 'we have nothing to say to the wages of the children – this is the same as if they were in their parents' own house ... wages properly so called are out of the question'.[73]

An 1864 report on handloom weaving in domestic workshops emerged from concern with the labour of children and young persons.[74] However, it was not until 1878 that domestic workshops were regulated by the Factory Acts. One explanation for this delay was the reluctance by the state to conceptualize homes as factories. The physical separation of the workplace from the home, characteristic of industrial capitalism, created a sharp ideological distinction between public workplaces and private homes. The unevenness of this process, exemplified by domestic handloom weavers dependent upon putters-out, presented a conundrum for reformers.

The case of domestic weavers was further complicated by the changes in the sexual division of labour. Although women increasingly wove linen cloth after the introduction of the fly-shuttle, the number of female handloom weavers increased dramatically after 1825 as an alternative occupation for displaced handspinners in the core linen weaving regions. The 1864 report reveals that women were employed as domestic handloom weavers in great numbers. However, they were rarely employed in large workshops or manufactories creating new divisions of labour 'within a previously unified craft to differentiate male from female work'.[75] Handloom weaving of fine linen in manufactories remained a masculine activity contrasting culturally with the feminine domain of the home. Although large numbers of women and girls wove linen cloth, the state was reluctant to regulate private home-based work.

Local labour availability, gendered conceptions of work and their reinterpretation made the appropriate gender of handloom weavers increasingly ambiguous in the period between 1825 and 1914.[76] As proto-industrial households struggled to meet the challenge posed by the elimination of handspinning and the decline in wages in the first half of the nineteenth century, a reformulation of the rigid sexual division of labour became imperative. However, this reformulation occurred in one direction only. It is significant that while the spread of the putting-out system increased the need for winders, winding remained an occupation filled by women and

73 *Children's Employment Commission*, Appendix to the Second Report (1843), Evidence Messrs. William Orr & Co. Weaving Factory, 1841.   74 H.C. *Report upon the Hand-loom Weaving and Hosiery Manufactures in Ireland and Scotland, Industrial Revolution: Children's Employment*, IUP ser., vol. xiv (1864).   75 Gay Gullickson, 'Love and power in the proto-industrial family', in Maxine Berg (ed.), *Markets and Manufacture in Early Industrial Europe* (London 1991), p. 221.   76 Joy Parr, 'Disaggregating the sexual division of labour: a transatlantic case', *Comparative Studies in Society and History*, 30, no. 3 (1988), 513–18.

children. In contrast, domestic handloom weavers became more diversified by age and sex since handloom weaving households required the earnings of several weavers to make ends meet. Nevertheless, the strength of the cultural association between men and handloom weaving remained powerful shaping perceptions of handloom weavers as skilled men struggling against the encroachments of the putting-out system, deskilling and mechanization.[77]

According to A. V. Chayanov and theorists who have extended his model to proto-industrial households, one aspect of the logic of simple reproduction is the inclination toward self-exploitation, meaning that during hard times peasants will intensify their labour efforts to increase productivity and consume less. Based upon her analysis of the machine made lace industry in Nottingham, Sonya Rose challenges this model arguing that we know little of the varied strategies of household members coping with the difficulties posed by factory production.[78] This call for a more complex analysis of strategies applies equally to handloom weavers in Tullylish. Rather than treating self-exploitation as a transhistorical indicator of pre- or anti-capitalist logic, it comprised only part of any household's changing strategies to survive and maintain ties to a particular place during hard times.[79]

Under capitalism, the existence of self-exploitation and sweated labour among domestic weavers and other homeworkers was explicit in the investigation of domestic workshops by Factory Inspectors in Ireland. Those seeking to extend the Factory Acts noted that all members of the household worked extremely long hours. Many women, young persons and children wove cloth and wound bobbins of weft yarn. Warps were supplied by manufacturers already wound by women, children or machinery. Children, who worked mostly for their parents, began winding from age six and stopped by age thirteen. Children were also employed by weavers for a few hours each week to help fasten the threads at the start of a new web. The age for beginning weaving varied with the nature and width of the loom and fabric. Easier work was begun by age ten, and the more difficult cloth from age twelve, the most common age to begin weaving. Handloom weaving was thought to be 'especially suitable for the young'. Where children and young persons wove for manufacturers, they were paid by the piece or web.

As in the eighteenth century, the composition of nineteenth century weaving households was flexible, frequently including extra winders who were boarded and paid a small sum for their work. By this time, pauper children residing in a nearby workhouse were a principal source of apprentice labour earning 5s. to 10s. a quarter year or simply fed in exchange for work. Journeymen weavers were also boarded at 'stranger's households' and were paid a small weekly sum for their board and looms.[80]

---

77 Sonya O. Rose, ' "Gender at work": sex, class and industrial capitalism', *History Workshop*, no. 21 (1986), 120–1. 78 Sonya O. Rose, 'Proto-industry, women's work and the household economy in the transition to industrial capitalism', *Journal of Family History*, 13, no. 2 (1988), 181–4. 79 Tessie Liu, *The Weaver's Knot* (Ithaca, NY, 1994), p. 228; Joan Vincent, 'Conacre: a reevaluation of Irish custom', in Jane Schneider and Rayna Rapp (eds), *Articulating Hidden Histories* (Berkeley, CA 1995), pp. 87–8. 80 *Report upon Handloom Weaving and Hosiery Manufactures*, pp. 216, 218, 222.

The terms of apprenticeship for male pauper children in the period are revealed in the following agreement concerning Hugh Bowen, a child residing at the Lurgan Workhouse, and Thomas Mawhinney of Tullyheron near Waringstown. Thomas received permission to take out Hugh Bowen, designated as no. 69, to teach him to weave diaper. He agreed to pay Bowen one guinea each year for the first four years and two guineas for the last or fifth year for clothing.[81] The Board of Guardians recommended that these terms be a precedent for boys in the future. The clerk was directed to keep a book for the purpose of registering the agreements between parents, the party taking in the boy, and to witness this agreement after their respective signatures or marks. The terms for girls varied. One included payment of 4 guineas during a four year period and in the final seventh year two guineas for clothing.[82]

The hours of work in small dwelling workshops were in the summer from 6am till dark (which could be as late as 11pm) and in the winter from 8am or earlier (when it was still dark) till 9 or 10pm. It was usual to find up to four looms per household in Ireland, three to four in the Lurgan region, usually owned by the weavers and costing between 15s. and £2. While weaving shops were not crowded, due to the size of the looms, the atmosphere was damp and 'loaded with the fluff which flies from the yarn'. Many were also extremely damp to keep the yarn supple. Floors were earthen, and water in wet weather filled the treadle holes where the workers placed their feet.[83] As a result, respiratory diseases and swelling of the legs were widely complained of by weavers.

While decreasing wages largely dictated the number of hours a household worked, proletarianization remained uneven with domestic weavers still retaining more control over the pace of work than factory weavers. If trade was good, little work was done after Saturday morning, or on Sunday or Monday. However, towards the end of the week 'many work longer, as till midnight, or early morning, and sometimes all night' with little time taken for meals.[84] Weaving remained a collective family enterprise with a hierarchical androcentric organization. Young persons sat the full day like their parents, who controlled their hours of work, learning to discipline both their bodies and habits, as Thomas Foy a weaver from Portadown described at length:

> I have four looms in my house, worked by my own family ... In summer we begin at 5 or 6 am and work till dark, about 8 or 9; in winter begin at 7 or daylight and work till 11pm ... We are scarcely off at all for meals – I suppose not over an hour altogether. If we take more, we are either in a hurry or must work later at night. I do this myself, and should not like it if my children did not do the same. The winders ... get a few minutes to spare now and then, but generally they must work as late. We fetch them to work just as soon as they are able-to ... keep one another going. My girl there, Mary Jane, aged 9 years 4 months, winds constant; another of 8 can wind for one or two; and Susan

81 Ibid., p. 199.   82 Ibid., pp. 26, 199.   83 Ibid., pp. 215–16, 222.   84 Ibid., pp. 217.

aged 7 years 2 months has wound a bit ... My children did not begin weaving until they were nearly 13, but one, aged 12, has wove handkerchiefs with me helping her. Heaps of nights we have to stay up the whole night through to get a web out, and you cannot do without a winder or someone to attend you ... Many a one suffers severely from the wet; its very bad for the stomach and bowels and gives pains ... My house with the loom shop costs me 14*d* a week, but the looms are my own, as it paid better to buy them for about £3 each than to hire them at 2*d* a week or 8/- a year ... I believe that we should do much better in factories, and wish that I had gone and got my family in ... there is no loss of time there as we have. There is a day lost in going to get the stuff out from the manufacturer and nearly another in putting it into the loom and starting ...[85]

In the 1880s, a period of recession in the linen industry, Factory Inspectors began to report on handloom weavers in a systematic way. By the late nineteenth century, wage payments were usually made in cash averaging 10*s.* per week for a cambric weaver. By 1885, they had fallen to 7*s.* per week as demand for cheaper cotton hand-kerchiefs increased.[86] In counties Down and Armagh, cambric weavers in 1886 were earning 5*s.6d.* for eleven hours of work a day with deductions for winding, paste dressing for the yarn, and lighting oil. Consequently, alternative survival strategies were necessary. During times of depression in the linen trade, earnings from the loom were supplemented by agriculture, fishing, animal grazing and turf cutting.[87] Many handloom weavers emigrated while others did not teach the trade to their children; alternative strategies to self-exploitation.

Although there is no precise information relating to the decline in the number of handloom weavers, the Flax Supply Association reckoned that there were 30,000 handloom weavers in Ireland in 1875. By 1898, Clara Collet estimated that there were only 2500 left in Ulster, where most would have been concentrated.[88] Collet pointed out that women, who were a very considerable proportion of handloom weav-ers, fared worse since they rarely owned their own looms. Under the patriarchal domestic system, looms were generally owned by their fathers to whom their daugh-ter's earnings were paid.[89]

Children who worked as winders in manufactories also worked with a parent or relative earning from 2*s.6d.* to 3*s.* per week. By fifteen or sixteen, young persons earned as much as adults and girls earned as much as boys. Wages paid to adult men were, however, low averaging from 6*s.* to 8*s.* per week and payment in grocery and goods instead of cash was practiced. Only the youngest children aged ten and below

85 Ibid., p. 219; Liu, *Weaver's Knot*, p. 224.   86 H.C. *Half Yearly Reports of the Inspector of Factories, Ending 31 October 1885, Industrial Revolution: Factories,* IUP ser., vol. 20 (1884–7), p. 9.   87 Francis X. McCorry, *Lurgan: An Irish Provincial Town, 1610–1970* (Lurgan 1993), p. 85.   88 Boyle, 'Economic Development', p. 117.   89 H.C. *Board of Trade Report by Miss Collet on Changes in the Employment of Women and Girls in Industrial Centers, Part I, Flax and Jute Centers,* vol. 88 (1898), p. 53.

were likely to be in school. When they did attend, their attendances were very irregular and few ever went beyond the first book or grade level.[90] The decline in wages also made it very difficult for cambric weavers to send their children to school. Although domestic weavers covered by Section 16 of the Factory and Workshop Act of 1878, were prohibited from employing children under ten, children as young as six were kept out of school and extensively employed by impoverished parents. The tension between poverty and schooling was noted by Inspector Woodgate who found weavers to be,

> ... hard working, not idle and keenly anxious to send their children to school, but with such earnings it would almost seem an impossibility for all of them to comply with provisions of the Factory and Workshop Act in this respect. The cost of schooling ... is a penny a week, and when children have got into the higher grades, this is increased to 1½ and 2*d* a week, and in cases of large families with a father earning 5*s*.6*d* a week and having 1*s* and 1*s*.6*d* to pay for rent, it will be seen, after providing food for the body, there cannot be much margin left to provide food for the mind.[91]

POWERLOOM WEAVING FACTORIES

Relative to Scotland, the powerloom was more slowly adopted in Ireland due to lower labour costs and technological problems in weaving fine linen cloth.[92] Handloom weaving of fine linen cloth was not weakened until after the Great Famine when the demographic toll had the effect of pushing up handloom weavers' wages. Before the Famine, both the difficulty in weaving linen yarn by power and the lack of incentive for capitalists to invest in powerlooms shaped their strategy. Under the putting-out system, capitalists had low fixed and variable capital costs, and they were able to earn considerable profits. The decrease in the number of weavers, coupled with the increased money needs of those weavers who were now without land, pushed up the average wages of weavers from 10*d*. to 1*s*. per day. Although the cost of food fell in the 1850s, labour costs were no longer held down by producers partially reproducing themselves.

Consequently, powerloom weaving began to look more attractive to capitalists. In 1856, the cost a bundle of forty leas yarn power-woven was only 1 per cent less than

90 *Report upon the Handloom Weaving and Hosiery Manufacture*, pp. 218, 220.   91 H.C. *Half Yearly Reports of The Factory Inspectors, Ending 31 October, 1886, Industrial Revolution: Factories*, IUP ser., vol. 20 (1884–7), p. 10.   92 Alastair Durie and Peter Solar, 'The Scottish and Irish linen industries compared', in Rosalind Mitchison and Peter Roebuck (eds), *Economy and Society in Scotland and Ireland 1500–1939* (Edinburgh 1988), p. 218.

hand-woven, while a capitalist could expect initial fixed capital costs of 6500 pounds to build and equip a weaving factory.[93] However, as yarn prices rose in the 1850s, and as they faced competition from powerloom linen weavers in England and Scotland, Irish manufacturers began to look for more efficient methods of production.

Although the general picture after the 1860s was a steady increase in the number of powerlooms, closer examination reveals a more complex uneven process. A new division of labour between hand and powerloom production of linen emerged with fine linen cloth, such as damask and cambric, remaining unmechanized until the 1880s. As in France, powerlooms limited the range of production in which hand work could continue.[94] At first, powerlooms produced drills and heavy linens forcing Irish manufacturers out of the home market since powerlooms could produce twice as much heavy cloth as a handloom weaver.

After the Famine, in the late 1860s, investment in powerlooms increased during the 'cotton famine' associated with the American Civil War, and the resulting increase in demand for a substitute for cotton cloth. This rise in demand ushered in the great 'linen boom', beginning in 1862, which effected the home and foreign markets. 'Linen cloth, which had almost disappeared from the wardrobes and bedrooms of the middle and working classes has again become a necessity for common wear'.[95]

In response to the spectacular increase in demand, the number of linen workers rose from 33,500 in 1862 to 57,000 in 1868. New flax spinning mills and weaving factories were rapidly built, including vertically integrated factories. Powerloom weaving capacity now grew at a faster rate than spinning. Between 1862 and 1871, the number of weaving factories in Ireland rose from thirty-four to sixty-nine and the number of looms almost trebled.[96] In 1864, a contemporary report celebrated prospects for the linen industry. 'New mills and factories are springing up on all sides; while as fast as can be started orders flow in, and such a thing as manufacturing for stock is almost unknown'.[97]

After the yarn arrived at the weaving factory from the spinning mill, it needed to be wound into a form suitable for weaving.[98] Bobbins with yarn intended for warp were wound onto spools by women and girls. Yarn was placed in a warping frame called a 'travers', that furnished the quantity of warp required for the length of the intended web. It was the function of male warpers to provide a sufficient number of parallel threads for a web of equal length. The warper caused the reel to revolve unwinding the yarn. The warps converged into a focus by means of a small machine

93 Boyle, 'Economic Development', p. 78.   94 Liu, *Weaver's Knot*, pp. 153–6.   95 Quoted in Oliver Greeves, 'The Effects of the American Civil War on the Linen, Woolen and Worsted Industries of the United Kingdom', Ph.D. diss., University of Bristol, 1969, p. 173.   96 Boyle, 'Economic Development', pp. 91–3.   97 H.C. *Half Yearly Reports of Factory Inspectors, Ending 31 October, 1864, Industrial Revolution: Factories*, IUP ser., vol. xii (1865–7), p. 47.   98 For descriptions of the production processes in weaving factories see W.T. Charley, 'Flax', in *British Manufacturing Industries* (London 1876), pp. 80–6; and Irene Margaret Thompson, 'Dust and Sensitivity in the Linen Industry: Investigations into the Health of Linen Workers', M.D. diss., Queen's University of Belfast, 1952, pp. 24–6.

called a 'heck-box' containing as many pins as separate lines of warp. At the top of each was a tiny eye through which the line of warp passed as it was wrapped evenly onto the beam.

Since the warp threads were subjected to much tension and friction, the warp beam yarn was treated with 'size' in the 'sizing shop'. There it was passed between a heavy pair of rollers, the lower one being partly immersed in a cold size solution while the upper rollers squeezed off the excess. The size was rubbed into the fibres and smoothed over by cylindrical brushes over and under the yarn in opposite directions to it. The yarn was then dried by passing it over steam heated cylinders. These workers were men assisted by boy apprentices.

Beaming, another male occupation, was the next process where the warp yarn was wound onto the weaver's beam. The lines of yarn were passed between teeth and distributed evenly over the warp beam to the width desired in the cloth. Next, the thread from the warp beam or weaver's beam were drawn through two structures – the 'heddle' and the 'reed'. This was called 'drawing-in', and was usually the job of women and girls. Heddles were the part of the loom mechanism used to raise and lower the warp in weaving. There were a number of varnished cotton strings supported above and below by two horizontal parallel wood strips approximately eight inches apart. Each string was looped near the middle to form an 'eye'. The weaver's beam was suspended by its ends to allow the lines of warp to hang down perpendicularly. Sitting on a stool, the drawer-in passed a hook into the eye to draw the warp thread through the eye. Next these threads were drawn through the reed, a comb with equally spaced steel strips held between two wooden or steel baulks. Threads in twos or threes were drawn by means of a reed hook through each space. The reed determined the closeness of the warp threads and guided the moving shuttle during weaving.

Weft yarn was wound onto 'pirns' or bobbins on a winding machine by women and girls. Full bobbins were removed, arranged on pirn frames attended by boys, taken to the weft office for checking, and distributed to the weaving room.

The weaving shed was arranged with the front of two looms facing the weaver, who was able to move freely between the two. Shuttles containing the full pirns were made of wood with one very sharp pointed metal tip. These shuttles carried the yarn back and forth at great speed. Shuttle guards at either side of the loom were supposed to prevent the shuttle from flying beyond the loom. Weavers attended the looms, mended the inevitable breaking threads, and took the finished web on their shoulders to the cloth office. There it was inspected and any defects resulted in fines deducted from their wage. Also, the raw ends were clipped and finished, the cloth was passed through rollers, and lapped or folded into shape. Relative to the declining wages of handloom weavers, wages in powerloom factories were high although there was a gap between urban Belfast and rural weavers' wages. In spite of higher wages, powerloom factory owners had lower variable capital costs. While the cost of a handloom was 30s. as compared with £3 for a powerloom, two powerlooms were ordinarily supervised by a single female weaver as compared with one male hand weaver per loom.[99]

Although powerloom weaving began to spread in Ireland during the 1860s, the first investigation of working conditions did not occur until 1892. In that year, Inspector Osborn, seeking to extend the regulations adopted under the Cotton Cloth Act with regard to artificial humidity, made enquiries into weaving sheds in Ireland. Due to the need for moisture to prevent breakage, Osborn found poor ventilation and high humidity levels in weaving sheds that increased with the fineness of the cloth woven. Jets of steam were infused into weaving sheds by means of uncovered pipes creating a hot humid atmosphere. In contrast, sizing or dressing rooms where the warps yarns were prepared were hot and dry. While the temperature in these rooms could be as high as 101 to 117°F., it was a dry heat permitting the body's perspiration to evaporate.[100]

As a result of Osborn's report, regulations to control the amount of humidity and for proper ventilation were enacted. In 1903, it was also recommended that requirements relating to ventilation be replaced by a standard of air purity to be measured by the amount of carbon dioxide in the air inside factories in excess of that found outside. In his report, Inspector Hamilton P. Smith recommended that the levels of humidity in weaving sheds and spinning rooms be the same, and that the water used to humidify the rooms be pure.[101] Refinements to the 1903 law were made in 1905 specifying precisely how much 'carbonic acid' could be in the air, and the heat and humidity levels allowable.[102] While weaving of flax and tow were labeled dangerous trades in 1905, a detailed report in 1914 attested to the overall lack of improvement in working conditions in both spinning mills and weaving factories. In weaving sheds, humidification coupled with the heat entering through the characteristic 'saw-toothed' shed roofs in the summer created a persistently hot humid environment. Weavers attended two or three looms for long hours on their feet with condensation dripping from the ceiling on them and the floors below.[103] The dangers posed by flying steel tipped shuttles remained and no attempts were made to protect weavers' hearing from the relentless deafening noise produced by powerlooms.

99 Greeves, 'American Civil War', pp. 355, 383. 100 *Report of Factory Inspector Osborn, Industrial Revolution: Factories*, IUP ser., vol. 23 (1894), pp. 192, 195. 101 H.C. *Report Upon the Conditions of Work in Flax and Linen Mills as Affecting the Health of the Operatives Employed Therein by Inspector Hamilton P. Smith, H. M. Superintending Inspector of Factories* (cd 1997), vol. x (1904), pp. 6–8. 102 H.C. *Report to His Majesty's Secretary of State for the Home Department on the Draft Regulations for the Processes of Spinning and Weaving Flax and Tow and the Processes Incidental Thereto by G.A. Bonner*, vol. xv, 1906. 103 H.C. *Report of the Departmental Committee on Humidity and Ventilation in Flax Mills and Linen Factories* (cd 7433), vol. xxxvi (1914), p. 192.

HEMSTITCHING FACTORIES

In the linen industry, the making-up end of production consisted of producing and decorating linen and cotton household articles, handkerchiefs, wearing apparel, embroidery and sewing. In and around the city of Derry, the adjacent districts of County Londonderry, Donegal, and Tyrone, it consisted of the manufacture of shirts, collars and ladies undergarments. Some of these items were decorated in various ways by hand or machine sewing mostly by women in their homes. Brenda Collins states that despite the annual gross value of sewed muslin and the numbers of women employed in embroidery, sewing or dressmaking (estimated to be between one in four and one in nine in every Ulster county between 1850 and 1914), the importance of the making-up trades to the history of the linen industry has not been adequately recognized.[104]

Women's ability to sew has long been held in high esteem, and many produced clothing, bedsheets and quilts for their families. During the nineteenth century, sewing remained a respectable occupation for women, offering an alternative to factory work. The sewing or needle trades can be divided into two categories, 1) embroidery which includes flowering, sprigging, parcelling and, 2) sewing which includes plain stitches and seams. Flowering, sprigging, parcelling, embroidery, sewing muslin and lace making had a long history in Ireland.[105] The sewing of plain and fancy work moved during the nineteenth century from the west of Scotland to the north of Ireland where it was concentrated in Counties Down, Donegal, Fermanagh and Tyrone. As in Scotland, sewed muslin in Ireland developed out of the cotton industry in and around Belfast.[106]

In Tullylish, hemstitching of handkerchiefs and tea towels by factory operatives and homeworkers was prevalent. Swiss embroidery machines began to dominate the higher end of the trade by the 1860s. Unlike other sewing machines operated by women, these were operated by one adult man with three female assistants. Swiss embroidery was a skilled occupation and men and women were taught by experienced instructors. Hemming tea towels was also performed by women operatives on sewing machines in small factories in and around Banbridge.

The number of women working inside hemstitching factories was greatly surpassed by women and children sewing in their homes. Most sewing in Tullylish was organized by a putting-out system where 'parcels' to be sewn were either delivered or picked up by women. In towns like Belfast, Lurgan or Portadown, women or

104 Brenda Collins, 'Sewing and social structure: the flowerers of Scotland and Ireland', in Rosalind Mitchison and Peter Roebuck (eds), *Economy and Society in Scotland and Ireland 1500–1939* (Edinburgh 1988), p. 242; Brenda Collins, 'The organization of sewing homework in late nineteenth-century Ulster', in Maxine Berg (ed.), *Markets and Manufacture*, p. 139. See also Cohen, 'Working Conditions'. 14–16; and Marilyn Cohen, 'Proletarianization and Family Strategies in the Parish of Tullylish, County Down, Ireland, 1690–1914', Ph.D. diss., New School for Social Research, 1988, Margaret Neill, 'Homeworkers in Ulster, 1850–1911', in Holmes and Diane Urquhart (eds), *Coming into the Light* (Belfast, 1994). 105 Elizabeth Boyle, *The Irish Flowerers* (Belfast and Cultra 1971). 106 Collins, 'Sewing', p. 247; 'Organization', p. 141.

their children came to the factory to pick up the work and brought it back when finished. In the countryside it was often mediated by the social ties formed between shopkeepers and their customers. Sewing was distributed by agents either from a shop, office, '... or from some spot where the agent arranges to meet the workers.'[107] In Tullylish and Seapatrick it was not organized by the agent, shopkeeper, or worker system as in Donegal.[108]

The predominant form of homework in Tullylish was drawn thread work, done either inside the homes or 'at their doors'. It consisted of drawing aside the threads of the fabric near the edge of the handkerchief with needle and thread at equal intervals, to form a pattern. All that was required was a needle or 'pricker'. Drawing threads produced a 'shire' rendering the finished article more open and attractive with a fancy, more expensive hem.[109] Lurgan and Portadown were the centres of the handkerchief industry, and there hemstitching, Swiss embroidery and lace edging were performed both in factories and by homeworkers.

A key difference in making-up work was the division between work performed inside factories and the sweated tasks performed by adult female and child home-workers. The making-up end clearly was not 'based on some unilinear progress toward a factory system'.[110] Like the garment industry generally, movements toward and away from centralized mechanized production can be traced in the various sectors of the making-up trades creating considerable ambiguity in both census classification of occupations and in relation to the Factory and Workshop Acts. To further complicate the picture, handsewing continued within factories while sew-ing machines after the 1890s spread into homes.[111] In 1912, Factory Inspector McCaughey specifically stated that thread drawing was formerly done in factories, gradually passing into the homes around Lurgan. As the trade increased and the supply of factory labour did not, thread drawing was put-out to women and chil-dren who performed the work for lower wages.[112] Employers were able through sweating and decentralization to decrease their variable capital costs and maximize profits.

In Ulster, the outcome of the expansion of embroidery and sewing was its exten-sion through decentralization into the countryside.[113] The report further specified which processes were performed in factories, which were performed by homework-ers, and which were carried on both in factories and homes indicating a level of

107 *Committee of Inquiry into ... Making-up Trades*, pp. 369–70.   108 Collins, 'Sewing', pp. 146–7.   109 Ibid., pp. 217, 222.   110 Ibid., p. 139.   111 Ava Baron and Susan F. Klepp, '"If I didn't have my sewing machine": women and sewing machine technology', in Joan M. Jensen and Sue Davidson (eds), *A Needle, a Bobbin, a Strike* (Philadelphia, PA 1984), p. 38.   112 *Committee of Inquiry into... Making-up Trades*, p. 407.   113 Collins, 'Sewing', p. 248.

flexibility open to employers. Only three processes – punch hemstitching, machine embroidery (Swiss Embroidery), and machine spoking – were always performed in factories. Those always done at home were hand spoking, hand embroidery, fancy sewing and lace undercutting. Most processes were performed both inside and outside the factory at the discretion of the employer. These included narrow and broad hemming, thread drawing, vice-folding, paring, hemstitching, top sewing, thread clipping, lace attaching, scalloping, nickelling, machine stitching of linen and cotton apparel and shirt and collar button holing. Employers frequently gave factory workers extra work to do at home or on Saturday in direct violation of the Factory and Workshop Act.

The near total lack of investigation by Factory Inspectors suggests that conditions inside hemstitching and embroidery factories were good. The work was clean, dry, quiet and was therefore, of the highest status.[115] However, this was not the case for homeworkers who drew the bulk of attention from Factory Inspectors after 1864. Similar to homeworkers generally, Irish industrial homeworkers were highly specialized sweated workers who earned extremely low piece wages. While homework was very poorly paid, it was perceived as a clean and respectable alternative to factory employment. In Ireland, Inspectors were concerned with the long hours spent at such work by married women and their children, the failure of employers to furnish homeworkers with 'particulars' relating to their wages, and violations of the Truck Acts.

Good workers at thread drawing earned from 4s. to 6s. a week and children about 2s.6d. per week.[116] Again, Inspectors were initially disturbed about the extensive employment of children. In the Second Report from the Commissioners on the Employment of Children and Young Persons in 1864, since simple thread drawing did not require formal teaching, women and children turned to it in great numbers. The extent of hemstitching around Lurgan and Portadown by 1889 was also noted by the District Inspector for the National Schools, who expressed an early concern regarding its negative effects on school attendance.[117]

> Within a few miles from there some thousands of females from 8 years old upwards are employed in sewing linen at their homes. Of these, probably one in three may be adults, mothers employing such children as they may have suitable for the work ... The handkerchiefs are either simply hemmed by sewing machines, or are what is termed hemstitched. For this latter threads must be drawn and this drawing is performed by children even of a very

115 Betty Messenger, *Picking up the Linen Threads* (Belfast 1975), p. 162; Nora Connolly O'Brien, *James Connolly*, p. 124.   116 *Report Upon the Handloom Weaving and Hosiery Manufactures*, pp. 217, 222.   117 *Report of the Commissioners of National Education in Ireland*, vol. 56 (1889), 190; Cynthia R. Daniels, 'Between home and factory: homeworkers and the state', in Eileen Boris and Cynthia R. Daniels (eds), *Homework* (Urbana, IL 1989), p. 18.

tender age. These children are paid by the dozen and sometimes toil from morning until night without any schooltime, earning a miserable pittance.[118]

Another complaint voiced by Factory Inspectors was that in violation of Section 40 of the Factory and Workshop Act (58 & 59 Vict. cap.37) employers were not furnishing homeworkers with particulars relating to piece wages. Under this Act, all textile factories and workshops were to provide this information so that workers could anticipate the amount of wages earned, but in 1905, Hilda Martindale found that in the Irish shirt collar and handkerchief trade such particulars were not furnished.[119]

In 1906, Factory Inspector McCaughey again drew attention to the area around Lurgan and to the extent of child labour. He complained in 1907 that outside of Belfast systematic inspection of the homes of homeworkers was not commonly undertaken by local authorities. Lists of homeworkers were not insisted upon by local magistrates, and when these lists were furnished, they were ignored. Even when McCaughey himself visited these homes and attempted to prosecute parents for overworking their children, magistrates were reluctant to consider these homes workshops because of the irregular working hours. He also found a general neglect of particulars 'was told by homeworkers that they did not know the rate of pay for the work in hand ...'[120] Finally, in 1909, Miss Young went door-to-door investigating the extent of homework. She found near complete disobedience of the Workshop Acts regarding child labour, piece rate particulars and the Truck Acts.[121]

Here too, part of the problem in both recognizing and rectifying the conditions faced by homeworkers was the ideological separation of workplace and home in which 'mothering and breadwinning were oppositional constructs'.[122] Homeworkers challenged this opposition posing a conundrum for the state who were unwilling to recognize as work this decentralized and irregular form of work.[123]

These ideological issues also negatively affected the gathering of accurate data about homeworkers. For example, in 1912–13, the Committee of Inquiry into the conditions of employment in the linen and making-up trades in the North of Ireland estimated that the number of women working in making-up factories was 22,000. The number of homeworkers, on the other hand, was not known but thought to exceed the number in factories.[124] Seaming and shirt-making were classified as dressmaking, while embroidery was included in the mixed materials class. Further, because homework was done mostly by married women with children, who com-

118 *Report of the Commissioners of National Education in Ireland*, vol. 56 (1889), p. 190; *Report Upon the Handloom Weaving and Hosiery Manufactures*, p. 216.   119 H.C. *Annual Report of the Chief Inspector of Factories and Workshops for the Year 1905*, vol. xv (1906), p. 323; Collins, 'Sewing', p. 146.   120 H.C. *Annual Report of the Chief Inspector of Factories and Workshops for the Year 1907*, vol. xii (1908), p. 132. 121 H.C. *Annual Report of the Chief Inspector of Factories and Workshops for the Year 1909*, vol. xxviii (1910), pp. 789–96.   122 Rose, *Limited Livelihoods*, p. 76.   123 Daniels, 'Home and Factory', p. 25. 124 *Committee of Inquiry into Making-up Trades*; Collins, 'Sewing', p. 140; and Bourke, *Husbandry to Housewifery*, pp. 109–41.

bined the work with their household tasks, it was difficult to ascertain the number of women engaged in industrial homework or the hours regularly worked by them. After 1841, census forms were completed by the head of the household, who was usually a man. Since most married women worked intermittently, supplemental wage earning activities were often not recorded rendering them invisible.

While the ideological strength of separate spheres led industrialists to pay higher wages to male breadwinners, it worked to the detriment of homeworkers were often widows, spinsters or married women whose husbands were either out of work or earning low wages. Obtaining homework was indispensable to these workers as it was either an essential supplement to the inadequate wage earned by the male head, or was the chief source of income for the household.

Homework was also indispensable to the employer, 'evidence shows that out-workers furnished the employer with a supply of labour on which, in times of pressure, he can make demands unrestricted by the Factory Acts; whilst in times of slackness he can turn them off without incurring the standard charges involved in the case of factory workers'.[125] Homeworkers functioned as a flexible supply of labour integral to the accumulation of profits by capitalists in this end of production. Even when the work was a household's sole means of support, employers were able to pay sweated wages because prevailing gender conceptions assumed that homework was supplemental. In all putting-out systems, profits are based partly upon sweating. Women engaged in thread drawing and machine stitching at home, earned between $1-2d$. per hour.[126] In addition to lower wages, employers did not have to expend time or money to train or supervise homeworkers which made the worker less valuable and easy to lay-off when demand was slack, which further increased their profits.

Comparative studies of homeworkers over time and space confirm that women 'choose' homework because it allows them to contribute to inadequate household budgets while caring for their homes and children, a strategy cast in rosy terms by Ada Heather-Bigg at the opening of this chapter.[127] Homework is also part of a decentralization process that is becoming increasingly common today. The employer's motive for decentralization is to maximize profits. This is achieved by either decreasing costs through decentralization, or increasing profits where costs are

125 *Committee of Inquiry into Making Up Trades*; Daniels, 'Home and Factory', p. 18; Collins 'Flowerers', p. 251. 126 *Committee of Inquiry into ... Making-up Trades*, p. 374. 127 Rose, *Limited Livelihoods*, pp. 83–4; Eileen Boris and Cynthia R. Daniels, 'Introduction', in Boris and Daniels (eds), *Homework*, p. 5; Robyn Dasey, 'Women's work and the family: women garment workers in Berlin and Hamburg before the First World War', in Richard J. Evans and W.R. Lee (eds), *The German Family* (Totowa, 1981); Victoria Goddard, 'Child labour in Naples: the case of homework', *Anthropology Today*, 1, no. 5 (1985), 18–21; 'Domestic industry in Naples', *Critique of Anthropology*, 3, nos. 9 & 10 (1977), 139–50; Catherine Haskin, 'Homeworking in Britain', in R.E. Pahl (ed.), *On Work* (New York 1988), pp. 609–32 and Kathleen E. Christensen, 'Women, families and home-based employment', in Naomi Gerstel and Harriet Engel Gross (eds), *Families and Work* (Philadelphia, PA 1987), 478–90.

relatively stable, and where the employer alone has access to the market. For the homeworker, decentralization allows for some control over the labour process and for some reconciliation of family and work demands. However, because technological complexity decreases along with wage levels, trade union activity and the organized collective consciousness of the labour force, the amount of labour time also increases.[128] Employers in the making-up end were well aware that homework was sweated work. When Mr Thomas B. Johnson, a linen handkerchief manufacturer at Lurgan was asked if the women in his employ drawing threads and over seaming earned a fair wage, he stated tersely, 'Well it is this way; they are not keeping the house with it'.[129]

128 Goddard, 'Domestic Industry', 140; Boris and Daniels, *Homework*; Pahl, *On Work;* and Christensen, 'Home-Based Employment', pp. 478–90.   129 *Committee of Inquiry into the Making-up Trades*, p. 543.

6

Paternalism and Emergent Industrial Capitalism in Tullylish, 1825–47

No expense is regarded that can promote the happiness or comfort of the workers. The medical attendant is there allowed a salary of £180 a year. A very superior school is attached to the factory, free of charge to the workers and their families, with a library; the working hours are limited to 11 hours a day and no reduction in wages.[1]   Sub-Inspector Hudson, 9 May 1846

In the early Victorian period, there was an attempt to bridge the gap between public and private ethics by 'infusing society with the harmonious spirit of family life'.[2] Industrial capitalism had replaced medieval forms of deferential paternalism with an economic link based on the exchange of labour power for wages. Henceforth, a tension emerged between belief in a free market economy and commitment to social ties and obligations. The popular revival of social and economic paternalism in the mid-Victorian period addressed this tension by looking backward to the patriarchal family, suggesting the model for harmonious class relationships be that of 'wise' father and 'dutiful' child.[3] Employer paternalism, as a managerial strategy, reflected and reinforced this deeply hierarchical and gendered world view held together by the glue of familial obligation.[4] Employers would provide not only for their own dependents but for their extended family of employees. Instead of the language of class conflict, 'all could be described in the language of paternalism, as the dependents and children of their father, their master, their guardian'.[5]

Analysis of social and economic paternalism in the Victorian period has been enriched by scholarly analysis over the past two decades. Patrick Joyce, for example, has analyzed how social processes in mid-Victorian England, including the need for security among the working class, deference and paternalism, coalesced to form a cultural hegemony conceptualized as the 'the culture of the factory'.[6] Building upon Howard Newby's notion of deference as social relationships that convert 'power

1 H.C. *Half Yearly Reports by Inspectors of Factories, Industrial Revolution: Factories*, Report by James Stewart, IUP ser., vol. vii (1842–7), p. 24.   2 Catherine Gallagher, *The Industrial Reformation of English Fiction, 1832–1867* (Chicago 1985), p. 115.   3 Ibid., pp. 115–26, quotes on pages 115, 117.   4 Ibid., p. 115; Judy Lown, *Women and Industrialization* (Minneapolis, MN 1990); Sonya Rose, *Limited Livelihoods* (Berkeley, CA 1992).   5 Leonore Davidoff and Catherine Hall, *Family Fortunes: Men and Women of the English Middle Class, 1780–1850* (Chicago 1987), p. 21.   6 Patrick Joyce, *Work, Society and Politics* (New Brunswick, NJ 1980).

relations to moral ones', Joyce defined a total factory 'milieu' based upon the penetration of work into family, neighbourhood and community life that partially explains mid-Victorian stability.[7] Experience had taught English capitalists that it was in their interest to have good workers and good men who were independent, self-reliant and could appreciate the 'natural' identity between capital and labour. In the words of one Irish capitalist, John Grubb Richardson, builder of the model factory town of Bessbrook in County Armagh, 'The better the village's living standards the more contented were the people in home and factory resulting in happier relationships between employer and employee'.[8] Philip Scranton has facilitated the comparative analysis of paternalism by defining and linking specific forms with particular economic and cultural contexts. He has specified three forms of paternalism; the 'familiar style', characteristic of family-owned mills and rural mill villages, is most applicable here.[9]

Because the social model for employer paternalism was the patriarchal family, feminist scholars have probed how gender distinctions were integral to paternalistic managerial strategies. Terms in common usage like 'master' and 'man' conveyed both class and gender hierarchies; 'an abiding sense of superiority' of fathers as heads of household over women and children.[10] Employer paternalism appealed to personal familial ties of dependency as a means for reconstituting traditional authority relations within the factory and its surrounding environment.[11] Employer paternalism as a cultural hegemony countered the ideological separation of workplace and home and helped 'to turn industrial capitalism into a way of life' where capitalists set the parameters.[12]

The Irish linen industry provides numerous examples of paternalistic endeavour by Victorian capitalists that have not received adequate scholarly attention. This chapter analyzes the emergence of employer paternalism in Tullylish between 1825–46. The culture of the factory at its peak between 1851–80 will be the subject of chapter five.

The rapid advancement of the linen industry between 1825–80 nurtured the growth of factory towns, villages and hamlets that reflected their owners' complex motivations for capital accumulation, class harmony, Protestant hegemony and the

---

7 Joyce, *Work, Society and Politics*, 92–3; Patrick Joyce, *Visions of the People* (Cambridge 1991). The hegemonic dominance of mid-Victorian paternalism suggested by Joyce is challenged by H.I. Dutton and J.E. King, 'The limits of paternalism: the cotton tyrants of north Lancashire, 1836–54', *Social History*, 7 (1982), 59–74.   8 Bessbrook Spinning Company Ltd and J.N. Richardson, Sons and Owden, Ltd., *Bessbrook: A Record of Industry in a Northern Ireland Village Community and a Social Experiment, 1845–1945* (Belfast, n.d.), p. 43.   9 Philip Scranton, 'Varieties of paternalism: industrial structures and the social relations of production in American textiles', *American Quarterly*, 36 (1984), 235–57. Quote appears on p. 247.   10 Joyce, *Work, Society and Politics*, p. 140.   11 Lown, *Women and Industrialization*, p. 3; Michele Perrot, 'The three ages of industrial discipline in nineteenth-century France', in John Merriman (ed.), *Consciousness and Class Experience in Nineteenth-Century Europe* (New York 1979), p. 154.   12 Rose, *Limited Livelihoods*, pp. 33–49, quote appears on pp. 37, 41.

extension of patriarchal familial norms to the workplace.[13] Paternalism was particularly suited to the Irish linen industry for a number of reasons. First, its labour force
was dominated by women and children, those considered most in need of paternal
protection. Second, many mills and factories were built in rural locations. Early
scholars of employer paternalism stressed the environmental and social structural
context. They argue that paternalism was most successful in isolated rural sites with
ample capital accumulation, where a very small number of large firms and a large
number of small ones co-existed, and where a large pool of semi-skilled and relatively
uneducated labour was available.[14] Third, rural industrial capitalists in Ireland and
elsewhere confronted challenges that were distinct from those in urban areas. Most
were dependent upon waterpower, were further from ports, warehouses, sources of
credit, and needed to attract and control a labour force. To attract a stable work
force, employers sought to build generational family commitment to the employer.[15]
Labour control was a particularly dynamic factor influencing managerial strategies
and the location of factories in sites that maximized an employer's control over the
process of production and minimized workers' resistance.[16] Finally, as in England,
paternalism was a strategy well suited to transitional periods when industrial discipline had to be imposed for the first time upon an essentially 'green' workforce.[17]

THE EMERGENCE OF A CAPITALIST ELITE BLOC IN TULLYLISH/SEAPATRICK

The process of transition from proto-industrial production to factories was condi-
tioned, by a number of variables that differed from one industrial region to another.
Such change depended on the degree of proletarianization, the extent of agricultural involvement on the part of workers, the nature of the competitive response,
the particular nature of the dependency in a locale, the power and influence of
entrepreneurial and landowning capital, technological imperatives and the ways
gender and ethnicity mediated class formation.[18] The capital accumulated by Protestant merchants, innovative bleachers and manufacturers prior to mechanized yarn
spinning was invested in a variety of industrial establishments along the Bann after

13 Denis S. MacNiece, 'Industrial villages of Ulster: 1800–1900', in Peter Roebuck (ed.), *Plantation to
Partition*; D.G. Lockhart, 'Planned village development in Scotland and Ireland, 1700–1850', in T.M.
Devine and David Dickson (eds), *Ireland and Scotland 1600–1850* (Edinburgh 1983); Marilyn Cohen,
'Paternalism and poverty: contradictions in the schooling of working class children in Tullylish,
1825–1914', *History of Education*, 21, 3 (1992), 291–306; 'Urbanisation and the milieux of factory life:
Gilford/Dunbarton, 1825–1914', in Chris Curtin, Thomas Wilson and Hastings Donnan (eds), *Irish
Urban Cultures* (Belfast 1993).   14 Howard Newby, 'Paternalism and capitalism', in Richard Scase
(ed.), *Industrial Society: Class, Cleavage and Control* (New York St 1977).   15 Louise A. Tilly, 'Coping
with company paternalism', *Theory and Society*, 14, no. 4 (1995), 413.   16 David Gordon, 'Capitalist
development and the history of American cities', in W. K. Tabb and L. Sawers (eds), *Marxism and the
Metropolis* (New York 1978), p. 40.   17 Joyce, *Work, Society and Politics*, p. 146.   18 Pat Hudson, *The
Genesis of Industrial Capital* (Cambridge 1986), p. 13.

1825. By 1834, the Ordnance Survey Memoirs for Tullylish list nine bleachgreens, two flax scutching mills, one spinning mill, one vitriol works, three corn mills and one flour mill along the Bann.[19] Samuel Lewis's 1837 description of Tullylish reveals the burgeoning state of entrepreneurship:

> The bleaching of cloth is the process peculiarly attended to; in the numerous bleachgreens which border the Bann in its progress through the parish upwards of 138,000 pieces of linen were finished for the market in 1834. A thread manufactory, carried on at Milltown on an extensive scale, gives employment to 170 persons, a mill at Coose for spinning fine linen yarn employs 200; each is worked by a combination of steam and water power; another for linen yarn is now being erected at Gilford on an extensive scale. Large works for manufacturing the chymical [sic] ingredients required in the various processes of the fabrication of linen cloth have been established at Moyallen and at Coose ... the vicinity of the Canal which skirts the parish on the West, and on which there is a wharf and stores about a mile from Gilford, contributes to the increase of this prosperity, by affording a vent for the manufactured articles throughout a large extent of inland country both to the North and South, and to the two great shipping ports of Belfast and Newry.[20]

The accumulation of capital by entrepreneurs in the region resulted in a concentration of wealth and power mobilized in collective and individual schemes to alter the physical environment to meet a variety of needs. For example, in 1836, the numerous mill owners along the Bann endeavoured to maintain and increase their profits by forming a joint stock company that met for the first time on 3 September. Since the geographical basis for industrial development was the River Bann, the members collectively sought to regulate the quantity of water, thus supplying their mills more effectively. The Bann Reservoir Act, passed in 1836, empowered these capitalists to raise the money required for building a Reservoir in £50 shares, and to levy a rate on each foot of occupied fall not to exceed £10 per annum. Three Reservoirs – Lough Island Reavy near Castlewellan, Dear's Meadow and Corbet Lough – were authorized with Dear's Meadow abandoned.[21] At the completion of the Lough Island Embankment on 6 January 1841, the Directors were confident that the supply of water would be efficiently regulated.[22]

Bleachgreen owner Benjamin Haughton will illustrate the entrepreneurial activities of Quaker capitalists in Tullylish during the early nineteenth century. By 1814, John Nicholson's large bleachgreen at Hall's Mill had faltered. An advertisement in

19 (PRONI), OSM, MIC.6/173, 20 October 1834.   20 Samuel Lewis, A *Topographical Dictionary of Ireland* (London 1837), p. 658.   21 John Frederick Bateman, 'Description of the Bann reservoirs, Co. Down, Ireland', *Minutes of the Proceedings of the Institution of Civil Engineers*, 7 (1848), 251–3.   22 (PRONI), D.1632/1/1, Bann Reservoir Co., Minutes of General Meetings, 1836–1864, 6 January 1841.

the *Belfast Newsletter* stated that all of Banford Green, containing 25 acres 1 rood 10 perches, Banford House and Demesne was for sale due to the owner's bankruptcy.[23] In 1815, the buyer of Nicholson's business and property was linen draper Benjamin Haughton (1781–1866). Haughton was characteristic of many bleachers in the mid-nineteenth century who were also drapers and putting-out manufacturers employing domestic handloom weavers. He had accumulated considerable capital that was invested in two bleach mills built in 1812 and described in the Ordnance Survey Memoirs. One was driven by a water wheel twelve feet by five feet in diameter that worked six single wash mills, three pairs of rubbing boards, a starching machine, cylinder and pumps. A second water wheel of 14 feet by 5 feet 6 inches in diameter worked two double beetling engines and a pump in a beetling mill 49 feet by 31.6 feet by 17 feet. Finally, a water wheel of 12 feet by 4 feet 6 inches drove two double washmills and a pair of squeezers in a second building.[24]

In 1834, Valuator John Hampton and his two assistants described the numerous properties owned by 'Ben Hutton' (Benjamin Haughton). In Loughans he owned a beetling mill that was currently out of use but part of a larger bleach works held by him at Moyallon. There he ran a large business with another beetling mill occasionally used valued at £7.9s., a bleaching and finishing house used mostly for yarn valued at £8.16s.9d., another beetling mill valued at 19s.4d., a cotton house valued at £2.19s.3d., and water power valued at £16.18s.10d. Finally, in Tullylish townland, along with a flour mill owned jointly with his in-law Joseph Malcomson, Haughton owned a bleachgreen called Benjamin Haughton & Company complete with lapping room.[25] There Fennell and Haughton carried on a cambric handkerchief bleaching business employing about seventy people. Haughton's sons, Thomas and Samuel, had a drill and sheeting manufacturing business until 1860.[26]

The principal competitor with Banford Bleach Works was Springvale Bleach Works in nearby Lawrencetown owned by the Uprichards, a Quaker family from Wales. About 1835, James Uprichard and his brothers Thomas and Henry founded Springvale. Similar to Banford, these bleachers were manufacturers of linen cloth. The bleachworks, which occupied 200 acres and employed abut 200 people, was powered by three iron water wheels and two steam engines. After the death of James in the 1840s and Thomas c.1850, James' son William took over, to be followed in turn by his son William Albert Uprichard.[27]

The challenge of mill spinning was taken up early in Tullylish by several capitalists in the 1830s. The key figures initiating the building of the first spinning mills were manufacturers and bleachers who had accumulated capital and experience.[28] For example, the first spinning mill on the River Bann was built about 1834 at

23 (PRONI), D.1286/Box 2/2, Beck Notebooks, p. 56.   24. E.R.R. Green, *The Industrial Archeology of County Down* (Belfast 1963), p. 21; and (PRONI), VAL.lB/350, Parish of Tullylish, Co. Down, Fieldbook. 25 Green, *Industrial Archeology*, p. 21; and (PROI), *Valuation of Mills in Co. Down, Mill Book 5, c.*1836. 26 Green, *Industrial Archeology*, p. 21.   27 R.S.J. Clarke, *The Heart of Downe: Old Banbridge Families* (Belfast 1989), p. 96.   28 Hudson, *Genesis*, p. 75.

Hazelbank by bleacher Samuel Law. Law was one of three brothers – along with John, a linen draper, and George, discussed previously – who in 1829 inherited his uncle Joseph Law's estate just prior to his death in 1831 at the age of 82.[29] About 1833, Samuel Law employed William Fairbairn to erect one of his iron breast water wheels first used for driving beetling engines. The 1834 Ordnance Survey Memoirs described Law's bleachgreen as having two large water wheels, one of which turned machinery for spinning linen yarn. The machinery at the mill consisted of 3000 mule spindles operating twelve hours a day, nine months of the year. An 1834 Valuation gave the dimensions of Law's spinning mill as 54 feet in length, 39 feet wide, and 36 feet high containing 210.6 square feet of space.[30] In 1838, the three story spinning mill was driven by a 25 horse power (h.p.) steam engine and a 30 h.p. water wheel and employed a workforce of 143 females and 42 males.[31]

Another example was William Hayes (1770–1827), who came as a young man to Banbridge taking over the Millmount bleachgreen owned by the McClellands and land at Edenderry. A corn mill located on the land was converted to a bleachgreen in 1800 and 1806. One building contained 4 feet of wash mills and 3 runners of rubbing boards driven by a breast water wheel. The other building housed the corn mill and the beetling mill. These bleach mills were taken over by William's eldest son Richard (1797–1864).[32]

William also acquired glebe land at Seapatrick where he established his third son Frederick W. Hayes (1802–53). Frederick was a pioneer of both spinning and weaving by power. In 1826, he was given a grant of 500 pounds by the Linen Board during its last years, for spinning fine yarn by power. It is probable that this spinning mill utilized the older dry spinning method. Also, by 1835, Frederick was weaving linen and cotton union cloth on 100 powerlooms at Seapatrick, at a time when there were only a few hundred powerlooms in all of Ireland producing cotton fabric. Seapatrick was the first powerloom factory on the Bann and perhaps in the Irish linen industry. Hayes' factory was described in the Ordnance Survey Memoirs as having a 50 h.p. iron water wheel that drove 82 looms, 4 dressing machines, a winding machine for 20 spools, 5 double sets of bobbin machines each winding 40 bobbins, 5 single beetling engines, a calender, 5 sets of scutches, a set of rollers, a pump, lathe and a circular saw. This water wheel was the second of William Fairbairn's wheels to be erected on the Bann, after Samuel Law's.[33]

For about ten years, Hayes concentrated on weaving union cloth, but ultimately he turned to the manufacture of linen thread. In 1840, he founded the Royal Irish Thread Mills, principally spinners of fine linen thread.[34] Thread making was first produced in Ireland in 1784 by John Barbour of Paisley and became an important branch of the linen industry in the Banbridge area. Successful manufacturers who

29 (PRONI), D. 104 6/517/2, Conveyance Regarding Estate of Samuel Law, late, of Hazelbank, Flaxspinner; Clarke, *Heart of Downe*, p. 22.   30 (PRONI), VAL.1B/350, Parish of Tullylish, Fieldbook. 31 Green, *Industrial Archaeology*, pp. 7, 19–20; and (PROI), *Valuation of Mills in Co. Down, Millbook 5*, *c.*1836.   32 Green, *Industrial Archeology*, p. 18.   33 Ibid.   34 Clarke, *Heart of Downe*, p. 109.

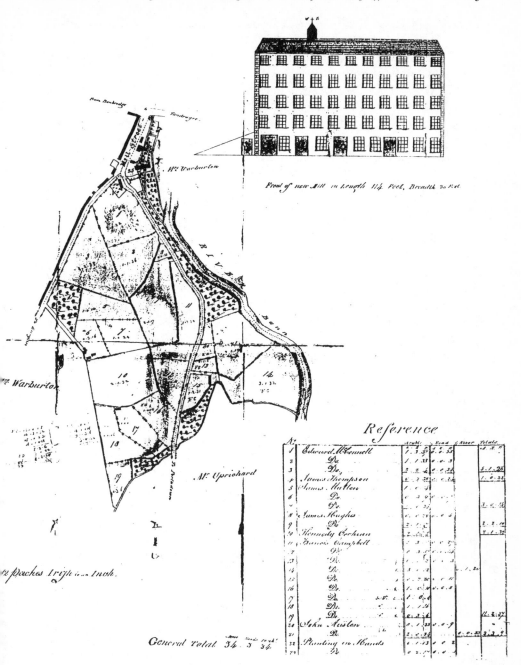

6   1831 survey of Hugh Law's property in Drumaran showing the front of the new yarn-spinning mill

earned profits through the putting-out system played a major role in the transfer to mechanized production in this branch.

Hugh Dunbar, son of linen draper Robert Dunbar, was one of the early capitalists manufacturing linen thread at Huntley Glen in Tullylish. Dunbar, who was to transform Gilford, was a successful linen manufacturer acquainted with the trade since 1805, employing 1700 handlooms by 1839. By 1824, he was listed in Pigot's directory as a thread manufacturer.[35] Dunbar reported to the Commissioners investigating the condition of handloom weavers in 1840, that from his perspective, the linen trade had never been in a 'more healthy and promising condition ...' as demand for linen was up and the wages for handloom weavers in this area were increasing.[36]

Thread manufacture, like yarn spinning, was revolutionized by the wet spinning process. In 1834, the competition from mill spun yarn compelled Dunbar to either erect his own spinning and twisting mill or go out of business. Since Dunbar did not possess sufficient capital alone for such an undertaking, in 1834, he formed a partnership with W.A. Stewart of Edenderry, Banbridge. He chose Gilford for the site of his new spinning mill, where an established bleachgreen with considerable water power existed.[37] The land on which the mill would be built was purchased from three men, all of whom were bleachers and drapers: Hugh Law, heir to George Law's holdings including the bleachgreen, 34 acres, 3 roods, 34 perches, and corn mill at Gilford; William McCreight who held land on the opposite side of the Bann; and James Uprichard, who held land at Banvale[38] (see figure 6).

Dunbar and Stewart's business commenced on 4 February 1836 in premises located on Mill Street. At this time, Dunbar continued to manufacture brown cloth at Huntley Glen until 1843. In 1837, W.A. Stewart died and Dunbar took in Robert Thompson as a partner. The firm then traded under the name Dunbar Thompson & Company. But the partnership was short-lived, and Hugh Dunbar soon brought in young John Walsh McMaster of Armagh just twenty years old. In 1839, James Dickson, another son of a linen bleacher and manufacturer, was also taken into partnership. At the time of the formation of this partnership, the mills at Gilford were in a sufficiently complete state to allow for the commencement of business. Completion of the yarn and thread spinning mills took place in November of 1841. In 1843, the firm divided into two sections, trading under Dunbar McMaster & Company for flax spinning and linen thread and Dunbar Dickson & Company for the manufacture of brown linen cloth.[39]

---

35 J. Pigot, *Pigot's Provincial Directory* (London 1824), p. 344.   36 H.C. *Reports of Assistant Commissioners on Handloom Weavers, Industrial Revolution: Textiles*, Part III, IUP ser., vol. ix (1839–40), Evidence of Mr Dunbar, p. 660.   37 (PRONI), D.1286/1, Beck Notebooks, H.C. Lawlor, 'Rise of the linen merchants in the eighteenth century', 2, no. 2 (1942), 91.   38 (PRONI), MIC.102/1, Hugh Law Esq. and Elizabeth Law to Hugh Dunbar, William A. Stewart and John Thompson, Merchants, Fee Farm Grant of the Water Corn Mill of Gilford, Co. Down, 12 February, 1835; M.P. Campbell, 'Gilford and its mills', Review: *Journal of the Craigavon Historical Society*, 4, no. 3 (1981–2), 21.   39 (PRONI), D.1286/1, Beck Notebooks, Lawlor, 'Linen Merchants', 91; and D.2714/8F, Genealogist Gilford Area, Notes on Dunbar McMaster & Co. of Gilford.

We know little about working conditions in these early mills in Tullylish and Seapatrick. In 1840 and 1841, Factory Inspector James Stuart visited the spinning mills at Hazelbank and Seapatrick. Although Hazelbank was not mentioned, Frederick W. Hayes was not attending to the Provisions of the Factory Act. He was taken to hearing for employing young persons without certificates of age, for employing them at night, and for a longer period than was allowed by law. Although Hayes could produce no evidence in defense of himself at the hearing (that is, he did not have the certificates of age), the magistrates dismissed the complaint against him. The reason suggested by Stuart was that the magistrates were 'John Lindsay, Thomas Crawford and John Welsh, Esq., the uncles and brother-in-law of Mr Hayes'.[40]

By this time, the industrial capitalists in Tullylish overshadowed their landlord in power and wealth. As landlords, the Johnstons continued to collect rents from their tenants who now included industrial capitalists like Hugh Dunbar. Rents also continued to be high for tenements in Gilford, ranging from £1 to £1.10s. per annum for a house with no land and £2–3 per annum for a house and garden.[41] Comparison of rentals on the Johnston Estate between 1840–46 show an increase in tenements with and without small gardens along Castle Street in Gilford.[42] While no evidence exists for Johnston's estate during the transitional 1830s, by 1840, many of his tenants appear to be abandoning the strategy of acquiring small fragments of land on which to grow potatoes and moved instead to tenements in Gilford, where they joined the newly expanding industrial proletariat working at Dunbar McMaster & Company. By 1840, the Commissioners on handloom weavers reported that 'the weavers in the neighbourhood of Banbridge do not, except in a few instances hold land; and a good number live in small cottages built for them, held under their employers'.[43]

HUGH DUNBAR: RURAL PATERNAL CAPITALIST

By the beginning of the nineteenth century, Evangelicalism was a force in Ireland and many Evangelicals recognized the need to address the enormous challenges posed by urban industrial capitalism. Like other British industrial cities, the working class population of Belfast rose dramatically in the first half of the nineteenth century, and many lived in over-crowded, squalid, unhealthy conditions. Through home visits and a variety of voluntary associations, Evangelicals 'spurred by a com-

40 H. C. *Reports by Inspectors of Factories, Industrial Revolution: Factories*, Quarterly Report by James Stuart, IUP ser., vol. 7 (1842–47). 41 H.C. *Reports from Commissioners, Poor Laws* (Ireland), Appendix E, vol. xxxii (1836), pp. 335–6; (PRONI), T.426, Myles MSS., Copy Rent Roll of the late Sir William Johnston Bart., 1 November, 1840. 42 (PRONI), T.426, Myles MSS., Copy Rent Roll of the late Sir William Johnston, Bart., 1 November 1840; D.1594/59, Burgess Documents, Rental of the Late Sir William Johnston's Estate, 1 November 1846. 43 *Reports on Handloom Weavers*, Evidence of Mr Carson and Mr Brice Smith, p. 660.

bination of missionary zeal and fear of the lower classes', campaigned for the spread of Sunday Schools, temperance movements, bible societies and town missions. The temperance movement in particular spread after 1829, with many of its strongest supporters being merchants and millowners who sought to promote class harmony and the sobriety of their workforces. Employers were called on to establish temperance societies in their factories and shops.[44] Evangelicalism also provided a scripture-based ethic that defined the class-specific obligations necessary to ensure social harmony. Protestant respectability was promoted among the working class as a reflection of personal morality while they 'reminded the material beneficiaries of industry of their social duties, stressing the responsibilities of man as God's steward and urging systematic exercise of benevolence'.[45]

One of Ireland's earliest factory towns, Dunbarton was built during this period by Hugh Dunbar (1790–1847), a Unitarian. Dunbar proved an ideal candidate for the familiar paternalist he was to become. He was reputed to have been an 'extraordinarily generous man with a list of fully 400 paupers whom he weekly served in his own house with pecuniary aid' and to have died dispensing alms. On his large memorial in Banbridge, Charity is depicted in high relief succouring the sick and needy with the inscription, 'Blessed is he that considereth the poor'.[46]

Dunbar laid the institutional foundations for religious identifications that cross-cut class among the town's population. Evidence suggests that from the start of his transition from putting-out manufacturer to industrial capitalist, Dunbar subscribed to a paternalistic managerial strategy emphasizing that concern about the human welfare of one's employees was 'morally desirable and practically profitable'.[47] He attempted to provide decent working conditions in his large spinning mill and retained exclusive ownership of the lands, mill buildings, and workers' houses until his death in 1847, in spite of a formal partnership between six men.[48]

Mention of Dunbar McMaster & Company (Gilford Mill) by Factory Inspectors began with James Stewart in 1839.[49] At that time, the mill was the largest or one of the largest in Ireland, employing about 2000 people. The architectural design of this massive five-story factory with its prominent factory gate indicates the concern with industrial discipline and a carefully calculated division of labour characteristic of the 'classical age of factory discipline'.[50] In his report of 9 May 1846, Stewart provides a glowing description (see the quotation introducing the chapter)

44 Elizabeth Malcolm, *'Ireland Sober, Ireland Free': Drink and Temperance in Nineteenth Century Ireland* (Syracuse, NY 1986), pp. 56, 76.   45 Hempton and Hill, *Evangelicalism*, pp. 105–21. Quote appears on page 119; Jane Garnett, "'Gold and the Gospel": systematic beneficence in mid-nineteenth century England; *Studies in Church History*, 24 (1987), 347–58; S. Peter Kerr, 'Voluntaryism within the Established Church in Belfast', *Studies in Church History*, 23 (1986), 347–62.   46 Captain Richard Linn, A *History of Banbridge* (Banbridge 1935), p. 171; Campbell, 'Gilford', 22; Clarke, *Heart of Downe*, pp. 12, 18; PRONI, D.1286/2/4, Beck Notebooks, History of Flax Spinning Mills in Ulster, p. 210.   47 Lown, *Women and Industrialization*, p. 95.   48 (PRONI), D.2714/8F, Gilford Genealogist, Notes on Dunbar McMaster & Co. of Gilford.   49 H.C. *Half Yearly Reports by Inspectors of Factories, Industrial Revolution: Factories*, Report by James Stewart, IUP ser., vol. vii (1842–7).   50 Perrot, 'Three Ages', 156–9.

confirming that Dunbar had made significant efforts to provide for the well-being of the workers both on and off the job. Although workers had forcibly removed them, splash boards had been installed on all spinning frames to help keep spinners dry.

Dunbar's attempts to build a community at Dunbarton coincided with a decade of extreme demographic upheaval associated with the Great Famine between 1841–51. The population attracted to Dunbar McMaster & Company consisted largely of former proto-industrial producers from the surrounding rural townlands. Prior to the opening of Gilford Mill in 1841, as table 4 shows, the population of Gilford grew relatively slowly, numbering 529 in 1831, and 643 in 1841.[51] However, between 1841 and 1851, the population grew by 217 persons per year.

Table 4: Population growth and density in Gilford, 1831–1901

	1831	1841	1851	1861	1871	1881	1891	1901
Gilford Town	529	643	2814	2892	2720	1324	1276	1199
Males	-	300	1247	1253	1182	588	602	527
Females	-	343	1567	1639	1538	736	674	672
Inhabited Houses	-	104	333	452	502	286	288	271
Uninhabited Houses	-	7	21	26	57	44	25	51
No. per house	-	6.2	8.4	6.4	5.4	4.6	4.4	4.4

Source: Aggregate Census of Ireland 1841–1901; Basset, Co. Down, p. 259.

The concentration of workers in factories rather than in dispersed cottages posed an immediate problem for those creating built environments for production and consumption – housing workers in the right locations. Capitalists in Ulster and elsewhere initially sought to resolve this problem by building company-owned housing consisting of rows of tenements located close to the mill gates ensuring a large measure of control over the social life of their employees.[52] In addition, shops and other social institutions were built close to sources of employment. The authority over the use of other aspects of social space in the effort to 'reform the whole man' not only kept the cost of living down, but was a crucial means by which the rhythms of work in the mill or factory dominated everyday life.[53]

Hugh Dunbar began building homes for his increasing workforce almost immediately after leasing the necessary land. Prior to the erection of Gilford Mill, the older town of Gilford had developed in a 'Y' formation. The land leased from Law, Uprichard, and McCreight in the 1830s, on which the mill and village of Dunbarton were to be built, was separated from the older village of Gilford by rising ground off

51 George Henry Bassett, *The Book of County Down* (Dublin 1888), p. 259.   52 David Harvey, *The Urbanization of Capital* (Baltimore, MD 1985), pp. 22–3.   53 Joyce, *Work, Society, and Politics*; Harvey, *Urbanization*, p. 50; Lown, *Women and Industrialization*, p. 68; Cohen, 'Paternalism and Poverty', 291–306.

to the left side of the 'Y'. Land in Castle Hill, off to the right owned by George Law, was leased in 1844.[54]

Gilford Mill was built on the low lying ground beside the river, and the land where the houses were built rose steeply upwards from the mill gates. The earliest mill-owned houses, completed by the 1838 Valuation, were arranged in terraces on the slopes above the mill. Among the earliest workers' houses owned by Hugh Dunbar were a group of terrace houses at Bridge Street at the base of the older part of the village close to the corn mill. These homes were in existence prior to the 1830s. Early streets built by Dunbar were Ann Street, consisting of seven houses built on a steep slope rising upwards directly from the mill gates, and High Street, consisting of 52 homes with 18 of these being 'back-to-back' style. The other side of the back-to-back houses was called Bann Street, facing the rear waste ground at the river. Finally, Hill Street consisted of homes that were narrower and smaller.[55]

Despite variations in the quality of housing, usually employer-provided housing in Ulster was of a higher standard than that provided by speculative builders. Company-owned housing was a lure to attract a present and future labour force consisting preferably of families. Although Judy Lown argues that company housing strengthened the position of men, Irish spinning mills offered greater employment opportunities for women. In Gilford/Dunbarton, employment of the male head at the mill was not a condition of occupancy.[56]

Unlike most privately-owned property, employer's housing was not necessarily expected to show a normal rate of profit on the capital invested. For the most humane employers it was recognized that the provision of a decent environment for their workers was a social obligation that would help create class harmony. For others, low quality housing was provided and the rents charged were high enough to take advantage of their monopoly position.[57]

Houses in Dunbarton were more typical of urban terraces than rural cottages. The houses built in the early 1830–40 period were sound, but without yards and in some cases without rear access. About half (51 per cent) of the total houses in Gilford/Dunbarton built by the mill owners and other speculative builders had no land attached for keeping animals or growing vegetables. Only 12.6 per cent of houses in Gilford/Dunbarton had piggeries while slightly more (19.7 per cent) had fowlhouses. Factory-owned houses, such as on Hill Street, were more likely to have simple outoffices for animals such as hens. Houses owned by other landlords were more likely to have both yards and outoffices such as on Castle Hill Street and Rutton's Row.

54 (PRONI), D.2714/5C, Genealogical Notes on Families in Gilford, Castle Hill. 55 Denis S. McNiece, 'Factory Workers' Housing in Counties Down and Armagh', Ph.D. diss., The Queen's University of Belfast, 1981, pp. 11–22. 56 Lown, *Women and Industrialization*, p. 158. 57 John Burnett, *A Social History of Housing, 1815–1970* (London, 1980), pp. 81–82; Sydney Pollard, 'The factory village in the industrial revolution', *English Historical Review*, LXXIX (1964), 513–31.

This period of building was unrestricted by laws regulating health and sanitation; housing standards are indicative of an individual employer's criteria for suitability. Room size, ceiling height, windows, and construction materials were important to the quality of life as was the degree of crowding. Denis McNiece, who extensively researched workers' housing in several Ulster factory towns, described the sizes and amenities found in the early mill-owned houses in Dunbarton:

> The 'back-to-back' houses were the most basic units available, having only two rooms 11' x 11' with single windows on each floor, they would have provided rather cramped living space for more than four occupants. The lack of rear doors and windows and the resultant reduction in ventilation ... was probably less critical in an open site which allowed unlimited circulation of fresh air ... they were adequate for single occupation or smaller family units and would have been a considerable improvement on the poorer type of rural dwellings. Living space in the houses in Hill Street was also cramped, particularly in the kitchens where the staircases and the projecting chimney breasts reduced the width to less than 8'. The ground floor rooms which spanned the rear of the houses had no back doors and were probably used as bedrooms. Where the staircases ran upwards from these rooms instead of from the front porches, privacy, which was already at a premium, was further reduced ... the kitchen houses in Ann Street had similar rooms spanning the full width of the rear ground floors, but were fitted with back doors and 'mouth organ' fanlights which suggests ... that this room was designed as a scullery. The adjoining houses had front parlours, but the frontages were no larger, and the status of a 'better' front room and a hall was diminished by the smaller amount of space available for each ... High street were adequate kitchen houses although ceiling height on the ground floors was limited to 6'6". Unlike Ann Street houses, the rear rooms on the ground floor were partitioned to make provision for small extra bedrooms adjoining the sculleries.[58]

While the owners of Dunbar McMaster & Company were building houses throughout most of the period of rapid population growth between 1841–61, they could not keep up with the demand, especially in the decade between 1841–51. In 1839, the mill only employed 215 workers; by 1870 this number had expanded to over 2000. During the period between 1836–62, the company built 200 houses at a cost of 10,000 pounds.[59] Still, in 1851, there was only a sufficient quantity of first class houses. Four hundred and sixty-six households were pressing into 220 second class houses (the classification for the vast majority of factory-owned housed); 122

58 McNiece, 'Workers' Housing', 23.   59 H.C. *Reports from Commissioners, Paris Universal Exhibition*, Part III, vol. xx (1867–8), pp. 60–1.

households into 63 third class houses, and 49 households into 29 fourth class houses.[60] Average weekly rents for these houses were 2s.3d. and 1s. for a single workman per week.[61] After 1867, building was sporadic consisting of another terrace of houses, and larger prestigious terraces.[62] All factory-owned houses were inspected monthly by the firm owners, annually limewashed, painted and repaired at the firm's expense.[63]

Before his death in 1847, Hugh Dunbar built a Fever Hospital at the top of Hill Street. This hospital consisted of two terrace houses under the supervision of Henry McBride, supervising surgeon for the factory, who was a physician, surgeon and apothecary.[64] Dunbar, a Unitarian, gave generously towards the building of the new Non-Subscribing Presbyterian Church in Banbridge. Dunbar's donation on 11 August 1846 of 2 roods and 23 perches for the cost of 1d. payable half yearly on Castle Hill, that later provided the sites for the Roman Catholic Church and school, suggests his tolerance of religious difference.[65] Lands for the Presbyterian, Methodist and Episcopal Churches were also donated either by Dunbar, or the McMasters, who were especially supportive of the Church of Ireland. Finally, before he died, Dunbar built a school that opened in 1846 consisting of three separate infant, male and female schools. The cost to the firm of providing the three room school house, teachers' salaries, fire, light, daily cleaning, repairs, annual painting and limewashing was 104 pounds per year.[66]

Schools and churches facilitated discourses promoting middle class values, class harmony, and gendered social spheres. Schooling was an integral part of a hegemonic factory culture since 'from his or her earliest days the operative was schooled into the reputation of a paternal elite, and ... into an environment dominated by a particular employer and factory'.[67] The five schools established early in nineteenth-century Tullylish were long affiliated with particular Protestant denominations.[68] In contrast, Dunbar's school was from its inception under the jurisdiction of the 1844 Factory Act and the National System of Education in Ireland beginning in 1831. Soon after Hugh Dunbar's death, the school was visited by Head Inspector Dr Patton, who reported to the Commissioners of National Education. Referring to the concern for working-class schooling displayed among Ulster's millowners, Patton singled out Dunbar McMaster & Company by then employing,

> ... nearly 2,000 hands in their spinning factories, and have erected a splendid and commodious school house consisting of three departments, for the instruction of children, boys, girls and infants – during the day, and for adults,

60 (PRONI), 1851 Census of Ireland.   61 *Paris Universal Exhibition*, pp. 60–1.   62 McNiece, 'Workers' Housing', pp. 18–21.   63 *Paris Universal Exhibition*, pp. 60–3.   64 McNiece, 'Workers' Housing', p. 31.   65 Campbell, 'Gilford', 36; Clarke, *Heart of Downe*, p. 18.   66 Cohen, 'Paternalism', 6.   67 Joyce, *Work, Society, and Politics*, p. 172.   68 These include Moyallon Male and Female established in 1788, Gilford Male and Female schools established in 1819, Bann school established in 1816, Ballynagarrick established in 1820, Clare school established in 1827, and Ballylough established in 1822.

and such as could not attend the day school, in the evening ... in the several departments of which 125 boys, 98 girls and 61 infants – total 284 are receiving a most efficient education and moral training. At the evening school there are at present 131 males, and 81 females on the books.[69]

In 1847, District Commissioner James Patton wrote a letter describing the need for the Gilford Mill Evening School, to meet the increasing schooling needs of adolescents, many of whom were illiterate.

> ... I visited these schools ... at 7½ o'clock, and found 56 males and 36 females; the cause of the small attendance on this and the evening before was in consequence of the mill working longer hours to make up for deficiencies caused by want of water and many from feeling tired were not inclined to attend this evening. Their average age might be 16 years or more – all employed at the mills. They all appear to have made rapid progress in reading and writing, also in arithmetic; few I understand, could read on the opening of the School in March last, and none could write and many only in the alphabet. There are at present 161 males and 123 females on the Rolls. The average for the last three months being 80 males and 75 females ... none of these pupils attend the Day Schools. The hours of attendance from 6½ till 9:00. The weekly payment 1 penny and for the Mathematics and the extra branches 5–7 pence. I think that these evening schools are likely to succeed and be productive of much good.[70]

Whether respected, feared or resented, familiar paternalists like Hugh Dunbar, John W. McMaster, and bleachgreen owners along the Bann were 'familiar figures, masters who knew their hands by name, pressed their souls toward church or chapel, commanded their political allegiance, and rewarded the virtue of the diligent, devout, deserving few'.[71] In the decade prior to the Famine, paternalistic employers emerged as generators of social structure and culture that constrained and resocialized the lives of first generation workers. Employer hegemony deepened when dislocation associated with the Great Famine pressed thousands into Gilford/Dunbarton and other developing industrial sites along the Bann. The influence of the Great Famine on capitalist development in Tullylish is the subject of the next chapter.

---

69 H.C. *Appendix to the Eighteenth Report of the Commissioners of National Education in Ireland* (1851), pp. 250–1.   70 (PRONI), ED.1/16, Down Aided Applications, 1846–1860, No. 27, Gilford Mill Evening School, 20 September 1847.   71 Scranton, 'Varieties of Paternalism', 241.

7

Capitalist Development during the Great Famine: Tullylish, 1847–51

> ... that having taken the opinion of the Medical Officer as regards the admission of more paupers into the workhouse, and he being decidedly opposed to further admissions, although all the applicants exhibited symptoms of starvation and some even of death ... and that previous to the applicants being turned away, each is to be supplied with some portion of food.[1]
>
> Banbridge Board of Guardians, 10 April 1847

> ... the Board beg leave to lay before them the real state of this part of the country. There are in this Union a great portion of rate payers or rather occupiers liable to rates whose sole dependence for the support of their families at this moment is a loom and nearly the entire amount of their furniture a bed, often of a most wretched description with only one or two cooking utensils. On these the collector may lay his hands in default of payment, but what must follow? Struggling industry will be driven forth upon the world, the addition of an entire family made to the pauper's list and a few shillings collected at the eventual cost of many pounds.[2]
>
> Lurgan Board of Guardians, 8 July 1847

Initial attempts to build a community at Dunbarton and the rapid expansion of industrial capitalism along the Bann at mid-century corresponded with the Great Famine – the watershed in Ireland's nineteenth-century history. Since the impact of the Famine was mildest in some parts of Ulster, particularly in the northeast, most analyses have focused on rural agricultural regions elsewhere in Ireland exploring its impact on mortality rates, evictions, emigration, agricultural production and output.[3] However, Ulster was Ireland's most densely populated province in 1841. The fact that mortality rates in some Ulster regions during the Famine were among the lowest in Ireland has resulted in scholarly neglect, erroneous assumptions and overgeneralization reinforcing the mistaken view that this catastrophe

---

1 (PRONI), BG.6/A/6 Minutes of the Banbridge Board of Guardians, November 1846–June 1847. 2 (PRONI), BG.22/A/6, Minute Book of the Lurgan Board of Guardians, 1 May 1847 to 27 March 1848, 98. 3 Joel Mokyr, *Why Ireland Starved: A Quantitative and Analytical History of the Irish Economy, 1800–1850* (London 1983); Cormac O'Grada, *Ireland Before and After the Famine* (Manchester 1988), p. 78; Cormac O'Grada, Ireland: *A New Economic History, 1790–1939* (Oxford 1994); Mary E. Daly, *The Famine in Ireland* (Dundalk 1986); Christine Kinealy, *This Great Calamity: The Irish Famine 1845–52* (Dublin 1994); Patrick McGregor, 'The impact of the blight upon the pre-famine rural economy in Ireland', *Economic and Social Review*, 15, no. 4 (1984), 289–303; S.H. Cousens, 'Regional variations in population changes in Ireland 1861–1881', *Economic History Review*, 2nd ser., 17 (1964–5), 301–21.

largely bypassed the Province. Further, although research on Counties Mayo and Fermanagh draw a strong connection between the decline of domestic handspinning after 1825 and the severity of the Famine's impact in the north and west, we know little about the connections between the Famine and linen producers east of the Bann.[4] There has been no attempt to connect Famine-induced demographic changes to divergent paths of capitalist development in the Ulster linen industry.

This chapter addresses these gaps at the microhistorical or regional level. Pat Hudson argues that regions emerge in the course of analysis.[5] The parish of Tullylish provides an ideal context for regional investigation of the Famine, since distinct subregional patterns of economic development had emerged by the end of the eighteenth century. Given the unevenness of industrial capitalist development in Tullylish, questions regarding the ways potato blight intersected with the linen industry are addressed. Following Joan Vincent, such questions require that we 'refine the categories of the suffering' by giving priority to class, gender and age rather than the 'landlord/other dichotomy'.[6]

THE POOR LAW AND CREATION OF POOR LAW UNIONS IN TULLYLISH

A state system of poor relief was introduced into Ireland in 1838 after prolonged debate on the nature of poverty in Ireland, its connection with overpopulation and the most effective means to alleviate it. After 1839, Ireland was divided into new administrative units called poor law unions, each consisting of various electoral divisions where rates were struck and raised. Unions consisted of a number of townlands, each with its own workhouse. These opened their doors in 1845 – just in time for the Famine – and were built to accommodate approximately 100,000 paupers.[7]

At this time, the parish of Tullylish was divided between two Unions: Banbridge and Lurgan.[8] The elected Board of Guardians in Banbridge Union included many prominent bleachers, drapers and manufacturers including Samuel Law, Isaac

---

4 Eric L. Almquist, 'Mayo and Beyond: Land, Domestic Industry and Rural Transformation in the Irish West', Ph.D. diss., Boston University, 1977; Joan Vincent, 'Linen in the Irish northwest: unfinished business, or lived experience in the 1830s', in Marilyn Cohen (ed.), *The Warp of Ulster's Past: Interdisciplinary Perspectives on the Irish Linen Industry, 1700–1920* (New York 1996); Joan Vincent, *The Culture and Politics of the Irish Famine: Fermanagh 1836–56* (forthcoming).   5 Pat Hudson, 'The regional perspective', in Pat Hudson (ed.), *Regions and Industries* (Cambridge 1986), p. 3.   6 Joan Vincent, 'Culture, history, place: local discourses and historical anthropologies', Paper presented at the annual meetings of the American Anthropological Association, New Orleans, 1990, 16.   7 Ibid., p. 107. 8 Banbridge Union included the thirteen townlands of Tullyrain, Tullylish, Moyallon, Loughans, Mullabrack, Drumiller, Lenederg, Drumaran, Knocknagor, Drumhorc, Lisnafiffy, Coose and Drumnascamph, that comprised the industrial mid-section along the Bann and the southern agricultural townlands. Lurgan Union included Ballydugan, Ballymacanallon, Ballynagarrick, Bleary, Clare, and Ballylough, all populated with handloom weavers oriented toward Lurgan and Portadown.

Stoney and John Christy from Tullylish. In Lurgan the original Board included Joseph Christy and Thomas Uprichard along with other local linen manufacturers.[9]

After 1847, the Poor Law became the major organ for poor relief during the Famine. The Temporary Relief Act allowed for the provision of soup kitchens in 1847 and outdoor relief regulated in part by the Quarter Acre or Gregory Clause.[10] Ireland's poverty was perceived to pose a considerable threat to British prosperity, acting as a sieve on British revenues. The aim of the Poor Law was limited to relieving symptom (destitution) rather than cause (poverty), and it was hoped that the extension of the Poor Law to Ireland would facilitate social engineering, meaning both an economic transition from subsistence potato farming to capitalist agriculture and a cultural transition in the social life and character of the Irish people. Irish paupers were, therefore, treated more harshly than the English, with no 'right' to relief and no outdoor relief.[11]

The prevailing ideology regarding Irish overpopulation, underdevelopment and poverty constrained the interpretation of the potato blight and subsequent famine. The government invoked only temporary relief measures to meet the exceptional distress. Providentialism, Malthusian ideas and political economy combined to generate a powerful ideology that interpreted the Irish Famine as a divinely ordained and inevitable social revolution. Debate centered on how best to relieve starvation among the poor while simultaneously discouraging 'a culture of dependency' and ensuring that the stigmatized Irish landlords would uphold their 'moral responsibilities'.[12] British public opinion was in favour of shifting the burden of Irish poverty away from the British treasury and onto the shoulders of Irish property. The administration of the Poor Law, with its emphasis on local responsibility through local taxation was regarded as the ideal mechanism to accomplish this shift.[13]

THE FAMINE IN TULLYLISH: A GENERAL OVERVIEW

The failure of the potato crop was partial in Ireland in 1845, general in 1846, and absolute in 1847. In County Down, by 1845, 46–50 per cent of the potato crop was affected with blight. In 1846, reports from both the Banbridge and Lurgan Boards of Guardians indicate that the potato crop had failed in their unions.[14] In Banbridge Union near Gilford, one-sixth of the district was planted with potatoes in 1844, one-fifth in 1845, and one-eighth in 1846, due to the high price and scarcity of seed.

9 (PRONI), B.G6/A/1, Minute Book, Banbridge Board of Guardians, 8 April 1839, to 25 July 1842; BG.22/A/1, Minute Book, Lurgan Board of Guardians, 22 February 1839, to 18 January 1842. 10 Ibid., pp. 116–17. 11 Christine Kinealy, 'The Poor Law during the great famine: an administration in crisis', in E. Margaret Crawford (ed.), *Famine: The Irish Experience 900–1900* (Edinburgh 1989); 'The role of the Poor Law during the famine', in Cathal Poirteir (ed.), *The Great Irish Famine* (Dublin 1995), pp. 104–6. 12 Peter Gray, 'Ideology and the famine', in Poirteir (ed.), *The Great Irish Famine*, pp. 95–6. 13 Kinealy, 'Poor Law', p. 112. 14 Daly, *The Famine*, p. 54.

In the electoral division of Tullylish in Lurgan Union, one-eighth was planted in potatoes in 1844, one-seventh in 1845 and one-tenth in 1846 when turnips and oats were sown to replace expensive potatoes.[15]

In Ulster, the south and west fared worst during the Famine due to high population pressure, subdivision of holdings, increasing reliance on the potato and narrowing economic opportunities in agriculture and rural industry after the elimination of handspinning. Intermediate levels of mortality were felt in Tyrone and Armagh. The northeast, a model of Anglocentric (and Anglo-dependent) progress, possessed the combination of a capitalist linen industry and a majority of Protestants, exempting it from prevailing stereotypes of lazy, Popish, potato-dependent peasants.[16] This region, with its stronger more diversified economic base, diet, better communications and food retailing system was generally better insulated from the Famine.

The connection between potato blight and famine varied according to social class with 'the great shoals of corpses swept into the Famine abyss ... primarily those of cottiers and labourers'.[17] Cottiers and cottier/weavers in the one to five acre range, who had for long provided cheap labour for manufacturers, were the most affected by the failure of the potato crop.[18] Holders of between one and five acres, who were so prevalent in pre-Famine Ulster, declined from 44.9 per cent of the population in 1841 to 15.5 per cent in 1851. Those who had a more substantial subsistence base with five to fifteen acres, fell from 36.6 per cent of the total to 33.6 per cent.[19] These were the better off linen weavers concentrated near Lurgan and in northeast Antrim clinging to independence.[20]

Liam Kennedy argues that, 'the severity of the Great Famine is best understood in terms of the impact of a natural disaster (potato blight and the subsequent destruction of the major food source) on weakened economic structures'.[21] This useful insight generates theoretical questions to guide this investigation of the relationship between the Famine and a capitalist linen industry in Tullylish. Since conceptions of gender are always integral to economic structures, I investigate how gender mediated the Famine's impact. What role did the Famine play in the uneven paths of capitalist development in Tullylish/Banbridge and Tullylish/Lurgan? What role did local economic structures play in the duration of the Famine? Since employment opportunities favoured females, how did gender affect the connection between natural disaster, internal migration and economic structures in Tullylish?

15 (PRONI), 1A/50/86, Constabulary Reports. The author wishes to thank Gerard McAtasney for this reference.   16 Christopher Morash, *Writing the Irish Famine* (Oxford 1995).   17 Liam Kennedy, 'The rural economy 1820–1914', in Liam Kennedy and Philip Ollerenshaw (eds), *An Economic History of Ulster 1820–1939* (Manchester 1985), p. 29.   18 Oliver MacDonagh, 'The Irish famine emigration to the United States', *Perspectives in American History*, 10 (1976), 357–446.   19 Ibid., pp. 357–446.   20 Emily J. Boyle, 'The Economic Development of the Irish Linen Industry', Ph. D. diss., The Queen's University of Belfast, 1977, p. 71.   21 Kennedy, 'Rural Economy,' p. 29.

How were middle-class Victorian cultural conceptions of gender affected by ideological explanations of Irish poverty and its alleviation during the Famine?

The records of the Boards of Guardians in Banbridge and Lurgan reveal the distinct economic characteristics of their Unions and their divergent paths of industrial capitalist development. In Tullylish, capital investment in mills was concentrated along the Bann in Banbridge Union where the transition to mill-based spinning had profoundly altered the organization of production. Here industrial capitalist structures were strengthening based on the exploitation of a growing proletariat. The weaving of fine linen cloth, such as damask or cambric, by dispersed petty commodity producers in Tullylish/Lurgan remained under the control of putting-out manufacturers usually based in Lurgan. Since fine linen weaving was not yet mechanized, in Tullylish/Lurgan, the relationship between fragmentation of holdings and linen weaving continued from the late eighteenth century. Landlords seeking to profit from leasing small high priced plots, let a large proportion of their land directly to weaving households eliminating middlemen. Since Tullylish/Lurgan remained enmeshed in this proto-industrial system, farms were smaller than the national average through the 1860s.[22] Comparison of the Board of Guardian records for Tullylish indicate that while many in Tullylish suffered and died, proletarians residing in industrializing Banbridge Union were better insulated by employment in mills and the provision of housing by employers than petty commodity producers in Lurgan Union. In fact, the population along the Bann was growing rapidly in certain areas at mid-century as the aggregate census figures reveal. Table 5 summarizes the population trends for the parish as a whole and for the Poor Law Unions separately. It can be seen that while growth slowed due to death and migration, Tullylish as a whole gained 740 inhabitants between 1841–51 when the population reached its nineteenth-century peak. Population figures remain high through 1861 reflecting the rapid growth of the linen industry. Of the 740, 61.6 per cent were female reflecting increased opportunities for female employment.

When we compare Tullylish's two electoral divisions, all of the gain occurred in the electoral division of Tullylish in Banbridge Union which gained 887 individuals, 62 per cent of whom were female. Most moved to Gilford to take advantage of employment opportunities at Dunbar McMaster & Company. In contrast, the electoral division of Tullylish in Lurgan Union lost 101 individuals during this time, the vast majority of whom (71.3 per cent) were female. Tullylish/Lurgan's population had reached its peak in the Pre-famine period of 1841.

When we probe beneath these aggregate figures to examine gender and townland differences, divergent internal migration patterns caused by the Famine are revealed. In Tullylish/Banbridge, the skyrocketing population of Gilford between 1841–51 from 643 to 2814 (see table 4) accounts for most of the increase. Although females predominated, the relative proportions of males (43.6 per cent) and females (56.3

---

22 W.H. Crawford, 'A handloom weaving community in County Down', *Ulster Folklife*, 39 (1993), pp. 3–4.

Table 5: Demographic change in Tullylish, 1821–91

Union	1821	1831	1841	1851	1861	1871	1881	1891
Tullylish Total	9259	10501	12660	13400	12908	11154	9228	7903
Males	4532	5161	6143	6427	6168	5244	4340	3754
Females	4727	5340	6517	6973	6740	6241	4888	4149
Inhabited Houses	1687	1850	2142	2181	2378	2366	1954	1765
Persons per House	5.5	5.7	5.9	6.1	5.4	*	4.7	4.5
Tullylish/Banbridge	–	–	7049	7936	7594	6859	5285	4923
Males	–	–	3388	3721	3563	3154	2439	2304
Females	–	–	3661	4211	4031	3075	2846	2619
Inhab. Houses	–	–	1232	1287	1446	1314	1110	1092
Persons per House	–	–	5.7	6.2	*	*	4.8	4.5
Tullylish/Lurgan	–	–	5217	5116	4969	4295	3943	2980
Males	–	–	2563	2531	2433	2090	1901	1450
Females	–	–	2654	2582	2536	2205	2042	1530
Inhab. Houses	–	–	897	914	981	852	844	673
Persons per House	–	–	5.8	5.6	*	*	4.7	4.4

Sources: Census of Ireland, 1821–1891, Co. Down, PRONI; Abstract of the Population of Ireland, vol. 14 (1822); Return of the Several Counties in Ireland as Enumerated in 1831, vol. 39 (1833). *Statistics based only on the number of inhabited houses.

per cent) suggest both sexes were moving to the town in large numbers. Of the fourteen townlands in Tullylish/Banbridge, only four – Coose, Drumaran, Drumna-scamph, and Lenaderg – had modest population increases during the Famine. All of these townlands flank the River Bann between Gilford and Banbridge and were the sites of long-established centralized mills. An expanding Milltown, the site of a large bleachgreen, absorbed 22 persons and another 40 moved to neighbouring Drumnascamph. Since the town of Gilford was located partly in Drumaran and partly in Loughans, we can assume that Gilford's gain spilled over into surrounding Drumaran explaining the small 15 person increase. The other townlands, especially those in the south of the parish, lost population during the Famine.

Turning to densely populated Tullylish/Lurgan, where production of fine linen by petty commodity producers prevailed, three of five townlands gained population during the Famine. Domestic handloom weaving of fine damask and cambric remained prevalent until the 1880s generating a gendered pattern of internal migration. With the exception of Bleary, which gained 88 men and women, all of the other townlands, including the two with modest gains, lost women. Ballydugan for example, which gained population during the Famine, absorbed 44 men but lost 21 women. Ballymacanallon, a townland flanking Gilford, lost 25 women but gained 10 men. Finally, Clare lost the most population during the Famine – 125 women and 90 men.

These gendered migration patterns suggest that the androcentric organization of handloom weaving households provided male weavers with somewhat more insulation. Although after 1825, increasing numbers of women were employed as handloom weavers providing essential wages for their households, female labour was regarded as more expendable, especially since employment opportunities for them in the nearby spinning mills were increasing.[23] Thus, more women were proletarianized as blight weakened the ability of weaving households to partially reproduce themselves by growing potatoes on small holdings.

An indirect source of information relating to the demographic effects of the Famine on children in Tullylish are the yearly Reports of the Commissioners of National Education in Ireland. These Reports, which began in 1834, list for each school the number of children on the rolls indicating which schools gained and lost children in the Famine years between 1846–9 (figures for 1850–1 are missing). Use of this data requires caution since each entry in a school's register did not necessarily represent a new distinct child. Any child who had been absent for thirteen consecutive weeks was removed from the books, and if he or she applied for readmission, then he or she would be enrolled as a new pupil under a new roll number. Being 'struck off' the register in this way was common and, in some instances, the same child was admitted as a new pupil twice or more times in a year artificially swelling the enrollment figures. Under famine conditions, it is reasonable to expect that frequent lengthy absences from school would increase.

Decreases in the number of children on the rolls suggest that children died, moved or were withdrawn due to illness or the need for children's paid and unpaid labour. Table 6 shows that during the peak Famine years, most of the Tullylish schools showed some decline in enrollment except the Moyallon Schools, located in a prosperous Quaker-dominated townland, and the Gilford Mill Schools which show a spectacular increase. By 1849, however, school enrollments in those schools located in Banbridge Union began to recover. The three schools in Lurgan Union: Ballynagarrick, Ballylough, and Clare still show fewer children in 1849 than in 1846 suggesting the greater likelihood of disrupted schooling among handloom weavers' children whose working conditions and schooling were not yet regulated under the Factory Acts.

The decline in enrollment in the Gilford No. 1 school, also located in expanding Gilford, requires explanation since Gilford's population was expanding so rapidly. Falling enrollment figures at this school were due to the opening of the Gilford Mill Schools in 1846 rather than Famine-related causes. The new Gilford Mill Schools had both a fine reputation and catered to the needs of halftimers, a sizeable propor-

23 Anne McKernan, 'War, gender, and industrial innovation: recruiting women weavers in early nineteenth-century Ireland', *Journal of Social History*, 28, no. 1 (1995), 109–24; Brenda Collins, 'The loom, the land and the market place: women weavers and the family economy in late nineteenth and early twentieth century Ireland', in Marilyn Cohen (ed.), *The Warp*.

Table 6: Demographic change in Tullylish during the Famine as revealed by
school enrollment figures, 1846–9

School/PL Union	1846	1847	1848	1849
Banbridge Union				
Bann (Mixed)	309	271	261	325
Moyallon	218	227	242	222
Male	96	110	110	117
Female	122	117	132	105
Gilford No. 1	289	215	173	200
Male	200	121	115	141
Female	89	94	58	59
Gilford Mill	189	410	701	554
Male	60	175	250	233
Female	66	132	206	99
Infant	63	103	245	222
Lurgan Union				
Ballynagarrick(Mixed)	204	105	157	166
Ballylough (Mixed)	130	123	–	111
Clare (Mixed)	135	111	119	127

Sources: Thirteenth Report of the Commissioners of National Education (Ireland) for the year 1846, vol. 17 (1847); Fourteenth Report ... for the year 1847, vol. 29 (1847–8); Fifteenth Report ... for the year 1848, vol. 23 (1849); and Sixteenth Report ... for the year 1849, vol. 25 (1850).

tion of the school-going population in Gilford/Dunbarton. The majority of these halftimers were young girls, reflecting the preference for young female labour in spinning mills. This is reflected in female enrollment at Gilford No. 1 which decreased drastically between 1847–8 while the male student population declined only slightly.

THE FAMINE AND CENTRALIZED INDUSTRY: TULLYLISH/BANBRIDGE

The records indicating most directly the extent of suffering in the Tullylish region are the actual workhouse records for the Banbridge and Lurgan Unions that list the numbers admitted, residing in the workhouses, and deaths on a weekly basis, along with comments on conditions, disease and the strain on resources. These data are tabulated in appendices 2a and 2b.

Looking first at appendix 2a relating to Banbridge Union, the data reveals that between 31 October 1846 and 6 October 1849, the effects of the Famine were most severe in 1847–8. By 1849, both new admissions and deaths had dropped dramati-

cally even though the average number in the Workhouse was still high both in absolute terms and relative to its 800 person capacity. While more than twice the number
of people were admitted in 1847 than in 1848, in the latter year more people could
expect to die in the workhouse prior to discharge. These figures and the comments
made by guardians indicate that while Famine-related distress did not bypass the
Banbridge Union, strengthening economic structures shortened and lessened its
destructive consequences.

The guardians' comments support current perspectives on death during the
Famine linking death to weakened immune systems and the spread of infectious
disease as opposed to actual starvation. Provisions for dealing with the sick in Ireland during this period were handled by two administratively distinct institutions
that became interdependent during the Famine – the Medical Charities including
dispensaries, permanent fever hospitals, and county fever hospitals, and the Poor
Law which included workhouses, infirmaries and fever hospitals.[24] Both medical
officers and guardians were alarmed by the spread of 'fever', meaning typhus and
typhoid and its 'inseparable companion' dysentery rendered more virulent under
famine conditions.[25] Attempts were made to separate dysentery patients and their
clothing from fever patients to reduce its lethal spread among inmates. While medical officers knew that fever was contagious and linked to both poverty and potato
crop failure, they had limited understanding of how or why. Contemporary methods of disease control and sanitary standards – isolation of the infected, thorough
cleansing of the body and clothes, fumigation and limewashing of housing, and
controlling population movement often proved impossible to maintain in chaotic
conditions.[26]

Christine Kinealy argues that many guardians responded to the distress in their
unions swiftly and compassionately. When work-houses were full, guardians provided other forms of relief such as admittance, free meals in the workhouse, providing food to take home and admitting parts of families.[27] To extend the provision of
workhouse relief, guardians had the power to erect temporary sheds and 'galleries'
in all parts of the workhouse where additional accommodation could be afforded.
Since outdoor relief was prohibited by the Poor Law, guardians faced with unrelenting
demand for workhouse relief, often provided it in 'ways categorically prohibited by
the legislature'.[28] Finally, in addition to the dire situation at the Workhouse, guardians addressed the needs of local Fever Committees and hospitals, such as in the
electoral divisions of Tandragee and Dromore, that were reporting high rates of
infectious disease.

In November 1846, a committee was formed in Banbridge Workhouse to estab-

24 Peter Frogatt, 'The response of the medical profession to the great famine', in E. Margaret Crawford
(ed.), *Famine: The Irish Experience 900–1900* (Edinburgh 1989), pp. 135–6.   25 Laurence M. Geary,
'Famine, fever and the bloody flux', in Poirteir (ed.), *The Great Irish Famine*, pp. 75–7.   26 Frogatt,
'Response', pp. 139, 150.   27 Kinealy, *This Great Calamity*, p. 107.   28 Kinealy, 'Poor Law', p. 111.

lish a soup kitchen by subscription in one of the probationary wards. This scheme was rejected by the Poor Law Commissioners because it would interfere with existing meal arrangements in the Workhouse and 'congregate together a number of distressed people to partake of food'.[29] In January 1947, the Banbridge Workhouse was so over-crowded that desperate people were being turned away and temporary space was required. The debilitated condition of those denied entry prompted the guardians to supply each with food consisting of 'dinner and one half pound of bread' not permitted under the Irish Poor Relief Act. The guardians were 'convinced that at this particular crisis of distress ... Poor Law Commissioners will not object when the motions which actuate the Board in pursuing this course are taken into consideration by them nor will the auditor in examining of the half yearly accounts disallow the expense'. They were mistaken, however, and the Commissioners denied their request on legal grounds. The guardians nevertheless resolved to continue the practice.[30]

The level of suffering in Banbridge Union still was not great enough for all of its electoral divisions to be included under the Temporary Relief Act of 1847. This Act called into operation the formation of working committees for relief by electoral divisions. Grants were given to distribute free rations or at the cost of 2½d. per ration during the period 24 May to 15 August. In Ireland, 1,677 of the total 2,049 electoral divisions were under the Act. In northeast Ulster there was relatively little expenditure on public works; in Banbridge Union, of the twenty-three electoral divisions only thirteen (Tullylish was not included) were under the Act.[31]

During the years 1847–9, Minute Book notes indicate that Banbridge Workhouse policies on work by inmates reflected both the structural dominance of the linen industry in the region's economy and an ideological perspective on poverty that stigmatized claims by the poor for assistance. Since hard work was linked with morality and respectable gender identity, paupers were seen to require a steady diet of it to improve their character. Banbridge guardians maintained that if 'prevented from carrying on active and unremitting industry in the House we will be wholly unable to keep the establishment from being crowded with a lazy, idle and demoralized population'.[32]

Workhouse inmates were engaged in a variety of regionally important manufacturing tasks including spinning flax, winding yarn, weaving cloth and sewing calico to lessen the burden of the poor on the rate payers and Workhouse resources. If they refused, as did Sarah Macken or Isabella Mathews, they were discharged. Supplies

29 (PRONI), BG.6/A/6, Extracts from the Minutes of the Board of Guardians of Banbridge Poor Law Union November 1846–June 1847, pp. 28, 34.   30 (PRONI), BG.6/A/7 Extracts from the Minutes of the Banbridge Board of Guardians, January–October 1847.   31 H.C. *First Report of the Relief Commissions Together with Treasury Minute of 10 March 1847*, vol. xvii (1847) ; and *Fifth, Sixth and Seventh Report of the Relief Commissions Constituted Under the Act 10 Vi ct. c. 7. and Correspondence Connected Therewith*, vol. xxix (1847–8).   32 (PRONI), BG.6/A/10 Extracts from the Minutes of the Banbridge Board of Guardians, 2 March 1850.

ordered include flax and yarn purchased from F.W. Hayes & Company in Seapatrick, looms purchased from James Hutchenson, and a hackler was hired to dress the flax.[33] In April, 1848, handbills were 'issued by the Board offering to Apprentice out 50 boys and 50 girls, inmates of the workhouse, to weaving and other trades for such period as may be agreed on not less than 3 years' to lessen the burden of paupers on the ratepayers.[34]

The practice of using the labour of pauper or charity children to extend household production of linen yarn and cloth extended back at least until the mid-eighteenth century.[35] A source of available apprentices for local residents or linen manufacturers in Banbridge Union was pauper children residing at the Lurgan Workhouse. In contrast to England, there was no statutory provision to allow Irish Boards of Guardians to apprentice children limiting their ability to intervene on behalf of a child. Although securing positions for girls was far more difficult than for boys elsewhere in Ireland, in northeast Ulster this was not the case.[36] In Lurgan Union, due to the prevalence of domestic weaving, many girl paupers were discharged from the workhouse to be taught winding bobbins, sometimes weaving and spinning yarn on spinning wheels. Pauper boys were also occasionally taught winding and frequently taught weaving.[37]

These strategies by the Banbridge guardians to keep inmates at productive work reflected laissez faire doctrines dictating that workhouses in Ireland should be self-supporting establishments rather than drains on the local ratepayers or the British treasury. Reflecting local entrepreneurial spirit, the Banbridge guardians eagerly sought to establish a profitable woollen manufacture within this linen-dominated region. They maintained that the use of cheap dependent pauper labour would not interfere with the employment of 'independent labour' or create unfair competitive advantage. In their view, the managerial strategies of workhouses should support capitalism by promoting industry, supplying cheap labour, and demanding a disciplined resident population imbued with the work ethic.[38] Again, the Poor Law Commissioners disagreed.

Although middle-class Victorian conceptions of gender firmly linked breadwinning to masculinity and domesticity to femininity, poor men and women were always expected to work hard, albeit in gender specific ways. Victorian cultural conceptions of respectable masculinity categorically excluded able-bodied male paupers. However, since dependence and motherhood were integral to respectable femininity, the treatment of able-bodied women with children requires further analysis.

33 (PRONI) BG.6/A/7,8, Minute Books of the Banbridge Board of Guardians, July 1847–February 1848, and July 1848–February 1849.   34 (PRONI), BG.6/A/9, Minute Book of the Banbridge Board of Guardians, December 1848–October 1849.   35 Joseph Robins, *The Lost Children: A Study of Charity Children in Ireland*, 1700–1900 (Dublin 1980), p. 68.   36 Ibid., 240–1.   37 (PRONI), BG.22/A/2B and BG.22/A/3, Minute Books, Lurgan Board of Guardians.   38 (PRONI), BG.6/A/10 Extracts from the Banbridge Union, May 1849–October 1850, pp. 720–1.

During the Famine, when the economy and character of the Irish people were believed to require profound alteration, gender distinctions relating to appropriate work roles and moral dilemmas over the implications of employing working class mothers outside the home were temporarily suspended when convenient. Although caring for children was central to middle-class conceptions of femininity, more pressing concerns with pauperization and increasing rates levelled the able-bodied poor regardless of sex and regardless of whether women were single or married, deserted or widowed, with or without children.

The Master at Banbridge Workhouse, for example, was ordered by the Poor Law Commissioners to 'employ the able-bodied women in any way he may deem proper' including the arduous and despised task of breaking stones. Although the commissioners at first were doubtful whether grinding corn at the corn mill was suitable work for women, the guardians ultimately were 'unanimously of the opinion that the employing of able-bodied women in the grinding of corn for their own use is not a severe or labourious employment nor likely to be injurious to their health'. After the permission of outdoor relief was granted in January 1848, the Banbridge guardians continued to deliberate over the duration of relief to able-bodied widows with two children and whether women whose husbands had been transported were legally entitled to outdoor relief. Women who were deserted temporarily or permanently were not, despite their hardship, considered equivalent to widows with two or more children and were denied outdoor relief.[39]

Given the prevalence of women in this region who migrated into Banbridge Union in search of employment, guardians periodically in 1848 and 1849 encouraged their emigration to lessen the expense of their upkeep on the ratepayers. Early in 1848, the Master of Banbridge Workhouse suggested that guardians try to reduce the number of young unemployed women in the Workhouse by invoking the 18th Section of the Irish Poor Relief Amendment. He was subsequently ordered to make a list of all girls in the Workhouse who were willing to emigrate and to write to the guardians of each electoral division requesting whether they would consent to a rate for that purpose. The active encouragement of emigration to Canada and Australia from the Banbridge Workhouse persisted until 1850.[40]

39 (PRONI), BG.6/A/8, Extracts from the Minutes of the Board of Guardians of Banbridge Poor Law Union, July 1848–February 1849, pp. 257, 276; BG.6/A/8 Extracts from the Minutes of the Board of Guardians of Banbridge Poor Law Union, July 1848–October 1849, pp. 8, 222, 357; BG.6/A/9, December 1848–October 1849, pp. 31, 47, 59–60, 80, 174–5.   40 (PRONI),BG.6/A/10, Extracts from the Minutes of the Board of Guardians of Banbridge Poor Law Union, May 1849–October 1850, p. 733.

LANDLORD STRATEGIES DURING THE FAMINE: THE JOHNSTON ESTATE

Since 1843, Irish landlords had been liable for paying rates on all property valued under four pounds, the tenant being exempt. Amendments to the Poor Law during the Famine attempted to make Irish property, particularly the stigmatized Irish landlord, responsible for Irish poverty.

Joan Vincent argues that most of the gentry in County Fermanagh were enmeshed in a 'weblike culture of dearth' that operated to avert periodic starvation on their estates prior to the Famine. Gentry families were 'part and parcel of demands and expectations' operating at the level of the locality. During times of distress, landlords set up local relief committees, organized private charity, postponed gale days and reduced rents.[41] What evidence do we have relating to this 'culture of dearth' during the Famine in Tullylish?

By 1847, the last Johnston, Sir William Johnston Bart., a bachelor, had been dead for six years leaving his estate to his two widowed sisters Marianne Burgess and Catherine Ormsby. On 30 October 1847, the Banbridge Board of Guardians wrote to Mr Franklin McCreight, estate agent to the late Sir William Johnston, for payment of rates valued under four pounds per annum that he had refused to pay in violation of the 1843 Act. Although estate agents complied in February, the Poor Law rates struck for the Johnston estate rose sharply between 1845–50. For example in 1848, poor rates were £11.10s.1d.; in 1849, they were £17.5s.; and £18.7s.5d in 1850, the latter rate struck on the Demesne and 'smallholdings of tenants.' In 1847, the Poor Rates on Johnston's Gilford demesne and castle were £5.18s.9d., and in that year McCreight listed a 'voluntary assessment for the poor' at £5.1s.3½d suggesting that landlords Burgess and Ormsby recognized their charitable responsibility to the poor in the locale.[42]

Rent Rolls for the Johnston estate in the heart of Tullylish/Banbridge for the Famine years provide further evidence relating to landlord strategies. Pre-Famine rentals indicate that it was not uncommon for Johnston's tenants to fall into arrears and sometimes tenants were perpetually in arrears for small sums. In 1844, nearly half (35) of Burgess and Ormsby's 72 tenants had arrears brought forward from the previous year. In November 1846, landlords Burgess and Ormsby collected rents from 72 tenants, 16 of whom lived in tenements in the town of Gilford. Although only 6 tenants were currently in arrears and served with eviction notices, 67 of the 72 had arrears brought forward from 1845. Arrears in the amount of one year's rent for one year were tolerated with ejectment notices served if tenants did not substantially meet their rent obligations the following year.[43] The 1849 rent roll is unique

41 Joan Vincent, 'A political orchestration of the Irish famine: County Fermanagh, May 1847', in Marilyn Silverman and Philip H. Gulliver (eds), *Approaching the Past: Historical Anthropology through Irish Case Studies* (New York 1992), pp. 84–5.   42 (PRONI), D.1594/59, Rental of the Estate of Sir William Johnston's Gilford Estates, 1846.   43 (PRONI), D.1594/59 Burgess Estate Papers, Rental of the Late Sir William Johnston's Gilford Estates, 1846.

since it lists arrears brought forward from 1847 and the amount due for two years, 1848-9. This suggests that during the most severe years of the Famine, landlords Burgess and Ormsby were prepared to make many allowances or reductions in rent due to distress.

They also were willing to extend part time employment to many tenants. An 1849 wages book for Gilford Castle indicates that weekly wages were paid to a number of male and female workers whose number ranged from thirteen in June to seventy-eight in September. Workers were engaged in a variety of tasks, some of which were associated with flax cultivation. The vast majority of those employed at Gilford Castle were women who worked part-time, as little as half a day in a given week.[44] Since only one such wage book exists, we can only speculate whether the provision of part-time employment by landlords Burgess and Ormsby increased during the Famine to better enable some tenants to meet their rent obligations.

Although Burgess and Ormsby appear to be part of the local web of obligations, during the Famine they did serve numerous tenants with eviction notices. The case of Joseph Adamson will illustrate since he was a long term tenant whose original lease for three lives commenced in 1774 when he leased 10 acres 2 roods in Loughans for the yearly rent of £6.15s. Due to the expanding linen industry, by 1795, the value of Adamson's holding had risen to £16.4s. In 1840, Adamson occupied a smaller holding of 8 acres 3 roods and 11 perches at will and paid an increased yearly rent of £9.5s.2d. This increase was apparently difficult for him to meet – in both 1840 and 1844 Adamson was in arrears for the previous year's rent. In the latter year, he paid only £17.1s. of the £18.10s.4d owed, but was not served with eviction papers. In 1846, although Adamson was in arrears for rents due in 1845, he paid the total amount of rent due, £35.6s.10d. During the peak Famine years between 1846–9, Joseph Adamson died. His widow, in arrears for half of her 1847 rent, could only pay £6 of the two year rental of £17.3s.2d and was served with eviction papers. Observations recorded on the Adamsons of Loughans by estate agents McCreight and Carleton state simply that, 'arrears are caused by poor people. I have served them with notice to quit. There is no distress on premises'.[45]

The Adamsons were not alone. By 1849, the number of tenants currently in arrears on the Gilford Estate had risen to 32 of 75 (excluding 13 tenements in Gilford town), 14 of whom still carried rental arrears from 1847. On 14 June, 1849, 6 tenants were served with 'ejectment decrees', and 20 more tenants (25 per cent of the total) were served with notices to quit in that year.[46] Most (17) of these lived in rural Drumaran, and, significantly, none resided in the town of Gilford, revealing that proletarians living in the town were better insulated than small farmers in the sur-

44 (PRONI), D.1252/20/8, Dickson Estate, 1849 Wages Book.   45 (PRONI), D.1594/76, Burgess Documents, 1795 Rent Roll of Sir William Johnston, Bart.; T.1007/237, Burgess Documents, 1814, 1844 Rentals of the Estate of the Co-heiresses of the late Sir William Johnston, Bart; D.1594/59, 1846, 1849 Rental of the Late Sir William Johnston's Gilford Estate.   46 (PRONI), D.1252/20/8 Dickson Estate, 1849 Wages Book.

rounding townland. In April, 1850, 12 notices to quit were served, another 11 in
July, and 6 in 1851.[47] Observations by estate agents reveal that when 'arrears are
caused by poor people' with no other signs of 'distress,' notices were served to quit.
However, cases showing distress, such as the orphans of the late John Hill, invoked
pity and the agents suggested that an allowance be made. Landlord Ormsby complied with an allowance of £10. Twenty-eight additional tenants were granted allowances of small sums deducted from their rent.[48] Thus, when we add those who could
not pay their rent to those who were granted allowances, we can conclude that the
majority (57 per cent) of tenants on the Johnston estate suffered some hardship
during the Famine.

By 1851, Gilford Estate rentals reveal that Famine-related disruption had abated.
Although 15 of 83 tenants were in arrears for their 1850 rent, only 8 remained so in
1851. Although no eviction notices were served, allowances were still necessary in
41 cases, suggesting that Famine-related ramifications continued at least until 1852.[49]
Evidence from Johnston estate rentals suggest that landlords in regions dominated
by the linen industry were less inclined than those elsewhere in Ireland to clear
their estates of smallholders and consolidate holdings since employment opportunities as weavers still enabled many small tenants to pay high rents either fully or
partially. Rather than a decrease in the number of tenants and smallholders between
1846–51, on this rapidly industrializing estate, their proportion increased.[50]

THE FAMINE AND PROTO-INDUSTRY: TULLYLISH/LURGAN

Amartya Sen argues that Famine is largely explained by the inability of groups to
purchase existing food due to inflated prices.[51] Since blight severely reduced the
quantity of food produced on small plots, farmer/weavers would be forced to purchase more of their food at inflated prices. In Lurgan Union, concern over the state
of the potato crop was voiced in November 1845, when guardians stated that the
quantity of potatoes was underaverage and a considerable amount injured by blight.
By April of 1846, the effects of blight, epidemic disease and cultural disruption
exemplified by deserted women and children were pressing heavily upon the Workhouse. Guardians were actively looking into substitutes for potatoes, such as Indian
cornmeal, to feed the growing number inmates and ways to expand the capacity of
the Workhouse, especially in the nursery and female apartments. Workhouse diets
consisting in 1844 of oatmeal, buttermilk, broth and potatoes, consisted in 1846 of
oatmeal, buttermilk, broth and white bread. The number of inmates with fever was
rising sharply generating alarm over crowded conditions in the fever hospital.[52]

47 (PRONI), D.1252/20/10 Dickson Estate, Day Book of Costs of Gilford Estate, 1849–1901.   48
(PRONI), D.1594/59, Burgess Estate Papers, Rental of the Gilford Estate ending 1 November 1949.
49 (PRONI) D.1594/189, Burgess Estate, Rental of the Gilford Estate, Property of Captain Ormsby
and Another.   50 (PRONI), D.1594/59, Burgess Estate Papers, Rental of the Gilford Estate ending 1
November 1849.   51 Amartya Sen, *Poverty and Famine* (Oxford, 1981).   52 (PRONI), BG.22/A/4,

Unlike the situation in Tullylish/Banbridge, the electoral division of Tullylish in Lurgan Union was included under the Temporary Relief Act. The maximum number of people so relieved in Tullylish/Lurgan in any one day was 712; 244 were still on the list when the rations stopped.[53] The Workhouse at Lurgan was more severely overcrowded during the Famine, and the prevalence of epidemic disease and death were widespread. During the Famine years, additional space was needed in the Portadown Hospital, the distillery and a temporary workhouse was built along with temporary fever sheds to relieve overcrowding in the permanent fever hospital.[54]

The minutes of the Lurgan Board of Guardians during the Famine reveal the extent of mortality in the Workhouse and region due to epidemic disease. By January 1847, the number of deaths in the workhouse due to epidemic disease was so high that the Poor Law Commissioners wrote expressing their concern and regret. During the week of 16 January 1847, 55 inmates died, 35 of whom were under the age of 15. Workhouse physician Dr Bell's explanation points to a combination of economic and cultural causes – the high cost of provisions, the 'great dislike of going to the workhouse among the lower classes', and the desire to be buried in a coffin by many who could not otherwise afford this expense. He maintained that many who arrived at the workhouse were already dead, close to death or died within 24 hours of being admitted.[55]

Sanitary conditions in the Workhouse, as described by the medical officer, were so poor, and knowledge about the spread of epidemic disease so limited that those fever patients admitted who were not close to death died soon after admission. In the Lurgan Workhouse, the number of corpses on a weekly basis was extremely high during the peak Famine years. The Chaplain, who visited the sick and dying routinely, reported on 18 March, 1847 that,

James Vaughan died about 12 o'clock last night and his remains were in the male infirm ward this afternoon at 4:00 ... his corpse was allowed to remain sixteen hours after his death in the ward, before it was removed to the dead house.[56] The medical officer states that from the great increase of inmates, being four times the ordinary number and from the crowded state of the house, it has been impossible to provide dry beds in many instances in cases of those wetted by weakly ill children and by persons in a sickly state. This sleeping upon damp beds also increased fever and bowel complaints which have in many instances proved fatal.[57]

Minute Books of the Lurgan Board of Guardians, 12 April 1845–28 March 1846, pp. 40, 58, 306, 365; BG.22/CJ/1, Half Yearly Abstracts of Accounts, 1841–51, Half Year Ending 29 September 1846. 53 *Fifth, Sixth and Seventh Reports of the Relief Commissioners*, p. 29. 54 (PRONI), BG.22, Lurgan Workhouse Statistics during the Great Famine. 55 (PRONI), BG.22/A/5 Minutes of the Lurgan Board of Guardians, April 1846–April 1847, p. 426. 56 (PRONI), BG.22/FO/2 Chaplain's Book, 31 August 1846 to 4 March 1848. 57 (PRONI), BG.22/A/5 Minutes of the Lurgan Board of Guardians, April 1846–April 1847, p. 426.

Although the guardians ordered a large supply of new beds and a proper drying house to be erected, in the interim they considered it their 'duty to have a consultation with two or more of the most eminent physicians which this part of Ireland can supply' to learn about the causes and treatment of the prevalent epidemic and 'to show the earnest desire of the Board to leave no means untried to meet this dreadful situation'.[58] Dysentery continued to increase nevertheless, along with measles and smallpox among children recovering from dysentery, prompting the medical officer to request immediate fundamental remedies including warmer clothing, and a more nutritious diet to counter extreme debilitation caused by inadequate food and sanitation.[59] In 1849, 'the proper discharge of the onerous duties entailed ... by the great amount of sickness that prevailed in the workhouse until within a very recent period' prevented Dr Bell's successor Dr William Ross MacLaughlin from submitting annual reports and attending to 'those prolific external sources of disease' – filthy yards, deficient drainage, proper ventilation and surface water.[60]

A comparison of Workhouse records (see Appendices 2a and 2b) for both Unions relating to admissions, residents and deaths on a monthly basis shows that the Famine crisis began to effect the people in Lurgan Union slightly earlier than in Banbridge, and continued longer. Banbridge began to cope with the Famine by December of 1846 when the workhouse was 81 persons over capacity. Better records for Lurgan Union reveal that the number of monthly admissions began to dramatically increase between February and March of 1846, and reached crisis proportions by December of that year when a full workhouse reported 58 deaths.

The best year to compare is 1847 due to complete records for both Unions. The early months of 'Black 47' were a time of severe distress in both Unions when Workhouse resources and staff were pressed far beyond their capacities. Large numbers of people were admitted during this time, and many of those who were admitted died mostly of infectious disease. Even though Lurgan Union had taken measures to increase its capacity from the original 800 to 1812 in October 1848, 634 more people died in Lurgan Workhouse and its fever hospital than in Banbridge. In Banbridge Workhouse, 18.7 per cent of those admitted died averaging 41.5 deaths per month. Lurgan Workhouse's death rate was 30 per cent of total admissions with 94.3 deaths per month, a figure more than twice that of Banbridge. Both workhouses had to resort to turning desperate people away to reduce the resident population and cope with those already sick and dying.

The crisis in Lurgan Workhouse abated somewhat in 1848 with the death rate dropping to 23 per cent of admissions and the average number of deaths per month dropped to a rate nearly equal to Banbridge's (30 for Banbridge and 31.3 for Lurgan). Nevertheless, Lurgan Workhouse still admitted 1,637 more people in 1848

58 (PRONI), BG.22/A/5, Minutes of the Lurgan Board of Guardians, April 1846–May 1847, p. 456.
59 (PRONI), BG.22/A/6, Minutes of the Lurgan Board of Guardians, 1 May 1847–27 March 1848, p.37.   60 (PRONI), BG.22/CJ/1 Half Yearly Abstracts of Accounts for the Lurgan Board of Guardians, Medical Report of Lurgan Union Workhouse, 29 September 1849 by William Ross MacLaughlin, M.D., Edin., Physician to the Lurgan Workhouse and Fever Hospital.

than Banbridge Workhouse. In Banbridge Union, the crisis at the level of the work-house was largely over by the summer of 1849, while in Lurgan Union large numbers of people were still being admitted to the Workhouse in 1851.

Indoor Relief Registers for Lurgan Workhouse permit more finegrained analysis of inmates from Tullylish presented in table 7. Between 1845 and 1848, the proportion of inmates from the five Tullylish townlands (Bleary, Clare, Ballynagarrick, Ballydugan and Ballymacanallon) was low ranging from 12–13 per cent of the total people admitted. In 1841, these townlands were all densely populated with handloom weavers. Domestic weaving allowed many to remain on the land who otherwise would have migrated to industrializing towns or elsewhere. It is significant that throughout the Famine, very few residents of Ballymacanallon, a townland flanking industrializing Gilford/Dunbarton, entered the Workhouse. It is reasonable to assume that instead, many displaced persons from this townland entered the expanding workforce of Dunbar McMaster & Company.

Table 7: Residence and sex characteristics of famine inmates from Tullylish in Lurgan Workhouse, 1845–8

Year	Ballymac %	Bleary %	Clare %	Ballyna %	Ballydu %	Male %	Female %	Total %
1845	5.2	15.5	51	12.1	17.2	45.8	54.2	59
1846	0	57.0	16.6	5.2	21.2	39.4	60.6	208
1847	1.0	51.2	15.0	10.0	22.6	51.0	49.0	349
1848	2.4	24.6	45.1	18.0	29.9	47.0	53.0	217

Source: PRONI, BG.22/G/1–2 Lurgan Workhouse Indoor Relief Register.

Despite the predominance of handloom weavers and winders in Tullylish, the proportion of inmates from Tullylish with these occupations was only 14 per cent in 1845, 29 per cent in 1846, 24 per cent in 1847 and 32 per cent in 1848. This suggests that wages earned by weavers of fine linen provided most with the ability to buy food.

However, a close examination of sex characteristics reveals that gender distinctions are important in the region. With the exception of 1847, the proportion of women inmates was greater than men due to the elimination of handspinning, greater economic expendibility and desertion by husbands. In 1845–6 the proportion of deserted women with children accounted for 10 per cent of inmates from Tullylish. Desertion posed problems for women and children since they were economically and socially dependent. Even soldiers were not legally held responsible for the maintenance of their wives.[61]

61 (PRONI), BG.22/A/6, Minutes of the Lurgan Board of Guardians, 1 May 1847–27 March 1848.

Another source of demographic data on the inmates is the half yearly abstracts of accounts for the various electoral divisions in Lurgan Union between 1845 and 1851. This data is summarized in table 8 allowing comparison between Tullylish and Lurgan Union as a whole.

Table 8: Abstract of inmates from the electoral division of Tullylish relieved in Lurgan Workhouse, 1845–51

Year	No. Relieved	Males	Females	Children<15
1845 half year 3/25	51	12	17	22
half year 9/29	14	4	5	5
1846 half year 3/25	73	14	19	40
half year 9/25	102	20	29	53
1847 half year 3/25	250	50	78	122
half year 9/29	251	52	65	134
1848 half year 3/25	170	29	46	95
half year 9/29	-	-	-	-
1849 half year 3/25	80	20	15	45
half year 9/29	53	11	12	30
1850 half year 3/25	26	6	11	9
half year 9/29	37	11	10	16
1851 half year 3/25	37	5	14	18
half year 9/25	28	10	15	3

Source: PRONI BG.22/CJ/1, Half Yearly Abstracts of Accounts for Lurgan Board of Guardians.

The data reveal that in Tullylish/Lurgan, as elsewhere in Lurgan Union, the effects of potato blight were felt by March 1846. Similarly, the division suffered the worst in 1847 and began to recover by March 1849. The very low numbers of people relieved from Tullylish in 1850 and 51 suggest that an expanding linen industry shortened its duration relative to elsewhere in Lurgan Union where large numbers of people still entered the workhouse in the closing years of the Famine.

The data also reveals the heavier toll taken on women and especially children with children consistently comprising roughly half of those relieved. More adult females were relieved than males since women, whose principal occupations in this region were winders, weavers and sewers, earned less wages than skill male weavers. Because widows with children and women with illegitimate children were particularly vulnerable to impoverishment, they figure prominently in the workhouse population.

The poor rate on Tullylish/Lurgan was 50*d*. per pound, 20*d*. for outdoor relief and 30*d*. toward indoor or workhouse expenses. The Poor Law Commissioners were determined to ensure 'vigorous collection' of these rates despite growing resistance. The

Lurgan Board of Guardians in July 1847, responded that it was senseless for rate collectors to press hard upon impoverished rate payers, as indicated in the quote opening this chapter. In fact, the Lurgan guardians were already in debt before the full impact of Famine was felt in the Union by Autumn of 1845. The economic base of much of Lurgan Union was handloom weaving of fine linen cloth such as cambric, damask and diaper organized by the putting-out system. Some weavers were highly skilled and earned wages which were sufficient to ensure independence and the retention of their land. Still, under the best of circumstances, this latter group's prosperity was not increasing, and under Famine conditions the burden of extra rates and high food prices was heavy.

By October, 1847 reports of local resistance to the collection of poor rates began. The following month, Robert Molling of Maralin reported to Dublin Castle that, 'a communication was forwarded to me stating a large meeting had taken place on the Shane Hill, Tullylish Division, Lurgan Union for the avowed purpose of giving opposition to the collection of the poor rates'.[62] Examination of the half yearly abstract of accounts for Tullylish/Lurgan between 1842–51 reveals that the rate struck for the electoral division of Tullylish was a persistent problem which reached crisis proportions during the Famine. Government loans to finance famine relief works in the Union were borrowed from the Board of Works and were to be repaid in twenty half yearly installments. Some local landlords such as Lord Lurgan and John Handcock offered interest free loans to farmers near Lurgan willing to undertake drainage, remove hills and fill in hollows for famine relief.[63] In some years, as table 9 shows, a pittance was collected despite rising expenditures on paupers between 1846–9.

Constabulary reports suggest increasing larceny in Lurgan Union, a form of desperate agency, as distress mounted in 1847. For example, on 13 January 1847 a report stated that,

> between the hours of one and two o'clock this morning a boat lying at a place called Madden's Bridge about half a mile from Gilford Castle, with flour in transit for Newry, the property of a miller in Tandragee was attacked by men to the number of five and twenty or thirty most of whom were armed with flint locks and nearly half of the freight that is to say 80 bags of flour was carried off.

62 National Archive, Dublin, Outrage Papers, 1845–50, Robert Molling of Maralin, Lurgan to Dublin Castle, 26 October 1847 and 8 November 1847. The author wishes to thank Gerard McAtasney for this reference.   63 Francis X. McCorry, *Lurgan: An Irish Provincial Town, 1610–1970* (Lurgan 1993), p. 75.

Table 9: Half-yearly abstract of accounts for the electoral division of Tullylish,
Lurgan Union, 1844–1850

Year		Rate	Collected	Uncollected	*Amt.Spent/ Paupers
		£ s.d.	£ s.d.	£ s.d.	£ s.d.
1844	3/25	207.1.0½	4.0.0	203.1.0½	39.0.8
	9/29	203.1.0¼	190.10.0	12.11.0½	39.17.11½
1845	3/25	12.11.0½	3.0.9	5.17.11½	45.17.8½
	9/25	203.14.6	152.10.0	51.4.1	48.4.9½
1846	3/25	248.12.1	24.17.7	223.14.6	74.14.6
	9/25	223.14.6	205.14.9	17.19.9	118.6.6
1847*	3/25	412.11.5	3.16.2	408.15.3	287.10.10
	9/25	408.15.3	393.8.4	15.6.11	274.18.3
1848	3/25	541.3.1	499.13.11	91.9.2	210.14.7
	9/25	–	–	–	–
1849	3/25	482.11.6	141.9.4	340.5.6	118.5.10
	9/25	340.5.6	299.6.0	40.19.6	74.15.10
1850	3/25	236.5.8	18.19.11	217.0.7	36.9.0
	9/25	217.0.7	193.10.10	23.9.9	32.18.0

Source: PRONI, BG.22/CJ/1, Half Yearly Abstracts of Accounts, Lurgan Union. *in 1847 expenditure on paupers includes outdoor as well as indoor relief.

After searching the area, the officer found high quality flour in many of the surrounding houses and concluded that it was the same flour stolen from the boat. However, since the bags were well hidden, he could not prove his allegations. About five or six weeks later, a similar attack was made on a cargo of Indian meal at Madden's Bridge and another theft of flour near Portadown.[64]

Despite higher levels of distress, Lurgan guardians were not as eager as those in Banbridge to promote or finance the emigration of female paupers. Although Inspector Mr Senior visited the Workhouse in March of 1848 and selected a number of young women for emigration, the guardians neither wanted to pay the cost of 3 pounds per head nor lose the contribution to be made by their labour. Part of the reason is that handloom weaving and winding remained labour intensive and prospects for employment temporarily brightened for those weavers who survived. In 1846, domestic linen producers comprised 26 per cent of the resident population of Lurgan Workhouse. In 1847, their proportion fell to 12 per cent. The combination of a decline in the number of weavers in the region and persistent demand for their labour caused wages to rise. A letter written on 10 August 1848 suggests that the

64 National Archive, Dublin, Outrage Papers, 1845–50. The author wishes to thank Gerard McAtasney for this reference.

Lurgan Board of Guardians recognized the growing labour supply problem and sought to do their part to relieve it by providing cheap child pauper labour.[65] On 6 September 1849, the Lurgan Guardians inquired whether they could 'apprentice out "orphans" or other pauper children for a given period of time, the applications for such are now getting numerous, the weaving trade being brisk'. Although the Commissioners replied that there was no provision in the Poor Law Act enabling guardians to do so, girls continued to be taken out as winders and servants.[66]

CONCLUSION

An expanding linen industry in east Ulster did not fully insulate Tullylish from the ravages of the Famine. Many suffered and died, particularly women and children. However, capitalist development strongly mediated its demographic impact and duration. The Famine accelerated proletarianization in Tullylish, permanently solving the labour supply problem for capitalists along the River Bann. Many domestic weavers died, while others were forced to give up their holdings and migrate to townlands closer to the mills or send their daughters. Since employment opportunities, particularly for women, were expanding, more women than men were involved in Famine-induced internal migration. The rapidity and scale of internal migration posed challenges for paternalistic employers like John Walsh McMaster, who not only needed to discipline a 'green' young female workforce, but house and 'improve' them through the provision of schools and churches. Although the demographic catastrophe in Tullylish/Banbridge was largely over by 1849, its long-term effects persisted throughout the 1850s as a displaced population intersected with the labour supply needs of capitalists along the Bann. These regions reached their population peak in 1861.

The Famine provided the second blow to a proto-industrial system already weakened by the generalization of putting-out. Although the decline in the number of handloom weavers decelerated the proletarianization of surviving handloom weavers in Tullylish/Lurgan in the short term, rising variable capital costs created a powerful impetus to mechanize linen weaving. This impetus was intensified by the boom in demand for linen cloth in the 1860s during the American Civil War, initiating a secondary wave in the innovation and development of the linen industry. Tullylish during the 'boom years' between 1860–80 is the subject of the next chapter.

65 (PRONI), BG.22/A/7, Minute Books of the Lurgan Board of Guardians, April 1848 to March 1849. 66 (PRONI), BG.22/A/8, Minute Books of the Lurgan Board of Guardians, 5 April 1849 to 28 February 1850.

8

Tullylish in the 'Boom Years': 1851–80

> The paternalism that mattered most widely was in fact a paternalism largely un-
> known to the historical record. Below the level of deliberate community-building
> and lavish provision in the factory, what took the greatest effect was a church here,
> a school or canteen there, and always the stream of social life that characterised all
> factories.   Patrick Joyce, 1981

In the quarter century following the Great Famine, the Ulster linen industry boomed.
With their labour supply problem permanently solved, paternalistic capitalists at
mid-century entered a period of rapid economic growth reflected in the number of
factory settlements mushrooming along the Bann (see figure 7). In particular, the
owners of Dunbar McMaster & Company profited, as their yarn and thread acquired a reputation for quality around the world. As enlightened paternalists committed to class harmony, part of the McMaster's profits was invested in creating a
complex factory-town driven by the gendered rhythm of work in their large spinning mill.

This chapter focuses on Tullylish at its economic peak between 1850 and 1880,
using case studies of particular firms to illustrate the degrees and contradictions of
paternalistic endeavour. By mid-century, capitalists in Tullylish had assumed cultural hegemony, in the extended sense of defining a total way of life and world view.
Their contradictory motivations for capital accumulation based upon exploitation,
class harmony, Protestant domination and the extension of patriarchal familial obligations to the workplace shaped their factory millieux.

As a historically specific form of hegemonic masculinity, employer paternalism
is a relational construct, the explanation of which demands contextualization within
a totality of gender relations. Paternalistic employers exploited their male and female employees for profit while simultaneously encouraging self-help and independence as indicators of male respectability. Among their predominantly young
female workforce, exploitation was coupled with paternal protection, deference and
dependence. Several questions will guide this chapter. How did employer paternalism as the dominant form of masculinity define standards of manliness and femininity among the working class? How did the contradictions between paternalism
and accumulation influence the hiring practices, division of labour, and factory
millieux along the Bann? How did reliance upon a young mostly female labour force
expose the contradictions in this familial model for paternalism?

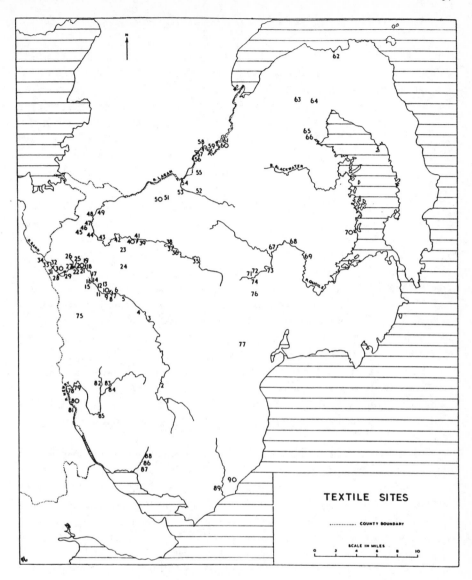

7   Textile sites in County Down showing density of industrialization along the River Bann in Tullylish/Seapatrick

DUNBAR MC MASTER & COMPANY AND GILFORD/DUNBARTON

Hugh Dunbar, the original owner of Dunbarton and partner of Dunbar McMaster & Company died on 17 April 1847. Under the 1847 partnership agreement, if Hugh Dunbar were to die, his share in the partnership would pass to his sister Anne with his four sisters – Anne, Isabella, Jane, and Elizabeth – inheriting his real and personal estate. From 1847–55, the second formal partnership consisted of Anne Dunbar, Jane Dunbar, J.W. McMaster, James and Benjamin Dickson, W.R. Massaroon and William Spotten, who were taken in as partners in 1855. The particular interest of the latter two men was in extending the merchandising of brown and bleached linens.

In December of 1855, John W. McMaster, with the consent of the other members of the firm, agreed to purchase the land, mills, houses and machinery from Anne Dunbar, who died in 1865, and Jane Dunbar, who died in 1874, for £55,663.18s.2d. This purchase came into effect on 3 November 1865, initiating a third partnership whereby all lands, houses and machinery were the absolute property of McMaster, and all future buildings were built and owned by him. In 1865, capital stock was valued at 75,000 pounds with the partners' shares as follows: 1) J.W. McMaster, 27,000 pounds; 2) James Dickson, 16,500 pounds; 3) Benjamin Dickson, 16,500 pounds; 4) William Spotten, 7500 pounds; and 5) W.R. Massaroon, 7500 pounds.

After 1865, the partnership between McMaster and the Dicksons ended. Dunbar Dickson & Company now traded, after a legal battle to keep their world-famous name, under the name William Spotten & Company. The Dicksons set up a new firm called Dickson Ferguson & Company. Both firms prospered until the 1880's recession.

The combined business of Dunbar McMaster & Company and Dunbar Dickson & Company 'flourished beyond measure ... and the firm made money in tubfulls'.[1] In the second half of the 19th century, the physical environmental and spatial arrangement of Gilford/Dumbarton reflected its particular intersection of production and commercial function, status-class stratification and religious sect. In 1849, a bleachgreen was added, and in 1856, John W. McMaster built a large warehouse in Belfast where the merchandising of white linen was carried on. Also, during this time, several of the partners built large mansions in Gilford. Dunbarton House was built prior to 1860 housing John W. McMaster, his wife Mary Heron McMaster and their four children – Hugh Dunbar (1843–1907), John George, Isabella, and Percy Jocelyn. Benjamin Dickson bought an extensive property from the Johnston's and built Gilford Castle, and James Dickson built Elmfield House.

---

1 H.C. Lawlor, 'Rise of the linen merchants in the eighteenth century', 2, no. 2 (1942), 92; and (PRONI), D.2714/8F, Notes on Dunbar McMaster & Company of Gilford.

8   Dunbarton Street, Gilford, *c.*1900

By 1867, building in the factory town of Gilford/Dunbarton was largely over, and the sporadic development thereafter consisted primarily of prestigious parlour houses offering better quality accommodation.[2] During the 1860s, the McMasters erected another terrace of houses at the foot of Hill Street called Sandy Row, another three large terraces on Dunbarton Street in 1878, large terraces on Main Street in 1898 and a final six houses called New Row off Stramore Road in 1901. The total capital invested in houses between 1836–62 was 10,000 pounds and all were inspected monthly, limewashed, painted and repaired by the firm annually (see figures 8, 9, 10, 11, 12).

The accumulation of great personal wealth by John W. McMaster did not temper the paternalistic tone set by Hugh Dunbar. The principal source of evidence relating to McMaster's paternalistic endeavours is the 1867 Report by the Parliamentary Commissioners on the Paris Universal Exhibition, containing detailed information on all participating British firms. The form completed by Dunbar McMaster & Company provides a snapshot of the firm and factory village at its peak.

By the 1860s, Dunbar McMaster & Company was engaged in flaxspinning, linen

2 Denis S. McNiece, 'Factory Workers' Housing in Counties Down and Armagh', Ph.D. diss., The Queen's University of Belfast, 1981, pp. 18–21, 23.

9   Whinney Hill looking towards Banbridge Road, Gilford, *c.*1900

10   Hill Street, 'Keady Row' in Gilford, 1970; showing derelict houses

11   Workers in front of the mill gates of Dunbar McMaster & Company, *c.* 1900

thread manufacturing, yarn bleaching and the manufacture of linen and cambric. They employed 369 adult males, 541 adult females, of whom 127 were married, 262 young males between the ages of thirteen and eighteen, 341 young females between thirteen and eighteen, 31 male children and 54 female children, who together totalled 1598 workers. All workers above the age of 13 worked 60 hours per week.

The 541 adult females at Dunbar McMaster & Company represented 33.9 per cent of the workforce. Of these 127 were married. According to Margaret Hewitt, only 13.6 per cent of married women in Ireland worked outside the home. At this firm, they represented only 8 per cent of the total workforce and 23.5 per cent of the adult females employed. Since these are the only precise figures relating to the age and gender breakdown of the workforce available, it is useful to compare them with demographic figures given for the linen industry in Belfast and Ulster exclusive of Belfast. While there is a twenty year span between the 1867 figures used for Dunbar McMaster & Company and the 1886 figures, there was not much change in the proportion of women, juveniles and children employed.[3] In 1868, the percentage of women, juveniles and children employed in the linen industry was 81.4 per cent. At that time Dunbar McMaster & Company's figure was 76.9 per cent, slightly lower than the average figure for Ireland.

3 Emily J. Boyle, 'The Economic Development of the Irish Linen Industry, 1825–1913', Ph.D., diss., The Queen's University of Belfast, 1977, p. 148.

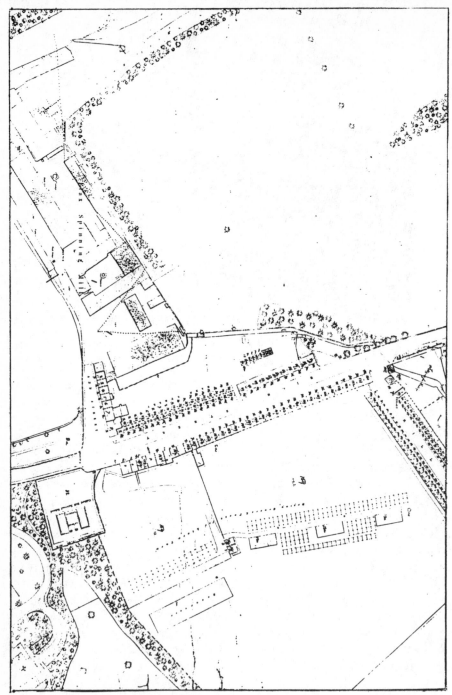

12   Valuation map of Dunbarton, 1862

Joy Parr argues that broad patterns of gender segregation in the economy frequently do not suffice at the level of the community, industry or firm. Instead micro-level approaches should recognize that men, women, capital and labour have heterogeneous interests that help explain 'why a job that is clearly and exclusively women's work in one factory, town, or region may be just as exclusively men's work in another factory, town, or region'.[4] Textile millowners dependent upon female labour had to reconcile their dependency with the prevailing cultural norm for adult men to provide for their families. Consequently, paternalistic employers recreated the patriarchal family in the mill through rigid occupational sex segregation and wage asymmetry.[5] Although doffing mistresses in spinning mills supervised other women and children, as did adult women in the home, women in the mills did not supervise men. Rather, the hierarchical relations of production in spinning mills reflected patterns of gender relations characteristic of the patriarchal family, with men occupying managerial and supervisory positions. Further, Victorian gendered assumptions about mechanical aptitude, and strength determined that all skilled occupations were male.

Evidence also suggests that employment patterns in the linen industry differed according to rural or urban locale. For example, when we compare Ireland, England, Scotland, and Rural Ulster, Rural Ulster and 'other places in England' had the lowest proportion of married women employed with 44.3 and 44.1 per cent respectively. When we compare adult male employment figures in the linen industry in Belfast, England and Scotland, Belfast had both the lowest proportion of adult men (13.8 per cent) and the highest proportion of adult women (59.1 per cent) employed. This supports contemporaries who complained of the large number of married women working in Belfast's linen mills and factories.[6] Further, as table 10 shows, because more adult women were employed, there were proportionately less juveniles and children employed in Belfast than in the rest of Ulster and at Dunbar McMaster & Company. In rural industrial sites, men were far less likely to find alternative sources of employment outside of the linen industry prompting rural employers to hire more of them and fewer married women. Hiring adult males conformed with prevailing gender conceptions favouring domesticity for married women and the male breadwinner role. Although the workforce was overwhelmingly female, fewer adult and married women were hired with more adult men, juveniles and children hired instead.

4 Joy Parr, 'Disaggregating the sexual division of labour: a transatlantic case', *Comparative Studies in Society and History*, 30, no. 3 (1988), 511–12.   5 Judy Lown, *Women and industrialization* (Minneapolis 1990), p. 8.   6 H.C. *Report by Miss Orme and Miss Abraham on the Conditions of Women's Work in Ireland, Industrial Relations: Labour Commission*, IUP ser., vol. xxxiv (1893–4), p. 349; Mary Galway, 'The linen industry in the north', in William G. Fitzgerald (ed.), *The Voice of Ireland* (Dublin and London: 1929), p. 297; and James Connolly, *Selected Writings* (Baltimore 1973), pp. 193—4.

Table 10: Age and gender breakdown of linen workers at Dunbar McMaster
& Co., (1867), Belfast (1886) and Ulster exclusive of Belfast (1886)

Type Worker	Dunbar McMaster		Belfast		Rest of Ulster	
	No.	%	No.	%	No.	%
Men	369	23.1	853	13.8	1939	18.3
Lads	262	16.4	576	9.3*	1660	15.7*
Boys	31	1.9 }18.3				
Total Males	662	41.4	1429	23.1	3599	34.0
Women	541	33.9	3661	59.1	4689	44.3
Women < 18	341	21.3	1103	17.8*	2305	21.8*
Girls	54	3.4 }24.7				
Total Females	936	58.6	4764	76.9	6994	66.1
Fem.Juv. Children	1229	76.9	5340	86.2	8654	81.7
Total Juv.Children	688	43.0	1679	27.1	3965	37.4
Total Workers	1598		6193		10593	

Source: Paris Universal Exhibition, 1867; Returns of Labour Statistics From the Board of Trade, Industrial Relations: Wages, IUP ser., vol. 20 (1887–92), 483. *workers under 18 years of age.

While hiring more adult men may seem incongruous with keeping variable capital costs at a minimum, this strategy promoted stability among families who depended upon the mill for wages. These families would both reproduce the labour force over generational time and continuously occupy employer-owned houses. Further, since reliance on child labour was normative in the linen industry, rural employers hired more juveniles and children who earned lower wages than adults. Finally, rural employers paid lower wages overall than employers in Belfast.[7] In 1867, Dunbar McMaster & Company reported that single workmen averaged 15s. per week while the average weekly family wage was 36s. Their range of wages began with a low of 4s., which was paid to a child, and increased to a high of 50s., paid to a select few of their skilled adult men.[8]

Thus, a distinctive labour recruitment pattern emerged in rural areas favouring adult male and juvenile labour to the extent possible. The earnings of the male head, given the wage differentials between the sexes, were most crucial to a household's survival. Victorian reformers were loath to see married women working outside the home and paternalistic employers were bound to subscribe to this view. Evidence

7 H.C. *Average Rates of Wages of Operatives Employed in the Linen Manufacture in Various Districts, at 1st October, 1886, Industrial Relations: Wages*, IUP ser., vol. xx (1887–92).   8 Ibid.; *Report From Commissioners: Paris Universal Exhibition*, vol. xxx (1867–8), p. 57.

that the McMasters were no exception can be gleaned from the low proportion of married women in their employ and in their policy of allowing these workers 'one hour daily ... extra for meals and the assistance of relatives and friends' so that they might 'attend to their family and domestic duties'.[9]

Although Victorian single women were presumed to be under the care and authority of their fathers, an expanding textile industry that employed female labour undermined this patriarchal ideal. As substitute fathers, the McMasters extended paternal concern to the 25 per cent of young single women who had made their way to Gilford alone to work in the mill. While the McMasters did not build separate boarding houses, young women in Gilford/Dunbarton were 'comfortably lodged with long resident and respectable families, and placed under the immediate supervision of their respective clergy'.[10]

The long arm of the McMaster family extended to all aspects of community life in Dunbarton and adjacent Gilford creating a distinctive culture of the factory. As the heart of Gilford/Dunbarton, the large spinning mill was connected to schools, churches, shops and numerous voluntary associations. In 1867, there was a cooperative society offering food and clothing for sale to the workers. It was under the immediate control and supervision of the proprietors but managed by a secretary, manager and assistants.[11] This cooperative society or store was not a truck shop as participation was not obligatory. There were numerous other shops in Gilford that ensured consumer choice.

Remaining independent of parish relief was a pillar of working-class respectability. Since wages were low, household members were vulnerable to destitution when the male breadwinner fell ill. The McMasters, as benevolent fathers, contributed to the spirit of self-help and independence among their workers in times of illness by establishing a sick fund, to which they contributed 250 pounds annually. The furnished hospital and dispensary were exempt from paying rates and made available rent free. The workers contributed 350 pounds annually in the proportion of ½d. to every 3s. earned. The funds were applied in allowances in case of illness for procuring efficient medical attendants at the hospital, dispensary, and houses of sick persons; for supplying medicines free at the dispensary, open for an hour and a half daily; for providing nurses for the sick; and for defraying the expenses of burial in case of death.[12]

The owners encouraged self-improvement among the workforce by providing churches and educational institutions. Houses of worship for the four leading denominations each with a Sabbath School attached were built by the owners. Hugh Dunbar had provided land free for the Roman Catholic Church, and the McMasters for the Church of Ireland, Presbyterians and Methodists. These churches and

---

9 *Paris Universal Exhibition*, p. 46. 10 Ibid., p. 47; Lown, *Women and Industrialization*, p. 143. 11 *Paris Universal Exhibition*, pp. 60–3; Patrick Joyce, *Visions of the People* (Cambridge 1991), p. 131. 12 *Paris Universal Exhibition*, pp. 65–9.

their respective clergy were supported by the proprietors and working people in the town.

By 1865, the population of Gilford had reached a level where J.W. McMaster proposed to the Ecclesiastical Commissioners that Gilford Town and certain adjoining townlands become a distinct Parochial District. It was McMaster's opinion that the distance between Gilford and the existing parish Episcopal Church in Tullylish townland discouraged church attendance. Furthermore, the other denominations in the town – Presbyterians, Methodists and Roman Catholics – all 'have respectively raised neat and commodious Churches'.[13] Because the town's population was 'almost exclusively of the operative classes' who were too poor to raise the money, and because McMaster felt 'so strongly the moral obligation existing on himself to aid to the utmost of his power the spiritual wants of the operative classes', he was willing to finance the endeavour. McMaster offered to contribute a site for the building valued at 250 pounds, an endowment of 1250 pounds, a sum sufficient to provide for repairs, and 750 pounds to build a 'neat and suitable house, offices and garden rent free for the Incumbent'.[14]

After legal haggling with Benjamin Dickson, the Parish of Gilford was created in 1867 consisting of Loughans, Gilford Town, Moyallon, Mullabrack and portions of Drumiller, Kernan, Drumaran and Ballymacanallon. The foundation stone of the new church was laid in 1868. Both J.W. McMaster, his son Hugh Dunbar McMaster and other members of the McMaster family remained committed to the Church of Ireland, and its Sunday school.[15] A member of the McMaster family served as vicar almost continuously between 1869 and 1904.[16]

The provision of schools clearly illustrates the contradiction between paternalistic ideology and the accumulation of surplus value produced by children's labour.[17] By the mid-Victorian period, education was to play a central role in legitimizing an emergent social consonance based upon the understanding of the laws of political economy and the harmony of interest between labour and capital. After Hugh Dunbar's death, J.W. McMaster purchased the schools. He too was reputed to have 'spared no expense or trouble in providing school accommodation, supplying all necessary apparatus and in procuring the services of highly qualified teachers'. His son, Hugh Dunbar McMaster later enlarged one of the schools.[18]

Concern by the McMasters for schooling was partly motivated by enlightened self-interest, partly by religious faith and partly by a belief that the mixed non-

13 (PRONI), D.2714/8E, Gilford Genealogist, 1865 Memorial of J.W. McMaster to Ecclesiastical Commissioners for Churches.   14 Ibid.   15 (PRONI), D.1769/8/1A, L'Estrange Brett Papers (Solicitors Belfast), Letter dated 27 March, 1866, from Hugh Dunbar McMaster to L'Estrange and Brett.   16 St Paul's Parish Church, Gilford, Bazaar Book and Calander, 1934.   17 Marilyn Cohen, 'Paternalism and poverty: contradictions in the schooling of working class children in Tullylish, County Down, 1825–1914', *History of Education*, 21, no. 3 (1992), 291–306.   18 (PRONI), ED.1/19 Down Aided Applications, 1873-1884, no. 144; (Letter) H.D. McMaster to L'Estrange & Brett, 27 March 1866; D.1796/8/1A, L'Estrange & Brett Papers.

denominational goals of the National Board would weaken 'party' feeling and promote religious toleration in their community and in Ireland.[19] John W. McMaster
considered schooling and facilitating self-improvement to be a wise investment essential to the advancement of the manufacturing system generally and of workers
individually. The following letter written on 12 January 1851 from J.W. McMaster
to the Commissioners of National Education in Ireland reflects his convictions:

> ... I consider our schools the most powerful engine we possess in connexion
> with our little colony for promoting the happiness, comfort, and independ-
> ence of our people, as well as the success of our concern. In fact, I look upon
> education as almost indispensable for the well-being of an establishment like
> this, not only from the beneficial influence which it imparts to the whole
> community, but also from the valuable training which the pupils receive in
> preparation for their various offices, and I find that the desire evinced by a
> scholar for learning and improvement is always a sure test of their value in
> the works; so much is this thought, that when a choice hand is required to be
> brought up in the factory for an important post, with a view to their promo-
> tion afterwards, it is from the schools they are usually selected; and this has
> now become so well known among them, that it forms the chief incentive to
> that perseverance and anxiety to learn with which they apply themselves
> particularly at the night-schools. I consider these even more useful than the
> day schools, and many of our best hands owe their present success and com-
> fort to the instruction received there. Those of our people who avail them-
> selves of the advantages of education, are generally distinguished for their
> good conduct, steadiness, neatness and self respect; and I perceive them after-
> wards becoming attendants in our reading room for their recreation and
> improvement instead of frequenting the ale-houses.[20]

In 1867, the cost to Dunbar McMaster & Company of providing the three room
school house, teachers' salaries, fire, light, daily cleaning, repairs, annual painting
and limewashing was 104 pounds per year. The National Board of Education contributed 270 pounds and the children 1*d*. per week.

Data relating to enrollment, attendance and grade levels for the various schools
in Tullylish between 1859–1865 suggest that the factory schools at Gilford Mill
managed by the paternalistic McMasters and the Milltown Day Schools managed
by bleachgreen owner John Smyth had the best daily attendance figures in Tullylish
of 70 per cent of the average number of children on the rolls.[21] When these are
compared with daily attendance figures of 33–50 per cent reported by the Powis

19 (PRONI), ED. 1/19 Down Aided Applications, 1873–1884, no. 144.   20 *Appendix to the Eighteenth Report of the Commissioners of National Education in* Ireland (1851), pp. 251–2.   21 For a fuller discussion of this data see Cohen, 'Paternalism and Poverty'.

Commission, we can conclude that the combination of the law, employer paternalism and working-class motivation had a positive effect on children's schooling in this region. Slightly more than one child for every two tabulated in the average number of children on the rolls attended school, a proportion high enough to inspire confident predictions by local school inspectors regarding the extension of literacy among those under twenty-one years of age.[22]

It is also significant that Gilford Mill Male Day School had the highest proportion of students (23 per cent) examined in Book 3 or higher. According to the Powis Report, only 7 per cent of children reached the Book 4 level. Forty-five per cent left after Book 1 without achieving full literacy. The vast majority of other schools in Tullylish followed this pattern with 45 per cent at the Book 1 level, 23 per cent at the Book 3 level, and only 7 per cent at the Book 4 level. While a lower proportion of girls at the Gilford Mill Female Day School were examined in the upper classes, attendance often equalled or surpassed that at the Male Day School.[23]

The Gilford Mills Schools also included the only separate infant school in Tullylish. According to District Inspector Samuel Brown, separate infant schools were one way in which the obstacle of early removal of children from school to work could be remedied.[24] The rate of attendance at this infant school was nearly equal to the day schools' as was enrollment. Infant schools were on the whole enthusiastically received in working class neighbourhoods because they served as cheap reliable sources of child care for working mothers where no institutional nursery existed.[25]

The Gilford Mill Evening Schools were also the first to open in the parish. Evening schools were characteristic social institutions advocated and provided by reformers who espoused self-improvement. While average attendances were always lower at the Gilford Mill Evening Schools than in the day schools under the regulation of the State, part of the reason for the success of these evening schools can be attributed to John W. McMaster. In an 1854 application to the Commissioners for additional funds for the Gilford Mill Male Evening School (attended by both males and females), Inspector George Fields noted that, 'as these respectable manufacturing proprietors prefer employing those who are comparatively educated – many young persons whose education had been neglected in childhood avail themselves of the evening schools ...'[26]

Working-class attendance at evening schools supports the position that learning was valued. Evening schools met a demand for learning among working class juveniles who did not receive adequate schooling during the day, since they were em-

22 *Thirtieth Report of the Commissioners of National Education in Ireland* (1863), p. 217. 23 H.C. *Royal Commission of inquiry into Primary Education, Ireland (Powis Report)*, Part iii, vol. xxviii (1870), p. 410; Cohen, 'Paternalism', p. 297. 24 *Thirty-Third Report of the Commissioners of National* Education *in Ireland* (1866), p. 258. 25 Mary Jo Maynes, *Schooling for the People* (New York 1985), pp. 150–1; Lown, *Women and Industrialization, p.* 143. 26 (PRONI), ED.1/16 Down Aided Application 1846–60, No. 159; ED.1/16 Down Aided Applications, 1846–60, No. 27.

ployed at the various mills and factories. Students who were frequently adults aged sixteen or older were taught the '3R's', money tables, grammar, geography, and spelling. Although on average their attendances were significantly lower than day schools, occasionally their average enrollments edged higher. Attending the evening schools (in session from 6:30 pm to 9:00 pm Monday, Wednesday and Friday) after a ten hour day which ended at 6:00 pm was difficult; even more so was concentrating on the school work. Nevertheless, Gilford Mill's Evening School sent more students for promotion to the next class in 1862 than did the Day School.

It is important to note that these attempts to achieve a basic education among the working class usually did not lead to upward mobility or future prosperity. Working-class parents who sent a child to school full time faced the double burden of school fees (at the Gilford Mill schools in mid-century, 1*d.* per week), and sacrificed a child's earnings.[27] In trying to grapple with the problem of irregular attendance, the Commissioners of National Education in Ireland found that whether the area was agricultural or industrial, the reasons for irregular attendance were the same – parental need for their children's labour and the lack of practical importance of education beyond reading, simple arithmetic and, in some cases, writing.

Children usually began school at the age of five or six and left at twelve or thirteen. However, because of the irregularity of their attendance, two-thirds did not advance beyond the second class or absorb more than three and a half years of school in total. Most only attended for four and a half months each year resulting in a child obtaining only a 'tolerable acquaintance with reading writing, and arithmetic, with perhaps a little grammar and geography ...'[28] While some improvement in average daily attendance occurred by 1863, the problem of irregular attendance persisted and, where employment opportunities presented themselves, children were withdrawn from school at earlier ages to begin earning wages.[29] As Inspector Brown explained in 1866 for District No. 16, that included Tullylish,

> The extraordinary demand for juvenile labour in the various departments of the linen manufacture and hem-stitching has an important bearing on the state and prospects of education in this district. Children are now withdrawn from school at a much earlier age than formerly.[30]

Because of the inherent contradiction between an employer's profit motive and financial pressure among the working class to send their children to work as early as possible, it was necessary for the state to extend laws regulating child labour and schooling. In the case of children employed in textile factories, partial attendance at school under the half-time system was enforced by law as of 1844. Only for these

27 *Paris Universal Exhibition*, p. 76.   28 *Seventeenth Report of the Commissioners of National Education in Ireland* (1863), p. 159.   29 *Thirty-third Report of the Commissioners of National Education in Ireland* (1866), p. 257; *Thirtieth Report of the Commissioners of National Education in Ireland* (1863), p. 159.   30 *Thirty-Third Report of the Commissioners of National Education in Ireland* (1866), p. 257.

children was schooling compulsory under the Factory Acts. In 1874, the minimum age of employment, set in 1819 at nine years, was raised from nine to ten, and those children who had not attained a given standard or class by age thirteen were required to remain another year. In 1891, the minimum was age was again raised to eleven. Not all employed children, however, were covered under the Factory Acts at the same time, and those children not employed in factories, such as agricultural laborers were not covered at all. Only in 1876 were education legislation and factory legislation co-ordinated in Ireland with uniform regulations for factory children and those employed elsewhere.[31] By 1892, moreover, compulsory fulltime attendance began to be implemented under the law.

While the halftime system provided factory children with some schooling, problems remained. National school hours, normally 10 am to 3 pm, did not harmonize well with the working schedules of linen mills and factories. Children often had to eat a hasty 'piece' (lunch) between work and school. Frequently, neither morning nor afternoon children's work shifts permitted sufficient hours in the classroom. Halftimers had to attend school for a minimum of 200 half days during twelve months to qualify for examinations while fulltime children had to attend for 100 days.[32] The children's youth and fatigue after hours in the mill meant lower achievement on the whole. Finally, the lower National Board allowance for halftimers (50 per cent of that for fulltime students) put a financial strain on factory schools. Such schools were forced to depend heavily on the good will of the manufacturer (who often served as manager).

Leisure activities in Gilford/Dunbarton also reflected the concern for working-class self-improvement, albeit in gender specific ways. Far more institutions were established for men since respectable women were defined in terms of domesticity. A Young Men's Mutual Improvement Society was in active operation at which lectures and debates were delivered regularly 'on scientific and useful subjects' by both the members and 'leading and influential public men in the vicinity'. A news room, library and public lecture room were provided by the proprietors who contributed free rent, light and heat. Finally, cricket, boating, handball and football clubs, and gymnastics were fostered and encouraged.[33]

It is significant that a Temperance Society was established at Gilford and lectures were given in connection therewith to about 18 per cent of the workforce who belonged. Spurred by the Evangelical revival of the 1850s, both temperance and teetotalism advanced during the second half of the nineteenth century. Although the Church of Ireland did not go as far as the smaller dissenting sects in championing teetotalism, an active temperance society was in operation and its hierarchy supported the campaign for reforming the licensing laws.[34] However, unlike

31 H.C. *Annual Report of the Factory Inspectors, Industrial Revolution: Factories*, IUP ser., vol. XVIII (1878–81), p. 89.   32 *Powis Commission Report*, XXVIII, Part i, p. 327.   33 *Paris Universal Exhibition*, p. 83.   34 Elizabeth Malcolm, *'Ireland Sober, Ireland Free': Drink and Temperance in Nineteenth Century Ireland* (Syracuse 1986), pp. 330–3.

13 Banford Bleach Works with linen bleaching on the grass

14 View of Banford House with linen bleaching on the grass

Bessbrook, where the lack of public houses reflected the long-time active support of total abstinence by the Quaker Richardson family of Moyallon, public houses were part of the economic and social life of Gilford/Dunbarton. Despite the proximity to Gilford of Moyallon where the Richardsons and other Quaker families resided, the rather small proportion of active members suggests only moderate influence by these prominent Quakers and the temperance movement over the consumption of alcohol among Gilford's working- and middle-class population.

The McMasters also attempted to facilitate self-help activities among their employees. It was the owners' belief that through self-help working-class men could improve themselves and advance above their class. To encourage such motivation, a penny bank was established in 1863 and a savings fund was in operation for thirteen years by 1867. McMaster acted as treasurer of the savings fund allowing 5 per cent interest per annum on deposits. One hundred and forty-eight working people contributed with an average savings of £12.2s. Others saved with the Post Office Savings Bank or invested with shopkeepers. The firm proudly stated that seven of these investors had acquired 87 houses, others owned shops, land and farming stock comprising 50 horses, 66 cows, 150 pigs and a great many poultry. Several of their officials had likewise invested their savings becoming mill owners and partners in mercantile establishments in their own right.[35]

Finally, under the Town Improvement (Ireland) Act of 1854 (17 & 18 Vic. Cap.103), that set up a system of electing Town Commissioners, the mill owners played a prominent role in the maintenance of the town of Gilford. These Commissioners first met in 1858 with J.W. McMaster, JP in the Chair. They adopted the cleaning and lighting sections of the Act and set rates to pay for these services. A 'scavenger', employed 'to constantly cleanse and remove all accumulated dirt and nuisance', was to be paid £2.2s. per month. Scavengers were also to dispose of beggars in the streets by committing them, and posting notices 'to the effect that all parties found begging in the streets of Gilford, be taken up and Prosecuted as the Law directs'. Lighting for the streets was provided by the Gilford Gas Company owned by the McMasters at the cost of 30s. per lamp per half year. Town Commissioners continued to handle these responsibilities until 1893 when they were also to appoint school attendance committees. Predictably, the first Chair of the Gilford School Attendance Committee was George Bingly Luke, part owner and manager of Gilford Mill.[36]

Town government reflected the structural divisions of status-class and religious sect while assigning such divisions a functional relevance in the town. The elite of land and mill owners such as Benjamin Dickson, John W. McMaster, and Hugh Dunbar McMaster always filled the leadership role of chair of the Town Commissioners since they provided the economic life blood of the town. However, the predominantly Protestant lower middle class of shopkeepers and professionals served

35 Ibid., pp. 87–92; Lown, *Women and Industrialization*, pp. 152–8.   36 (PRONI), D.2714/3A, Minutes of Meetings of Ratepayers, Gilford Town Commissioners, 1859–1915.

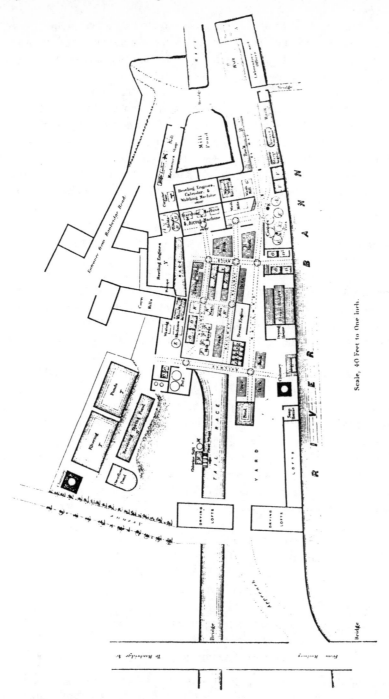

15 Map of Milltown Bleachworks, 1864

under them and played a vital role in organizing community life. From its inception in 1859, the majority of Gilford Town Commissioners were small property owners and professionals, most of whom were Church of Ireland serving continuously for years. In 1859, petty bourgeois Commissioners included physicians George Henry Acheson and Henry McBride; Thomas Thompson, grocer and spirit dealer; Benjamin T. Parkes, grocer and spirit dealer; James Doak, pawnbroker; Hugh McConnell, grocer, spirit dealer, woollen draper and pawnbroker; and John Byrne, a Catholic hotel keeper.[37] A half century later in 1901, under the chairmanship of Hugh Dunbar McMaster, Commissioners included Terence Fox, grocer and spirit dealer; Samuel Joyce, confectioner; butchers Moses and George Kinlay; Charley Hanvey, hotel keeper; and George Livingstone and George B. McConnell (son of Hugh McConnell), drapers.[38]

Although the motivations of paternalistic employers were partly humane, linen capitalists as a class had as their first motivation the accumulation of profits. Opportunities for self-improvement were made available, but these were only partially beneficial to the working class who were in demand as cheap labour. Paternalism offered a solution for some employers to the 'moral dilemma' inherent in the capitalist class system through urging 'reform, not in the mill but in the institutions of the community, and particularly in the educational system'.[39] Such efforts were considered a wise investment in the reproduction of a mutually beneficial economic system.

In Gilford/Dunbarton, the power of the mill owning family over social life continued uninterrupted by the deaths of Hugh Dunbar in 1847 and John Walsh McMaster in 1872 at the age of fifty-three. McMaster's eldest son Hugh Dunbar McMaster took control at the tender age twenty-nine for another quarter century until the family-owned firm joined the new Linen Thread Combine in 1898. Hugh Dunbar McMaster died in 1907. At the death of Gilford's last linen lord on 29 July 1907, George Hillen, a thirty-four year old shoemaker, keeper of a lodging house on Mill Street and son of shopkeeper Isaac Hillen, composed a poem to memorialize the town's paternal icon entitled, 'In Loving Memory of Hugh Dunbar McMaster, Esq., JP'

> Heaven has gained and earth has lost
>   A good kind-hearted friend,
> Unto the poor hath on him called
>   He freely did extend ...
> And we viewed with heart-felt sorrow
>   The last respects to him were paid;
> Round the little Town of Gilford
>   Never shall his memory fade.

37 Ibid.; Isaac Slater, *Slater's Directory of Ireland* (London 1856).37.22   38 (PRONI), D.2714/3A Minutes of Meetings of Ratepayers 1859–1915, p. 294; William MacDonald & Co., *MacDonald's Irish Directory and Gazetteer* (1902–03 edition), p. 436.   39 Anthony F.C. Wallace, *Rochdale* (New York 1978), p. 334.

BLEACHGREENS: THE EXAMPLE OF BANFORD BLEACH WORKS

There were no other factory villages of the size and complexity of Gilford/Dunbarton in Tullylish. Bleachgreens were small enterprises and their owners provided only housing and occasionally a shop or a school. However, resident bleachgreen owners and employment at the bleachgreen dominated their workers' rhythm of life in much the same way as in Gilford/Dunbarton.

The land on which Banford Bleach Works was built was owned by Benjamin Dickson, a partner in Dunbar McMaster & Company, who had purchased the land from the Johnston's. Banford Bleach Works was built on the site of what was probably the oldest bleach mill on the Bann owned by the Quaker John Nicholson and mentioned by Walter Harris in 1744. John Nicholson was succeeded by his son Thomas, and Banford House was built soon after in 1780. In 1863, Daniel Jaffe joined Thomas Haughton to form the Banford Bleach Works Company, and in 1883, John Edgar bought out Benjamin Haughton's interest. He and Thomas Haughton, who died in 1888, ran the business on the 177 acre site until its purchase by Frederick Sinton about 1890.[40] The firm remained in the Sinton family, many of whom were connected to the linen industry, until it closed after World War II (see figures 13,14).

Information about Banford Bleach Works during the nineteenth century is contained in various business records that provide evidence for this successful bleachgreen during the peak years between 1862–72. At this time, bleaching and finishing linen was still a lengthy process taking about three months. It was also a very particular and exact process catering to customers' specialized requirements. Foreman bleachers kept 'Full Books' listing each customer's specific bleaching specifications, and important details about the cloth such as the size, type and fineness, accompanied by samples. Also, each company's linen had exact time requirements relating to each process including grassing.

Evidence relating to the Company's progress during the 'Boom years' of 1862–72 and subsequent industry depression can be drawn from three sources. One source is 'Bleach Books', listing Banford's customers' names, the amount and description of linen bleached and the prices paid with discounts given to each customer. The second is 'Invoice Books' from which billing information by the month and year can be tabulated. When we look at the yearly total of charges between the years 1864–1887, it is evident that Banford Bleach Works' business expanded during the 1860s and 1870s, and declined during the depressed 1880s.[41] By 1880, the firm's capital was worth 30,000 pounds and its customers included locals such as Pat McCosker of Gilford or Robert Bell of Banford who sent their linen remnants to be bleached, and

40 E.R.R. Green, *The Industrial Archaeology of County Down* (Belfast 1963), p. 21.   41 (PRONI), D.1136/EC/l, Bleach Book no. 4, 1863–5; D.1136/EC/2, Bleach Book no. 5, 1873–7; D.1136/CE/l, Invoice Book no. 4; D.1136/CE/2, Invoice Book No. 5; D.1136/CE/3, Invoice Book no. 6; D.1136/CE/4, Invoice Book no. 8.

16   Halls Mill, Lawrencetown, *c.* 1910

17   Old Spinning Mill, Hazelbank Weaving Co., Ltd, Coose

industry giants like Dunbar Dickson & Company of Gilford who sent their award winning linens.[42]

The three principal areas sending linen to be bleached at Banford were Belfast, Manchester, and London. Ireland's bleachgreens had a reputation for quality along with lower prices. Consequently, many English companies sent their linen and union cloth to be bleached and finished there. Banford's English customers were listed in a separate book with a specialty in bleaching union cloth.[43]

While the various greens along the Bann must have competed with each other to some extent, Parliamentary and oral evidence suggest that the greens tended to specialize. In the 1850's, the Parliamentary Commissioners, interviewed two Tullylish bleachers, Messrs. J & W Uprichard and Messrs. Haughton & Fennell of Banford Green. Springvale bleached linen cloth, diaper, and damask while Haughton & Fennell, describing themselves as 'general linen bleachers', bleached linen cloth, cambric handkerchiefs and other types of linen[44] (see figure 16).

Oral evidence relating to specialization confirms that Uprichard's green at Springvale continued to bleach heavy linens like damask and sheeting. Banford green, while more or less in competition with Springvale, bleached cloth that was not quite as wide or heavy. Both firms used similar processes, holding to the older methods of bleaching which made more use of the atmosphere as opposed to chemicals. This method took longer but better preserved the quality and strength of the cloth.[45]

During the 1860s, the partners of Banford Bleach Works owned thirteen houses. The 1865 Griffith's Valuation lists thirteen houses owned by Thomas Haughton in Knocknagor in which seventeen heads of household lived, suggesting crowded housing conditions.[46] In 1865, Banford Bleach Works was valued at 160 pounds. The larger Springvale occupying 260 acres, with three iron waterwheels and two steam engines to provide power, and employing about 250 people, was valued at 235 pounds. Springvale's owner William Uprichard built considerably more houses. In Knocknagor, Uprichard owned ten, at Mill Park fifteen and at Coose twenty-two. By 1886, Banford's owners Thomas Haughton and John Edgar had expanded the number of company-owned houses to thirty-two and they employed 150 people.[47] There is also evidence that in 1865, a sick fund was begun at Banford with contributions from the workers' wages deducted each fortnight to be used in case of need by a worker's family.

The largest green in Tullylish located at Milltown, was owned by the Smyths.

42 (PRONI) , D.1769/33/1B, L'Estrange Brett Collection, 14 February, 1880; D.1136/CE/1 Invoice Book No. 4, 1870-72.   **43** (PRONI), D.1136/CE/5, Invoice Book No. 1 English, 1 January 1876 to 11 October 1877.   **44** H.C. *Report of the Commissioners Appointed to Inquire how far it may be Advisable to Extend the Provision of the Acts for the Better Regulation of Mills and Factories to Bleaching Works Established in Certain Parts of the United Kingdom and Ireland*, vol. xviii (1854–5), p. 77.   **45** Interview with former bleachgreen owner Albert Uprichard, July, 1983.   **46** (PRONI) , Griffith's Valuation for the Parish of Tullylish, 1865; D.1136/FA/l, Wages Book no. 4, 1863-5.   **47** Griffith's Valuation; Clarke, *Heart of Downe*, p. 96, George Henry Bassett, *The Book of County Down* (Dublin 1888), p. 261.

About 1824, John Smyth (1798-1890) purchased the land for Milltown Bleachworks and built Milltown house for himself and his family. His eldest son William (1826–1894) started the firm William Smyth & Company, linen manufacturers, and he and his brother John's (1830–1914) business eventually occupied 220 acres and employed 260 people. They had six iron water wheels, a foundry to serve the neighbourhood and also owned Banville Beetling Mills. The Milltown bleachworks was valued at 300 pounds, with the Smyths owning seventy-two houses in Drumnascamph and Lenaderg[48] (see Figure 15).

Evidence from wage books, beginning on 30 January 1909 and continuing until 1926, reveals that sums for housing, coal, and a sick fund were deducted from the workers' wages. Prior to July 1912, the sick fund was contributed to only by employees. After July 13, 1912, a new system was set up where a category of deductions were made for unemployment insurance and insurance that included the sick fund. This system was sustained by both employees and the employer with the amount contributed to unemployment insurance by the workers matched exactly each pay period by the owner Frederick Sinton. Sinton contributed a slightly larger proportion to the sick fund.[49] Workers could also turn to their employers for small loans. While these concrete expressions of paternalism were small and largely unnoted in the historical record, they reflect the level of dependence on owners by their employees.

During the transition to industrial capitalism, the position of working-class men rested both on their class exploitation by capitalists and women's subordination and dependency within the home.[50] At bleachgreens there was a tight fit between the paternal model underlying employer/employee relations, the prevalence of male workers and their ability to keep wives at home. In 1909, only two wives of Banford employees worked for wages outside the home, one in a spinning mill and one in a powerloom factory. One was the wife of a 'fieldman' with no children and the other the wife of a labourer with three wage earning children in their mid-teens. Both of the women employees listed on Banford's wagebooks were widows with young children currently residing with their fathers who also worked at Banford. These wage-earning widows operated within an androcentric logic, living in households headed by their fathers and probably obtaining their jobs through being 'spoken for' by him.

Women were never hired at Banford in large numbers. In the 1863–5 wagebooks, a period of rapid growth, only eight women were employed at Banford as markers of cloth. In 1909, during a period of contraction in the linen industry, only twelve women were employed at Banford – ten of whom worked in the stockroom and the other two as markers. Women's occupations did not require the strength (a 'natural'

48 Griffith's Valuation; Clarke, *Heart of Downe*, p. 30. 49 (PRONI), D.1136/FA/2, Wages Book, 30 January 1909 to 29 November 1913. 50 Keith McClelland, 'Masculinity and the "representative artisan" in Britain, 1850–80', in Michael Roper and John Tosh (eds), *Manful Assertions* (London 1991), p. 77.

male trait) necessary to alternately bleach, and grass large quantities of heavy often wet linen cloth. Their occupations also did not require the skill (another male attribute) required in the application of various chemicals used to whiten brown linen, or the careful judgement involved in providing linen's smooth patent finish.

Since males were key wage earners and expected to work continuously to support their families, it is not surprising that the family labour system was strongest at bleachgreens. Although small, bleachgreens were relatively good places to work, where men earned slightly higher pay and status than in spinning mills. Getting a boy into a skilled trade or occupation was an important means of obtaining security and a respectable masculine identity since they retained autonomy and craft knowledge.[51]

Methods of production and working hours at bleachgreens strongly reflected gender conceptions relating to craft skill and work roles. Due to the length of time required by the open-air bleaching process in Ireland, much of the work was not subjected to the interrelated processes of mechanization, deskilling, and feminization as had occurred in many spinning mill and powerloom weaving occupations. The bleaching process in the early twentieth century at Banford or Springvale bore a remarkable similarity to the process in the eighteenth century, although the use of chemical bleaching agents reduced the time linen was exposed to the atmosphere. As proletarians, bleachgreen workers were dependent upon wages and could not control working hours, rates of pay or exposure to hazardous chemicals and noise. These workers were not labour aristocrats; their wages did not permit a significantly higher standard of living or increased life chances. However, most were able to achieve androcentric cultural definitions of independence – steady employment and support of one's family without recourse to public charity and retention of skill.

After the boom years of the 1860s and 70s, Banford Bleach Works' business appears to have declined and leveled off. Although part of the explanation is the recession of the 1880s, equally significant is a withering of innovation in the bleaching and finishing end of production. The methods of production at Banford at the end of the nineteenth century bore a remarkable similarity to those a century earlier; the small linkages established in the eighteenth century between the temporal requirements of bleaching and mechanical or chemical advances did not continue in the nineteenth.

POWERLOOM FACTORIES: HAZELBANK WEAVING COMPANY

The weaving of linen by powerlooms in Ireland did not begin in earnest until the 1860s. Powerlooms had been present in the 1830s in fairly large numbers mostly engaged in weaving cotton and union cloth. According to E.R.R. Green, in 1836, of

51 Harry Braverman, *Labor and Monopoly Capital* (New York 1974).

the 1516 powerlooms in Ireland, one-third were located in County Down. Shrigley Cotton Mill had 425 powerlooms, and 100 were located at Hayes' mill in Seapatrick which he considered unsatisfactory. After the death of the cotton industry in Ulster by 1850, there were no powerlooms in County Down and only 518 in all of Ulster.

Powerloom linen weaving factories began to reappear in numbers by 1862 when the increased demand for linen cloth fueled by the 'cotton famine' brought about the third wave of industrialization after bleaching and spinning. Eight weaving factories were built during these years increasing the number of powerlooms to 930 in County Down and 4108 in Ulster. By 1868, the number of powerlooms in Ireland was almost equal to Scotland, and far ahead of England, with 8971 of the 12,149 located in Counties Down and Antrim. By 1905, there were twenty weaving factories in County Down with 5286 powerlooms.[52]

Tullylish's handloom weavers produced fine linen not woven on powerlooms until the 1880s. However, by the 1880s, these weavers also faced competition from powerlooms and needed the combined earnings of three to four weavers to live in comfort.[53] In the Lurgan and Waringstown regions, all labourers' cottages had three to four loom weaving shops. After the 1880's, handloom weaving declined for a number of reasons – competition from powerlooms, competition from cheaper cotton handkerchiefs that greatly reduced demand for linen cambric and competition from the rural poor who were migrating to towns like Lurgan in search of employment. By 1897, it was estimated that there were only about 500 handloom weavers in County Down, 800–1000 in County Armagh including the border of Tyrone and Monaghan, and about 1,000 in County Antrim including the border with Derry.[54]

There were two powerloom factories located in Tullylish, and several more in or around Banbridge. One was owned by Dunbar Dickson & Company and the other was located at Hazelbank in Coose near Lawrencetown. The powerloom factory at Hazelbank had, since the early nineteenth century, been owned by the Law family. Samuel Law, a bleacher, erected the earliest spinning mill on the site at Hazelbank (see figures 16, 17). This spinning mill continued to run at least until his death in 1867 and, perhaps, until the mid-1870s. From that point, the spinning mill was occupied by Mr McTier and Susan Law. Griffith's Valuation in 1865 valued the land and buildings that comprised the Hazelbank flax spinning mill at 290 pounds. Law had also built thirty-six workers' houses at Coose known as 'Law's Row' and owned another nineteen in Drumnascamph. The populations of Law's Row reached 107 by 1861, a figure large enough to warrant separate listing in the census.

52 Green, *Industrial Archaeology, p.* 11.   53 H.C. *Royal Commission on Labour, Reports from the Assistant Agricultural Commissioners, Industrial Relations*, Ireland, vol. 4, Parts 1–4, IUP ser., vol. 40 (1893–4), p. 86.   54 H.C. *Board of Trade Report by Miss Collet on Changes in the Employment of Women and Girls in Industrial Centers, Part I: Flax and Jute Centers*, vol. 88 (1898), pp. 52–3.   55 (PRONI), Griffith's Valuation, 1865; VAL.12B/16/25B, 1879–86; and D.1286/2/4, Beck Notebooks, History of Flax Spinning Mills in Ulster.

At some point between 1875–9, after Samuel Law's death, Thomas Dickson and William Walker, a linen merchant from Banbridge, purchased the premises and most of the workers' houses, establishing the Hazelbank Weaving Company. At the time of the 1879 Valuation, the buildings were valued at 230 pounds and there were still thirty-six company-owned houses. Dickson and Walker increased the number of powerlooms from seventy-five to 200 and built two preparing sheds. The weaving shed in which Messrs. William Law & Company had manufactured fine linens was already there.[55] By 1886, Hazelbank Weaving Company, employed 200 people, mostly young women, weaving drills, rough browns, buchrams and glass cloths as the following description indicates.

> When the Hazelbank Weaving Co. entered into possession, there were only 75 looms. This number has since been increased to 200, all having the very latest improvements. During the winter and spring, an iron breast-wheel 15 feet in diameter and 8 1/2 feet fall, produces about 65 horse power, and works in conjunction with a steam engine of 70 horse power ... The buildings of modern character consist of a weaving shed, 135 feet long and 100 feet wide; and two preparing sheds, one 135 feet long and 23 feet wide; and the other 135 feet long and 36 feet wide. The weaving shed was in existence previous to 1880, and the preparing sheds were built by the Hazelbank Weaving Co. Extra warerooms are also among the latest improvements, the whole necessitating an extensive outlay. The mill premises and grounds cover 17 statue acres. Included in this area is the house of Mr Walker and 43 workmen's cottages, all built by the firm. About 200 people are employed. A majority of this number are daughters of small farmers residing at a convenient distance from the factory.[56]

Increases in the population of adjacent Lawrencetown reflect the growth and influence of Hazelbank. Lawrencetown's population was not high enough prior to 1851 to be listed separately in the census. By 1851, as part of the Famine-induced population explosion along the Bann, Lawrencetown had a population of 129, with thirty-five households pressing into twenty-four houses. Thereafter, the population fluctuated at 126 in 1861, 143 in 1871 (with the number of houses rising to thirty-two), and 139 in 1881.

The owners of Hazelbank Weaving Company provided only housing for their workers.[57] Since the workforce of Hazelbank was relatively small in comparison to Dunbar McMaster & Company or F.W. Hayes & Company, it was common for women in a given household to work in the weaving factory, men at a nearby bleachgreen, and children either in the above factories or at a yarn spinning mill depending on

56 Basset's, *Co. Down*, pp. 270–1. 57 (PRONI), D.1764/2, Cash Book, no. 3, 26 February 1909 to 9 June 1913.

their sex. Thus, mill settlements along the Bann were connected by overlapping work and kinship ties.

The labour force of powerloom weaving factories was predominantly female. Although the majority of powerloom weavers were female, more male powerloom weavers were employed outside of Belfast due to the lack of alternative employment opportunities.[58] Rural employers also hired males for jobs such as weft winders, warpers, pirn cleaners and givers-in, which were exclusively female in Belfast. Further, certain job categories, notably various 'assistants', do not appear in the Belfast statistics. These assistants were usually young boys further supporting the argument that rural linen factory owners tended to hire more males and juveniles than urban owners.[59]

Powerloom weavers were paid by the piece according to a scale of prices that equalized their pay, regardless of the type of cloth woven. This was in contrast to handloom weavers whose prices could vary dramatically according to the type and fineness. Generally, piece rate workers earned slightly better wages than time workers with some exceptions. Weaving factories paid all of their weavers, warp and weft winders by the piece, and they earned slightly better wages than most female spinning mill workers.

However, the wages of powerloom weavers were often held down through frequent fines. Weavers, who were piece workers, received their work in the shape of a beam of warp divided into so many 'cuts' or lengths. The number of cuts varied considerably, and with each beam weavers received particulars stating the number of cuts and the length of time each cut should take to weave. Note was made of the time when weaving of the cut began. Powerloom weavers, thus, made few independent decisions during the production process with a number of men including tenters, cloth passers and management, responsible for overseeing productivity and quality control.

Fines were generally small but could amount to a considerable deduction from the worker's weekly wage. Workers could be fined for late attendance, reelers were fined for reeling either too much or too little yarn (short or long count), weavers were fined for damaged webs, hemstitchers were fined for damaged work and deductions were made for thread and needles used in their work.[60]

The 1896 Truck Act attempted to control and regulate fines and deductions from wages. Where these were imposed, certain necessary conditions were required. All fines or deductions due to bad work, damaged goods, or materials and articles used during work, were illegal unless made in pursuance of a contract between the employer and the worker. This contract had to be in writing and signed by each worker and each worker was to receive a copy. In the case of fines, the contract had to specify clearly the matter in respect of which a fine was to be imposed

58 Parr, 'Disaggregating', 517.   59 H.C. *Return of Labour Statistics from the Board of Trade, Part II, Industrial Relations: Wages,* IUP ser., vol. xx (1887–92).   60 H.C. *Annual Report of the Chief Inspector of Factories and Workshops for the Year 1902,* vol. xii (1903), p. 148.

and the amount. No fine or deduction was legal unless it was reasonable. Written particulars were to be given to the worker on each occasion when a fine or deduction was made.[61] In most spinning mills and weaving factories, a contract notice was exhibited showing the various deductions that could be made.

The loophole in the Truck Act allowing for evasion was to designate as 'bonus' a certain part of the sum contracted to be paid to the worker, and to attach certain conditions to its payment. According to Factory Inspector Deane, a woman whose wage was 1s.4d. per day or 1½d. per hour had 2s.4d. deducted for being a few minutes late in the morning. A combination of the bonus system and the custom of 'locking out' from the moment of commencing time till breakfast time resulted in the loss of one quarter of her day's earnings. She received 7s.8d. instead of 10s. for her 55½ hour week because the 2s.4d. deducted that represented a 'bonus' of 2s. and the loss of 4d. for one quarter of the day. Usually a bonus ranged from 6d. to 1s. per week, however the amount varied and could be as much as 2s. This whole system was exempt from the Truck Act.[62]

In the case of spinning mills, the bonus was a time bonus or a certain amount given for making full time in a week and was part of the sum contracted to be paid. Workers considered the bonus to be part of the wage because without it, weekly wages were far too low to reproduce the worker. Each mill had a different method of formulating this bonus. In some mills, workers were allowed entrance to the mill for five or ten minutes after commencing time and at the end of meal hours by paying a fine of 1d. or 2d. if they were any later they were locked out until the next meal hour losing both that part of the day's wage and the bonus. In the majority of mills however, workers who were not at the entrance gates at the exact commencing time or after meal hours were closed out until the next meal time, losing both wages and bonus. This held even if the worker was absent due to illness.[63]

Hazelbank's wage books confirm that a system of fining was in place from 1881. Although all workers except cloth passers and managers were open to fines, skilled male tenters were fined very infrequently. Weavers, weft and warp winders, beamers, warpers, and drawers-in were all fined anywhere from 1d. to 1s.1d. Weavers were the group most subjected to fines although they appear to be compensated for time lost due to loom breakdown as a concession to the piece rate system. Weavers received 64.2 per cent of 467 fines followed by weft winders. Fines tended to be small at Hazelbank with 87.4 per cent between 1–4d., and 66.2 per cent between 1–2d. This suggests that generally Hazelbank complied with the 'reasonable fine' requirement of the Truck Act. By 1882, there was also evidence of a bonus system.[64]

61 H.C. *Annual Report of the Chief Inspector of Factories and Workshops for the Year 1906*, vol. x (1907), p. 322. 62 Ibid., pp. 240–2. 63 Ibid., pp. 240–2; Hilda Martindale, *From One Generation to Another, 1839–1944* (London 1944), pp. 138–41. 64 (PRONI), D. 1764/10B, Wage Book 11 April, 1892 to 27 March, 1893 and Wage Book 21 March 1881 to 15 August, 1887; Lown, *Women and industrialization*, p. 108.

Each weaving factory had a different bonus system and fines for lateness varied between factories.[65] On the whole, weaving factory workers were not quite so strictly treated as spinning mill workers. Usually they were allowed entrance if they were two or three minutes late, and up to five or ten minutes upon paying a fine. Those later than this were locked out losing their bonus, even in cases of illness. Weavers received a bonus of 2s.6d. a fortnight. If shut out of the factory, losing 1s.3d. of the day's wage, they lost 1s.6d. of the bonus for the first offense and 2s.6d. if they were late again. Winders often did not receive a bonus, and when they did, it was in accordance with the number of hanks wound. A weft winder would receive weekly 1s.5d. for winding 100 hanks for the first 500 and then 1s.6d. per additional hundred. A warp winder would receive 10d. per hundred hanks for the first 800 and then 6d. per hundred extra. In some factories a weaver could earn a bonus for perfect cloth, but deductions were made from it for bad work. If the cloth passer complained once per fortnight about flaws in the cloth the weaver was fined 1s.6d. and twice she lost the whole 2s.6d. Thus, few weavers were ever able to earn this bonus. Inspector Hilda Martindale was skeptical of owners' justifications for the bonus system.

> I have been told that it has been the practice for many years and arose owing to a scarcity of women's labour, the manufacturers holding this out as an inducement to their workers to remain with them. Again, I was informed that it was a difficult matter to ensure that workers came regularly, and that it was imperative from a manufacturers point of view that spinning frames and weaving looms should not stand idle and that these ends could only be gained by the adoption of a system of this kind. It seems to me curious that in Ireland, where there has always been rather a dearth of employment than of employees, that this reason of scarcity of workers should be put forward, and again, if it is so important that looms and frames should be at work, it is surprising that it is politic to shut out workers and not allow them employment for several hours if they happen to be a few minutes late.[66]

Henry Patterson states that, 'mechanisation allowed an influx of women and young workers into weaving. This meant that the weaving trade began to suffer a lowering of status as it became defined as "women's work."'[67] Fining reflects this lowering of occupational status. It comprised one aspect of a larger proletarianization process in which weavers of linen, once relatively autonomous skilled male workers, were deskilled and feminized.

---

65 Martindale, *From One Generation*, pp. 242–3. 66 Ibid. 67 Henry Patterson, 'Industrial labour and the labour movement, 1820–1914', in Liam Kennedy and Philip Ollerenshaw (eds), *An Economic History of Ulster* (Manchester 1985), p. 160.

HEMSTITCHING FACTORIES: SEVERAL EXAMPLES

Finally, there were two hemstitching factories in Tullylish, again employing mostly women. One was located in the handloom weaving townland of Ballydugan called Blane's, and the other was located near Banbridge called Bell's. In 1910, a hem-stitching factory was started by James Blane who had previously been a linen manu-facturer employing handloom weavers. Hemstitching of handkerchiefs was performed in the factory while drawn thread work or shire stitching was done by homeworkers who lived near by. Local women, usually mothers at home, came to the factory to pick up the handkerchiefs and returned them finished.

In 1912, Blane introduced Swiss embroidery machines and opened Ireland's first Swiss embroidery school in Ballydugan. There were only two such schools in Ireland, the other one located in County Londonderry.[68] A 1912 Valuation assessed the hemstitching factory at 157 pounds, the embroidery factory at 83 pounds, and the Embroidery School at 18 pounds. At that time, Blane did not own any workers' houses. Swiss embroidery was a skilled occupation and, consequently, the machin-ery was operated by one adult male with three female assistants. All were taught their skills in the 'Theory Room' or Embroidery School by an experienced Swiss instructor named Hans Siefert. Hemstitching factories paid their workers piece rates and, in the case of Swiss embroidery, the wages of the female assistants de-pended on the speed of the embroiderer. A proficient embroiderer could embroider as many as thirteen dozen handkerchiefs at one time.[69] In 1915, the following de-scription of the Embroidery Schools at Ballydugan and Maghera was provided by George Fletcher:

> These schools are well designed, light and airy buildings, offering pleasant conditions for work. No motive power is required other than that provided by the worker. The worker sits at one end of the machine, which is operated by hand and foot. The enlarged design is mounted on a board, and the opera-tor follows it, point by point, with an indicator which operates a pantograph and moves the long frame holder containing the handkerchiefs, which are held in position by metal frames. In the six and three-quarter yards machine as many as 234 handkerchiefs are embroidered simultaneously. The needles, pointed at either end, with an eye in the middle, are held by clips in a frame which moves to and fro on wheels. The 234 needles pass through the hand-kerchiefs at the precise points required, and are seized by corresponding clips at the other side, which slide back, pulling taut the threads. The opera-tor moves the pantograph indicator to the next point of the design, and, by

68 Marilyn Cohen, 'Working conditions and experiences of work in the linen industry: Tullylish, County Down', *Ulster Folklife*, 30 (1984), 14. 69 Ibid., 15; (PRONI) , Val.12B/21/8/E, Valuation Revision List, Tullylish, 1909–1920.

the movement of a lever, the frames containing the needle clips repeat the operation. The needles are threaded, and the thread knotted and cut automatically by a beautiful and cunningly-designed machine. These schools have been very successful. Before they were started, there were scarcely a dozen of these machines in Ulster. Now there are, I am informed, something like 140, and we are well on the way to capture the industry, and thus provide employment for our own workers.[70]

Although wage books for Bell's or Blane's are not available for public inspection, another wage book from John Johnston Hemstitcher in Banbridge exists for the period 1899–1900.[71] In addition to giving information about wages paid to inside and outside workers, we can also glean evidence relating to the different patterns of work among factory and home workers.

At Johnston's firm, inside stitchers were single women who were paid regularly by the piece. They were fewer in number then the outside stitchers who included married women. These outside workers were intermittently paid, indicating that they hemstitched when they could. For example, for the week 5 January 1900, 37 outside stitchers were on the books. Only 15 of these were paid that week, and of the 15, only 11 were paid more than once during the whole month of January. Eleven of the 37 were married women, and of these only 3 were paid more than once in the month. Only one married woman worked continuously and was paid weekly.[72]

Because stitchers were all paid by the piece, we would expect to see substantial differences in the amounts paid to each worker. The last complete entry for 16 November 1900 shows that the wages paid to the 25 inside stitchers ranged between a low of 3s.5½d. and a high of 12s.3d. with an average of 6s.4d. The range among the 36 outside stitchers was much greater from 2s.5d. to £1.0s.9d. due to the varying circumstances affecting homeworkers' productivity. Although the number of hours outside stitchers worked is unknown, the small piece rates paid of 1½d. per dozen and the attention demanded that women worked long hours frequently assisted by their children after or during school hours. Finally, although the exact number of women in Tullylish engaged in homework is unknown, oral evidence suggests that homework provided by hemstitching factories was a principal source of supplementary wages among married women in the parish.

CONCLUSION

Following David Harvey, 'money creates an enormous capacity to concentrate so-

---

70 Quoted in W.H. Crawford, 'A handloom weaving community in County Down', *Ulster Folklife*, 39 (1993), 7,9.   71 (PRONI), D.1042, John Johnston Hemstitcher, Banbridge Co. Down, Factory Wages Book, 1899–1900.   72 Cohen, 'Working Conditions', 15; Joanna Bourke, *Husbandry to Housewifery* (Oxford 1993), p. 122.

cial power in space'.[73] In Tullylish, the construction of built environments was molded in varying degrees by paternalism. While enormous demographic shifts between 1841–61 constrained paternalistic endeavours, the continued expansion of the linen industry until 1880 provided huge profits partially invested in building factory-owned housing and communities along the Bann.

Gilford/Dunbarton represents extensive paternalistic investment, but all of the factory villages and hamlets along the Bann had similar factory milieux. Since all of the mill and factory owners were resident, each reflected the pervasive influence and power of the employer.[74] Although each settlement was distinct, they were closely connected as phases in the production process, as parts of the complex regional linen conurbation, and as working-class communities with minor distinctions in standard of living, life chances and life style. Many families were linked through kinship ties to residents in nearby hamlets, and through ties with co-workers since household members frequently worked in different workplaces along the Bann.

Cultural constructions of gender, which had their roots in an older patriarchal domestic system, profoundly shaped these factory milieux. Paternalistic employers were fathers writ large playing roles similar to the male household head. They controlled the economic system and demanded deference from those provided with the basis of material and social life. The ideological conception of capitalists as benevolent distant fathers partly legitimized the rigid class inequality characteristic of these communities. As linen industry occupations became increasingly deskilled and feminized during the nineteenth century, masculine work identity was reconstructed as men retained roles as supervisors and skilled workers. More finegrained analysis of the feedback between gender, family, community and work relations – the fabric of social life along the Bann – is the subject of the next Part.[75]

73 David Harvey, *Consciousness and the Urban Experience* (Baltimore 1985), p. 12.   74 Joyce, *Visions*, p. 131.   75 William Lazonic, 'Industrial relations and technical change: the case of the self-acting mule', *Cambridge Journal of Economics*, vol. 3 (1979), 231–62; Sonya Rose, '"Gender at work": sex, class and industrial capitalism', *History Workshop*, 21 (1986).

PART III

WORK, FAMILY AND COMMUNITY IN TULLYLISH, 1900–14

9

Work, Demography and Social Structure,

1901

The first decade of the twentieth century fell within a longer pattern of stagnation in the linen industry, lasting from the 1880s to World War I.[1] There were no significant changes in the laws regulating working conditions or major technological advances. Consequently, the period can be treated as a continuation of the late nineteenth century discussed in the previous chapter. This part focuses on actual households and families of linen workers in Tullylish between 1900 and 1914 to illuminate the historically specific connections between work, family and community, and the problem of structure and agency. The analysis of factory culture is deepened by analyzing how work in the mills and factories influenced social life and the formation of identities. This chapter provides a demographic context examining how demographic and social structural patterns in Tullylish were shaped by occupation, kinship, region, religion and gender.

GENERAL CHARACTERISTICS OF THE STUDY POPULATION IN 1901

The study population in 1901 consisted of 3601 individuals living in 751 households. The majority (61 per cent) of the people resided in the factory town of Gilford/ Dunbarton included in its entirety. Sixteen per cent lived in the handloom weaving townland of Ballydugan, or in the townlands of Bleary or Clare close enough to have attended Ballydugan National School. The remaining 23 per cent lived in the rural hinterland of Gilford or the townlands closest to Banford Bleach Works and Hazelbank Weaving Company (see appendix 1).

Most (70 per cent) of the employed population were semi-skilled factory operatives. Eleven per cent were skilled workers, 11 per cent were unskilled labourers and the remaining 9 per cent were property owners, shopkeepers, clerks and other professionals who mostly resided in Gilford. Also, because the labour market favoured young females, we would expect the population to reflect this preference. The sex ratio was 79.9, and 50 per cent of the total population was under 21 with a mean age of 27.

1 Emily J. Boyle, 'The Economic Development of the Irish Linen Industry, 1825–1914', Ph.D. diss., The Queen's University of Belfast, 1977, p. 6.

The religious breakdown of the population reflected the long history of Protestant settlement, especially among adherents of the Church of England in East Ulster and County Down. In Tullylish, 49.2 per cent of the population were Protestant Episcopalians, 19.9 per cent Presbyterians, 29.2 per cent Roman Catholic and 1.5 per cent Quakers and Methodists.

By the turn of the century, 67 per cent of the population in Tullylish could read and write. Only 10 per cent were illiterate and another 9 per cent could read only. These literacy figures were affected by how many years a child attended school, the regularity of attendance and the final class or booklevel attained before leaving school. Since attendance and attainment varied by gender and religion, literacy rates varied among these groups as table 11 shows.[2]

Table 11: Literacy rates by sex and religion in Tullylish, 1901

Literacy	Males		Females		Catholic		Protestant	
	No.	%	No.	%	No.	%	No.	%
Cannot read or write	139	10.2	221	12.7	154	16.6	205	9.5
Can read only	108	7.9	227	13.0	102	11.0	233	10.8
Can read and write	1111	81.8	1291	74.2	673	72.4	1726	79.6
Totals	1358		1739		929		2164	

Source: 1901 Census Enumerators' Schedules for the parish of Tullylish. *Percentages were based on individuals five years of age and above.

Households on the average were small with a mean size of 4.8 persons. This is compatible with Peter Laslett's 4.75 mean for England and L.A. Clarkson and Brenda Collins' figure for Lisburn.[3] However, since this mean tells us little about the changes in size over the life cycle, it is useful to look at certain stages such as the middle years of child raising. When we exclude both the first life cycle stage when the young couple was childless, and the 'empty nest' stage when the older couple's children have left, the mean houseful size rose to 6.2 and the mean nuclear family size to 5.8 persons. This evidence suggests that a family strategy of bearing children who would later become wage earners was prevalent.

2 Analysis of variance supported the hypothesis that the final booklevel, years in school, meeting the 100 minimum days required for promotional examinations, and removal from the attendance register due to excessive absence was affected by religion. The statistics are as follows: 1) booklevel: F ratio = 11.6078, F probability = .0007; 2) struck off: F ratio = 15.2842, F probability = .0001; 3) years attended: F ratio = 13.9469, F probability = .0002; 4) 100 days: F ratio = 16.3756, F probability = .0001. These factors were also affected by gender. 1) booklevel: F ratio = 5.9178, F probability = .0357; 2) Years attended: F ratio = 15.9414, F probability = .0001; 3) 100 days: F ratio = 5.4154, F probability = .0202.   3 Peter Laslett, *Household and Family in Past Time* (Cambridge 1972). Leslie Clarkson and Brenda Collins, 'Protoindustrialization in a northern Irish town: Lisburn 1820–21', in *Proceedings of the International Economic History Conference*, 'A' Theme on Proto-industrialization: Report No. 8. (Budapest: Akad. Kaido 1982).

The formation of households in the parish was shaped by kinship, the family wage economy and religion. Kinship was the principal means by which individuals came together to live. Most people formed households through marriage resulting in households composed of simple nuclear units defined as married couples with or without children and widows or widowers with children. Only 9.5 per cent of the population lived in households without other kin, with 8.1 per cent of this total living alone, and 1.4 per cent living with other unrelated men and women. While most (62.9 per cent) of the population did live in such simple nuclear units, as table 12 illustrates, a significant minority did not. Many individuals remained single and lived either with other members of their family or lived with other non-kin. The number living alone was quite small.[4] This is to be expected given the lack of state support at this time for the sick, elderly or others like single women, whose wages were insufficient for them to make ends meet alone.

Table 12: Types of households in Tullylish by religion, 1901

Type	Total Population		Catholic		Protestant	
	No.	%	No.	%	No.	%
Solitaries	60	8.1	31	13.4	29	5.6
Co-res. siblings and/or other kin	59	7.9	31	13.4	38	7.3
Co-resident non-kin	10	1.4	3	1.3	7	0.9
Nuclear family households	472	62.9	132	57.1	340	65.4
Extended family households	110	14.7	30	13.0	78	15.0
Multiple family households	31	4.1	11	4.8	22	4.2
Indeterminate	9	1.2	3	1.3	6	1.1

Source 1901 Census Enumerators' Schedules for the Parish of Tullylish.

A high percentage of the population above the age of twenty (37 per cent) were single. Because of the unbalanced sex ratio, we would expect to find higher proportions of single women. However, when we examine which women remained single, religion becomes relevant. More Catholic men and women remained single than Protestants with Catholic women the group most likely to remain unmarried. This deviation in marriage patterns affected the types of households formed and material strategies as shown in table 11.[5] Catholics were more likely to live in non-nuclear family households and female-headed households than Protestants. The latter in particular were smaller with fewer male wage earners.[6]

4 For comparison with Counties Clare, Meath, Wicklow and Mayo see Timothy W. Guinnane, 'Intergenerational transfers, emigration, and the rural Irish household system', *Explorations in Economic History*, 29 (1992), 460–6.   5 Glassie argues that the 'Irish' pattern of postponed or late marriage and high rates of celibacy pertains more to Catholics than Protestants. See Henry Glassie, *Passing the Time in Ballymenone* (Philadelphia, PA 1982), p. 25.   6 Analysis of variance supported the hypothesis that the mean size of households was affected by religion. The F ratio = 4.0095 and the F probability = .0458.

The extended kin most likely to be residing in nuclear family households were grandchildren, sisters, brothers, nieces and nephews. These are lateral or descendent kin who made strategic sense given the preference for juvenile labour in linen mills and factories.[7] While ascendent kin, like parents or grandparents, could function as childminders, or help with housekeeping, lateral and descendent kin were more likely to be employed and contribute their wages to the household purse.

DIFFERENTIATION OF THE STUDY POPULATION: REGION

A focus on four subregions within the Parish reveals distinct demographic patterns. While females outnumbered males in all regions, Gilford/Dunbarton had the highest proportion of females followed by the Banford/Hazelbank region. These were areas dominated by the spinning mill of Dunbar McMaster & Company and the Hazelbank Powerloom Weaving factory respectively. There was little variation in the types of households with the exception of Gilford where more individuals lived alone. Catholics, however, were not evenly distributed in the parish with 80 per cent of the Catholic study population living in Gilford or Lawrencetown.

As table 13 shows, Ballydugan, located in the handloom weaving subregion, had the highest illiteracy and partial literacy rates. This townland was late relative to the other regions in providing an evening school for older children and young adults. The first group of young persons attending were 19–20 years of age. Many had not attended day school and achieved literacy at the evening school. In this period, material constraints strongly influenced who attended school, the regularity of attendance and the number of years children remained in school. Handloom weaving households still relied on the labour of all household members with children often functioning as winders, weavers, givers-in and with setting up the complicated patterned cards used by damask weavers on their Jacquard looms. If parents needed their children to help with these tasks they were kept home from school. Consequently, the children of handloom weavers attended school more erratically and for less years than those in the other regions. The mean years for children in Ballydugan was 5.8 as compared with 7.5 in Gilford/Dunbarton and Banford/Hazelbank.

Children in Gilford/Dunbarton, whose attendance at school was regulated by the Factory Acts, attended school most regularly followed by those in Banford/Hazelbank where some halftimers were also employed. Rural areas such as those surrounding Gilford and, Ballydugan had the most erratic attendances. Children of both sexes were kept at home if they were needed as childminders, if they did not have adequate or suitable clothing and shoes, to help with preparing the loom prior to weaving and to help with agricultural work during peak times of the year.

7 Michael Anderson, *Family Structure in Nineteenth Century Lancashire* (Cambridge 1971), pp. 9–16.

Table 13: Literacy rates in Tullylish by region, 1901

Literacy	Gilford %	Rural %	Banford/Hazel %	Ballydugan %
Illiterate	10.2	9.8	7.5	11.7
Can read only	8.5	5.2	6.5	17.5
Literate	67.4	73.2	72.9	56.0
Too young*	13.9	11.7	13.1	14.9

Source: 1901 Census Enumerators' Schedules for the Parish of Tullylish. *those under five years of age.

   Less years in school and erratic attendance would affect overall achievement levels. Table 14 shows, while the vast majority of children in all four regions left school after the 5.1 Booklevel, in Ballydugan most left after the fourth class. They were less likely to meet the minimum 100 days necessary to qualify for promotional exams, were more likely to be 'struck off' the register for missing thirteen consecutive weeks and were less likely to advance into higher classes.[8] Although all four schools facilitated literacy, Ballydugan was the least successful.

Table 14: Final booklevel achieved by region, 1901

Booklevel	Gilford %	Rural Gil %	Banford/Hazel %	Ballydugan %
Infant only	6.8	3.5	3.4	9.7
1st class	17.7	19.6	12.5	22.2
2nd class	33.2	37.1	26.1	34.0
3rd class	50.8	52.5	42.0	55.5
4th class	74.7	72.1	63.6	79.8
5.1 class	87.4	88.9	84.1	97.2
5.2 class	92.2	97.3	93.2	97.9
6.1 class*	100.1	100.1	99.9	100.0
Total pupils	2194	325	512	567

Source: 1901 Census Enumerators' Schedules for the Parish of Tullylish; SCH.162/1/1,2 Attendance Registers for Ballydugan National School; SCH.325/1/1,2 Attendance Registers for Gilford No. 1 National School; SCH.325/1/4–11 Attendance Registers for Gilford Mill National School; SCH/327/1,2 Attendance Registers for Knocknagor National School. *includes all children in classes 6.1 and above. Percentages are cumulative.

8 Analysis of variance supports the hypothesis that the booklevel, years attending school, removal from the register for irregular attendance, and meeting 100 minimum days was affected by place. The Tukey test revealed that variation in the means significant at the .05 level between Ballydugan and the other three National schools.

DIFFERENTIATION OF THE STUDY POPULATION: RELIGION

Elsewhere, I have analyzed the multidimensional ways in which religion mediated social structure in Tullylish.[9] Skilled workers included mechanics, artisans, craftsmen and all other occupations which required a period of apprenticeship. As in Belfast and Dublin, there were proportionately more Protestant skilled workers (17.3 per cent) than Catholic (10.5 per cent).[10] There were twice as many Protestant mechanics as Catholic and three times as many Protestant artisans and craftsmen. Relative to their numbers, more Catholics were to be found among the 11 per cent of lower paid, lower status unskilled jobs such as labourers or domestic servants.

Within the spinning mill of Dunbar McMaster & Company, religion mediated the ranking of occupations to some extent. For example, flaxdressers or 'hacklers' were the highest paid and highest status male employees. Among male workers, who were the principal wage earners in a household, the main criterion for status was wages earned. Unlike roughers, flaxdressers and sorters were skilled occupations requiring an apprenticeship of seven years. Protestant flaxdressers outnumbered Catholics by four to one. In contrast, sixteen of the twenty-six roughers were Catholic.

This intersection between occupational status and religion characterized female occupations to a lesser degree. The few women professionals such as nurses, teachers or postmistresses were mostly Protestant. Status criteria among the majority of semi-skilled female occupations differed since variations in pay between them were small. On the whole, piece workers, such as reelers, weavers, winders and hemstitchers, earned slightly higher wages. These occupations were also of a higher status than yarn spinners because of the small difference in pay, greater sense of autonomy while working and the degree of cleanliness (meaning the lack of dust, water and oil) associated with them. Among female spinning mill occupations, religion was not a significant variable with nearly the same number of Catholic reelers (twenty-eight) as Protestant (thirty-one). Oral evidence suggests that only in hemstitching factories did religion influence employment opportunities for women. These were also higher status jobs due to the clean, quiet, less strenuous working conditions and were predominantly filled by Protestants.[11]

---

9 Marilyn Cohen, 'Religion and social inequality in Ireland', *Journal of Interdisciplinary History*, 25, no. 1 (1994). 10 Richard Jenkins, *Lads, Citizens and Ordinary Kids* (London 1983), pp. 26–7; Richard Jenkins, 'Ethnicity and the rise of capitalism in Ulster', in Robin Ward and Richard Jenkins (eds), *Ethnic Communities in Business* (Cambridge 1984), p. 57; Mary Daly, *Dublin: the Deposed Capitol* (Cork 1984), p. 124; E.A. Aunger, 'Religion and class: an analysis of 1971 census data', in R.J. Cormack and R.D. Osborne (eds), *Religion, Education and Employment* (Belfast 1983) pp. 34–7; A.C. Hepburn, 'Employment and religion in Belfast 1901–1951', in R.J. Cormack and R.D. Osborne (eds), *Religion, Education and Employment* (Belfast 1983), p. 45; A.C. Hepburn, 'Work, class and religion. in Belfast, 1871–1911', *Irish Economic and Social History*, 10 (1983), 37–42; Denis P. Barritt and Charles F. Carter, *The Northern Ireland Problem* (Oxford 1962), p. 53; and Cohen, 'Religion and Social Inequality'. 11 Marilyn Cohen, 'Working conditions and experiences of work in the linen industry', *Ulster Folklife*, 30 (1984), 6–15;

Due to the low wages prevailing in the linen industry, of the 429 wives with resident husbands in Tullylish, 20.7 per cent worked in factories, a number significantly higher than the 13.6 per cent reported for Ireland by Margaret Hewitt.[12] However, skilled workers such as mechanics and bleachgreen workers were better able to keep their wives at home and children in school.[13] In households headed by unskilled laborers proportionately more were required to work. Since proportionately more Catholic men filled lower paying unskilled jobs, twice as many Catholic wives (33 per cent) worked outside the home as Protestant (17 per cent).[14]

Religion also shaped residence and marriage patterns. Religious endogamy in Tullylish was nearly absolute strongly determining the formation of households. Further, because Catholics were more likely to remain single (due partly to prohibitions against remarriage and greater legitimacy for celibacy), there were proportionately more of them living in female-headed households (29.1 per cent) than Protestants (18.7 per cent).

Most of the Catholic study population were concentrated in Gilford/Dunbarton or Lawrencetown.[15] Finegrained analysis of Gilford/Dunbarton street-by-street revealed considerable residential clustering.[16] All but one of Gilford's eighteen streets were relatively homogeneous with 70 per cent or more of the population either Catholic or Protestant.[17] Seven streets in Gilford/Dunbarton were entirely Catholic or Protestant accounting for 8.0 per cent of Catholic households and 12.9 per cent of Protestant households. Catholic households were in the majority on only five streets. Sixty-one per cent of all Catholic households lived on these streets with 48.8 per cent living on two – Castle Hill Street in Gilford and Hill Street in Dunbarton. Protestant households formed the majority on the remaining thirteen streets. In only five streets did the proportion of Catholic households approximate the proportion (21.6 per cent) of Catholics in the town.

Religion also strongly dictated where a child went to school. In 1901, there were three schools in Gilford/Dunbarton. The oldest was the Gilford No. 1 school established in 1819. While the religious composition of this school prior to National Board statistics is unknown, by mid-century, it became and remained overwhelmingly

Betty Messenger, *Picking Up the Linen Threads* (Austen, TX 1975), p. 72; Nora Connolly O'Brien, *James Connolly: Portrait of a Rebel Father* (Dublin, 1975), p. 124; and interview with former hemstitcher, Mrs Fry, July, 1983. **12** Margaret Hewitt, *Wives and Mothers in Victorian Industry* (London 1958) p. 13. **13** Analysis of variance supported the hypothesis that the mean number of girls in school over age twelve would be affected by the occupation of the household head. The F ratio = 2.6492; F probability = .0075. The Tukey test revealed differences in the means significant at the .05 level between skilled and other workers. See also Peter N. Stearns, 'Working-class women in Britain, 1890–1914', in Martha Vicinus (ed.), *Suffer and Be Still* (Bloomington, IN 1972), pp. 101–2. **14** Hepburn, 'Work, class and religion', 41–2. **15** See Anthony C. Hepburn, 'Catholics in the north of Ireland, 1850–1921: the urbanization of a minority', in Anthony C. Hepburn (ed.), *Minorities in History* (New York 1979), 86, for an analysis of working class residential segregation in Ulster towns. **16** Hepburn, 'Catholics', 91–2; Hepburn, 'Work, class and religion', 36–7. **17** Patrick O'Flanagan, 'Urban minorities and majorities: Catholics and Protestants in Munster Towns c.1659–1850', in William Smyth and Kevin Whelan (eds), *Common Ground* (Cork 1988), p. 129.

18　Castle Hill National School, Gilford, 1924

19　Knocknagor National School, 1920

Protestant, managed by the local Presbyterian minister. The Gilford Mill National Schools, owned and managed by the paternalistic owners of Dunbar McMaster and Company, were from their inception in 1846 under the direction of the National Board and strongly committed to its goal of integrated schooling. These schools remained denominationally mixed (in spite of their use as the Church of Ireland Sunday School) largely because they catered to the needs of halftimers of all faiths working in the mill. Finally, in 1879, the Castle Hill National School was established on the grounds of the Roman Catholic Chapel and managed by the curate of the parish (see figure 18). The demand for this school by Catholics who raised funds by subscription, reflected strong sentiments among Catholic residents that the religious education needs of their children were not being met by the other two National Schools.

In the Banford/Hazelbank region there were two schools, both of which were highly segregated. Knocknagor, long associated with the Church of Ireland, was almost exclusively Protestant (see figure 19). The older Bann National School, located in Lawrencetown, had a predominantly Catholic student population in its Day School while its Evening School was mixed. The religious composition of other schools in the parish such as Ballydugan, reflected older settlement patterns in the townland where they were located.

A.C. Hepburn and Brenda Collins point out that differential illiteracy between Catholics and Protestants was, at the turn of the century, a much discussed topic. They found that in Belfast twice as many Catholics were illiterate as Protestants.[18] Aggregate census data for Tullylish in 1901 reveal that illiteracy rates varied by religious group in proportions similar to Belfast with roughly twice as many illiterate Catholics. Deviation was most pronounced in Gilford where 17.4 per cent of Catholics were illiterate as compared with 6.8 per cent of Protestants. In the study population, 16.6 per cent of Catholics were illiterate as compared with 9.5 per cent of Protestants. However, Catholics (11 per cent) were equally likely to be partially literate as Protestants (10.8 per cent). Part of the explanation is that proportionately more Catholic children (47 per cent) attended for only one to five years and 77.9 per cent left after eight years. Fewer Protestant children (27.7 per cent) left after five years and 40.8 per cent remained for up to ten. This meant that fewer Catholic children were in the higher level classes above the fifth class. While more years in school did not at this time translate into vertical social mobility, the ability to keep children in school reflects subtle but meaningful distinctions in status and standard of living among the working class.

18 Hepburn and Collins, 'Belfast', 218–19; and Hepburn, 'Catholics', 96.

DIFFERENTIATION OF THE STUDY POPULATION: GENDER

Gender represents another way in which the working class was stratified since women earned about half the wages of men.[19] Households headed by women were among the poorest segments of the population. In Tullylish, there were 236 women who headed households, representing 31.3 per cent of the total.[20]

While the factors promoting the formation of female-headed households have been debated, the link between female-headed households and poverty has been repeatedly affirmed.[21] In her study of Irish female paupers in the mid-nineteenth century, Dympna McLoughlin has shown that the majority of workhouse inmates were able-bodied females comprised of single pregnant women, deserted wives, and older women with children.[22] For these women, temporary residence in the workhouse formed part of a complex strategy for survival.

A theoretical relationship between the growth and poverty of female-headed households as a consequence of proletarianization is revealed by a comparison of census data just prior to mill-based spinning in 1821 with data beginning in 1851. In 1821, female-headed households represented 14.1 per cent of the total 121 households in the nearby townland of Derryhale in Kilmore parish with widows comprising fourteen of seventeen female heads. This suggests that prior to mill-spinning the commodification of labour power was not yet sufficiently advanced to be a factor generating households headed by *single* women. Clarkson and Collins' study of Lisburn, based on the 1821 census, found that opportunities for employment as spinners, tambourers, embroiderers, lured widow-headed households from the countryside.[23]

Such commodification intensified after 1825. During the period of most rapid proletarianization between 1825 and 1851, female-headed households in the region were created by complex factors including death, desertion, migration, individualized earning and expanding employment opportunities for females. The 1851 Census provided demographic data relating to male and female-headed households. In

19 Jane Lewis, *Women in England* (Bloomington, 1984), pp. 162–73. 20 Marilyn Cohen, 'Survival strategies in female-headed households: linen industry workers in Tullylish, County Down, 1901', *Journal of Family History*, 17, no. 2 (1992), 303–18. Brenda Collins found that more than 20 per cent of all people in Belfast lived in female-headed households with the availability of employment largely accounting for this high proportion. See Brenda Collins, 'Families in Edwardian Belfast', Unpublished paper presented to the Urban History Group of the Economic History Society annual meeting, University of Aberdeen, March 1982, 4. 21 Marietta Morrissey, 'Female-headed families: poor women and choice', in Naomi Gerstel and Harriet Engel Gross (eds), *Families and Work* (Philadelphia 1987), pp. 302–14; Martha T. Mednick, 'Single mothers: a review and critique of current research', in Arlene S. Skolnick and Jerome H. Skolnick (eds), *Families in Transition*, 6th ed. (Glenview, IL 1989), pp. 441–56; Nancy Folbre, 'The pauperization of motherhood: patriarchy and public policy in the United States', *Review of Radical Political Economics*, 16, no. 4 (1984) pp. 72–88; Lown, *Women and Industrialization*, p. 77. 22 Dympna McLoughlin, 'Workhouses and Irish female paupers 1840–70', in Maria Luddy and Cliona Murphy (eds), *Women Surviving* (Dublin 1989), pp. 119–24. 23 Clarkson and Collins, 'Proto-industrialization', 10–11.

Gilford/Dunbarton, 55.3 per cent of the population was composed of female-headed households; only 44.7 per cent lived in male-headed households. The predominance of female-headed households can partly be explained by both the death of and desertion by many married men during the Great Famine and the rapidly expanding labour force of Dunbar McMaster and Company after 1841. Many households headed by women were attracted to the employment opportunities at the spinning mill. Elsewhere in Tullylish, the proportions living in female and male-headed households were nearly equal.

Throughout the period between 1871 and 1891, single and married females outnumbered single and married men in the Banbridge Poor Law Union. An unbalanced sex ratio coupled with abundant employment opportunities along the River Bann encouraged the formation of households headed by single women. Both opportunities for employment, and social contact with other single women tend to concentrate never-married women in cities and towns.[24] While women earned about half the wages of men, resulting in a precarious existence for women living alone, pooling resources (spinster clustering) allowed for the survival of households composed of single women.[25] A preference for female labour would also encourage both single and married males to migrate out of the region effectively creating female-headed households for short or long periods of time. Finally, widows outnumbered widowers throughout the period. Due to the unbalanced sex ratio, widowers who wished to remarry had a larger field of either single women or widows from which to choose perpetuating widow-headed households.[26]

Seventy-two per cent of the female-headed households in the 1901 study population resided in Gilford/Dunbarton where the principal attraction was employment in Dunbar McMaster & Company. The importance of employment for these women, who were often providers for themselves and other dependents, is confirmed when we see that of the 236 female heads, 60.2 per cent were employed, a figure far exceeding the 20.7 per cent figure for wives with resident husbands.

Although all female-headed households faced financial difficulties due to asymmetrical wage scales, it enhances our understanding of the economic strategies, and household composition of female-headed households to distinguish between households headed by widows and single women. Because 'marriage remained the normative expectation of women of all classes', widows were in an ideologically superior position *vis-à-vis* never married women.[27] At the turn of the century, widowhood was a common experience marking the transition of many women to later life cycle stages.

---

24 Ruth B. Dixon, 'Late marriage and non-marriage as demographic responses: are they similar?' *Population Studies*, 32, no. 3, 464; Christine Stansel, *City of Women* (New York 1986), pp. 83–5.   25 Judy Lown, *Women and Industrialization* (Minneapolis, MN 1990), p. 77.   26 Cohen, 'Survival strategies', 307, 310–11; Alexander Keyssar, 'Widowhood in eighteenth century Massachusetts: a problem in the history of the Family', *Perspectives in American History*, 8 (1974), 84–94.   27 Lewis, *Women in England*, p. 3.

In Tullylish, 60 per cent of female heads of household were widows, 36 per cent were single and 4 per cent were listed as married but not residing with their husbands, possibly due to their emigration to Greenwich, New York. When we distinguish between widows and single female heads of household, we find divergent patterns of employment. Beginning with widows, 41.7 per cent were employed; a proportion twice that of wives with resident husbands. Historians have long recognized the significance of widows among the female paid labour force.[28] This higher proportion of employed widows can be explained by the difficulty in making ends meet after the death of the principal wage earner and the commitment of older people to maintaining the headship of their households. Since most of the working class had little or no property or savings to leave to their survivors, loss of a spouse necessitated major adjustment.[29] Few household heads employed in the linen industry would have been able to save enough to provide for a widow and her children beyond a limited period of time.[30]

Jane Lewis states that widows, along with deserted wives and unmarried mothers, were considered under the 1834 Poor Law to be able-bodied. They, therefore, posed 'baffling problems' for local guardians who contemplated whether widows should be encouraged to work. This would have necessitated either taking their dependent children into the workhouse, or providing assistance through outdoor relief. While the attitudes of local guardians toward able-bodied widows and deserted wives varied along with rates of relief, both were more likely to be employed than married women with resident husbands.[31]

Among the working class, widowhood frequently exacerbated the poverty they had known while married to men in low-paying jobs. The best economic solution for a widow was remarriage simply because men earned higher wages. Where remarriage did not occur, economic interdependence was critical due to the lower wages earned by women (about two thirds those of an unskilled man) and the smaller size of female-headed households (3.3 persons) as compared with 5.4 persons in male-headed households.[32]

It is significant that the majority (58.3 per cent) of widows heading households in Tullylish did not work outside the home, reflecting the prevailing family wage

28 Leslie A. Clarkson and E. Margaret Crawford, 'Life after death: widows in Carrick-on Suir, 1799', in Margaret MacCurtin and Mary O'Dowd (eds), *Women in Early Modern Ireland* (Edinburgh 1991); Leslie A. Clarkson, 'Love, labour and life: women in Carrick-on Suir in the late eighteenth century', *Irish Economic and Social History*, 20 (1993), 18–34; Clarkson and Collins, 'Lisburn', 11–13; Wilson, *Life After Death*, p. 63; Lown, *Women and Industrialization*, p. 83.   29 Sonya O. Rose, 'The varying household arrangements of the elderly in three English villages: Nottinghamshire, 1851–1881', *Continuity and Change*, 3 no. 1 (1988), 102.   30 Leslie Woodcock Tentler, *Wage-earning Women* (Oxford 1979), pp. 166–8.   31 Lewis, *Women in England*, pp. 62–4.   32 Clarkson and Collins, 'Lisburn', 10, found a similar distinction in widow-headed households in Lisburn, 1821. The mean size of households headed by spinners was 2.8 as compared with 5.1 for weaving households headed by men.

ideology stressing female dependence on a male wage earner.[33] Evidence suggests that widows tried to maintain the conventional pattern of female employment terminating after the birth of children, but under conditions of poverty, nearly half were unsuccessful. Widows on the whole remained part 'part of a family economy of varying degrees of viability', and tried to retain headship by functioning as housekeepers and relying on the wages earned by older children, other resident kin, or earnings from taking in boarders.[34]

The principal supporters of widow-headed households were children.[35] Carole Turbin suggests that in widow-headed households the contributions of children, and especially daughters were more substantial than in families with resident fathers. While sons usually earned higher wages, daughters contributed a greater proportion of their earnings for a longer period of time. In the mid-nineteenth century, there was broad consensus among the middle class that unmarried women should remain at home fulfilling their obligations as daughters and sisters. This ideology often ran counter to the contingencies of daily life among the middle class, and it was tempered further by economic interdependence among working-class families.[36]

Familial values among the working class in Tullylish were strong and a large proportion of unmarried employed daughters and sons remained home helping to support widowed parents and unmarried siblings. In Tullylish, where opportunities for female employment in the linen industry were prevalent, we would expect daughters to play a substantial role in the support of families. Of the 209 daughters living with widowed mothers, 10.1 per cent were over the age of thirty-five and employed. In spite of higher rates of celibacy and age at first marriage in Ireland, we can, following Susan Watkins, conclude that many unmarried daughters over the age of thirty-five would remain single. We can also assume that their residence in the household represented a strategy of postponed marriage, ensuring a prolonged

33 Lisa Wilson, *Life after Death: Widows in Pennsylvania, 1750–1850* (Philadelphia 1992), p. 2; Daniel Scott Smith, 'Life course, norms, and the family system of older Americans in 1900', *Journal of Family History*, 4 (1979), 287; Peter N. Stearns, 'Old women, some historical observations', *Journal of Family History*, 5 (1980), pp. 48–9.   34 Olwen Hufton, 'Women without men: widows and spinsters in Britain and France in the eighteenth century', *Journal of Family History* (Winter 1984), 364; Tamara Haraven and Louise Tilly, 'Solitary women and family mediations in two textile cities: Manchester and Roubaix', *Annales de Demographie Historique* (1981), 270; Carole Turbin, 'Beyond conventional wisdom: women's waged work, household economic contribution, and labor activism in a mid-nineteenth century working class community', in Carol Groneman and Mary Beth Norton (eds), *To Toil the Livelong Day* (Ithaca 1987), p. 52; Carole Turbin, 'Beyond dichotomies: interdependence in mid-nineteenth century working-class families in the United States', *Gender and History* 1, no. 3 (1989), 301; Tamara Haraven, 'Life-course transitions and kin assistance in old age: a cohort comparison', in David Van Tassel and Peter N. Stearns (eds), *Old Age in Bureaucratic Society* (Westport, CT 1986), 114; and Timothy Guinnane, 'The Poor Law and pensions in Ireland', *Journal of Interdisciplinary History*, 24, no. 2 (1993), 278–81.   35 Keyssar, 'Widowhood', 99–112; Lown, *Women and Industrialization*, p. 83.   36 Martha Vicinus, Independent *Women: Work and Community for Single Women 1850–1920* (Chicago 1985), pp. 4, 10.

contribution to the household budget.[37] Daughters who postponed marriage, either temporarily or permanently, represented a substantial proportion of single daughters who diverged from the conventional pattern by working for most of their adult lives.

While the daughters of widows contributed their earnings for a long period of time, the economic contributions of single sons were also significant. Of the 151 sons living with widowed mothers, 6.6 per cent were over the age of thirty-five and employed. Given the unbalanced sex ratio, the nearly equal proportions of sons and daughters over the age of thirty-five suggests that the economic necessity for all household members to contribute wages and the cultural commitment to help support widowed mothers and other family members was strongly felt by all children. Finally, due to the strength of age domination in Ireland and the degree of economic interdependence, it is reasonable to suggest that patriarchy would be tempered in widow-headed households.[38]

Significantly more widows headed their own households in Tullylish than moved into the households of their children. This supports the argument that in the late nineteenth century older men and women struggled to retain the headship of their households as a way of maintaining relative independence.[39] In households already coping with low wages and cramped living space, taking in a dependent widow meant additional economic burden and loss of privacy. As in the United States during this period, the principal strategy for widows to remain household heads was to be gainfully employed. In cases where the widowed head was unemployed (in Tullylish nearly half), adult children resided with them more often than widowed parents moving in with children.[40]

When we focus on the twenty-four households headed by males where elderly widows resided, we find that similar to England and the United States, widows were more likely to live as dependents in the households of their children than were widowers. Widows overwhelmingly resided with sons, and the vast majority (nineteen) were unemployed continuing the conventional pattern of support by employed children and males.[41] In contrast, of the four elderly widowers residing with their sons, three are listed as employed. There were also seven households where a widowed daughter and her young children were taken in. All of these younger widows

37 Alexander Humphries, 'The family in Ireland', in M.F. Nimkoff (ed.), *Comparative Family Systems* (Boston 1965), p. 237; Hufton, 'Women without men', 362; and Susan Cott Watkins, 'Spinsters', *Journal of Family History* (Winter, 1984), 310; Haraven, 'Life-course transitions', 115; Anderson, 'The Impact', 38.   38 Turbin, 'Beyond Dichotomies', 295; Tilly, 'European Perspective', 310; Guinnane, 'Poor Law', 280.   39 Haraven, 'Life-course transitions', 114–15; Michael Anderson, 'The impact on the family relationships of the elderly of changes since Victorian times in governmental income-maintenance provision', in Ethel Shanas and Marvin B. Sussman (eds), *Family, Bureaucracy and the Elderly* (Durham 1977), pp. 50–1; Rose, 'The varying arrangements', p. 111.   40 Smith, 'Life course', 290–1; Haraven, 'Life-course transitions', 114–15.   41 Smith, 'Life Course', 291; Joanna Bourke, '"The best of all homerulers": the economic power of women in Ireland, 1880–1914', *Irish Economic and Social History*, 17 (1991), 44–5.

were employed. It is not known whether these young widows had followed a conventional employment pattern only to be forced back into the workforce after the death of their husbands or if they worked continuously. It is likely that residence with parents was a temporary strategy on the part of young widows enabling them to achieve a more secure financial footing prior to forming an independent female-headed household. We can assume that the strength of kin ties and the poverty faced by widows living alone motivated the decision by male heads of household to take in elderly widowed parents or young widowed daughters. Such a decision represents a strategy to avoid or deter destitution.

When we turn to single female-heads of household, socio-cultural norms defining conventional employment patterns for women break down completely. In these households, nearly all (88 per cent) women over twelve years of age were employed, thus assuming the role of providers for themselves and other household members. Due to the low wages earned by female linen industry workers, these women were heavily interdependent requiring that they remain employed continuously rather than temporarily or intermittently.[42] When single sisters or sisters-in-law resided with married brothers and their families, nearly all (five of six) were employed suggesting that the continuous pattern of employment among single women also characterized this group. We do not know if their residence was permanent or temporary, but living with a married brother suggests that independence was weighed against greater financial security.

Hepburn and Collins found that in Belfast, 'female-headed households tended to have markedly different demographic characteristics from the households headed by men'.[43] The evidence from Tullylish confirms this differential pattern with the high proportion of female-headed households substantially accounting for the variation in household types. Looking first at the sex composition of female-headed households, only 26.9 per cent of the total members were males while in male-headed households the proportions of males and females were nearly equal (49.3 per cent males and 50.7 per cent females).[44] Female-headed households were often composed of older females averaging 30.8 years of age as compared with 25.3 years in male-headed households. Finally, only 7.9 per cent of the individuals over the age of eighteen residing in female-headed households were married as compared with 57 per cent in male-headed households. The vast majority were either single (66 per cent) or widowed (26.1 per cent). In male-headed households, 35.9 per cent were single and only 7.1 per cent were widowers.

42 Clarkson and Collins, 'Lisburn', 13; Bourke, 'Home Rulers', 45; Bourke, *Husbandry to Housewifery*, 52; Smith, 'Life Course', 287, found high proportions of about one third of all single women employed between the ages of 55–64 and higher proportions of employed single women between the ages of 65–79 than among married women in these age categories.   43 A.C. Hepburn and Brenda Collins, 'Industrial society: the structure of Belfast, 1901', in Peter Roebuck (ed.), *Plantation to Partition: Essays in Honour of J. L. McCracken* (Belfast 1981), pp. 216–17; Collins, 'Families', 4; Clarkson and Collins, 'Lisburn', 10; Mary Daly, *Dublin: The Deposed Capitol* (Cork 1984), p. 307.   44 Clarkson and Collins, 'Lisburn', p. 10.

Expectedly, there were very few female-headed households (5.2 per cent) who were recently married or raising young children. The proportion of female-headed households increased with age reflecting the prevalence of widows at later stages of child raising (16.7 per cent) and old age with children (27.8 per cent). In contrast, most male-headed households were at the early (14.3 per cent), middle (27.1 per cent), and later stages of child raising (26.6 per cent).

When we distinguish between households headed by widows and single women, we also find differences in composition. At the turn of the century, the Poor Law required that children support their aging parents. At times families absorbed their dependent ageing relatives and, at other times, the elderly might have expanded their own households with relatives to bring in more wage earners.[45] The vast majority of widows in Tullylish (84.8 per cent) lived with their children.[46] The remaining 15 per cent lived alone, with other kin, or with non-kin in two-family dwellings. Also, it was not uncommon for widow-headed households to include such descendant kin as grandchildren or nieces and 10 per cent were augmented with boarders. Such adjustments in living arrangements represent economic strategies among those too old to work or to work regularly.

While the composition of households headed by single women was more varied, kinship was still the principal organizing factor. Forty-two per cent of single women lived with their siblings usually their sisters. Another 19 per cent lived with other employed relatives such as cousins or nieces. Only 13 per cent lived alone and another 7 per cent lived with non-kin or as boarders. These attempts not to live alone, or 'spinster clustering', helped ensure survival during a time when state assistance for the poor was minimal and stigmatized.[47] Further, the rigid sexual division of labour underscored economic interdependence in households comprised of single individuals, especially men. As Joanna Bourke states, 'unmarried men always needed a woman – a *relative* – to perform those activities men seem incapable of providing for themselves ...'[48] Never-married women, in particular, support the argument that life-course effects are cumulative.[49] Banbridge and Lurgan Workhouse records confirm that the failure to marry or have living children had negative economic consequences for older women, with childless women more likely to become dependent on parish support.[50]

Turning to the link between poverty and literacy rates among female-headed households, we find higher illiteracy rates than in the population generally. Looking first at literacy rates among female heads of household, we find 27 per cent were illiterate, 30 per cent could read only, and 43 per cent could both read and write, a

45 Rose, 'Varying Household Arrangements', 114; Smith, 'Life Course', 288–91.   46 Hufton, 'Women without men', 362; Richard Wall, 'Women alone in English society', *Annales de Demographie Historique* (1981), 314.   47 Hufton, 'Women without men', 361; Michael Anderson, 'The social positions of spinsters in mid-Victorian Britain', *Journal of Family History* (Winter, 1984), 390; Haraven, 'Life-course transitions', 115.   48 Bourke, 'Home Rulers', 45.   49 Haraven, 'Life-course transitions', 111.   50 Smith, 'Life Course', 292–3.

proportion significantly lower than in the population generally. When all members of female-headed households are included, both partial literacy and illiteracy rates were higher due to the increased need for wage contributions by children reducing the amount of time they spent in school.[51]

While these households contained fewer school-aged children, when we find them, schooling patterns diverged significantly. Children living in female-headed households attended for approximately one year less (6.3 years) than those living in male-headed households (7.2 years). A significantly greater proportion of children living in female-headed households (42.3 per cent) only attended school for five years or less as compared with 26.4 per cent of children in male-headed households. While the vast majority of children would have stayed in school for approximately eight years, 19.2 per cent of children living in male-headed households were able to remain for ten or more years while only 9.6 per cent in female-headed households were able to do so. As the number of years in school increased, the proportion of children living in female-headed households diminished.

Further, daily attendance figures suggest that children in female-headed households attended school more erratically. Halftimers were required to attend school for a minimum of 200 halfdays to qualify for promotional exams. Children who attended school fulltime were expected to attend for 100 days. The data suggest that proportionately more children from female-headed households did not meet the minimum attendances necessary to qualify for promotional exams. These children were more often struck from the register due to thirteen weeks of consecutive absences than those with resident male heads.

Fewer years attending school and more erratic daily attendance translated into lower proficiency or booklevels. Children in female-headed households were less likely to reach the higher level classes of 5.1 and above than those in male-headed households. Seventy-nine per cent of the children living in female-headed households left school after the fourth class as compared with 73 per cent of the latter's children. Children who passed Booklevel four had a fair level of competence at reading, writing and arithmetic. Those leaving before the fourth class would have been only partially literate. Again, 56.4 per cent of the children of female-headed households, compared with 49 per cent of the children of male-headed households left prior to achieving literacy, mastery of arithmetic or the ability to write.

CONCLUSION

Both religion and gender structured access to resources in Tullylish. Since the family wage ideology assumed a temporary or intermittent employment pattern among women, all women workers were paid insufficient wages. As a result, they were

51 Susan J. Kleinberg, *In the Shadow of the Mills* (Pittsburgh 1989), pp. 126–8.

dependent on men – husbands, fathers and employers. The ramifications of these gender-segregated employment practices for female-head households were severe – poverty, heightened economic interdependence and reduced schooling among children.[52] Religion functioned to designate and reproduce who occupied strategic positions within the social and technical relations of production. The evidence presented here supports conclusions reached for Belfast that 'Catholic male householders were disadvantaged in that area of the manufacturing sector of the economy ... where the best paid employment was available'.[53] The next chapters explore the implications of economic constraints for social identity and household strategies.

52 Lown, *Women and Industrialization*, p. 77.   53 Hepburn and Collins, 'Belfast', 228.

10

Dimensions of Factory Culture in Tullylish:
The Shop Floor

> They must have ruled Northern Ireland, the linen lords somehow.
> Sarah Ewart, former reeler, 1983

By the end of the nineteenth century, the permanence of capitalist industry was recognized by many workers in Great Britain, the United States and elsewhere including an acceptance of the legitimate role of capital, notions of rightful profits and the 'laws' of supply and demand. In northeast Ireland, in the second half of the nineteenth century, capitalist control over all phases of linen production was extensive, penetrating even the preserve of fine linen cambric and damask by handloom weavers.

In this context of capitalist hegemony, Patrick Joyce argues that workers attempted to moralize existing stratified social relations between masters and men, propagating such notions as a community of mutual rights and obligations.[1] In small rural factory millieux, where employers were resident, webs of social obligation between social strata were dense. Workers constructed their social identities and relationships in terms of occupation, class and 'extra-proletarian' identifications such as place, religion and gender that included class and gender-specific notions of respectability, camaraderie and sociability often extending beyond the mill or factory gates[2] (see figure 20). This chapter focuses on the social interactions and forms of work-based identities among working-class men and women emphasizing how their work ideologies and subjectivities were strongly mediated by the social construction of gender in the family.

PERCEPTIONS OF CLASS STRATIFICATION

Perceptions of rigid social-class stratification ran deep in Tullylish. Factory owners led materially secure and privileged lives, while the majority of working class households struggled to make ends meet. Low wages throughout the industry negated any notable difference in standard of living or life chances between most categories of linen workers. To some, class privilege by employers, perceived as distant 'linen

---

1 Patrick Joyce, *Visions of the People* (Cambridge 1991), pp. 88–90.   2 Ibid., p. 5.

20   Tullylish Flute Band, *c.*1930

21   Class stratification: Members of the Richardson family of Moyallon pictured with local children at the Moyallon National School, *c.*1900

lords', was understood as 'natural', reflecting a deep consent regarding profit-earn-
ing and domination by property-owning male elites. Although others expressed re-
sentment at this chasm, the lack of alternative employment outside the linen industry
exacerbated workers' dependency on their paternalistic employers.[3] As a former
reeler explained, 'It [the mill] was the only source of income people had at that time.
You had no other ways or means of living'.[4]

A small number of people were farmers, shopkeepers, dressmakers, tailors,
artisans, or publicans. In mill villages, middle-class shopowners were nearly as
dependent upon the mill as workers since both relied upon the provision of wages
spent each week or fortnight in their shop. Such economic interdependence mag-
nified the influence of capitalists – the McMasters, the Sintons, the Dicksons, the
Uprichards and others. The McMasters were considered 'aristocrats' who expected
formal displays deference from their employees.

> ... yes that's where Mr. McMaster lived and he was lord of the manor, if you
> know what I mean by that ... Everybody was bowing and scraping to him if
> they saw him coming. They just had to get their hats off immediately ... if
> they didn't take their hats off it was just ... and everybody was just poor
> things.[5]

Resident employers interacted frequently albeit formally with their employees.
They would talk to and take a friendly interest in their workers' lives, and workers
could turn to them in times of need for small loans. But on the whole, a worker's
experience of the factory owner was as a distant 'gentleman'. 'He was always up
high. You were just a poor thing'. When owners were involved in community level
activities, their formality and artificiality was perceived as 'snobbish'. Employers'
wives often showed an interest in the schools managed by their husbands (see figure
21). Mrs McMaster took a particular interest in the girls' sewing class taught at the
mill school and once a year she would visit the school and examine the
sewing. Children would show her their 'specimens', material on which they practiced
their sewing, and she would reward the girl whose specimen was the best with a pair
of pearl-handled scissors.[6]

> ... once a year the McMasters gave to the Sunday School children at the
> church ... what they called a tea party. And I can remember there were four
> forms put this way, you know, edge to edge, no backs on them, and you put
> your foot over onto that, and you sat in that, and tea was passed round, and

---

3 See Mary Blewett, *The Last Generation* (Amherst 1990), p. 31 for similar expressions of resignation
among the last generation of Lowell, Massachusetts textile workers.   4 Interview with Mary McCusker,
former reeler and resident of Gilford, July, 1983.   5 Interview with Sarah Ewart, former reeler and
resident of Gilford, July 1983.   6 Ibid.

you got a piece a slice of fruit loaf and you never saw fruit loaf until the next year. We didn't have it. We thought it was our birthday to have a piece of this fruit loaf.[7]

As in other parts of rural Ulster, three social classes were relevant in Tullylish – the gentry, the middle class and the working class. The life style of the gentry was separate and distinct from the other classes. The capitalist and property owning gentry, 'didn't mix much with the common people'. Rather they lived above, physically and symbolically, in a large mansion with substantial surrounding property, staffed with servants and the accoutrements of wealth and status. Children of the gentry class were able to obtain the advantages of a higher education, and many attended boarding schools outside of Ireland. At that time, England was a common place where upper class children were sent to be educated, perpetuating the hegemony of English culture along with social isolation from the resident population.

Among the gentry, there were distinct gender-defined domains. As Leonore Davidoff argues, both gentility and its 'lesser derivative respectability' were gendered categories in which men were expected to be independent breadwinners.[8] Men were involved in the public domain including running the family business, working at other occupations appropriate to their class, involvement in politics, and social activities such as hunting or shooting. Local gentry families had a set social routine with a different family in turn holding a bridge or tennis party depending on the season. Nearly all homes had tennis courts. Men also played golf, but the great love of many gentry men in this area was hunting with horses and hounds and shooting pigeons.

Women led lives of leisure in a more private domain defined by the home. Wives were not usually informed about the day-to-day running of the business or their husband's work, and most would not have inquired about such things. Gentry women were also not expected to engage in housework or 'activities which could be classed as labour'.[9] Although the gentry led lives removed from the working class, their power to define a cultural hegemony shaped how working-class men's and women's self-identities.

THE WORK IDENTITIES AND SUBJECTIVITY OF MALE WORKERS

Luisa Passerini highlights several points useful in exploring men's work-based identities in Tullylish: 1) skilled workers' subjectivity includes pride in their manual abilities, quality of product, an attitude of superiority toward unskilled, young and

7 Ibid.   8 Leonore Davidoff, 'The role of gender in the "first industrial nation": agriculture in England 1780–1850', in Rosemary Crompton and Michael Mann (eds), *Gender and Stratification* (Cambridge 1986), p. 191.   9 Interview with Albert Uprichard, former bleachgreen owner and resident of Halls Mill, July 1983.

female workers and mutual respect between themselves and bosses; 2) part of accepting the ideology of the free and equal exchange between worker and employer, involves internalized acceptance of stratification; and 3) work ideologies often facilitated expressions of equality emerging from 'the recognition of a solidarity independent from the division of labor'.[10] These attitudes toward wage earning, the division of labour, and managerial strategies were mediated by gender and the pervasive family labour system.[11]

Under industrial capitalism, working-class men could retain a respectable masculine identity by supporting households, and constructing sexual divisions of labour in the workplace that linked authority, skill and strength with manliness.[12] The retention and recognition of craft skill and occupational sex segregation by successive generations of males strongly shaped male workers' subjectivity and work ideology since their relatively high position in the mills and factories was linked to merit.

For example, in spinning mills, the occupation of flaxdresser or hackler was a skilled job requiring the ability to dress flax properly and an eye for determining the quality of the yarn or thread into which it would eventually be spun. Although the flax was initially rough dressed by another group of male employees, 'roughers', roughing was not considered skilled. Roughers received neither high pay nor high status within the mill. In contrast, flaxdressers' skills were considered the most important in the mill earning flaxdressers the highest pay ($£2.12s.6d$ per week) and status.

Flaxdressing skills were picked up by young apprentices on their own through practice and watching other men at work during their seven year apprenticeship. Skilled workers were able to exert a degree of control over the labor process, chiefly by restricting entry. Knowledge and work practices were confined to those who had served apprenticeships effectively restricting the supply of labour and justifying their wage and status superiority.[13] Flaxdressers began as poorly paid machine boys, may of whom were halftimers dividing their time between school and employment under the Factory Acts. At age thirteen, they moved to the flaxdressing department to begin their apprenticeship. Apprenticeships at Dunbar McMaster & Company lasted for seven years and young apprentices worked at their own berths under the supervision of the foreman. Like the other flaxdressers, apprentices were paid by the piece and dressed about 73–100 pounds of flax.[14]

In the early twentieth century, machines rapidly replaced flaxdressers (see figure 22). Displaced hacklers, and other skilled workers such as mechanics and foremen, maintained that 'the machine can't do the same as the hand for quality ... A

10 Luisa Passerini, 'Work ideology and consensus under Fascism', *History Workshop*, 8 (1979), 92, 95.
11 Joan Acker, 'Hierarchies, jobs, bodies: a theory of gendered organizations', in Judith Lorber and Susan A. Farrell (eds), *The Social Construction of Gender* (Newberry Park, CA 1991), p. 167.   12 Peter N. Stearns, *Be a Man!* (New York 1979), pp. 44–5.   13 John Rule, 'The property of skill in the period of manufacture', in Patrick Joyce (ed.), *The Historical Meanings of Work* (Cambridge 1987), pp. 100–1.
14 Interview with William Quinn, former flaxdresser and resident of Gilford, July 1983.

22   Machine Heckling, F. & W. Hayes & Co., Seapatrick, *c.*1910

machine can do a certain amount but it can't give as true value as the hand'.[15] A former flaxdresser explained that he sorted flax into differently graded piles, 'by the feel of it'.[16] Not only was this judgement valued, but as a former assistant manager at Dunbar McMaster & Company pointed out, it warranted flaxdressers a degree of influence over decision making not shared by other machine operatives.[17]

Relations between managers and skilled male workers in Dunbar McMaster & Company were characterized in terms of mutual respect for skill and reciprocal rights and obligations. Managers 'respected a man for what he knew' or his skill and for his reliability. Workers respected a manager both because he too had served an apprenticeship and because he was expected to 'help a worker out in trouble'.[18]

Mechanics, who built and repaired machinery, were the archetypical skilled male worker. A former textile engineer at Dunbar McMaster & Company served both a seven year apprenticeship and went to technical school at night in Banbridge (after a full day in the mill) between 6:30 pm and 9:00 pm. His skilled labour earned him two pounds for a fifty-five hour week.[19] 'Fitters' were mechanics employed by various bleachgreens serving five year apprenticeships under engineers.[20]

15 Interview with Tom Vaughan, former mechanic and resident of Dunbarton, July 1983.   **16** Interview with William Quinn.   **17** Interview with Bob McElwaine, former assistant manager of Gilford Mill and resident of Dunbarton, July 1983.   **18** Ibid.   **19** Interview with Tom Vaughn.   **20** Interview with Howard Nelson, former fitter and resident of Banford, July 1983.

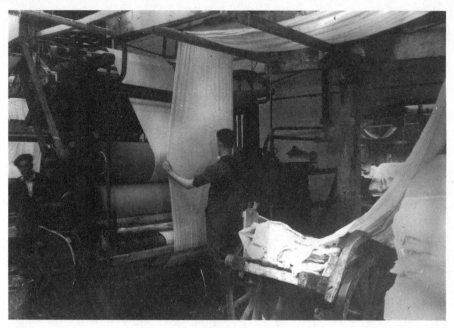

23   H. Cowdy and Sons, Bleachworks, Millmount, 1937

24   Banford Bleachworks showing the processes of stinting and grassing linen. Note pony and cart in the background

Work at bleachgreens required skill, considerable physical strength, and night work, which were all male preserves. During the summer months, when daylight hours were long, bleachgreen workers were expected to work long into the night, stopping only briefly to eat.[21] Although only mechanics required a formal apprenticeship, other skilled occupations at bleachgreens included the head bleacher and his assistant, the bluer, the finisher (the dry equivalent of the bleacher), the head beetler and the calender man. Skills at these and other jobs were largely picked up by the young men or boys through observation and practice.

Although work in bleachgreens was considered relatively healthy, bleaching and finishing did have their hazards. For example, young 'stinters' who carried and spread the wet webs of linen weighing 100–200 pounds, required considerable strength.[22] A beetler could expect his hearing to be impaired due to the noise of the pounding wooden beetles. At that time, no device was provided or worn to protect a beetler's hearing. Kievemen used very strong chemicals referred to as 'the black sour' to bleach the cloth which could injure the skin. 'You had to wear gloves to draw them out. It woulda burned the hands off ye if you hadn't had gloves to wear'.[23]

In all of the bleachgreens there was a unity of labour experience shaped partly by the conformity of open-air bleaching methods in Ireland and partly due to the reputation of the region for high quality bleaching. However, according to the men interviewed, there was a clear status difference between the bleachgreens between Gilford and Banbridge. Milltown bleachgreen at Lenaderg was the best paid and the 'swankiest'. Cowdy's large green near Banbridge was the lowest paid and was considered less safe. Cowdy's also employed the most women and Catholic workers. Banford and Springvale were nearly equal in most respects with Springvale paying slightly better wages (see figures 23, 24). Both had a reputation for high quality work, and kept to the old method of grassing linen to maintain its strength. Cowdy's green was more modern in its techniques suggesting a cultural association among some men between inferior worksites, mechanization or deskilling, and the sex and religious composition of the workforce.

The final skilled male occupation to be analyzed, handloom weaving, differs from the above in that much of the fine linen cambric and damask was, in the early decades of the twentieth century, still woven on handlooms in dispersed rural cottages located in the vicinity of Lurgan and Portadown.[24] Although many handloom weavers worked in dispersed sites rather than concentrated together, here again there was widespread recognition of the unity of labour experience among skilled handloom weavers of fine linen damask and cambric. This experience of unity was,

---

21 Interview with John McCusker, former kieveman and resident of Gilford, July 1983. See also Blewett, *The Last Generation*, p. 203.   22 Interview with Arthur Patrick Burns, former stinter, calender man and resident of Lawrencetown, July 1983.   23 Interview with John McCusker.   24 Marilyn Cohen, 'Working conditions and experiences of work in the linen industry: Tullylish, County Down', *Ulster Folklife*, 30 (1984), 1–21; W.H. Crawford, 'A handloom weaving community in County Down,' *Ulster Folklife*, 39 (1993), 1–15.

however, strongly gendered (see figure 25). Despite the large number of women handloom weavers by the early twentieth century, popular perception of skilled handloom weavers as skilled and male remains firm reflecting the androcentric bias of linen weaving households.[25]

Handloom weaving was not deskilled; weaving on Jacquard looms was a highly skilled craft, and knowledge of the whole process was retained and executed by the worker. Prior to weaving, weavers meticulously prepared the flour and water dressing for the yarn making sure there were no lumps in it. This dressing was carefully applied to as many threads as the weaver thought he could weave in a day. Its function was to make the yarn 'slippey ... to make these wee hairs that a been on the yarn stick together that the shuttle would go through and none of them catch the shuttle'.[26]

The technology involved in handloom weaving had remained largely unchanged for more than a century resulting in very long work days with little time for breaks. A cold moist environment was necessary for handloom weaving, and hence, the earthen floors in weaving shops and manufactories were kept moist with water in the summer. The reason for the long hours was the low wages paid to these highly skilled workers. Handloom weavers often worked from 8:00 am to 8:00 pm to be sure to finish the amount of cloth on the beam within a two week period. Weavers were also not paid for the time consuming work of drawing in the many threads through the reed and tying them, that could take as long as two or three days. As a result, weavers often kept sons home from school to help with this preparatory work.[27] Once the loom was prepared, the actual weaving of fine damask required intense concentration. 'He was watching everything. He was watchin' the cards, he was watchin' the pattern, he was watchin' the shuttle'.[28]

Handloom weaving skills were learned both at home and in manufactories. At first, a weaver would weave on a narrow loom until he had learned to 'throw shot'. Then as he got bigger and stronger he was able to work at the bigger loom.[29] The feet of handloom weavers were used to a great extent to supply the power for the looms. Weavers often kept their feet free and comfortable by cutting the fronts out of shoes or leaving their right foot entirely bare. Once weaving, the rhythmic movement of the weaver and shuttle was compared to that of a church organist.[30]

25 Brenda Collins, 'The loom, the land and the market place: women weavers and the family economy in late nineteenth and early twentieth century Ireland', in Marilyn Cohen (ed.), *The Warp*. 26 Interview with Lucy Green. 27 Interview with Frank O'Dowd, farmer and resident of Ballydugan, July 1983. 28 Interview with Lucy Green, former powerloom weaver, wife of former handloom weaver and resident of Ballydugan, July 1983. 29 Interview with Mrs Moore, former powerloom weaver and resident of Ballydugan, July 1983. 30 Interview with Lucy Green.

25 Handloom weavers selling cloth; location and date unknown

26 Banford five-a-side football team, *c.*1886

Cottage weavers obtained their bobbins from manufacturers, often located in Lurgan, and took their cloth back when finished. This putting-out system of production still gave to handloom weavers a nominal independence since they controlled the weaving process. Although they retained a degree of independence, low wages undermined their autonomy, the satisfaction they derived from craft knowledge, and from producing commodities of beauty such as linen damask.

> If he wasn't sittin' workin', there was nothin' to earn, no money. It wasn't as if you coulda took an hour off. If you did you paid for it. You were short at the week end. There was no leisure. You got your dinner and away you go again as hard as you could.[31]

Because many handloom weavers worked in dispersed cottages, a key element in male linen workers' subjectivity – the strong camaraderie formed on the shop floor – was absent. The relationships formed between men at work in centralized mills and factories tempered their drudgery, religious division and provided the basis for

31 Ibid.

male solidarity and sociability inside and outside of work (see figure 26). Although the noise of pounding wooden beetles at bleachgreens would have reduced the conversation and 'crack' that flowed between flaxdressers, beetlers expressed their spontaneous camaraderie in other ways such as watching that the beetles did not tear off a selvage that was 'hanging' or out of line when a worker walked outside to have a smoke.[32]

THE WORK IDEOLOGIES AND SUBJECTIVITY OF FEMALE WORKERS

Patrick Joyce argues that for women, the culture of the factory was less about the 'organized event' such as apprenticeships (from which they were often excluded), than the 'fundamental activities of human sociability'.[33] With the sole exception of doffing mistresses, who supervised young children in spinning mills, no women held supervisory positions or skilled occupations in linen mills and factories. Women were either semi-skilled machine operatives or homeworkers who learned their skills from other co-workers or relatives informally through observation and practice. Since cultural conceptions of femininity were antithetical to masculinity, stressing agility as opposed to strength, presumed mechanical ineptitude as opposed to skill and dependence as opposed to autonomy, women's work ideology and subjectivity reflected an ambivalent and sometimes paradoxical combination of class and gender domination and spontaneous pride and satisfaction in the linen product.

The archetypical female linen operative, the spinner provides an initial example. Spinners were workers subject to deskilling and persistently poor working conditions for a century between the 1830s and the adoption of ring spinning after World War II. They laboured for long hours bare foot, soaked with water and perspiration and smeared with oil.

Spinners usually began as doffers. Upon entering the spinning mill, an 'unskilled' cager, who was usually a child or halftimer, would teach the newcomer. After the newcomer learned the requisite skills she replaced the previous cager who then became a doffer, another 'unskilled' occupation. As a doffer, the necessary skills involved with removing full bobbins were picked up by observation and practice. Doffers continued doffing for two to three years before becoming 'semi-skilled' spinners.

The main skill a spinner had to learn was how to 'lay up ends' or joining threads together when they broke in such a way as to look smooth. This took some time to learn and had to be performed with speed. The male overseer in the spinning room would have watched the doffer, and when he thought she had acquired sufficient skill, he would give her a start as a spinner on an end frame. Doffers began working

---

32 Betty Messenger, *Picking Up the Linen Threads* (Belfast 1975), pp. 82–120; Interview with Adam Davison, former beetler and resident of Gilford, July 1983.   33 Joyce, *Visions*, p. 132.

27   Staff at Bell's Stitching Factory, Lenaderg, 1930

on this end frame for half a day, again under the supervision of the overseer. If she spun sufficiently well, she would be given a second frame.

Spinners and spinning room supervisors, in spite of the wet, the noise and smell of the oil, all of which were linked to various maladies, considered their occupations to be healthy. According to an assistant manager, 'there was always an excessive amount of heat in the spinnin' rooms ... The girls were soakin' with sweat and damp. But still with all they were healthy ...'[34] The main criterion used to evaluate healthy working conditions was the presence or absence of dust that was not found in wet spinning rooms.

The seven spinners I interviewed did not express a uniform sense of satisfaction at work. All emphasized the poor working conditions and the strict factory discipline at Dunbar McMaster & Company. Working hours were from 6:00 am to 6:00 pm. If workers were late, they found the gates locked, and were not admitted until after breakfast. If such lateness occurred too often, a worker was fired. Finally, all were conscious of their relatively low status, compared with reelers, winders, weavers, and making-up workers. As one former reeler stated, 'If you had started in the reeling you were considered better class', because cleaner working conditions enabled women to dress more respectably and wear shoes.[35]

34 Interview with Bob McElwane   35 Interview with Mary McCusker.

Nevertheless, like Betty Messenger, I also found that these spinners spontaneously evaluated their work experience largely in positive terms. Messenger suggests that part of a material explanation for this apparent paradox is the method of payment. Spinners were time workers in contrast to reelers and weavers who earned piece rates, an individualized system of payment under capitalism which links productivity to wages earned.[36] Piece-rate workers were under more pressure to maximize the time spent working and minimize conversation if wages were to be maintained. 'You wanted to drew your breath, but you wanted to go on to make your pay'.[37]

Another reason accounting for satisfaction among spinners explored by Messenger was the strong sense of camaraderie and lively atmosphere that prevailed in spinning rooms, where spinners sang and conversed together creating a lively 'fun' atmosphere.[38] While managers expected spinners to keep steadily at their work, when they were not around, such pressure relaxed a bit. Spinners would converse leaving 'two or three ends flyin' before stopping the machine to fix them.[39] Spinners were also quick to help when a co-worker was in a 'bog' or 'if you had a friend changin' from a coarse work onto a finer work, the person that was nearest to ye woulda come round and help to put the big bobbins on, and woulda helped you to tie them down and pull them through'.[40]

Spinners' subjectivity was rooted in a recognition of equality and unity of labour experience between female workers who were all equally messy, low status, deskilled and underpaid. Although spinners were keenly aware of these oppressive conditions, as time workers they did not bear the additional pressure of 'making your own pay'. Further, spinners were able to interact more freely with their co-workers than weavers.

Powerloom weavers' subjective evaluations of their work at Hazelbank Weaving Company are less paradoxical than spinners, expressing an expected negativity rooted in oppressive structural conditions. However, unlike spinners, weavers conveyed a submerged pride in their skills and product. While conditions in weaving factories were neither as dusty nor as wet as in spinning mills, they were not considered good. Weaving sheds were extremely noisy impairing hearing and impeding conversation. They were kept humid to keep the yarn supple, some dust or 'fluff' from the yarn was present, and the sharp metal tip of the shuttle could pose considerable danger when 'flying'. Since weavers could not talk to each other easily, they invented, as Messenger vividly described, a variety of ways to communicate including hand signing and lip reading.[41]

36 Ibid.   37 Interview with Molly Finnegan, former thread drawer and resident of Gilford, July 1983.   38 Interview with Mrs Fry, former spinner, hemstitcher, and resident of Banford, July 1983.   39 Ibid.   40 Ibid.   41 Interview with Sarah Campbell, former powerloom weaver and resident of Lawrencetown, July 1983.

Factory discipline was perceived as strict and a time bonus system of 6*d*. per week was lost 'if you were one minute late'. Weavers, who operated two powerlooms, were paid by the piece at so much per cut or 100 yards. All faults detected in the cloth by the cloth passer resulted in fines which were deducted from the wage. When the cut was completed, the weaver carried the heavy cloth on her shoulder to the office where it was marked down. As piece rate workers, weavers were under pressure to maintain concentration watching and repairing broken yarn.[42]

Each weaver pointed out the particular aspect of her job which was most annoying. To one it was the fluff and dirt. To another it was standing on the cold tiled floor on a winter morning and having to handle the cold machinery. To another it was the heat in the sheds during the summer. One former weaver summed up her opinion of Hazelbank succinctly. 'It was a dungeon ... only thing was, you were glad of the money'.[43] A particularly oppressive requirement at Hazelbank was that weavers and weft winders were required to stand constantly.[44]

In spite of these negative evaluations of working conditions, when asked about the relationships formed between co-workers, all maintained that they were friendly and helpful. More experienced weavers were quick to help a young learner. At Hazelbank, a new learner was given a fortnight to four weeks to learn the necessary skills before she got a loom of her own. Learners were expected to pick up much of this skill on their own, but certain skills had to be mastered. These included how to change a shuttle, how to draw in broken ends of warp through the headle and reed and how to tie a weaver's knot.[45]

Among the weavers at Hazelbank, the family labour system was normative, and it was very common for a learner to be taught by a member of her family, often a sister. This was the case for four of the five weavers interviewed.[46] After the initial learning period was over, and the young learner was considered to be ready by the weaver teaching her, she would be given one loom for a few weeks with her progress monitored by the boss and tenter, both of whom were men. Tenters, while not actually supervisors, were very important to the weaver, often enabling her to make her wage. Tenters were skilled workers responsible for the beam they had started, and made sure that the loom ran properly fixing any malfunction. Looms at that time broke frequently, and weavers were not allowed much in terms of compensation for time lost due to repairs. Most weavers at Hazelbank had two looms, but a few of the most experienced had three. Thus, although powerloom weavers were deskilled workers with little autonomy, they frequently expressed pride in their finished linen cloth.[47]

The final group of female workers to be considered are 'making-up' workers who in Tullylish worked either in nearby hemstitching factories or as homeworkers

---

42 Ibid.   43 Interview with Lucy Green.   44 Interview with Sarah Campbell.   45 Ibid.   46 Interview with Mrs Nelson, former powerloom weaver and resident of Banford, July, 1983.   47 Interview with Sarah Campbell.

at home. Working conditions in hemstitching factories were considered the best for women industry wide. According to a stitching factory owner, they were considered 'better' since they were 'more amenable to a girl because they were dry footed in a nice atmosphere'.[48] Stitching factories were clean, dry and relatively quiet. One women, who worked as a spinner in Gilford Mill, and enjoyed her work there, was quite clear that she would not have left Bell's stitching factory in Lenaderg to go back to Dunbar McMaster & Company (see figure 27). At Bell's, the work, which consisted of hemming tea towels, table cloths and napkins with sewing machines, was considered 'lovely'. Workers carried their 'ticket' or quantity to be sewn, up a flight of stairs to their sewing machine and sent their ticket down a chute when finished.[49]

It seemed the only troublesome aspect of the work was the occasional poorly woven piece of cloth that was difficult to stitch on the machine. She maintained that the only noise was the low hum of the sewing machines, and the atmosphere was lively and relaxed; a combination of the fun of spinning rooms without the restrictive managerial pressure.[50]

At Blane's in Ballydugan, the work consisted of both hand and machine work. Machine embroidery of handkerchiefs was performed by highly skilled men and their female assistants. Other finishing tasks such as marking, folding and thread drawing were often performed by female homeworkers.[51] Workers at both Blane's and Bell's earned piece rates, and would often bring extra hankies home to bolster their wage. Since homework was very poorly paid, child labour was frequently used, often at the expense of schooling. The work did not require much skill, but speed was necessary to counter low wages. Drawn thread work was learned by many children of both sexes in this area prior to entering the factory. Children in and around Ballydugan would have gone to Blane's factory to pick up the hankies and brought them back when finished while Bell's distributed and collected homework by pony and cab.[52]

THE SIGNIFICANCE OF THE FAMILY LABOUR SYSTEM

The notion of family was integral to factory culture on many levels. The prevalence of the family labour system figured prominently in the subjective evaluations of work. Being 'spoken for' by relatives was always an important way of obtaining employment in the linen industry.[53] It also strengthened the links between work, family and

48 Interview with Mr J.M. Blane, hemstitching factory owner in Ballydugan, July 1983.   49 Interview with Mrs Fry, former spinner, hemstitcher and resident of Banford, July 1983.   50 Ibid.   51 Interview with Molly Finnegan, former thread drawer and resident of Gilford, July 1983.   52 Interview with John McCusker, former kieveman and resident of Gilford, July 1983.   53 Leslie Clarkson, 'The city and the country', in J.C. Beckett (ed.), *Belfast: The Making of the City* (Belfast 1983), p. 156; Michael Anderson, *Family Structure in Nineteenth Century Lancashire* (Cambridge 1971), p. 228.

community. In small factory villages and hamlets, the overlap between co-worker, kin and neighbour was extensive. In Tullylish, kinship was indispensable to both job recruitment and training, contributing to close personal relationships among co-workers. Kinship enhanced the quality and quantity of social interactions both on and off the job and reduced the pressure and anxiety felt by newcomers. The ideal was to have as many of one's children and other relatives working in the same mill and, where possible, in the same section or occupation.[54]

Among the weavers at Hazelbank, it was very common for a learner to be taught by a member of her family, often a sister. The one exception, whose first job was a learner at Hazelbank, emphasized the importance of her aunt's personal interest in her progress.

> My aunt learned me. My mother's sister. She worked there all her life. [Was it common for a person to be taught by a member of her own family?] Yes, nearly everybody was. They put me first till a girl to learn, and the girl that they put me till to learn ... she was left handed and that was awful awkward on me you see. Well, my aunt then said to the manager, 'You know my niece can't pick this up at all because you put her till a woman thats left handed and its very very awkward on her, you know'. So then my aunt took me and learned me.[55]

The family labour system was strongest and most clearly recognized at bleachgreens by both employers and employees. It was mentioned as far back as the 1857 Parliamentary Report, and continued to be maintained at all of the bleachgreens in Tullylish. Sons did not always follow fathers or brothers into the same occupation, but the fact that a father worked at a particular green was enough to ensure a strong boy a job when he left primary school. A former kieveman at Banford followed his father who worked at the washmills. His three sisters and brother were also employed at Banford. When asked if it was a common practice for sons to follow their fathers into a job at Banford he replied,

> The whole family, they were started, you see, just on your father's account. You would have went in when you left school. You just walked in you see ... He has hardly to say I was ready for startin' work, and he'd a said, 'send em'.[56]

The family labour system was also strongest among handloom weavers, with 90 per cent of handloom weaver's children having the same occupation as their parents. This is not surprising given the domestic organization of production. However, this

54 Blewett, *Last Generation*, p. 147.   55 Interview with Mrs Nelson, former powerloom weaver and resident of Banford, July 1983.   56 Interview with John McCusker.

pattern was normative throughout the parish with 82.5 per cent at Dunbar McMaster & Company, 83.1 per cent in Banford and 87.5 per cent at Hazelbank.

Table 15 reveals how gender mediated the family labour system. Although employment opportunities were more prevalent for females, normative job recruitment through relatives was stronger among males since they were expected to be continuous breadwinners for their families. It was essential to a household's long-range goals that existing jobs for males be filled by male children and kin. However, in the short run, families relied on the earnings of all their children, resulting in both sexes being 'spoken for' and hired.

Table 15: The relative strength of the family labour system among male and female workers, 1901

MALES

Type Family Labour Pattern*	Yes	No
Sons & brothers	359 (79%)	98 (21%)
Male relatives	28 (62%)	17 (38%)
Male boarders	14 (44%)	18 (56%)
Total males**	534	

*based on relationship to male household head **all working males excluding males heads and sole male wage earners

FEMALES

Type Family Labour Pattern*	Yes	No
Wives	89 (63%)	53 (37%)
Daughters & sisters	440 (74%)	156 (26%)
Female relatives	34 (71%)	14 (29%)
Female boarders	19 (83%)	4 (17%)
Total females**	809	

*based on relationship to male household head and to other female kin **all working females excluding female heads of household and sole female wage earners. *Source* 1901 Census Enumerators' Schedules for the Parish of Tullylish.[58]

57 Aker, 'Hierarchies, Jobs, Bodies', 166–7.   58 For each census household with more than one wage earner, I assumed a family labour system if children either had the same occupation as a parent, as a sibling, other co-resident relative or if they had an occupation clearly within the same factory. Ascertaining kin-based recruitment patterns among wives was less clear because some would have obtained their jobs through kinship links with their families of origin, while others obtained theirs through their families of procreation.

Among extended family households, it was more common for female relatives than male relatives to be spoken for. This is to be expected given the prevalence of employment opportunities for females in the spinning mills and weaving factories. It made strategic sense to take in a female relative who could easily be employed in the same factory as oneself. This preference for female labour was more evident when the occupations of male and female boarders are compared. Although most male boarders did not follow other males in the household either into the same occupation or factory, among female boarders we find the opposite. This suggests that many of the female boarders were actually relatives, and that paternalistic influence over co-residing single females was strong.

Among males, the greatest tendency for sons and brothers to follow a family labour system was among bleachers, where 83.3 per cent did so, and among handloom weavers, where 83.8 per cent followed into the same occupation. The fewest men following this pattern were among Hazelbank's employees with 64 per cent due to the predominance of females in powerloom weaving factories and the availability of employment for males at nearby bleachgreens. Among females, the greatest tendency for daughters and sisters to follow a family labour system was among spinning mill employees with 78.9 per cent and among handloom weavers with 78.1 per cent. Among wives, 75.4 per cent of handloom weavers' wives were handloom weavers themselves. In the Hazelbank area, women could either work in the weaving factory, in the spinning mills or at Bell's stitching factory. The pull of these other factories partly accounts for the lower percentage (62.2 per cent) of daughters and sisters following kin-based employment patterns at Hazelbank.

CONCLUSION

Unequal gender relations in the family are at the core of work based identities and shop floor culture. All working-class men, women and children accepted the necessity and inevitability of hard work. Adult men expected to be breadwinners for their families, adult women expected to be both supplemental wage earners and performers of unwaged domestic work and children expected to contribute wages as halftime, fulltime or outworkers.

An acceptance of hard work was fundamental to various work ideologies that linked self-identity to forms of work and conceptions of gender. For men, who expected to be breadwinners, waged work, skill and working knowledge provided the foundation for a respectable masculine social identity. The retention of skill and craft knowledge about the production process by many male workers countered alienation and increased their autonomy and satisfaction. Male workers not only took pride in their skills and the quality of their work, but in possessing and recounting a detailed understanding of the entire linen production process from flax plant to finished cloth. Some men gained working knowledge formally through

apprenticeships and others through informal observation and 'hands-on' instruc-
tion by co-workers. This distinction in the methods of learning job related skills was
culturally significant separating and legitimizing hierarchical levels between managers and rank-and file workers, skilled working men from other 'lesser skilled' men
and men from women, since no female occupation required an apprenticeship or
was recognized as skilled.

Although working women's identities were also shaped by forms of waged work,
the intermittent nature of many women's waged work and the rigid sexual division
of labour in the household, resulted in their identity being as powerfully shaped by
unwaged work and roles in the household and community explored fully in the next
chapter. Women expected and accepted domination by men at work as they did in
the family. Since managers were exclusively male while females comprised the vast
majority of the workforce, theoretical analysis of consensus and deference needs to
recognize the historically specific intersections of class and gender subordination.[57]
For female linen workers, gender distinctions and class distinctions between rank-
and-file worker and manager overlapped. Because they were female, no female worker
was perceived to possess mechanical aptitude, exercised autonomy or decision making power. Hence, these factors did not figure prominently in women's subjective
evaluations. Rather we find relationships with co-workers and the cleanliness of an
occupation, defined by the presence of dust, damp and oil, directly associated with
satisfaction and relative status. The subordination and drudgery associated with
factory work was partly counterbalanced by the formation and satisfaction derived
from relationships with co-workers for both men and women. To the extent that co-
workers and kin overlapped, camaraderie among all workers increased tempering
the experience of class exploitation at work.

'It Wasn't a Woman's World':
Women's Contributions to Household
and Community Survival

> At the end of the fortnight, do you know how much I got? Three shillings and five pence then. I thought I could never get home quick enough to give it to my mother. I always gave it to my mother. Now, I worked till I was twenty-six and never kept one penny out of my pay.   Sarah Campbell, former powerloom weaver, 1983

> At all times, wives' skill and energy provided the only real barrier between mere survival and a decent level of comfort.   Ellen Ross, 1982[1]

Since the 1970s, scholars have theoretically addressed two interconnected phenomena under capitalism: the relationship between waged and unwaged work and the relationship between workplace and home. Under capitalism, the proletariat as a social class is constituted at two locations: the workplace, where the exchange of labour power for a wage occurs, and the home where reproduction occurs.[2] Since this renewal occurs privately in the home by means of unpaid work, two interconnected ideologies emerge: the separation between workplace and home and the invisibility of unwaged work.

Those performing unwaged reproduction work are usually women, and the social institution accomplishing reproduction is usually the family. Kinship is the primary means through which people come together in households to meet the needs of reproduction and consumption. Therefore, the social relationships people form with members of their families are constrained by the larger world of work.[3]

Jane Collins has clarified why unwaged work lies outside the logic of capitalist relations and how it articulates with capitalism in specific contexts. She focuses upon: 1) the points where forms of unwaged work articulate with labour and commodity markets; 2) the social arrangements that control unwaged work; 3) the implications for class relationships; and 4) the contradictions that arise in lived

1 Ellen Ross, "'Fierce questions and taunts": married life in working-class London, 1870–1914', *Feminist Studies*, 8, no. 3 (1982), 576.   2 Wally Seccombe, 'Domestic labour and the working class household', in Bonnie Fox (ed.), *Hidden in the Household: Women's Domestic Labour Under Capitalism* (Toronto 1980), p. 36; Joanna Bourke, *Husbandry to Housewifery* (Oxford 1993), pp. 1–22.   3 Rayna Rapp, Ellen Ross and Renate Bridenthal, 'Examining family history', in Judith L. Newton, Mary P. Ryan and Judith R. Walkowitz (eds), *Sex and Class in Women's History* (London 1983), p. 234.

experience between the 'logics' and demands of waged and unwaged work regimes.[4] These points, along with Patrick Joyce's concept of a working-class 'culture of control', will inform the presentation of this chapter. Joyce argues that the need to manage and bring dignity to lives spent in poverty among the working class generated a 'culture of control' characterized by order, strict gender roles and clear boundaries between the respectable and rough. Women were pivotal in the orchestration of these cultural norms since they were the managers of the household's resources.[5]

There is a growing literature relating to English working-class women's family roles and the varied effects of gender inequality on their lives.[6] At the turn of the twentieth century, women were crucial actors in the formation of working-class culture at the family and neighbourhood level. Through women's networks, various forms of paid and unpaid work were exchanged that ensured material survival. Men and women experienced class differently performing different types of work, conforming to different work schedules and rhythms. Women's work formed the basis of family and community sociability partly because they shouldered the heavy burden of coping with working-class material realities. Women-centred networks provided 'the interface between the formal economy and the web of interpersonal community and familial relationships' helping to explain how working-class families made ends meet.[7]

COPING WITH LOW WAGES

Although it is well known that the vast majority of workers in the linen industry earned low wages, contemporary studies of working-class family budgets in Ulster, such as those conducted in England by Seebohm Rowntree in York, or Maud Pember

---

4 Jane L. Collins, 'Unwaged work in comparative perspective: recent theories and unanswered questions', in Jane L. Collins and Martha Gimenez (eds), *Work without Wages* (Albany 1990), p. 11.   5 Patrick Joyce, *Visions of the People* (Cambridge 1991), pp. 151–64.   6 Maud Pember Reeves, *Round About a Pound A Week* (London 1979) Clementina Black, *Married Women's Work* (London 1983); Margery Spring Rice, *Working Class Wives* (London 1981); Peter N. Stearns, 'Working-class women in Britain, 1890–1914', in Martha Vicinus (ed.), *Suffer and Be Still* (Bloomington 1972) ; Mary Lynn McDougall, 'Working-class women during the industrial revolution, 1780–1914', in Renate Bridenthal and Claudia Koonz (eds), *Becoming Visible* (Boston 1977); Laura Oren, 'The welfare of women in labouring families: England, 1860–1950, ' in Lois Banner and Mary Hartman (eds), *Clio's Consciousness Raised* (New York 1974); Elizabeth Roberts, 'Working class standards of living in Barrow and Lancaster, 1890–1914', *Economic History Review*, 2nd ser., 30 (1977), 306–14; Elizabeth Roberts, 'Working wives and their families', in Theo Barker and Michael Drake (eds), *Population and Society in Britain, 1850–1980* (Batsford, 1982) ; Ross, 'Fierce Questions', 575–602; Ellen Ross, 'Women's neighbourhood sharing in London before World War I', *History Workshop Journal*, no. 15 (1983); Ellen Ross, *Love and Toil* (Oxford 1993); Jane Lewis, *Women in England* (Bloomington 1984); Standish Meacham, *A Life Apart* (Cambridge, MA 1977); Sonya Rose, *Limited Livelihoods* (Berkeley 1992).   7 Pat Ayers, 'The hidden economy of Dockland families: Liverpool in the 1930s', in Pat Hudson and W.R. Lee (eds), *Women's Work and the Family Economy in Historical Perspective* (Manchester 1990), p. 271.

Reeves in Lambeth, do not exist.[8] The sole attempt to calculate a poverty line for Ulster households at the turn of the century was made by Emily Boyle. She calculated the 'minimum comfort' cost of living for a family of two adults and two children to be 13s. 6¼d. per week in 1905. By 1913, this had risen to 15s. 10d.[9] Age statistics for linen industry workers in 1901 reveal that all male linen industry occupations, with the exception of labourers, were above Boyle's minimum. Nevertheless, most males did not earn enough to support their families alone, especially given the prevalence of large families. All female occupations were below the minimum with obvious implications for female-headed households.

Poverty was a repeated theme among the working people interviewed. The most common way this was expressed was, 'it was just a matter of slavery at that time', or 'they talk about the poverty line now. Nearly everybody was on the poverty line at that time'. Two factors were seen to be of paramount importance in shaping family strategies to cope with poverty. One, was the narrow employment base outside of the linen industry; 'there was nothing else for you'. If someone left a job, there was always someone ready to take their place.

The second factor was low wages demanding multiple contributions to make ends meet. A nearly universal household employment strategy emerged in male-headed households centring on the wage earned by the male head supplemented by the earnings of his children and, at times, his wife.[10] Female-headed households were even more dependent upon the wages of children since adult women earned about half the wages of men.

The number of children working was a function of the family life cycle.[11] After a family reached the middle years of child raising, parents began to reap the benefit of their children's wages only to lose them again as children married and left. Thus, all working-class families expected and needed their children to begin earning wages immediately after finishing primary school. Many children began contributing wages before finishing school under the halftime system usually at either Dunbar McMaster & Company or F. W. Hayes & Company in Seapatrick. In 1900, the minimum age for halftime work was twelve.

The concept of family strategy, which analyzes the actions of working-class men and women from the perspective of their position within the family, is appropriate and useful explaining regularities in working-class behaviour in Tullylish. However, problems arise when considering the family as the unit of analysis. Functional interdependence and the assumption that families are corporate groups can mask gender and age inequality and conflict based on individual interests.[12] For example, that the

8 Pember Reeves, *A Pound a Week*; B. Seebohm Rowntree, *Poverty: A Study of Town Life* (London, 1922); Lynn Hollen Lees, 'Getting and spending: the family budgets of English industrial workers in 1890', in John M. Merriman (ed.), *Consciousness and Class Experience in Nineteenth Century Europe* (New York 1979), pp. 168–86; Ross, *Love and Toil*.   9 Emily J. Boyle, 'The Economic Development of the Irish Linen Industry', Ph.D. diss., The Queen's University of Belfast, 1977, p. 166. Use of this minimum is somewhat problematic since many working-class households were larger than four members.   10 Ross, 'Fierce Questions', 576.   11 Lees, 'Getting and Spending', 172–3.   12 Nancy Folbre,

individual interests of children could be in conflict with those of their parents and the household as a whole was explicit in the State's effort to regulate the working hours, ages and schooling of working-class children. While the principal targets of legislation were employers who exploited child labour, parents urgently needed their children's wages. Children were fully aware of their financial importance. Still, for many, leaving school was a major sacrifice ('I remember I cried because I had to leave school'), as were regular infringements on their play time.

The concept of family strategy has been clarified by those scrutinizing the levels of meaning implicit in the military metaphor.[13] Laurel Cornell addresses how a household can have a strategy, by distinguishing between three essential elements: 1) policy or the formulation of long-term goals; 2) strategy or the ability to identify opportunities, mobilize resources, and take advantage of them; and 3) tactics or the everyday choices throughout the duration of the engagement.[14] The 'policy' or long-term goal of working-class families in Tullylish was partly economic – size and security of income, and partly cultural – achieving respectability – a complex set of values that reproduced the culture of control including independence, cleanliness, order neighbourliness and the male household head as breadwinner. The 'strategies' of households in Tullylish included moving to take advantage of employment opportunities; if, when and how a married woman contributed wages; the family labour system; the tension between the need for children's wages and the duration of schooling; and the establishment of various self-help networks. While these strategies functioned to achieve the long range goals, we can assume in this patriarchal context that power over strategic decision making was not evenly distributed. Finally, tactics, the daily decisions that operationalized strategies, involved the webs of social interactions necessary to stretch tight budgets. Tactical decisions were often made independently by married women who managed household finances.

FAMILY STRATEGIES: WORKING WIVES

While contemporary upper- and middle-class reformers argued that working wives could not properly care for their children, homes, or their hard working husbands, economic necessity often required that 'married women worked while others argued about whether or not they should'.[15] In Tullylish, as in Ireland generally, the majority of women chose not to work outside the home after marriage and the birth of their children conforming to Victorian middle class norms. However, a significant minority of wives (20.7 per cent) did continue to work.[16]

'Family strategy, feminist strategy', *Historical Methods*, 20, no. 3 (1987), 116; Louise A. Tilly, 'Beyond family strategies', *Historical Methods*, 20, no. 3 (1987), 123.   13 Daniel Scott Smith, 'Family strategy: more than a metaphor?' *Historical Methods*, 20, no. 3 (1987), 118.   14 Laurel L. Cornell, 'Where can family strategies exist?' *Historical Methods*, 20, no. 3 (1987), 120–1.   15 Meacham, *Life Apart*, p. 95: Lewis, *Women in England*, pp. 45–52.   16 This figure is considerably above the 11 per cent figure reported by Lees, 'Getting and Spending', 173–4, for working wives among English textile workers in 1890.

The occupation of the male head of the household was a principal indicator of social stratification within the working class. At the turn of the century, it was a sign of financial well-being and status to have the women of the household remain outside of the mills and factories. In addition to the wives and daughters of the middle class remaining unemployed, skilled workers, the majority of whom were Protestant, and bleachgreen employees were better able to keep their wives at home. Only 6.8 per cent of the wives of skilled workers were employed, while 23.1 per cent of the wives of semi-skilled workers, and 20 per cent of wives of unskilled workers were employed. Skilled workers were also more likely to have daughters over the age of twelve in school.[17]

Given the reality of insufficient wages and the double burden of employment and family responsibilities, paid employment did not lay the foundation for freedom or independence among working wives in Tullylish.[18] To the contrary, keeping a woman at home increased her ability to maintain order in the household. As Joanna Bourke argues for rural Ireland, 'the increasing movement of women into full-time housework was a sensible strategy for reducing the risk of poverty and for maximizing possible control over their own lives and the lives of their family'.[19] At the turn of the century, a working-class wife and mother who worked fulltime was not emancipated in any meaningful sense of the term. Women who were able to remain at home often viewed working wives with pity, as did contemporary reformers.[20]

Census data suggest that wives were least likely to work after the birth of their children, and their numbers in the workforce drop steadily until they reach the empty nest stage. Table 16 shows that 38.7 per cent of the households where wives worked were either recently married childless couples or at the stage of early child raising, when all children were under seven years of age. As children began to enter the workforce during the middle and later years of child raising, fewer wives remained in the workforce.

Since household chores were very time consuming, frequently another female filled this role if the wife worked outside the home – usually the eldest or second daughter, mother or sister of the household head. Daughters 'learned early about the double job of adult women; paid work in the mill and unpaid housework for the family'.[21] Women and girls, who were more likely to help both with housekeeping duties and wages, were also more likely to augment a nuclear family. For example, mothers and mothers-in-law were more likely to be taken as were sisters and granddaughters of the household head or his wife. In no case did a male function as housekeeper.

---

17 Analysis of variance supported the hypothesis that the mean number of girls in school over age twelve would be affected by the occupation of the household head. F ratio = 2.6492, F probability = .0075. The Tukey test revealed differences in the means significant at the .05 level between skilled and other workers. 18 Judy Lown, *Women and industrialization* (Minneapolis 1990), p. 61. 19 Bourke, *Husbandry to Housewifery*, p. 271. 20 Meacham, *Life Apart*, p. 96; Lewis, *Women in England*, p. 46. 21 Blewett, *Last Generation*, p. 38; Ross, *Love and Toil*, p. 154; Bourke, *Husbandry to Housewifery*, p. 202.

Table 16: Family life cycle and patterns of work among wives
in Tullylish, 1901

Wife-work	Recent marriage	Early cr	Middle cr	Later cr	Old age with children	Empty nest	Total
No	24	64	132	163	141	31	555
	(57.1%)	(80%)	(81.5%)	(92.6%)	(96.6%)	(81.6%)	(86.2%)
Yes	18	16	30	13	5	7	89
	(42.9%)	(20%)	(18.5%)	(7.4%)	(3.4%)	(18.4%)	(13.8%)
Total N	42	80	162	176	146	38	644
	(6.5%)	(12.4%)	(25.2%)	(27.3%)	(22.7%)	(5.9%)	(100%)

Source 1901 Census Enumerators' Schedules for the Parish of Tullylish.

FAMILY STRATEGIES: SUPPLEMENTARY WAGE EARNING

A working wife indicated the difficulties many working-class men faced living up to middle-class standards of respectable manhood defined in terms of breadwinning. Economic uncertainty was widespread among the working class. In her study of working-class standards of living in Barrow and Lancaster, Elizabeth Roberts illuminates how households with incomes below prevailing poverty line calculations were able to make ends meet. She concluded that married women's economic activities as supplemental earners and financial managers (which are impossible to accurately quantify), enabled households to survive.[22]

Other scholars have analyzed the various means by which working-class women, in the role of 'chancellor of the exchequer', supplemented their family's income and eased tight budgets.[23] Since many of these supplemental activities were extensions of women's domestic labour, they articulate with the labour and commodity markets in numerous ways. For example, providing childcare for a woman who worked outside the home for wages in Tullylish would both enable that mother to work and earn the child-minder about 2s.6d. per week. Other wives took in laundry, cleaned the homes of wealthier families, dug potatoes, pulled flax and gathered wild blackberries for 2s. a stone.[24]

Because many of these supplementary wage earning activities were undocumented, their full extent cannot be determined. Both the census and valuations

22 Roberts, 'Working Class Standards', 306–14.   23 Lewis, *Women in England*, pp. 52–62; Ross, 'Survival Networks', 11; Ross, 'Fierce Questions', Ross, *Love and Toil*; Rowntree, *Poverty*, p. 145; Seebohm Rowntree, *How the Labourer Lives* (London 1913), 87, 94; Black, *Married Women's Work*; Ayers, 'Hidden Economy', 277–81.   24 Roberts, 'Working Class Standards', 316.

provide important evidence, however, they are problematic sources of evidence for women's wage earning activities. The ideology surrounding the separate spheres of work and home impinged upon the definitions of work counted in the census. Income earning strategies were linked to family position and since married women's economic roles were often not publicly visible, their contributions were more likely than men's or single women's to be hidden. Finally, it was assumed that men would work for wages continuously and women intermittently. The consequent under-counting of women's supplemental wage contributions hid the fact that most married women earned small amounts of money continuously.[25]

Taking in lodgers was a common supplementary earning strategy among working families in Great Britain and the United States in the nineteenth and early twentieth centuries.[26] Caring for lodgers was principally women's work because it was an extension of their housekeeping tasks. Taking in boarders was probably wide-spread in the industrializing areas of Tullylish and Ulster between 1841–71, due to the enormous demographic shifts and shortages of housing associated with the Fam-ine and industrialization. However, by the time of the 1901 Census, only sixty-four people were listed by the enumerators as boarders living in fifty-three households. Most (forty) of these lived in Gilford.

A more common and important way of supplementing the household budget in Tullylish was, as table 17 reveals, keeping animals such as hens, pigs, goats or cows and growing vegetables in garden plots.[27] Census Enumerator's schedules mention the type of outbuildings attached to each dwelling, and valuations provide informa-tion on how much land was attached to a dwelling. These small patches of land were often used to grow vegetables and keep animals. Among the total population, 48.1 per cent of the households had land, small gardens or yards attached to their houses.

25 Christine E. Bose, 'Devaluing women's work: the undercount of women's employment in 1900 and 1980', in Christine Bose, Roslyn Feldberg and Natalie Sokoloff (eds), *Hidden Aspects of Women's Work* (New York 1987), p. 96; Bourke, *Husbandry to Housewifery* also discusses the limitations of the Irish census as a source for women's economic contributions. 26 Michael Anderson, 'Family, household and the industrial revolution', in Michael Anderson (ed.), *Sociology of the Family* (Harmondsworth 1971), 78–96; Michael Anderson, *Family Structure in 19th Century Lancashire* (Cambridge, 1971); Tamara Haravan and John Modell, 'Urbanization and the malleable household: an examination of boarding and lodging in American Families', *Journal of Marriage and the Family*, 35, no. 3 (1973), 467–79; Ayers, 'Hidden Economy', 277–8; Carol Groneman, 'She earns as a child: she pays as a man: women workers in a mid-nineteenth century New York community', in Milton Cantor and Bruce Laurie (eds), *Class, Sex and the Woman Worker* (Westport, CT 1977), pp. 83–100. 27 Conrad Arensberg, *The Irish Coun-tryman* (Gloucester, 1959); Eileen Kane, 'The changing role of the family in a rural Irish Community', *Journal of Comparative Family Studies*, 10, no. 2 (1972), 141–62; Joanna Bourke, 'Women and poultry in Ireland', *Irish Historical Studies* (May 1987), 293–310; and Bourke, *Husbandry to Housewifery*, pp. 145–98. For England see Roberts, 'Working Class Standards', 316. For the United States see Margaret F. Bying-ton, *Homestead: The Households of a Mill Town* (Pittsburgh 1974) who points out that beans, squash and vegetables were raised to decrease the family's cost of living, and hens were kept to sell eggs or provide eggs for the husband. For Germany see John C. Fout, 'The woman's role in the German working-class family in the 1890s from the perspective of women's autobiographies', in John C. Fout (ed.), *German Women in the Nineteenth Century* (New York 1984), p. 308.

Table 17: The frequency of gardens and outbuildings for animals in Tullylish,
1901

Outbuilding/ Land	Gilford		Rural Gilford		Ban/Hazelbank		Ballydugan	
	yes %	no	yes %	no	yes %	no	yes %	no
Land	48.9	51.1	77.4	22.6	82.4	17.6	84.5	15.5
Cow house	8.2	98.1	47.3	52.7	17.8	82.2	39.7	60.3
Calf house	1.1	98.9	16.4	83.6	0	100	6.0	94.0
Piggery	12.6	87.4	21.8	78.2	11.9	88.1	39.7	60.3
Fowl house	19.7	80.3	58.2	41.8	65.3	34.7	9.7	60.3

Source 1901 Census Enumerators' Schedules for the Parish of Tullylish. Val.12B/16/13A Annual Revision Lists Gilford, 1899–1903; Val.12B/16/25/E,F Annual Revision Lists for Banbridge Rural, 1887–1908; Val.12B/21/8/C,D Annual Revision Lists for Tullylish, Lurgan Union, 1885–1909.

The frequency of small patches of land varied according to region. For example, in the Hazelbank area, nearly every house owned by the Dicksons had a fowl house attached. In Gilford/Dunbarton, only some houses had fowl houses. Denis McNiece found that the houses on Hill and High Streets had fowl houses for keeping hens.[28] Hens were also kept in the field behind the houses on Stramore Road. According to the census, only three streets had no fowl houses, but the main concentration of them was to be found on Hill Street, Castle Hill Street and Rutton's Row. Factory-owned houses were more likely to only have outoffices for animals like hens, while those owned by other landlords more frequently had both land and outoffices.

The town of Gilford also had the fewest houses with land attached, while in the other areas the vast majority of dwellings had small patches of land. Within Gilford/Dunbarton, the incidence of gardens and land varied according to street. Some streets like Bann View Court, Brown's Row, Thompson's Row, High Street and Hill Street had no land or few houses with land while the other streets had at least some houses with land attached.

Although gardening was done by both men and women, keeping animals like hens, pigs, and goats was women's work.[29] According to the census, poultry was the most common animal kept. People who kept hens had fresh eggs in their diet or extra cash through their sale. Many people kept goats which provided milk. Goats were inexpensive to keep since they ate hedge vegetation. Pigs were also kept in pens beside the river and in front of back-to-back houses on Bann Street. Pigs were also inexpensive to keep, and were frequently sold as a Lawrencetown man explained.

28 Denis S. McNiece, 'Factory Workers' Housing in Counties Down an Armagh', Ph.D. diss., The Queen's University of Belfast, 1979, p. 26.   29 Mary Cullen, 'Breadwinners and providers: women in the household economy of labouring families, 1835–6', in Maria Luddy and Cliona Murphy (eds), *Women Surviving* (Dublin, 1989), pp. 92–106; Bourke, 'Women and Poultry', 293–310; Bourke, *Husbandry to Housewifery*, 145–98.

A good many of the people whose husbands worked in the bleachgreens they kept hens and they laid eggs and sometimes they could sell the eggs to supplement their husband's earnings, which weren't very big.[Was it a common thing to keep hens at that time?] Oh, it was. Nearly everybody and a good many people would have kept a pig. Now a pig didn't eat a whole lot of money. Where there's a family there's always refuse, and it didn't take too much of their own refuse to feed the pig. Over the months then it was sold. There was a man went round and killed the pig. The pig was killed and brought to market. They bought the pig for maybe five shillings or something and sold it for maybe a couple of pound or forty shillings or something. There was always a few bob extra.[30]

Perhaps the most important way a married woman could contribute additional earnings was through homework.[31] Homework articulated with labour and commodity markets chiefly as a poorly remunerated alternative to the factory system. Women who remained home could turn to homework sporadically, as available time arose in the course of their daily domestic routine. Unfortunately, this form of work was undocumented by Census Enumerators, and it is difficult to determine its extent. According to oral evidence, in areas close to hemstitching factories it was very common, but in other areas, less is known. Some women in the Gilford area made shirts at home with sewing machines for a firm called Pentland's, but, like drawn thread work, it was very poorly paid. Consequently, young children of both sexes worked long hours, assisting their mothers sometimes at the expense of attending school. Other children were expected to draw threads after school.[32]

While it is difficult to determine the extent of homework, it has long been a convenient way married women could contribute additional income. Homework was still done in the Ballydugan area in the 1980s, mostly by married women who regulated their own hours. Sewing machines and handkerchiefs are supplied by Blane's, and women do the work when they can. The company earns additional profits by reducing variable capital costs; sickness or unemployment benefits are not provided.

30 Interview with Arthur Patrick Burns, former stinter, calander man and resident of Lawrencetown, July 1983.   31 Miriam Cohen, 'Italian-American women in New York City, 1900–1950: work and school', in Milton Cantor and Bruce Laurie (eds), *Class, Sex and the Woman Worker* (Westport, CT 1977), pp. 120–43; Barbara Franzoi, 'Domestic industry: work options and women's choices,' in John Fout (ed.), *German Women in the Nineteenth Century* (New York, 1984); Fout, 'The Woman's Role', 311; Roberts, 'Working Class Standards', 310; Lewis, *Women in England*, pp. 55–62.   32 Interview with Sarah Campbell, former powerloom weaver and resident of Lawrencetown, July 1983; Interview with Mrs McCusker, former powerloom weaver and resident of Gilford, July 1983.

WOMEN'S STRATEGIES: MANAGING HOUSEHOLD EXPENSES

According to Laura Oren, there were essentially two ways of dividing the household money in British working-class households during the nineteenth century.[33] One
way gave the wife control. Her husband handed over all of his earnings and received
back a fixed sum used as pocket money. The second way, more common in England, was when a husband gave his wife a fixed sum each week based on his average
minimum earnings. In this latter case, wives did not always know the amount of
their husband's earnings. Oral evidence suggests that in Tullylish the first system,
where all family members handed over their pay to the wife and received back pocket
money, was the most common arrangement. A former beetler described how this
system worked in his parents' household.

> They would just bring it home and give it to her and they would've had
> whatever she wanted to give them out. The man, husband, never opened his
> pay. Brought it home and give it to her and she would've opened it. And she
> managed that, so she did. She'd give them their pocket money.[34]

Pocket money given to husbands, often spent on smoke and drink was considered 'wasteful' by contemporary investigators of poverty. It also enabled 'moments
of potential excess' that threatened a wife's careful control over financial order.[35]
When wives were faced with tight budgets, they often had to make do with less
since they could not refuse their husband's personal requests. Drinking among men
in particular was a factor affecting working-class standards of living and marital
tension.[36] 'The poor man's drink was at the expense of his family's food and sometimes his own'.[37] As in London, alcohol was integral to male sociability in Tullylish.
A former powerloom weaver described the marital tension that could arise.

> She hadn't have enough money to pay for the food and clothes. And he
> would've wanted his tobacco, his smoking money, and he woulda had to get
> that. And then maybe there'da been words over that you know. He'd expect
> her just that she should have the food on the table whether she had the money
> to pay for it or not. He expected but he didn't forget his pint of beer or
> whatever it was. He woulda got that. The men wanted their own way. In some
> cases there mighta been men who drank their money, you know, before they
> come home with their pay. They used to have to work up till dinner time on
> Saturdays in those days. Then with all these mills and factories, you see, they

33 Laura Oren, 'The welfare of women in laboring families: England, 1860–1950', *Feminist Studies*, 1,
nos. 3–4 (1973), 112; Meacham, *Life Apart*, pp. 72–3; Lewis, *Women in England*, pp. 26–8; Ross, 'Fierce
Questions', Ross, *Love and Toil*, pp. 76–8.   34 Interview with Adam Davison, former beetler and resident of Dunbarton.   35 Joyce, *Visions*, p. 151.   36 Roberts, 'Working Class Standards', 318; Ross,
'Fierce Questions'.   37 Ross, *Love and Toil*, p. 42.

were near the pubs. There was a pub up there and two down Hall's Mill. Maybe when they got drunk and come home they never turned round. No money. Separations too. True. They used to drink an awful lot in those days. It was so cheap too. It was only 4*d.* for a glass of whiskey or something and 2*d.* for a stout or something and the men were all goin' home, you see, and had a drink. Some of them stayed on and then they come home darting across the road. God help them. God help their wives.[38]

When households had to make do with less, it was usually the wife who ate less so that her husband and children did not feel the pinch. Members of a single family did not always share a single standard of living. Working-class women obtained a disproportionately smaller share of food, medical care and leisure time.[39] The structure of the family economy, in which men worked and women stayed home, gave men an illusion of independence and control while women were buffers. Thus, following Ellen Ross, the working-class family was not the 'bulwark against capitalist wage labor'.[40] Wives 'absorbed the blows of an insecure existence', ensuring the survival of breadwinners and children out of their own standard of living.[41] As in other working-class communities, providing food for husbands and children was a major preoccupation of women in Tullylish, which at times meant denying themselves food, as described by a mother of six.

[I] Wouldn't take an egg keepin' it for the children. Wouldn't take this or that keepin' it for the children. I remember one time. I don't remember if it was during the time he was in the hospital, musta been. And I wasn't eatin'. I was gettin' all for them. So long as I got food for them until I let myself down too far. I didn't feel like I was ever hungry. I suppose I was nibblin' at bits and pieces, but I was never sittin' down to a big meal. It was all for them, six of them.[42]

At the midday meal (dinner) and at the evening meal (supper), wives often did not sit down and eat with the family. Instead, they served making sure everyone else had enough, having a quiet meal by themselves later. Those who were working were usually served first, or sometimes wives fed the small children first, sent them out to play, and set the table again for the workers. It was essential to get the workers fed and on their way within an hour. Sometimes men who worked at the bleachgreens had to remain past 6:00 pm, perhaps until midnight, to get the work finished. They ate their tea at their place of work.

38 Interview with Sarah Campbell.   39 Oren, 'Welfare', 107; Lewis, *Women in England*, pp. 23–6; Ross, 'Fierce Questions', 585–7.   40 Ross, *Love and Toil*, p. 9.   41 Ibid., p. 121. Rowntree also found that among poor labouring families meat was rare. When cheap cuts were purchased, the wife and children had a small portion on Sunday while the rest was 'kept religiously for the breadwinner'. See Rowntree, *How the Labourer Lives*, p. 49.   42 Interview with Sarah Campbell. See Ross, *Love and Toil*, pp. 28–9 for London examples.

Bread, butter, buttermilk, potatoes, cabbage and bacon were prominent in the diet of workers in Tullylish. A former calander man described his food as 'plain' but healthy.

> There wasn't a terrible lot of meat. It wasn't used every day in those days. Maybe they got a pound of boilin' meat and had soup or broth on Sunday. And if there was much made on Sunday it was on Monday again. And usually the principal meal woulda been cabbage. There was alot of cabbage used, bacon and cabbage and potatoes. And some days just butter in it and a wee bit of butter. Nearly every house used buttermilk.[43]

Although wives in Tullylish often made due with less, managing the household money did give them a measure of control and influence over decision making that middle-class wives did not share. If any money was left, she might have bought something for herself. Extra money earned through supplementary earning activities could be spent by wives on themselves if circumstances allowed. Likewise, some men earned extra money at odd jobs, like gardening in the summer, and this money was considered theirs to spend as they liked. Daily decisions regarding purchases needed by the household were made by wives independently of their husbands. Both men and women acknowledged that money management was the special talent of women.[44] As a result, only women really knew how far wages would stretch.

> Long ago the men didn't even realize like what was the value of the money. It took the women really for to know the value and how far the money was goin' to go. Men didn't like take any interest such as I'll pay this for you this week and I'll pay that. The men never knew the value of money because they never really had any money.[45]

The biggest chunk of a household's budget went to food and clothing. Clothing was an expense some women were able to reduce by sewing clothing for their children.[46]

> My mother was a dressmaker. She could have made our clothes, all our dresses out of very little. She could have gotten the train for 4*d.* up to Banbridge to the drapery shop and she used to get bargains of remnants. She made all her own quilts, patchwork quilts, and thats out of rags and made a design on them. She had great hands.[47]

---

43 Interview with Arthur Patrick Burns, former stinter, calander man and resident of Lawrencetown. 44 Ross, *Love and Toil*, p. 51.   45 Interview with Mrs. McCusker. For similar views of working-class men as notoriously poor shoppers see Ross, 'Fierce Questions', 588.   46 Roberts, 'Working-Class Standards', 317.   47 Interview with Sarah Campbell.

Rents were low since many lived in company-owned houses.[48] Other landlords' rents were comparable. In 1867, the houses owned by Dunbar McMaster & Company were let at 1s. to 2s.3d. per week.[49] Oral evidence suggests that rents did not change in the early decades of the twentieth century ranging from 1s.6d. to 2s.6d. per week. At Banford, during the 1860s, wage books show rents ranging from 1s.8d. to 2s.4d.[50] By 1909, the range was wider and the rents higher from 2s.6d. to 7s., with the most common rent 3s.6d. to 4s. per fortnight.[51] Finally, Hazelbank's wage books for 1881–7 show rents ranging from 1s.3d. to 2s.1d. per week.[52] Thus, with the exception of Banford, rents were below those in Belfast where four-roomed 'kitchen houses' ranged from 3s.6d. to 4s. per week.[53]

WOMEN'S STRATEGIES: CREDIT AND SHOPS

Most of the commodities consumed by households were purchased in shops by women. These shops were open late, until 7:00 pm or 8:00 pm to accommodate those wives working until 6:00 pm. For the employees of Gilford Mill, there was a mill-owned shop across from the main factory gates where both food and clothing could be purchased with sums deducted from the wage. There were also numerous other shops in Gilford/Dunbarton.

Gilford and Banbridge were the main sources of shops for the households in this study. Women in the Banford/Hazelbank area usually came either to Gilford or Banbridge, and these shops delivered goods purchased by horse and van, as a Lawrencetown resident recalled.

When I was a boy at school my mother would have went to town with one pound with her and got their goods. Most people got their goods from Banbridge. There was a train went to Banbridge at quarter of four on a Saturday and they'd be back at 6:00. They done their shoppin' and the goods were sent out in a horse and van to the different houses. The woman woulda went with a pound and got their fortnight's goods, the eatables, you see, and had change back. They had to have bought their coal and paid their rent and all.[54]

48 For comparison with English industrial workers' rents see Lees, 'Getting and Spending', 177. 49 H.C. *Reports from Commissioners: Paris Universal Exhibition*, vol. xxx (1867–8), p. 61. 50 (PRONI), D.1136/FA/1, Wages Book no. 4. 51 (PRONI), D.1136/FA/2, Wages Book no. 16. 52 (PRONI), D.1764/10, Hazelbank Weaving Co. Wages Book. 53 H.C. *Report of an Inquiry by the Board of Trade into Working Class Rents, Housing, and Retail Prices, together with Standard Rate of Wages Prevailing in certain occupations in the Principal Industrial Towns of the United Kingdom*, vol. 107 (1908), p. 341; Brenda Collins, 'The Edwardian city, in J.C. Beckett et al., *Belfast: The Making of the City* (Belfast 1982), p. 172. 54 Interview with Arthur Patrick Burns.

Since wages were paid either weekly or fortnightly, credit relationships were established with shop owners. While the importance of credit to working-class women's financial strategies has been noted, most discussion has focused on pawnshops and moneylenders.[55] Evidence relating to pawnbrokers in Gilford/Dunbarton is scant. There is mention of two pawnbrokers serving as Town Commissioners in 1859. One, Hugh McConnell, was both a grocer and pawnbroker suggesting that shopkeepers many have established a variety of credit relationships with their working class patrons.[56]

Far more evidence relates to a credit strategy in which women patronized the same shop to begin a credit arrangement called her 'book.' This would enable a woman to take what she needed for her household and pay the shop on a Friday when wage packets were received. Banford paid their workers fortnightly, as did Dunbar McMaster & Company for a time. Later Gilford Mill began to pay weekly as did Hazelbank. For all households, but especially among those whose primary wage earner was paid fortnightly, this credit relationship was critical to enabling wives to maintain financial order.

> The women would do the shoppin'. She would get the stuff or send some of the children to the shop or send the book. It was marked in the book and they marked it in their own ledger and at the end of the fortnight they paid the bill and the shop people woulda usually give a wee packet of sweets for the children. They brought it home with them each time. Each time they went to buy something they brought the book. It got marked in the book and then the shopkeeper went back to see if it corresponded to the house ledger and the book was marked paid then till the end of the fortnight.[57]

Such credit relationships formed between a particular shop and a household by the wife or other female member, were one of the primary methods women attempted to stretch tight budgets and make ends meet.[58] Everyone stressed the importance of credit, and no one felt that shopkeepers were exploitative, even though it was not uncommon for households to fall into debt. People were tied to a particular shop through credit and debt. If a family fell into debt, usually due to the illness of the primary wage earner, shopkeepers usually saw the family through this difficult period. The family paid off their debt with 6*d.* or 1*s.* a week. Shopkeepers expected debts to be repaid. However, some debts were never fully paid off, and, occasionally, people moved from the area partly to avoid paying off their debt. According to a former calender man, whose sister's family owned a shop,

55 Roberts, 'Working Class Standards'; Lewis, *Women in England*, pp. 52–3, Ross, 'Fierce Questions', 588–90; Ross, *Love and Toil*, pp. 81–4. 56 (PRONI), LA.86/4CC/1 Gilford Town Commissioners, Income Expenditure Book, 1859–1906. 57 Interview with Mrs McCusker. 58 Roberts, 'Working Class Standards', 316; Ross, 'Fierce Questions'; Ross, *Love and Toil*, pp. 52–3.

If a man was off sick, well the way they worked was they put it to the back of the book, whatever was that couldn't be paid at the fortnight, and whenever he went to work again they paid their fortnightly goods and so much off what was at the back of the book till that bill was reduced. Sometimes it took nearly a year. If a man was out for two weeks it took a year nearly to get that. They took a shilling each time or two shillings each time till the end of it cleared. As a rule there was never too many heavy debts unless a man was off for months.[59]

Although the social relationship between shopkeepers and clients reflected class, religious, and credit-based inequality, oral evidence supports Conrad Arensberg and Solin T. Kimball's conclusion that customers did not experience shopkeepers as exploitative. Rather they were enmeshed in the local web of social obligations. In theory, shopkeepers had the power to refuse credit and the profits earned from the sale of commodities ensured them significantly higher incomes and social status. However, shopkeepers were under considerable pressure not to refuse credit, since they needed loyal customers. Thus, it was an important strategy for working-class wives to become familiar with a particular shopkeeper, and they relied on this familiarity to make ends meet.

The vast majority of middle-class shopkeepers in Gilford were Protestant in the early twentieth century. Only four Catholics sold food or clothing as compared with twenty-four Protestants. Catholics filled less prestigious niches such as publicans. According to the 1901 census, all of the public houses in Tullylish were owned and staffed by Catholics. It is unknown whether or not pubs were as lucrative as other shops, but pubs owners did not maintain credit relationships with their customers. Thus, the majority of Catholic and Protestant working-class households in Tullylish were indebted to Protestant shopkeepers for essential commodities.

According to a Gilford shopkeeper, who inherited his father's shop, shopkeepers were not competitive in terms of prices. There was no price cutting between them, and they did not try to capture one another's customers as shopkeepers expected and depended on customer loyalty. As elsewhere in Ireland, shopkeepers began to build a clientele by attracting their own family members or friends. They then expanded their clientele through contacts.[60] Some shops, for example, would have a

59 Interview with Arthur Patrick Burns.   60 See Conrad Arensberg, *The Irish Countryman* (Gloucester 1959) and Conrad Arensberg and Solin T. Kimball, *Family and Community in Ireland* (Cambridge, MA 1968) for the classic functionalist account of the social ties between shops located in town and the country farmers. For critique see Peter Gibbon and M.D. Higgins, 'Patronage, tradition and modernization: the case of the Irish "Gombeenman" ', *Economic and Social Review*, 6 (1974), 27–44; 'The Irish "Gombeenman": reincarnation or rehabilitation', *Economic and Social Review*, 8 (1977), 313–20; Lawrence Taylor, 'The merchant in peripheral Ireland: a case from Donegal, *Anthropology*, 14, no. 2 (1980), 63–76. For an indepth analysis of shopkeepers see Marilyn Silverman and P.H. Gulliver *Merchants and Shopkeepers: A Historical Anthropology of an Irish Market Town* (Toronto 1995).

reputation for special items like butter. Farmers then would pay off their bill in butter, and this commodity would attract additional customers.

Although shopkeepers were dependent on the mill as the provider of money spent in their shops, they were middle class and some were small property owners in their own right. If a working-class child secured a place as an apprentice in a shop, this was considered superior to factory work. Apprenticeships in shops lasted for five years, and for the first two years they received no pay, only meals. Thereafter, apprentices were paid very little, but eventually they would have a higher standard of living with their wives remaining home, their children better educated, and leisure activities like tennis, which required money for fees and proper attire, were possible.

WOMEN'S TACTICS: HOUSEWORK AND CHILDCARE

Women's unwaged domestic work includes food preparation, housekeeping, childbearing, and child rearing, all of which restore and renew the 'labouring capacity of potential and actual workers'.[61] One principal reason why so few wives worked outside the home was that labour intensive unpaid reproduction work was the sole responsibility of women.[62] Eileen Kane links this sexual division of labour in the West Gaeltacht to cultural conceptions of manliness.

> The responsibility for farm and family rests with the husband who does all outdoor and strenuous labour, as well as maintenance of the farm. The wife controls the kitchen, the children and the small animals and fowl. Men will have no part in women's work; masculinity is defined not by what he does as much as by what he does not, and the tabooed area includes the whole range of women's work. Women, conversely, can do men's lighter tasks; if a woman takes on heavier work, she is an object of respect and pity, and her husband, if he is living and able is despised.[63]

In Tullylish, while some men helped their wives, the culture of control included a clear demarcation between women's and men's work. There was little daily change in the routine or quantity of women's work resulting in the elimination of their leisure time. Even on the weekend there were particular tasks that had to be done,

61 Emily Blumenfeld and Susan Mann, 'Domestic labour and the reproduction of labour power: towards an analysis of women, the family and class', in Bonnie Fox (ed.), *Hidden in the Household* (Toronto 1980), p. 293.   62 See Elizabeth Bott, *Family and Social Network* (London 1957) Carol Adams, *Ordinary Lives* (London 1982); Thea Vigne (ed.), *Family History Issue, Oral History: Journal of the Oral History Society* 3, no. 2 (1975); Lewis, *Women in England*; Meacham, *Life Apart*; Ross, 'Fierce Questions', 578; Ross, *Love and Toil*, pp. 69–80.   63 Eileen Kane, 'The changing role of the family in a rural Irish community', *Journal of Comparative Family Studies*, 10, no. 2 (1972), 150.

such as ensuring that the children and their clothes were clean for Sunday School and Church. Although wives could expect help from their children, especially their daughters, many tasks would necessarily be done after hours, on weekends and by lamplight in the winter months. For working wives, weekends were a time to catch up with domestic tasks. Consequently, a frequent reply to the question, 'What did your mother do in her spare time?' was either another task like darning socks, knitting or that she hadn't any spare time. Women's long silenced feelings about gender inequality and their burdensome domestic responsibilities were revealed by a Lawrencetown woman:

MC. Did your father help with the childcare at all?

A. Well, you see with him bein' out workin'. He was workin'. He would be tired when he come home. Fathers in those days didn't take the same interest I think in the children as they do now. And they would hardly have held a child. They thought it was too much like a woman's work. And even after when I got married, the husbands wouldn't wheel a pram or anything. No, they wouldn't do that. They thought that was too womanish to do that. We were just killed. Looking after children and doin' all that bakin', and washin', and ironin'.[64]

Joanna Bourke argues that nineteenth-century reforms in the quality of Irish housing contributed to pulling women into unwaged housework. Such reforms were linked to health issues; cleanliness was promoted to combat disease and to address 'social and moral questions' associated with a 'moral, sober, intelligent, healthy and industrious people'. It was expected that improvements in housing and sanitation would increase women's workloads.[65] High standards of cleanliness clearly prevailed in Tullylish, including the outside toilets over the Bann at Banford disinfected regularly with lime provided by the Sintons. 'Everybody would just to see who would have the whitest'.[66]

In the early decades of the twentieth century, household chores were very labour intensive, the difficulties of which were compounded by the lack of space in the rows of company-owned houses. Extra flour for baking bread was kept in bags in the living room, since usually there was no separate scullery or working kitchen. Old flour bags were washed and put over the currently used bags to keep the contents clean. Furniture and decor were simple, both because houses were small and incomes limited.

But then houses was that small, you see, you couldn't put a whole lot of furniture in them. You needed your kitchen for to do your cookin', do your

64 Interview with Sarah Campbell. 65 Bourke, *Husbandry to Housewifery*, pp. 210–13. 66 Interview with Mrs McCusker.

washin', and all. And they were only small kitchens then in Banford and you
had to have that just free. You had your coal and all in that livin' room. Everything was in the livin' room and you just had the table and chairs. There was
no such a thing as settees or anything like this and instead of having units and
things they had these shelves on the walls. Well, then you put all your delft
up on them. They weren't even cupboards. You had to take them all down
and wash them and all. And above your doors they had all these big boards
across there. Well then you woulda put all the ornaments across there. You
hada wash them all.[67]

Most women in Ireland prior to World War I cooked over an open hearth fire
whether they resided in the countryside or in rural industrial regions.

They did the cookin' in the livin' [room] just on your own on the open fire.
There was no such a thing as ranges or cookers then. Even baked your bread
on an open fire. You would have had like a griddle, you see, and there was a
sort of a hook up on this and you hang your griddle on it and you put your
fire, and the heat went up round and thats where you done all your bakin'
and all. And fryin' was the same. It was all over the open fire.[68]

Standish Meacham states that among English working-class women, 'no ritual
assumed a greater importance in the eyes of respectable working-class women than
the weekly house cleaning'.[69] Wives in Tullylish were no exception, and they expected to be assisted by their daughters. The heaviest burdens fell on daughters in
succession with younger ones taking over the lion's share from older daughters when
they worked fulltime.[70] This asymmetrical division of labour was reproduced through
socialization practices. Daughters were taught by their mothers how to perform
domestic tasks such as washing floors, tables and chairs that varied on a daily basis.
Sons were expected to do some of the heavy chores, like carrying water or fire wood,
but they were allowed more free time to play and engage in sports like football.
Daughters, 'got very little time to play any when you were growin' up'.[71]

The family's clothes were washed by hand in a tub without the convenience of
running water in the houses. By the turn of the century, the location of water supplies to meet rising standards of cleanliness was a consideration when planning new
cottage construction. The President of the United Irishwomen, Mrs. Harold Lett,
estimated that an '"ordinary family" required nine gallons of water a day with an

---

67 Ibid.   68 Ibid.   69 Meacham, *Life Apart*, p. 87; Lewis, *Women in England*.   70 Interview with Mrs
Fry, former spinner, hemstitcher and resident of Banford; Ross, *Love and Toil*, p. 151.   71 Interview
with Mrs Fry.

extra nine on washing day'.[72] In Tullylish, boys fetched water at least once a day to meet a household's various needs. Those living in Gilford obtained their water for drinking and household uses in the following way:

> There was no water laid on in those days. There was a pump and you had to carry the water from the pump. Well then, that water was spring water which is not too good for washin' clothes, you know, it doesn't take the soap. So then, we had to maybe carry it up the field from the River Bann to get the softer water, which wasn't too terrible clean now, but you just had to do with it.[73]

Ironing clothes was a particularly arduous and disagreeable task done inside the house on tables covered with sheets.

> And the irons, do you know what they were like then? [No, tell me.] Well, they were box irons. Well, there was flat irons, and you had to heat them in the fire. There was the heater in the box iron the shape of the iron and you put them down into the fire. You hada wait till the fire was sort of red so they would go black, you know, the gas comin' out of it. And Oh, the summer-time, it was murder. You hada get the tongs, and you opened up the iron at the back, and you lifted out the bright red, as red as that there, and drop it into the iron, and then let this wee door snap down, and you had the other one in when you were ironin' till that one got cool, and then you dropped it in and lifted the other one out. And the sweat, it was just terrible.[74]

Daughter's tasks, like those of their mothers, were never finished.[75] Since girls in Tullylish were not allowed to go out at night after dark, time in the evening was often spent helping their mothers.

> When you were at home at night, you know, you were in the lamplight and there was really nothin' for anybody to do outside. There was no electric lighting or nothin'. When it got dark the girls didn't go out at night and my mother used to make all the boys socks, black socks, and I would sit and I would had took one from the top of the leg to the ankle. My mother woulda turned the heel in for me and then the next night I woulda sat and done from the ankle to the toe, and she woulda knotted off the toe. Like when I was young, I didn't know how to knot the heel or the toe and then she did that. We all helped her out with the knittin' and everything.[76]

72 Bourke, *Husbandry to Housewifery*, pp. 213–14.   73 Interview with Sarah Ewart, former reeler and resident of Gilford, July 1983.   74 Interview with Sarah Campbell.   75 Ross, *Love and Toil*, p. 154.   76 Interview with Mrs Fry.

In addition to mothers, schools also played an important function in gender role socialization. All schools admitted 'infants' from age three. Usually women teachers taught the infants and girls while male teachers taught the boys. Children were taught basic literacy, arithmetic, writing skills, spelling, geography and the prevailing ideology relating to the 'laws' of political economy. In addition to this, girls learned sewing and cooking to prepare them for their future roles as wives and mothers. By the turn of the twentieth century, due to the demand for domestic training classes in Ireland, the Commissioners of National Education began to include such domestic classes in the curriculum. By 1914, nearly half of all Irish schools taught domestic training classes. According to Bourke, cooking, in particular 'was popular amongst the parents and there was widespread agreement that the classes increased female enrolment and attendance at school'.[77]

Girls in Tullylish were taught to cook foods like queen of pudding with bread crumbs and apples or turnips and potatoes with bacon. Schools were equipped with ovens and stoves and cooking was taught by the mistress. Girls were also taught sewing and knitting. A former pupil at Bann School in Lawrencetown described these sewing lessons.

> We had to sew. We had to bring in a piece of material and make a little apron and she brought the wool. It was always red wool and made it into wee small balls. And we had to buy that wee ball for a ha'penny. And at first we had to knit what she called a garter, do you know the plain stitch at the beginnin'. Then she would teach us to knit little socks, that sort of thing. And then as we got older she taught us to sew, to make little aprons and things, and she had small pieces of material, and she cut a hole in the centre, and then she would get another piece and make a little pouch.[78]

WOMEN'S TACTICS: SOCIAL NETWORKS

Establishing a vital credit relationship between a household and a shop was only one example of how working-class women generated social organization and ties in their communities. The web of female-centred social relations between neighbours provided another support network equally vital to survival. For example, in Tullylish, when wives worked, childcare for their young children was a primary concern. Infant schools did not provide care for the whole time wives were away from home, nor would they provide care for children below age three. Therefore, working wives often turned to nearby kin, neighbours or to an older child to act as a care giver. Although a small fee of about half a crown a week was usually paid to the child minder,

77 Bourke, *Husbandry to Housewifery*, pp. 245–6.   78 Interview with Sarah Campbell.

if this sum could not be afforded, neighbours helped one another anyway. A former hackler, whose mother worked in the mill, had his meals cooked by his grandmother while an aunt looked in as well.[79] He stressed how 'neighbourly' people were, and that these ties between neighbours transcended religious boundaries.

> Every door was open. And if I were short of sugar next door or flour or somethin' like that enough to do the bakin', I'd get the neighbour to give in. Didn't ask any questions who you were. You were a neighbour and you worked in the mill beside them everyday in the week. Any trouble next door you were in just the same as the other side, the Roman Catholic was in to you.[80]

The importance of kinship and neighbourhood ties among poor families has been shown in a growing body of historical and anthropological literature.[81] The cultural evaluation of a neighbour often depends on the general importance assigned to the role. The specific type of neighbouring to be found in an area reflects local expectations about what neighbours should be or do. In areas like Tullylish, where the neighbour's contribution was indispensable, the role was strictly defined and highly significant. [82]

Henry Glassie states that while there are two social categories in Ballymenone – friends meaning blood relatives, and neighbours – neighbourliness is a greater organizing force in the community than kinship. Since 'neighbors are those with whom you work, those who can be trusted to help' in times of need, they provide the model for the proper behaviour of a relative.[83] Anthony Buckley similarly argues that among farming families in the village of Kearney in the Upper Ards of County Down, the neighbourliness of the past was a powerful custom rooted in chronic economic uncertainty.[84] In Tullylish, the two social categories of friends (relatives) and neighbours were also central to social organization. When a family faced difficulty making ends meet they turned to their 'friends', and neighbours for help.[85]

MC. During those times, how would a family make ends meet?
A.   Well, generally your friends give you a handout. You see, it was far more neighbourly then it is now. If there was a neighbour really far down, like you went around and you collected the whole locality. Just put your penny

79 Interview with William Quinn, former flaxdresser and resident of Gilford, July 1983.   80 Ibid.   81 See Carol B. Stack, *All Our Kin* (New York 1974) Susan E. Brown, 'Love unites them and hunger separates them: poor women in the Dominican Republic', in Rayna R. Reiter (ed.), *Toward an Anthropology of Women* (New York 1975); Ross, 'Survival Networks', 4–27; Ross, 'Fierce Questions', 587; Anthony D. Buckley, 'Neighbourliness – Myth and History', *Oral History Journal*, 11, no. 1 (1983), 48; Suzanne Keller, *The Urban Neighborhood: A Sociological Perspective* (New York 1968); Lewis, *Women in England*, p. 54.   82 Keller, *Urban Neighborhood*, pp. 20, 21, 24.   83 Henry Glassie, *Passing the Time in Ballymenone*, pp. 142, 292, 581, 583.   84 Buckley, 'Neighbourliness', 48.   85 Ross, 'Survival Networks', 9.

or tuppence or six pence or shilling. Then you went to the big boys and maybe he give you a pound or something. Well that due them maybe till someone got a job or something like that.[86]

Everyone interviewed stressed that the past was far more 'neighbourly' than now, a statement that conveys the strength of social obligation rooted in the material realities of the time.[87] Prior to 1920, services to the poor provided by the State were few and people depended on one another in times of crisis such as illness, unemployment, childbirth and death, and for daily needs like childcare, food exchanges and companionship. The networks between neighbours were another form of working class self-help, essential at a time when state support for the unemployed, aged, ill or deserted was largely absent and stigmatized.

Married women were at the core of family and neighbourhood based self-help, although men were also involved.[88] Men visited with their families and neighbours and would readily help when a crisis arose. Married women's social activities were circumscribed by the sheer amount of work they were responsible for and by a rigid cultural demarcation between male/public and female/domestic social spaces.[89] Public spaces were largely male. We do not find women or girls playing football, attending pubs, hunting or even going out much after dark. Visiting with neighbours and kin to share experiences and resources was a form of social interaction open to married women. Women were more likely to visit one another in their homes, while men usually met in groups outside along the road, went for walks with their dogs to get buttermilk or sat on a wall to have a chat. Since visiting was a central activity for married women, many preferred to do so alone. Visiting was a time when mothers could take a break from childcare, and seek the company of their peers.

> The children were put to bed early to have them ready for school in the morning. And, sometimes maybe after the children would go to bed, my father would sit in and let my mother go out and see some of her friends. I remember in the afternoon her sometimes goin' out. Sometimes she took us with her and sometimes she didn't because she thought that children could be a bit of a nuisance. I can well remember an old woman used to come to see my mother once a week and we would have loved to have sat and listened to all this conversation, but we weren't allowed to. She used to give us a piece of bread and jam and tell us to go out and amuse ourselves outside and don't come back till I call you. Wanted to talk to this woman, you see.[90]

86 Interview with Adam Davison.   87 Glassie, *Ballymenone*, p. 298.   88 Meacham, *Life Apart*, p. 60.   89 Kane, 'Changing Role', 158; Ross, 'Fierce Questions', 578.   90 Interview with Sarah Ewart, former reeler and resident of Gilford, July 1983.

In contrast to London pub culture that included women, Tullylish women would never enter a pub to drink.[91] Women who publicly drank violated norms for respectable female behaviour.

> Down to Hall's Mill there was always two pubs there. But women never went. Oh, no, women never went to a public house in those days. Even if you had somebody sick that you wanted to get brandy, you might go down to the public house and if anybody outside you might send them in. People thought if you were seen comin' out of a public house, you were drinkin'.[92]

The public spaces open to married women included workplaces, shops and church. It was important for families to be seen in church on Sunday. All women attended either separately from their children or together as a family.[93] Young single people of both sexes did a lot of walking with friends of the same sex during the summer evenings when the daylight could last until 11:00 pm. Friends would walk for miles not realizing until the next morning, when they woke up tired and sore, how many miles they covered.[94]

Women neighbours always helped one another when they were giving birth since babies were born at home.[95] Whenever possible a woman's friends and neighbours were there to help her both during delivery and her postpartum recovery. The birthing room was strictly a women's domain, and men, with the possible exception of a physician, were not present. A former weaver remembered that her grandmother would get up at any hour of the night to go and help a woman in labour.

> [She was] what you called 'handy women'. And people who lived out the way on a farm, way out, not in the village, she used to go. And the doctor, was an old doctor, would have to sometimes attend at the birth if it was a serious birth. The doctor, he wanted her to go to London for a bit of training. He said there was nurses not as good as what she was.[96]

Another weaver also recalled how her mother-in-law helped women deliver babies and cared for the sick.

---

91 Ross, 'Survival Networks', 10; Ross, 'Fierce Questions,'; Meacham, *Life Apart*, p. 93.   92 Interview with Sarah Campbell.   93 Interview with Mrs McCusker.   94 Ibid.   95 Kane, 'Changing Role', 155; Linda May Ballard, 'Just whatever they had handy: aspects of childbirth and early childcare in Northern Ireland prior to 1948', *Ulster Folklife*, 31 (1985), 59–72; Judith Walzer Leavitt, 'Under the shadow of maternity: American women's responses to death and debility fears in nineteenth-century childbirth', *Feminist Studies*, 12, no. 1 (1986), 142.   96 Interview with Sarah Campbell.

There was never anything such as doctors running, you know if you were expecting childer or anything like that. I don't believe there was ever a nurse with any of them women in Banford. She woulda went to deliver all them childer herself. Johnny's mother was very good at that. And very good at sickness. Anybody was ill and in bed she could make them comfortable and done for them, you know. Just the same as a midwife, as we call them, now. She was something like that. You see, you had to pay your doctor. Every time your doctor come into your house it cost you. We always would've said you have to have the money for the doctor when he comes. It woulda been half a crown then. In case, you hada keep that because he wouldn't have come into your house. We had a doctor here and he did say it to me, 'Did your mother have the money to pay for this?' And you had to pay that two and six for him comin' to visit you. And if you needed medicine, or if you needed anything, you had to pay him another two and six. It cost you what we would've said five shillings then.[97]

Judith Leavitt has argued that women-centred networks formed during the nine-teenth century to assist during childbirth and postpartum recovery, were a way in which women were able to regain a measure of control over their lives. Women spent much of their fertile lives pregnant and delivering babies, facing considerable risks to their health. Women's networks provided care and comfort, and by assum-ing control over the birth process, midwives and other female assistants were able to save their family the cost of a physician.[98] Even if the doctor arrived after the baby was born to 'cut the string', families had to pay. Consequently, women provided care for the sick, delivered babies and collected money to aid one another during confinement.

And then they started up a fund. You paid into this, you see, so much and like it wouldn't a been maybe a whole lot of money, maybe as we'da called it 10*d*. And maybe it was only 5*d*. you paid. Well then when your confinement came then you would have the money then. One of these ones that would start it up and all they give you the money then to pay your doctor for your confinement. There was no such a thing as 'I'm pregnant and I have to get free milk', or 'I have to get my money' or anything like that. I seen women comin' out of their work on a Friday night and them expecting a baby and havin' their baby on Saturday morning. Then they maybe woulda had to go into their work beginning maybe the next week. The next day maybe they woulda had to get up out of bed. They would stayed in bed the one day and they woulda been outa bed the next day to have done their washin' and had to

97 Interview with Mrs McCusker.   98 Leavitt, 'Under the Shadow',146–8; Meacham, *Life Apart*, p.69; Ross, *Love and Toil*, pp. 111–22.

look after themselves. You see, there was nobody who could stay at home for to look after you.[99]

The importance of self-help networks in defraying the cost of health care cannot be overstated. Working-class people in Tullylish did not turn to doctors unless it was absolutely necessary. There was a dispensary with an attending doctor for two hours on Mondays and Fridays. However, to receive this form of medical care, a person to obtain a certificate or 'line' from the Board of Guardians. Given the cost of medical care and the prevalence of contagious diseases, many forms of do-it-yourself healing were devised. For example, the wild herbs that grew in the hedge did not go to waste and were used for medicinal purposes by both men and women.[100] Portar and castor oil were used to cure jaundice, and flaxseed was boiled with licorice balls to cure whooping cough.[101]

When people became too ill with contagious diseases such as scarlet fever, typhoid fever or typhus they went to the fever hospital attached to the Banbridge Workhouse. Such fever epidemics were common at the turn of the century, and the care given at the Banbridge Fever Hospital was minimal as one man who convalesced there described.

It was quite a lot of it around here alone. Just in Lawrencetown there was maybe twelve, fourteen maybe twenty cases typhus epidemics on and off. When I was with scarlet fever, was 1911, there was seventy scarlet patients at Banbridge hospital at that time. So much so that the fever hospital didn't hold us all. We had to let into some parts of the infirmary. The locals called it the idiot wards that were just almost insane. These wards were vacant at the time and when they hadn't enough room in the fever hospital those of us were convalescent were transferred over. There was only one nurse for the fever hospital permanently, another woman that helped in the kitchen, and they got a temporary nurse from Belfast that year and one from somewhere above Banbridge. One to help at night and one to help the permanent nurse during the day. Well these old women, they would've helped with meals and that sort of thing. There was only one doctor and he wasn't resident. He lived in town and he had a private practice as well as being the infirmary doctor. [How were you treated for fevers?] Well, at that time you got no treatment really at tall. Only you were kept in bed for a few days after you went in and I remember well the night I went in. I remember it was about 7:00. It was October and it was quite dark. There wasn't motors to bring them at that time. It must have been a horse, a horse drawn ambulance

99 Interview with Mrs McCusker.   100 Anthony Buckley, 'Unofficial healing in Ulster', *Ulster Folklife*, 26 (1980).   101 Interview with Arthur Patrick Burns.

and I myself fit in one. There was another girl. I never was so cold in my life. I think I was comin' from a good warm bed at home, and it wasn't too warm in the ambulance. I had my own clothes in the ambulance and then I was put into the bath and I got these home made shirts, night shirts, and it didn't feel altogether properly aired but that what we got, and we were in between two linen sheets in bed so there wasn't much coverin', and there was no central heatin' or anything at that time. I didn't sleep too much the first night ... When you went in with scarlet fever in those days you had to stay at least six weeks. With scarlet fever the skin peels off the palms of your hands and your feet and you couldn't be discharged from the fever hospital until your hands and feet were clear of this skin, you see.[102]

In Gilford, there was a doctor who was paid by means of 2*d*. per week deducted from the workers' wages. He was available to those who worked at the mill. A mill-owned hospital with a resident nurse was located at the top of Hill Street. There was also the 'Jubilee Nursing Society', a voluntary society that met in a mill-owned house in Gilford. Volunteers went around to the houses every year to collect money to pay the district nurse who treated everyone, including women in labour.

Finally, if anyone died, it was women neighbours, not kin, who came to help prepare the body. It was strictly taboo for kin to be involved with laying out the dead body.

Oh, they would go to their neighbours if there was anything wrong. Oh, yes. Oh, they were the first to be there. If anybody died they would have people engaged to lay them out and all. Its not like now with the under-taker. No, my mother was always on call for that. The people who died, their own people wouldn't touch them. Oh, no. There was always two women went and did it. Fixed the bed. It was white. Two women would go out and the undertaker would come out with the coffin and the women in those days always left white sheets. If anything should happen see, if the paper was faded on the wall where the bed was, they'd put a big white sheet against the wall and everything was pure white. The women done that.[103]

THE LIMITS OF FAMILY STRATEGIES: OLD AGE AND PARISH ASSISTANCE

Kinship ties and neighbourly interactions were, and still are, important in the care of the elderly. Often elderly relatives lived with members of their family. When the

---

102 Ibid.   103 Interview with Sarah Campbell.

elderly lived on their own, their children, grandchildren, nephews and nieces were expected to assist and visit them regularly. For example, their fire wood was gathered, their water carried and their errands run.

Census evidence suggests that elderly people tried not to live alone.[104] Most elderly widows and single women either lived with co-residing kin or with non-kin. When households reached the stage of old age with children, they began to contract in size as children married and left. At this stage there was an increase in the proportion of households (35.3 per cent) with co-residing extended kin. Only 12.3 per cent of households at the middle years of child raising had co-residing kin. This proportion rose to 19.9 per cent at the stage of later years of child raising when all children were above age seven. In keeping with the prevailing belief that children were responsible for the care of aging parents, co-residing children and other kin helped maintain the independence of the aging couple or widowed individual.[105]

In 1908, the Old Age Pensions Act was passed entitling persons at age seventy residing within the United Kingdom for twenty years to 5s. a week. Elderly pensioners living alone and trying to survive on 5s. a week led precarious lives. Neighbours did what they could, as did community institutions such as local schools.

> There was one old lady lived just a few yards from the school, an old pensioner, and the day that we made our dinner she got the dinner. It was brought down to her. And there was a half door on the house where she lived and she'd be waitin' every Tuesday to see there was dinner. She'd a been disappointed if there was no dinner.[106]

Children frequently ran errands for elderly people living on their own.

> My mother used to say to me, 'Now don't you be takin' anything off those old people for bringing them the pension'. One old lady in particular she made me take a wee white three penny piece. That was silver. Every six weeks she had that waitin' for me. That was at the rate of a h'penny per week. But she changed it into silver to make it look somethin'. And I thought something of that.[107]

---

104 Guinnane, 'The Poor Law and pensions in Ireland', *Journal of interdisciplinary History*, 24, no. 2 (1993), 271–91. For England see Sonya O. Rose, 'The varying household arrangements of the elderly in three English villages: Nottinghamshire, 1851–1881', *Continuity and Change*, 3, no 1 (1988), 101–22; Michael Anderson, 'The impact on family relationships of the elderly of changes since the Victorian times in governmental income-maintenance provision', in Ethel Shanas and Marvin B. Sussman (eds), *Family, Bureaucracy and the Elderly* (Durham 1977); Jill Quadagno, *Aging in Early Industrial Society* (New York 1982). For the United States see Smith, 'Life Course', and Haraven, 'Life Course Transitions'.   105 Quadagno, *Aging*, pp. 121–4.   106 Interview with Sarah Campbell.   107 Ibid.

At the turn of the century, the link between old age and poverty was being investigated. Charles Booth's detailed study revealed the strength of this link.[108] He inquired into the condition of the aged poor, available employment and the types and extent of assistance from relatives, neighbours, church and parish. Beginning with children, the extent and form of assistance depended, in large measure, on the financial situation of that child and whether he or she had their own family to support. At times, money was given to pay the rent and to help maintain an elderly parent, but this form of assistance was irregular. More frequently, aged parents were taken in and given room and food in exchange for some type of assistance. Because elderly women were potentially more useful in the house as childminders and housekeepers, they were more frequently taken in. The strength of kin ties and a myriad of small forms of assistance were vitally important to maintaining 'the struggling lives of the old'.[109]

Evidence from an Outdoor Relief Register for the Banbridge Board of Guardians suggests that the link between old age and poverty was indeed strong in Tullylish.[110] Of the 519 people who applied for outdoor relief in 1899, 440 or 84.8 per cent were over age sixty. Poverty among the elderly also had a female face. Stearns states that, 'the tendency of the industrial economy to withdraw women from productive labor left them cruelly exposed, insofar as they outlived their earning spouses'.[111] In Tullylish, of the fifty-four recipients, 68.5 per cent were female, and only eight were under age sixty.

Individuals from Tullylish receiving outdoor relief between 1899 to 1911 were linked to the 1901 census enumerator's schedules. When we look at the types of households most likely to collect outdoor relief, table 18 shows that women and men living alone had the most difficulty making ends meet. Of the forty-six households headed by females living alone, 41.3 per cent received outdoor relief at some point. Men were better able to maintain themselves through employment than women and far more men had occupations listed for them on the outdoor relief register. Consequently, of the fourteen households headed by males living alone, a smaller proportion (35.7 per cent) received outdoor relief with labourers most likely to need parish assistance. Of the 118 labourers, 13.6 per cent had to rely on outdoor relief at some point. Finally, relative to their numbers in the population, outdoor relief was an option turned to more frequently by Catholics (15.2 per cent) then Protestants (6.6 per cent). Two explanations are Catholics were more likely to fill the lowest paid labouring jobs and more remained single with no children to assist them.

108 Charles Booth, *The Aged Poor in England and Wales: Condition* (London 1894); Quadagno, *Aging*; Guinnane, 'Poor Law', 272–4; Ronald V. Sires, 'The beginnings of British legislation for Old Age Pensions', *Journal of Economic History*, 14, no. 3 (1954).   109 Booth, *Aged Poor*, p. 327; Anderson, 'Impact', 50–1.

Table 18: The marital status of outdoor relief recipients in the Banbridge Poor
Law Union, 1899

Marital Status	Number	%
Widows	187	36
Employed	17	
Unemployed	170	
Widowers	56	10.8
Employed	11	
Unemployed	45	
Single women	163	31.4
Employed	15	
Unemployed	48	
Single men	49	9.4
Employed	7	
Unemployed	42	
Married couples	64	12.3
Employed	29	
Unemployed	35	

Source 1901 Census Enumerators' Schedules for the Parish of Tullylish; BG.6/EA/1, Outdoor Relief
Register, 2 October 1899–14 June 1948.

Those who reached old age with 'no one belonging to them' would probably live
out their final years in poverty on outdoor relief or in the workhouse.[112] While it was
considered a disgrace to have to enter the workhouse, parish assistance in the form
of outdoor relief did not carry the same stigma. Poor Law practices varied from
union to union, but in all cases, outdoor relief was never meant to be the sole means
of support since it was too meager a sum to live on.[113] Conditions in the Banbridge
Workhouse, recalled by a Lawrencetown resident, clarify why it was deplored.

110 (PRONI), BG.6/EA/1, Outdoor Relief Register for 2 October 1899 to 14 June 1948.   111 Stearns,
'Old Women', 48.   112 Booth, *Aged Poor*, p. 330; Anderson, 'Impact', 45.   113 Quadagno, *Aging*, pp.
102, 105, 115, 131.

I got a good idea of what was goin' on in the workhouse ...I was able to knock about and I was able to see what happened to these people all the time. They had a meal of porridge and buttermilk in the morning. At dinnertime they had a potato and buttermilk and in the evening they had porridge and buttermilk again. And anybody was a wee bit feeble or in poor health, they got a wee drop of tea in the evening. But what they called 'able bodied paupers' they got porridge in the morning, porridge in the evening and a potato and buttermilk. And now in addition to that there was what they called the tramps. They would get a night's lodging. I think they hada be in before seven in the evening and I don't know if they got any meal in the evening or not but they got a bed. And in the morning they hada do three hours work before they left. That was the men folk. I don't know what way the women were treated. There were women tramps on the road at that time too. I could see them from our window. I could see these men outside workin'. [Was one part for the men and one part for the women?] It was. I remember one morning there were quite alot there. I think what happened was a small circus, and times were bad, and the circus broke up the night before so they had no money to pay for lodging or anything and a good many of them come and got a night in the workhouse. So the next morning we could see these fellows from our window from the hospital. They were working. They would make work for them. They got alot of old rubble that come from an old building to put up a screen and they were mixin' this stone from the sand and lime and the mortar. Well, they hada stay there till 10:00 and before they could be discharged there hada been a policeman come up from the barracks had a word with each one of them before they went out. I think that was in case some of them mighta been law breakers or might of done something summoned in the court that didn't appear for some offense, but before they were discharged from the workhouse in the morning at 10:00, they had to go through the hands of the police. There was usually just one policeman come up to see them discharged.[114]

He pointed out that female residents were responsible for the laundry and for washing the floors. Also, some women helped the nurses in the infirmary or hospital. The category of people most likely to receive relief inside workhouse were people with no relatives or 'poor unfortunate girls who had a baby'.[115]

114 Interview with Arthur Patrick Burns.

CONCLUSION

For women, 'there was little distinction between work and home life ... their families' survival depended on their incessant efforts'.[116] Since women shouldered the full burden of reproduction work, they were key actors in the creation and reproduction of the culture of control and the social ties between families, neighbours and co-workers. The web of women-centred networks structured forms of self-help that ensured survival, modified resignation associated with low wages and limited alternatives, tempered women's drudgery and provided satisfaction for many.

Because women were household financial managers, supplemental wage earners, and, at times, fulltime wage earners, men and women were economically interdependent, a reality that modified patriarchy in significant ways. Men were clearly household heads and the extent of wives' influence was seen by women to depend partly on how 'agreeable' their husbands' temperament was. Nevertheless, major decisions affecting the family were largely arrived at by both husband and wife. Control over the daily household spending, establishing vital lines of credit with shops, and taking control over the birthing process were wholly in women's hands which increased their power *vis-à-vis* their husbands and children.

The 'logics and demands' of women's unwaged and waged work and between forms of women's and men's work created distinct ways of coping with material constraints. There was unanimous recognition that the realities of working-class life were experienced differently and unequally. While working-class men were expected to work hard as the primary wage earner, their work was over at the end of the work day. In contrast, childcare, high standards of cleanliness and the labour intensive nature of domestic work resulted in long hours of hard work for married women whether or not they worked outside the home. The succinct evaluation of gender inequality that forms the title of this chapter will also close it: 'Men didn't give women a very good deal in those days. The women got it very very hard. It wasn't a woman's world.'[117]

115 Ibid.; P. Townsend, 'The effects of family structure on the likelihood of admission to an institution in old age', in Ethel Shanas and G.F. Streib (eds), *Social Structure and the Family* (New Jersey 1965). 116 Blewett, *Last Generation*, p. 38.   117 Interview with Sarah Ewart, former reeler and resident of Gilford, July 1983.

Conclusion: Intersections:
Local Contexts and Global Process

> ... you knew everybody in the factory, where they were from and all about them. And everybody was friendly and stopped and talked to you. There was no closed doors the way they are now. The door was left open and they could've brought whoever they liked in.   Mrs McCurtin, former powerloom weaver, 1983

Historical ethnography, like microhistory, clarifies the historically specific nature of dependency in particular regions, invites linkages between specific historical contexts and broader historical processes, and the reassessment of conclusions based upon generalization and global perspectives. Since the economic history of the Irish linen industry is well documented, local studies suggest new questions, perspectives, methodologies and comparisons. Analysis of the factors determining structural change at the regional level helps explain how regions of 'revolutionizing industry' like Tullylish differ from those with alternate economic trajectories.[1]

Tullylish was typical of early Victorian rural industrial regions in terms of the challenges confronting capitalists seeking to tap and control local sources of water and labour power. However, it was atypical in other respects. First, contradictions within proto-industrial production undermined the system earlier in the Banbridge region than elsewhere in Ulster. By the late eighteenth century, due to the concentration of bleachgreens along the Bann, paths of capitalist development in the parish began to diverge. Many farmer/weavers in the townlands flanking the Bann abandoned their small plots of land to concentrate on weaving for putters-out prior to 1825. In this industrial mid-section, drapers and bleachers had long been engaged in entrepreneurial activity and were ready to invest in the reorganization of production along capitalist lines before cheaper British mill-spun yarn demanded defensive response. After 1825, bleachers and drapers who had accumulated capital, invested in building dams, mills and factories. In contrast, the northern townlands remained embedded in petty commodity production organized by manufacturers in Lurgan until the early twentieth century. Second, although nearly all rural entrepreneurs in Ulster provided housing, the factory community at Dunbarton was atypical, comparable with only a handful of large-scale factory villages and towns in Ireland and Great Britain.

---

1 Pat Hudson, 'The regional perspective', in Pat Hudson (ed.), *Regions and Industries* (Cambridge 1986), p. 20.

After the spread of mill-based spinning in 1825, regional distinctions deepened. The economic structures of the industrial mid-section in Banbridge Union strengthened based upon factory production of linen yarn and thread. The new spinning mills represented a fully capitalist production system based upon the exploitation of permanent wage labourers. Male and female handloom weavers in Lurgan Union remained dispersed with production organized by an older weakened putting-out system.

The full ramifications of strengthening versus weakening economic structures in the two sub-regions were evident between 1846–51. The demographic upheaval caused by the Great Famine was a watershed in Tullylish as it was in Ireland generally. However, due to the dominance of the linen industry, the affects of this watershed were mediated by regional capitalist development. Although the parish as a whole gained population during this tragic time, townlands along the industrializing Bann, and especially the town of Gilford, attracted many people in search of employment. In this context, Famine-induced demographic shifts contributed to the process of primitive accumulation by reducing the number of proto-industrial producers, many of whom provided cheap labour for factories in the region, Ulster, England and Scotland.[2]

The Great Famine also lowered the supply of handloom weavers through death, proletarianization and migration temporarily raising the wages of those who survived. Handloom weavers in Tullylish/ Lurgan fared worse during the Famine than proletarians in Tullylish/Banbridge. More people died in Lurgan Workhouse and over a longer period of time. The increase in weavers' wages coupled with the huge rise in demand for alternatives to cotton cloth during the American Civil War initiated a secondary wave of economic growth in the linen industry, based on the spread of powerlooms.

Thus, while capitalisms everywhere share a similar coherent structure, they are shaped by historically specific forces. In Tullylish, the social forces propelling capitalist development in the eighteenth century centred on dependency on English markets, the activities of an elite bloc of Protestant landlords, drapers and bleachers and a highly differentiated group of producers. Efforts to promote the linen industry among the elite were motivated by distinct class interests. As a class, large and small landlords in Ulster were quick to see and act upon the potential of an expanding linen industry to ensure a stable and increasing rent roll. Helping to promote the linen industry defined 'improving landlords' in this context. Smaller landlords, like the Johnstons, facilitated and underpinned the development of the linen industry through favourable terms of tenure granted to those tenants investing capital in expanding linen production and circulation.

In Tullylish, bleachers in particular benefitted from such favourable tenure

---

2 Karl Marx and Frederick Engels, *Ireland and the Irish Question* (New York 1972), pp. 133–4; Karl Marx, *Capital* (New York), p. 174.

arrangements and took full advantage of water power along the River Bann and the excellent location relative to market towns and sources of transport. Bleachgreen owners in Tullylish were thus enabled to be innovative in several ways. Although bleaching was not fully mechanized during the eighteenth century, it supplied the principle innovative impulse for the linen industry as a whole. As capitalists faced with the lengthy temporal requirements associated with bleaching linen cloth, bleachers contributed important technological and chemical innovations that reduced the time and cost of the bleaching and finishing process. By employing local labour in centralized mills, they encouraged the concentration of population close to their bleachgreens and actively reorganized relations of production along capitalist lines. Since many bleachers were also linen drapers and manufacturers, they accumulated merchant capital through the putting-out system and market. Bleachers required substantial capital, and were on the cutting-edge of capitalist development affecting change at the points of production and exchange.

According to Marx, capitalism is a mode of production, and merchant capital derived from trade or exploiting the market cannot alone transform a pre-capitalist mode of production. Although the historically specific case of Tullylish does not refute this enduring theoretical position, a more nuanced analysis of the logic of merchant capital supports the conclusion that drapers were a progressive force. In addition to the typical functions served by merchants – opening new markets, spreading the use of currency and increasing dependency upon wages – drapers in Tullylish/Seapatrick were a differentiated group including bleacher/drapers and small scale manufacturers who emerged from the ranks of proto-industrial producers. If we define or deconstruct the category drapers contextually, in Tullylish/Seapatrick, this heterogenous group were penetrating the production process through the putting-out system early. When faced with the choice of innovation or elimination after 1825, wealthy merchant manufacturers, exemplified by Hugh Dunbar, invested accumulated capital in building centralized mills.

Although wealthy and powerful bleachers and drapers won the competitive battle over smaller manufacturers, we should not overlook the small and hidden ways producers contributed to the emergence of capitalist relations of production. Peasants and proto-industrial producers are not uniformly motivated by the logic of simple reproduction. Nor can their economies be understood as 'natural', a complex term laden with ideology. As the complexity of yarn and cloth producers in eighteenth century Ulster reveals, some were motivated by accumulation, emerging as petty capitalists and petty landlords in their own right who employed proletarianized cottier weavers. Others sought to maximize their market advantage by taking in apprentices, extended kin and itinerants to maintain independence and expand the productive capacity of their households. Proto-industrial producers employed a range of strategies including self-exploitation, hiring additional labour, and abandoning farms altogether to meet the challenges posed by a developing capitalist linen industry. For most of the long eighteenth century, leasing land, however small, was an active strategy that worked against proletarianization.[3] However, by the close of the eighteenth century, this strategy was eroding in the region, initiating its antithesis, primitive accumulation.

The narrow employment base characteristic of rural industrial regions sharply differentiated them from a more diverse urban industrial Belfast. Rural factory owners faced distinct challenges that defined their class strategies. To ensure a stable labour force reproduced by future generations of family members, employers along the Bann needed to create a larger labour market for adult men than existed in Belfast. Unlike Belfast, which had a ready pool of available experienced labour to work in the new spinning mills, rural factory owners had to recruit and retain a largely green labour force through the provision of built environments consisting minimally of housing and extending at times to schools, churches and other social institutions. Because the built environment of factory villages reflects a combination of capitalist accumulation, cultural hegemony and subaltern cultural forms, they provide a rich opportunity for extending our understanding of paths of capitalist development, specific cultural hegemonies and working-class lives.

In the early nineteenth century, most of the rural Irish population had never worked in factories; hence, they were ripe for paternalistic endeavour. The two principal interrelated differences between rural factory towns such as Gilford/Dunbarton and urban industrial Belfast, were the lack of alternative sources of employment and the pervasive influence of mill owners. The expansion of Gilford/Dunbarton reflects the historically specific forces involved in the formation of an Irish industrial proletariat in the first half of the nineteenth century, and the contradictory motivations of mid-Victorian paternalistic employers. Hugh Dunbar died just prior to the Famine-induced deluge of people into Gilford/Dunbarton. While this population ensured his successor, John W. McMaster of an ample workforce, scarcity of housing and transience created dislocation and crowding. By the boom years of the 1860s, a rapidly expanding linen industry ensured the powerful McMasters of an enormously profitable business and solidified their cultural hegemony over social life in Gilford/Dunbarton.

Mid-Victorian paternalism, as a form of cultural hegemony, clearly reflected prevailing cultural conceptions of masculinity and femininity rooted in the patriarchal family. Looking backward to aristocratic deference and forward to the possibility of class mobility through self-improvement and self-help, paternalistic employers legitimized their domination partly in terms that expressed 'natural' gender relations in the family. The McMasters earned enormous profits as capitalists and status as patriarchs. They provided the means to support material life and facilitate self-improvement. As supportive fathers, they expressed satisfaction when

---

3 Jane Gray, 'Rural Industry and Uneven Development: The Significance of Gender in the Irish Linen Industry', *Journal of Peasant Studies*, 20, no. 4 (1993), 52; Brendan Collins, 'Proto-industrialization and pre-famine emigration', *Social History*, 7, no. 2 (1982), 131.

one of their own rose above humble origins. Hiring more adult men and fewer married women supported cultural norms regarding proper gender roles since the wages earned by male heads of household were key to its financial viability.

Paternalistic employers did not, however, significantly alter working conditions. In all cases, wages were low, hours were long, and many phases of production remained injurious to workers' health. Rural mills and factories were less likely to be routinely visited by Factory Inspectors allowing for evasions of the Factory Acts. While it is reasonable to assume that paternalistic owners made an effort to comply with attempts by the paternal state to regulate the working conditions of women and children, low wages resulted in evasions of child labour laws throughout the industry, especially regarding schooling. Further, paternalistic concern stopped short of including adult men, and supporting trade unions – a form of organized working-class self-help.

Wage systems, as Judy Lown argues, are 'deeply imbued with cultural and moral significance' with differences in the amount and methods of payment reflecting older gendered divisions of labour at the household level.[4] During the 1880s and 1890s, allegations were made that in several branches of the linen industry, wages were totally insufficient to enable workers to maintain a decent standard of living and should be considered 'sweated' trades. The definition of 'sweating' presented by the 1907 Select Committee on Homework, was wages that were 'insufficient to enable an adult person to obtain anything like proper food, clothing, and house accommodation'.[5] Wage statistics published in 1906 by the Board of Trade and those compiled by Emily Boyle show that earnings in the linen industry generally were extremely low, particularly in factories outside of Belfast.[6]

The reasons why wages and working conditions in the linen industry remained stubbornly poor are complex. First, processing flax into linen cloth was difficult. Second, the vast majority of the labour force were consistently women and young persons ideologically presumed to be supplemental wage earners.[7] The prevalence of children and young single women in all branches except bleaching suggests that the majority of workers were considered (and likely considered themselves) dependent rather than free agents.[8] Third, while many employers complied with the Factory Acts, there were far too few Factory Inspectors to ensure regular inspection

4 Judy Lown, *Women and Industrialization* (Mineapolis 1990), p. 106.   5 H.C. *Report from the Select Committee on Homework*, vol. 6 (1907), p. 3.   6 Emily J. Boyle, 'The Economic Development of the Irish Linen Industry, 1825–1914', Ph.D. diss., The Queen's University of Belfast, 1977, Appendix 10; John Harris, 'The Working and Effects of Trade Boards in the Linen Industry of Northern Ireland', M.A. diss. Queen's University of Belfast, 1924, pp. 20–2. In 1906, fulltime employees worked a 55 hour week. Among adult men, 44.4 per cent earned under 20s. a week; 36.7 per cent earned between 20s. and 30s. a week; 13.6 per cent earned between 30s. and 40s. a week; and only 5.3 per cent earned 40s. and above. Among adult women, 41.7 per cent earned under 10s. a week; 49.1 per cent earned between 10s. and 15s. a week; 8.5 per cent earned between 15s. and 20s. a week; and only 0.7 per cent earned 20s. and above. Ninety per cent of all women earned below 15s. a week.   7 Boyle, 'Economic Development', p. 148.   8 Carole Turbin, *Working Women of Collar City: Gender, Class, and Community in Troy, 1864–86* (Urbana 1992), p. 7.

and enforcement of the law. Factories and workshops located in rural areas, were seldom inspected and, when they were, securing cooperation was problematic.[9] Fourth, trade unions were slow to form and weak in the nineteenth century. By 1910, just over 11 per cent of the total workforce were members.[10] The earliest unions were established in male occupations such as flaxdressers and roughers (a numerical minority in comparison with female workers), since male workers were expected to be free agents and permanently employed. Men in these occupations were part of the Amalgamated Transport and General Workers Union at the turn of the twentieth century. While a proportion of female textile operatives were organized later, their unions were not strong enough to radically improve working conditions or wages. In many phases of production, union membership was not general until World War II. It took a general strike in 1946, which lasted six weeks, for all of Dunbar McMaster & Company to be unionized. Because the majority of linen industry workers remained unorganized prior to World War II, they were dependent upon the good-will of factory owners to comply with the Factory Acts and to take the initiative to lessen the health risks associated with linen production.

Bleachgreens were never closed shops. Some of the workers at Banford were unionized, but neither it nor Springvale were ever entirely unionized. Although Milltown was reputed to have paid their workers enough to have discouraged unionization, after World War I unionizing efforts by men from Belfast began.[11] Before that time, workers along the Bann risked being fired if they joined unions or tried to organize.

By the mid-nineteenth century, north east Ulster was, in some respects, typical of industrial regions in Great Britain. Comparisons between working-class life in England, Scotland and east Ulster reveal significant similarities in cultural responses to low wages and poor working conditions in the textile industry. Accounts of long hours of arduous labour on the job and at home, job related health hazards, paid and unpaid attempts to make ends meet by wives and the reliance upon child labour in working-class London, Liverpool, or Lancashire are analogous with working-class Belfast or Gilford.

However, the similarities between the Ulster linen industry which 'represents the only true case of industrialization in Ireland', can mask its economic domination by England, its underdevelopment and dependency upon British markets.[12] For more than two centuries, community and household life in Tullylish was wholly reliant on the linen industry. Although the industry was strong enough to support these communities fo two centuries, the danger of reliance upon a single industry was evident during periodic economic recessions, such as that in 1880, and in the

9 Hilda Martindale, *From One Generation to Another, 1839–1944* (London 1944), pp. 106–7.   10 Boyle, 'Economic Development', p. 155.   11 Interview with Arthur Patrick Burns, former stinter, calander man and resident of Lawrencetown, July 1983.   12 Jane Gray, 'Rural Industry and Uneven Development in Ireland: Region, Class and Gender, 1780–1840', Ph.D. diss., Johns Hopkins University, 1991, pp. 5, 33.

second half of the twentieth century when most of the mills and factories along the
Bann closed their doors.[13]

England's political and economic domination of Ireland generated distinctions
in the social structure and everyday life of working-class communities in Ulster,
more typical of its semiperiphery. This colonial legacy created additional layers of
insecurity on top of the financial insecurity characteristic of British working-class
life generally in the nineteenth and early twentieth century. Both owners and workers were well aware of the necessity for strong British demand to support continued
accumulation and employment.

Cleavages or 'extra-proletarian identifications' within the working class characteristic of labour relations in Ulster were also fundamentally the outcome of British
colonial domination.[14] Although poverty often created social linkages between Catholics and Protestants, periodic demonstrations of political loyalties, cultural difference
and conflict were deeply ingrained in the region. Church and chapel-based identifications in Tullylish cross-cut class identifications in significant ways.

To be Protestant was a resource yielding concrete economic, political and social
compensation. The ascendancy of Protestants in Ulster ensured that the elite of
landlords, merchants and capitalists in Tullylish were Protestant as were most of the
petty bourgeoisie of smaller landlords, shopkeepers and professionals. Protestants
dominated local politics, serving on the Board of Guardians and as Gilford Town
Commissioners. Although the powerful presence of paternalistic capitalists overshadowed the middle class of shopkeepers, small property owners and professionals
in Gilford/Dunbarton, the Protestant petty bourgeoisie, played a vital role in community life.[15]

Because middle-class Protestant shopkeepers supplied working-class households
with essential credit, they buffered the class exploitation between linen capitalists
and their employees. Wages were low and those who extended essential credit were
key participants in working-class women's strategies to make ends meet between
pay intervals. This widespread cultural pattern in Ireland was as rooted in familiarity, mutual obligation and ties to a locale as in class inequality. The social ramifications of upper-class stature largely removed capitalists from the everyday web of
social obligation existing between working and middle-class people. Although middle-class shopkeepers were a class above, with a higher standard of living and social
status, they were accessible on a daily basis, extending credit and seeing customers
through hard times.

Small indicators of wealth or status, such as occupational skill, autonomy, living

13 For an analysis of migration from Gilford to New York initiating in the depressed 1880s see Marilyn
Cohen, 'From Gilford to Greenwich: the migration experience of female-headed households at the
turn of the century', in Patrick O'Sullivan (ed.), *The Irish World Wide, vol. 4, Irish Women and the Irish
Migrations* (Leicester 1995).   14 Patrick Joyce, *Visions of the People* (Cambridge 1991), p. 5.   15 (PRONI),
D.2714/3A Minutes of Meetings of Ratepayers 1859–1915, p. 294; William MacDonald & Co.,
MacDonald's Irish Directory and Gazetteer, 1902–3 ed., p. 436.

in a slightly larger parlour house on 'Mechanic's Row', located close to the mill in Dunbarton or keeping one's children in primary school longer, were also unequally distributed between Protestants and Catholics. These distinctions were important despite the fact that opportunities for social mobility remained limited for all members of the working class. Thus, religion had a profound effect on the formation of cultural hegemony, social structure and forms of identity in the town, mediating androcentric conceptions of power at work and in the community.

This study of industrialization underscores the importance of gender as a category in the analysis of emergent capitalism. Innovations that bring about qualitative changes in the organization of production are never gender neutral. Although the first centralized industrial proletariat in Tullylish were male bleachgreen workers, their numbers were small and impact on the organization of production minimal. In contrast, the spread of mill-based spinning revolutionized relations of production creating a vast pool of cheap female labour comprised of former handspinners. These women and girls either entered the new spinning mills or were dependent upon the putting-out system as winders or handloom weavers. In Tullylish, where mill-based spinning advanced, winding yarn for manufacturers and handloom weaving were important alternative sources of employment for displaced female handspinners inhibiting emigration.

The spread of mill spinning spelled the loss of independence among the members of proto-industrial households. Women felt this change more directly since they lost spinning as an enduring occupation. They were now 'free' to form the first industrial proletariat in Ulster's cotton and linen yarn spinning mills and, for them, changes in working conditions were profound. Under the domestic system of production, women and girls worked under the direction of the male head whose conception of time was fundamentally task-oriented. Women were able to alternate between spinning, winding and other domestic responsibilities. Despite the familial and patriarchal character of early spinning mills, capitalist relations of production forced women to adjust to dependence on wages, long hours of work, synchronized time, unhealthy working conditions and strict factory discipline.

Although changes associated with work under capitalism were profound, forms of gender and generational inequality were remarkably persistent in the period between 1700–1900. Looking first at generational factors, children in the family-based economies of proto-industrial households were expected to work under the direction of their parents as soon as they were able. Their contributions were vital to the productive strategies of their family economies. While changes in the relations of production characteristic of factory production partly eroded parental control over their children, evidence suggests that many children in Tullylish were firmly rooted in the family-wage economy and resided with their families of origin and contributed to its resources until marriage. Children continued to be central to household strategies to retain independence and respectability since many working-class households could not make ends meet without their wages. Consequently, the vast majority of children in Tullylish began working as full or halftimers as soon as they reached legal age.

For working-class children of both sexes, leaving primary school to begin earning fulltime wages was a *rite of passage*. Evidence from Tullylish suggest that most working-class parents supported a basic education for their children. Still, the limitations poverty placed on the schooling of working-class children in Tullylish were, for them, the quintessence of class stratification. The vast majority of working-class children, whether they wanted to leave school or not, were forced to terminate their schooling after the fifth class. Even when a bright child demonstrated the ability and desire to continue learning at the secondary school level, the sacrifice of their wages, the cost of books and the cost of residence outside the community made it impossible. In many respects, when school was over so was childhood, since children then entered the adult world of waged work where they abandoned childhood games and concerns for the structure of factory culture. As elsewhere in Ireland, this transition to adulthood after leaving primary school was abrupt bypassing the 'teenage' or adolescent stage.[16] This life cycle transition was experienced by many as an ambivalent combination of sadness at leaving school and pride in contributing to the household's resources.

Cross-culturally, the best predictor of the division of labour between children is the division of labour between adults.[17] Moving to a consideration of gender over two centuries, one is no less struck by the endurance of gender inequality and its structural effects upon women's lives. In both the eighteenth and nineteenth centuries, there was a rigid sexual division of labour with women responsible for housework and childcare. In proto-industrial households, females were responsible for spinning and winding yarn and males for weaving cloth. While the fly shuttle and mill-spun yarn enabled more women to weave, men did not turn to winding. Within the new spinning mills and powerloom factories, occupations continued to be characterized as male or female even though more men filled occupations designated as female in rural industrial regions.

Continuities in the sexual division of labour shaped working-class women's dispositions – their values, understandings of the social system and what is possible.[18] Because women were responsible for domestic work in both centuries, the discontinuous rhythm of their waged work remained persistent. Although some eighteenth-century women spun yarn continuously and some nineteenth-century married women continuously worked for wages, generally, women's paid work was more intermittent than men's. Eighteenth-century women spun linen yarn alongside their other domestic responsibilities. Married women in the nineteenth century were often engaged in a variety of supplemental wage earning activities, such as home-

16 Eileen Kane, 'The changing role of the family in a rural Irish community', *Journal of Comparative Family Studies*, 10, no. 2 (1972), 156.   17 Candice Bradley, 'Children's work and women's work: a cross cultural study', *Anthropology of Work Review*, 8, no. 1 (1987), 3.   18 Ira Katznelson, 'Levels of class formation', in Patrick Joyce (ed.), *Class* (Oxford 1995), pp. 145–6.

work, performed alongside their domestic responsibilities. Eighteenth-century daughters probably spent more time spinning than their mothers, but they too were expected to help with household chores and childcare. Nineteenth-century daughters usually spent more time working for wages than their mothers, but were also expected to help with domestic work. When a wife worked outside the home, it was most often her eldest or second daughter who took over the functions of housekeeper. In no case did males fill this role.

In both centuries, women's underpaid work was crucial to maintaining an independent household and culture of control. The small wages earned by handspinners provided rent payments that helped insulate proto-industrial households from destitution and proletarianization and facilitated small-scale accumulation among manufacturers and yarn jobbers. The budgets of proletarian families in the nineteenth century were stretched by the myriad of underpaid sweated work performed by women that enhanced their ability to make ends meet without parish or informal community support. Finally, the many forms of unpaid work performed by women such as making clothing, establishing credit relations with shops, caring for the sick or helping women during confinement were self-help activities that contributed to the financial and emotional stability of their households and communities. In both centuries, women's undervalued and undercounted contributions secured the slim margin of survival.

There is also much similarity in the private domestic forms of female sociability in the two periods. In the eighteenth century, women gathered in someone's home to spin and converse. They were not part of the weavers' public work culture centring upon reading societies and hunts. In the nineteenth century, forms of public sociability open to men such as pubs, sports or pigeon shooting were closed to women. Single women were freer than married women to socialize in public places attending dances, evening school or taking long walks on summer evenings with their friends. Married women's public social space was confined largely to workplaces, shops, churches and certain recreational venues such as Catch-My-Pal Hall. Due to the demands of domestic work and childcare, married women spent most of their time at home enmeshed in visiting networks with kin and neighbours who provided conversation, a break from childcare and assistance. The private domain for women provided the foundation in both centuries for men's public forms of sociability, providing them with free time.

Since males in both centuries earned higher wages than females, we can assume that female-headed households in both centuries faced difficulties making ends meet. While evidence relating to female-headed households in the eighteenth century is scant, the 1821 census suggests that most were widow-headed. Since handspinning was poorly remunerated, households headed by widows engaged in handspinning were likely to be poor, even if land enabled them to partially reproduce themselves. In the nineteenth century, an industrial capitalist linen industry compounded the forces operating to generate female-headed households. Due to increased employment opportunities for women, the proportion of households headed by single women increased dramatically, as did those formed by husbands' desertion or migration.

Analysis of the strategies of female-headed households, who comprised a substantial minority, enriches our understanding of the Irish working class. In households headed by widows and single women, employment patterns diverged significantly from households headed by men. Due to asymmetrical wage scales, more female heads of household needed to work for wages than married women whose husbands were resident. The absence of a principal male wage earner increased the economic interdependence of all co-residing members. Because female-headed households were heavily dependent upon child labour, the schooling of these children suffered; their attendance was more erratic, and their attainment levels were below children of male-headed households. Thus, female-headed households in the nineteenth century were symbols of poverty as they are today due to the persistence of unequal wages.

Widows were more firmly embedded both ideologically and concretely in the prevailing sex/gender system since they had fulfilled women's primary roles as wives and mothers. Most tried to remain within the family wage economy relying on the wage contributions of their children. However, the strategies of single female heads of household countered prevailing cultural norms in two key ways. As spinsters, they did not fulfill women's paramount function and duty. Second, since they were not dependent on male breadwinners, they followed a continuous employment pattern similar to men. Therefore, questions regarding the household division of labour, work satisfaction and the degree to which patriarchy was tempered in these households requires further scholarly attention.

Part of dispelling the myth of the family as a seperate haven from the workplace involves documenting the labour intensive unpaid work performed by women in the home and analyzing the connections between waged and unwaged work. In addition to the economic link between unpaid domestic work and the value of labour power, the structure of family time strictly conformed to that of industrial time with schedules regulating sleeping, awakening and meals dictated by the punctual factory time clock. The unpaid work women performed to reproduce their household members on a daily basis orchestrated the rhythms of family and industrial time.

Such work was time consuming and arduous in the nineteenth and early twentieth centuries. Since conditions of work in the home were poor, as they were in factories, working wives were exposed to heavy and often unhealthy toil in two sites. Consequently, most women preferred to leave waged work after the birth of children looking upon those shouldering two work loads with pity.

Men's and women's work identities were deeply connected with cultural conceptions of gender and role expectations in the family. The history of Protestant domination in the region generated a form of hegemonic masculinity privileging

Protestant men, who owned or controlled the means of production, and were expected to exercise authority over subordinates defined in class, religious and gender terms. All men expected to be paternal authority figures and principal wage earners, leading them to emphasize wages, skill and autonomy in their subjective evaluations of work. As decision makers, men expected to acquire considerable working knowledge about their work process and the linen industry as a whole. Those whose occupations reflected and reproduced these masculine attributes, more often expressed positive evaluations of their work. Male respectability increased with independence and skill, since skilled workers, the majority of whom were Protestant, were better paid, regularly employed and better to keep wives out of the workforce.

Although acceptance of hard work was fundamental to men's and women's work ideologies the relative importance of waged work to self-identity varied. For men, who expected to be breadwinners, waged work was the foundation of their masculine identity. Waged work was also important to women's self-identity, however, the intermittent nature of their waged work and the sexual division of labour that placed unwaged domestic work squarely on their shoulders, created self-identities framed as much by extra-proletarian roles and relationships. Wives, who were responsible for the reproduction of their families, needed to utilize kinship and neighbourhood networks on a frequent if not daily basis. Ties between and among women tempered their drudgery and provided emotional satisfaction as they turned to one another for assistance, conversation and a break from chores.

This active purposeful structuring of self-help activities by women moderated patriarchy in significant ways. First, due to the degree of interdependence in working class household, the money earned by working-class wives was an important contribution to household budgets. Second, as managers of household finances, wives were adept at stretching tight resources since they knew the prices of necessities and established lines of credit with shopkeepers. The autonomous decisions made daily gave working-class wives a measure of power and autonomy *vis-à-vis* their husbands. These contributions by women to the survival of their families and working-class communities existing 'in conditions of chronic uncertainty' are as central to our understanding of working-class culture and survival as the trade union movement. As Aihwa Ong argues, by recounting women's stories of 'setbacks, courage, resourcefulness and inventiveness ...' we 'recognize informants as active cultural producers in their own right, whose voices insist on being heard and can make a difference in the way we think about their lives'.[19]

Similar to other capitalisms, the expansion of the linen industry developed unevenly fostering different workplaces, occupations and experiences. By the turn of the twentieth century, handloom weavers were proletarians, but their experience was distinguished chiefly by the decentralized nature of their work and the extent

19 Jane Lewis, *Women in England* (Bloomington 1984), p. 248. Aihwa Ong, 'Women out of China: Traveling Tales and Traveling Theories in Past Colonial Feminism', in Ruth Behar and Deborah Gordon (eds), *Women Writing Culture* (Berkeley 1995), pp. 353–4.

of craft knowledge they retained. Domestic weavers lived in dispersed rural cottages and worked for manufacturers. Therefore, they did not experience the workplace culture or camaraderie found in rows of employer-owned terraces and shop floors. Removed from the factory millieux along the Bann, handloom weavers remained difficult to organize into trade unions. Poor remuneration eroded the satisfaction they derived from craft knowledge and producing Ireland's fine linens.

All operatives, despite the process of deskilling reflected in such labels as semi- and unskilled labour, have to acquire working knowledge about their machinery, the materials to be processed, the formal organization of production and management where they work, working conditions, health hazards and issues at the macrolevel affecting their industry. That the majority of women's waged work was not socially recognized as skilled has as much to do with cultural conceptions of gender as the breakdown of craft knowledge and mechanization under capitalism.

Work ideologies relating to skill and the acceptance of social inequalities based upon class, gender and religion help explain the lack of working class militancy and trade unionism in the region. Skill established a common ground of mutual respect between managers and skilled male workers that mollified class antagonism. While some worked in more than one factory, many workers remained under the employ of the same owner for much of their working lives intensifying his and his managers' control over their working life.

Due to the lack of census enumerator's schedules for the nineteenth century, it is difficult to draw conclusions regarding the effects of industrial capitalism on kinship patterns in Tullylish. The social dislocation brought about by the Famine clearly disrupted many families due to increased death, desertion and migration rates. While the provision of housing by paternalistic employers may have encouraged the stability of families migrating to industrial settlements along the Bann, the preference for young female labour created an unbalanced sex ratio that encouraged the formation of extended households, households comprised of single individuals, and households headed by women. Further, the shortage of housing stock 1841–61 necessitated alternative residential strategies where lodgers were probably prevalent.

The depth of paternalism and prevalence of the family labour system, however, confirms the strength of kinship ties throughout the period. Reliance upon familial networks served important functions for the working class helping them to realize the policy goal of making ends meet. Given the narrow employment base in rural industrial Tullylish, and the extent to which households relied on the wages earned by children, it was essential for a family to ensure that available job openings were filled with their children. The presence of kin at the workplace helped ease the anxiety of young children first entering employment and learning new skills at eleven or twelve years old. The overlap between kin and co-worker, significantly increased camaraderie and work satisfaction.

From the perspective of the working class, the norm of being 'spoken for' allowed a measure of security to exist alongside the overall insecurity of working-class life. A family labour system also served the class interest of linen industry capitalists to coordinate employers and workers in the creation of surplus value. There was a link between paternalistic strategies and the reconstitution of familial relations at work as well as that between paternalism and the relative class calm of the mid-Victorian period. Filling job openings with worker's children greatly enhanced the power of paternalistic employers and workforce stability since dependence was, in fact, intergenerational. As one generation of workers left, an employer could expected a smooth transition of replacements from the next and continuous occupancy of their houses. Such a system tended to dampen both individual worker resistance and collective action since militant employees would risk their own jobs, along with those of their present and future kin.

This familial system of recruitment and training can be understood partly in relation to the process of 'manufacturing consent' through the creation of an internal labour market.[20] In rural industrial Tullylish, both populations were scarce enough for the allocation process to approximate an internal labour market where new recruits are drawn from the families of present employees. We know that familial recruitment patterns were predominant in the bleaching end of production at least by the mid-nineteenth century and probably long before.

We cannot, however, make similar assumptions about Dunbar McMaster & Company. Its large labour force and factory village expanded rapidly during a decade (1841–51) of severe dislocation and proletarianization. Therefore, it is likely that a largely external labour market prevailed until the end of the 1860's linen boom. Thereafter, recruitment via a more stable internal labour market spread and solidified between 1870–1914. While this internal labour market was not 'perfectly sealed', it was, by the late nineteenth century, a relatively secure system since workers frequently remained with one factory for many years.[21] Thus, in Tullylish, a kin-based internal labour market facilitated accumulation by diminishing insecurity defined in their respective class terms by workers and capitalists.

The generation of workplace and community culture by men and women reveals the depth of working-class agency. The symbiosis between work, family and community, was symbolized in people's memory by open doors through which friends, neighbours and kin were free to enter and receive hospitality. The insistence that communities were close-knit glosses over the deep well-known religious cleavages and may prompt a familiar criticism of popular memory as unreliable, biased or seeing the past through 'rose-colored glasses'. However, 'memory is, by definition, a term which directs our attention not to the past but to the past-present relation'.[22] This 'common sense' of the past as close-knit conveys important historical and cultural information about working-class interdependence and strategies at the turn of the century while it simultaneously 'contains elements of good sense', in

20 Michael Burawoy, *Manufacturing Consent* (Chicago 1979), p. 96. 21 Ibid., p. 97. 22 Popular Memory Group, 'Popular memory: theory, politics, method', in Richard Johnson, Gregor McLennan, Bill Schwarz, and David Sutton (eds), *Making Histories* (Minneapolis 1982), p. 211.

the troubled historical present.[23] Attempts to preserve respectability, defined in mid-Victorian gendered terms, were at the heart of working-class agency and subjectivity. Because working-class women led lives of purpose and dignity readily acknowledged in the community, perceptions of hard toil were somewhat tempered by memories of good times and close social ties.[24] Neighbourliness and interdependence, despite their links to rigid and oppressive class and gender inequality, were missed – considerably more so than the local linen lords whose wages tightly constrained their lives.

23 Ibid., p. 210.   24 Lewis, *Women in England*, p. 66.

Appendix 1

This appendix will briefly outline the methodology used in Part IV. Beginning with the quantitative evidence, the parish was divided into four sub-regions – Gilford/ Dunbarton, the townlands of Drumaran and Loughans surrounding Gilford (referred to as Rural Gilford), the Banford/Hazelbank area and the handloom weaving townland of Ballydugan. These sub-regions corresponded to the spinning, powerloom weaving, bleaching and handloom weaving processes of production respectively and were selected and defined by the availability of documents.

The Gilford/Dunbarton region and the surrounding rural townlands were quite homogeneous with regard to occupation since the area was dominated by the large yarn spinning mill, Dunbar McMaster & Company. This mill was still operating during the period of research and very few business records were retained by the Public Record Office of Northern Ireland (PRONI). The entire population of Gilford, as enumerated in the 1901 Census for Gilford Town, was therefore, included in this study. These Census Enumerators' schedules were linked to school attendance registers for the Gilford Mill and Gilford No. 1 National Schools, Valuations and a 1901 Outdoor Relief Register for the Banbridge Board of Guardians to obtain a data base for analysis.

The Banford/Hazelbank region was composed of the workforces of Banford Bleach Works, Hazelbank Weaving Company and other nearby bleachgreens. Many of these workers lived in company-owned houses close to the worksites and in the surrounding townlands. For Banford Bleach Works, there were wage books for the early twentieth century, beginning in 1909, available at the PRONI. The workers listed in the 1909 wagebook comprised the study population and these were linked to the 1901 Census Enumerator's schedules. Also, linkages were made between the Protestant children of Banford workers and attendance registers for Knocknagor National School. Catholic children would have attended Bann National School in Lawrencetown. Since this school, like the Catholic Castle Hill National School in Gilford, is still operating, records were not then available at the PRONI. Linkages between the children of Catholic workers and school attendance registers could not be made. They are the subject of my current research.

The owners of Hazelbank Weaving Company also deposited wage books for public inspection at the PRONI. I chose the population from the latest 1890 wagebook since it was closest to the 1901 census year. Again, Protestant children of Hazelbank employees were linked to school attendance registers for Knocknagor National

School. Catholic children attending the Bann National School could not be linked for the reasons given above. Thus, due to the lack of school attendance registers for two key Catholic schools – Bann and Castle Hill – I have more complete information on attendance and achievement for Protestant children in Gilford, Banford and Hazelbank.

The last region was the handloom weaving townland of Ballydugan. The methodology here was the same as for Gilford. I included the 1901 Census for the whole townland of Ballydugan, chosen specifically to correspond with a school attendance register for the Ballydugan National School. Children listed in the school registers were linked to census households.

Turning to oral evidence, contact was initially made with a local Tullylish resident, educator and historian, Mr Michael P. Campbell. He provided an initial list of names he had interviewed, and through them I received the names of others. In total, thirty-five interviews were collected with elderly men and women of both religious faiths who had worked in the various linen mills and factories. Some of these individuals were interviewed more than once due to a person's expertise. Formal questionnaires were not used. I was somewhat concerned with the issue of reliability; hence everyone was asked certain questions. However, I also tried to move beyond the level of oral history as empirical evidence toward interpretation of the individual's unique experiences and perspectives by allowing interviews to evolve.

Appendix 2

A. Monthly Totals of Admissions, Residents and Deaths in the Banbridge Workhouse, November 1846–October 1949

Month/Year	No. Admit.	No. Residents	Deaths	Av/wk Admiss.
Nov. 1846	172	564	7	43.0
Dec. 1846	401	881	29	100.0
Jan. 1847	403	1013	89	80.6
Feb. 1847*	198	1044	64	49.5
Mar. 1847*	51	899	72	12.8
Apr. 1847*	153	915	51	38.3
May 1847*	207	975	42	41.4
June 1847*	142	992	25	35.5
July 1847	224	989	41	44.8
Aug. 1847	136	818	22	34.0
Sept.1847	225	767	21	56.3
Oct. 1847	322	963	28	64.4
Nov. 1847	332	1200	20	83.0
Dec. 1847	276	1362	23	69.0
Totals	2669		498 (18.7% died)	
Averages (Mo.)		994.8	41.5	
Jan. 1848	373	1489	84	74.6
Feb. 1848*	103	1324	47	25.8
Mar. 1848	167	1303	44	41.8
Apr. 1848	191	1230	44	38.2
May 1848	148	1192	31	37.0
June 1848	163	1178	26	40.8
July 1848	76	1100	14	19.0
Aug. 1848**	36	928	7	–
Sept.1848	9	786	1	–
Oct. 1848	–	–	–	–
Nov. 1848	–	–	–	–
Dec. 1848	20	995	2	–
Totals	1286		300 (23.3% died)	
Averages (Mo.)		1152.5	30	

Month/Year	No. Admit.	No. Residents	Deaths	Av/wk Admiss.
Jan. 1849	103	1052	8	–
Feb. 1849	31	1057	6	–
Mar. 1849	65	1052	6	–
Apr. 1849	18	1049	9	–
May 1849	41	1061	4	–
June 1849	41	1058	4	–
July 1849	39	1020	5	–
Aug. 1849	12	865	2	–
Sept. 1849	10	696	2	–
Oct. 1849	20	643	2	–
Totals	380		48 (12.6% died)	
Averages (Mo.)		953.3	4.8	
Grand Totals 4908		882 (18% died)		

Source PRONI, BG.6/A/6,7,8, Banbridge Board of Guardians, Charts Showing Workhouse Admissions, 31 October 1846–6, to October 1849.
* During these months the medical officer would not permit further admissions for at least one week due to extreme crowding affecting the number admitted and average admissions per week figures.
** After August 1848, weekly entries are no longer given, only monthly or bi-monthly entries.

B. Monthly Totals of Admissions, Residents, and Deaths in the Lurgan Workhouse, January 1846–December 1850

Month/Year	No. Admit.	No. Residents	Deaths	Av/wk Admiss.
Jan. 1846	20	285	2	–
Feb. 1846	28	344	2	–
Mar. 1846	97	409	4	32.3
Apr. 1846	117	489	10	39.0
May 1846	125	447	16	31.3
June 1846	105	440	7	35.0
July 1846	59	351	15	14.8
Aug. 1846	94	286	10	18.8
Sept.1846	130	318	13	32.5
Oct. 1846	230	418	18	46.0
Nov. 1846	273	566	31	68.3
Dec. 1846	482	799	58	120.5
Totals	1760		187 (10.6% died)	
Averages (Mo.)		429.3		15.6

Jan. 1847	601	949	235	120.2
Feb. 1847*	37	656	223	9.3
Mar. 1847*	141	604	88	35.3
Apr. 1847*	44	562	47	11.0
May 1847	428	669	41	85.6
June 1847	442	1047	90	110.6
July 1847	313	952	119	62.6
Aug. 1847	191	850	81	47.8
Sept.1847	216	808	49	54.0
Oct. 1847	476	957	49	95.2
Nov. 1847	399	1132	44	99.8
Dec. 1847	481	1323	66	120.3
Totals	3769		1132 (30% died)	
Averages (Mo.)		875.8		94.3
Jan. 1848	607	1334	88	121.4
Feb. 1848	352	1345	77	88.0
Mar. 1848	235	1192	54	58.8
Apr. 1848	271	1004	49	54.2
May 1848	203	914	16	50.8
June 1848	159	861	14	39.8
July 1848	129	773	13	25.8
Aug. 1848	105	638	13	26.3
Sept.1848	138	608	9	27.6
Oct. 1848	152	661	8	38.0
Nov. 1848	229	774	20	57.3
Dec. 1848	343	910	14	68.6
Totals	2923		375 (12.8% died)	
Averages (Mo.)		917.8		31.3
Jan. 1849	244	1022	15	61.0
Feb. 1849	189	1008	22	47.3
Mar. 1849	183	897	26	36.6
Apr. 1849	165	829	30	41.3
May 1849	209	748	23	52.3
June 1849	251	662	36	62.8
July 1849	157	634	27	39.3
Aug. 1849	102	533	15	25.5
Sept.1849	81	424	9	16.2
Oct. 1849	69	443	6	17.3
Nov. 1849	94	457	5	23.5
Dec. 1849	142	492	7	28.4
Totals	1886		221 (11.7% died)	
Averages (Mo.)	679.1	18.4		

Month/Year	No. Admit.	No. Residents	Deaths	Av/wk Admiss.
Jan. 1850	200	597	8	50.0
Feb. 1850	143	568	9	35.8
Mar. 1850	103	489	16	20.6
Apr. 1850	91	458	15	22.8
May 1850	102	424	13	25.5
June 1850	128	411	16	25.6
July 1850	87	365	14	21.8
Aug. 1850	80	294	9	16.0
Sept.1850	40	275	6	10.0
Oct. 1850	57	282	3	14.3
Nov. 1850	153	351	9	30.6
Dec. 1850	121	371	9	30.3
Totals	1305		124	(9.5% died)
Averages		407.1		10.3
Grand Totals	11643		2039	(17.5% died)

Source BG.22, Lurgan Workhouse Statistics during the Great Famine, PRONI.
* Here again the medical officer was limiting the number of admissions. From October 1847 extra capacity was added at the Portadown Hospital and in December of that year capacity for 300 was added in the distillery, and in June and October of 1848 capacilty was increased with an additional temporary workhouse and fever sheds. The figures for the number residing in the workhouse reflect these changes.

Index